PERSPECTIVES ON
DEATH AND DYING

PERSPECTIVES ON
DEATH AND DYING

*Cross-Cultural and
Multi-Disciplinary Views*

EDITED BY

Arthur Berger, JD
Rev. Paul Badham
Austin H. Kutscher, DDS
Joyce Berger, MA
Ven. Michael Perry, DD
John Beloff, PhD

90-2179

The Charles Press, Publishers
Philadelphia

The Charles Press, Publishers
Post Office Box 15715
Philadelphia, Pennsylvania
19103

Library of Congress Catalog Card Number: 88-063424

ISBN 0-914783-26-2 (hardbound)
ISBN 0-914783-27-0 (softbound)

Managing Editor: Sanford Robinson
Editorial Assistant: Audrey Bedics
Compositor: Cage Graphic Arts, Inc.
Designed by Sanford Robinson
Printed by Princeton University Press

5 4 3 2

Special thanks to Lawrence McFadden and Reba Bartash for their invaluable help and cooperation.

CONTENTS

Editors vii
Contributors ix
Preface xi
Acknowledgment xiii

Part 1   Cross-Cultural Perspectives

1 Mythological Aspects of Death and Dying 3
   Stanley Krippner, PhD

2 African Perspectives on Death and Dying 14
   Kofi Asare Opoku, BA, STM

3 Death and the Afterlife in African Culture 24
   Kwasi Wiredu, PhD

4 Islamic Perspectives on Death and Dying 38
   Ahmad Anisuzzaman Muwahidi, PhD

5 The Concept of Death and the Afterlife in Islam 55
   Jan Knappert, PhD

6 The Good Death: Approaches to Death, Dying, and Bereavement
   among British Hindus 66
   Shirley Firth, PhD

7 The Hindu Concept of Death 84
   Jamuna Prashad, PhD

8 Upanishadic Eschatology: The Other Side of Death 89
   William A. Borman, PhD

9 Conquering Death. 101
   Daya Shanker, PhD

10 Rebirth and Afterlife in Buddhism 108
   Carl B. Becker, PhD

11 Chinese Perspectives on Death and Dying 126
   Wei Wei C. Huang, RN, EdD

12 Death in the Maya Cosmos 131
   Harold B. Haley, MD, and Francis X. Grollig, SJ, PhD

13 The Ethics of Certain Death: Suicide, Execution, and Euthanasia . . . 149
       Charles Davies, PhD

14 Do We Have a Right to Die? 163
       John Beloff, PhD

15 Voluntary Active Euthanasia: An Individual's Right to Determine
       the Time and Manner of Death 173
       Marvin E. Newman, JD

16 Jungian Psychology and the Nature of Death 188
       Alfred Ribi, MD

17 Problems Raised by the Concept of the Survival of Personality
       After Death 199
       Gertrude R. Schmeidler, PhD

18 Does Religion Need Immortality? 209
       Rev. Dr. Paul Badham

19 The *Ars Moriendi* and Breaking the Conspiracy of Silence 221
       Ven. Michael Perry, DD

20 A Postmodern Mythology of Death 232
       Michael Grosso, PhD

21 People and the Paranormal 244
       David Cockburn, PhD

22 The Near-Death Experience: Cross-Cultural and Multi-Disciplinary
       Dimensions 256
       David Lorimer, MEd

Index *269*

EDITORS

Arthur S. Berger, JD
Director, International Institute for the Study of Death, Pembrooke Pines, FL

Rev. Dr. Paul Badham
Chairman, Department of Theology and Religious Studies, Saint David's University College, University of Wales, Lampeter, Wales, UK

Austin H. Kutscher, DDS
President, The Foundation of Thanatology, New York, NY; Professor of Dentistry (in Psychiatry), Department of Psychiatry, College of Physicians and Surgeons, Columbia University, New York, NY

Joyce Berger, MA
Administrator, International Institute for the Study of Death, Pembrooke Pines, FL

Ven. Michael Perry, DD
Archdeacon of Durham Cathedral, Durham, UK

John Beloff, PhD
Professor (Emeritus), Department of Psychology, University of Edinburgh, Edinburgh, Scotland, UK

CONTRIBUTORS

Rev. Dr. Paul Badham
Chairman, Department of Theology and Religious Studies, Saint David's University College, University of Wales, Lampeter, Wales, UK

Carl Becker, PhD
Professor, Institute of Philosophy, Tsukuba University, Tsukuba City, Japan

John Beloff, PhD
Professor (Emeritus), Department of Psychology, University of Edinburgh, Edinburgh, Scotland, UK

William A. Borman, PhD
Independent Scholar, The Foundation of Thanatology, New York, NY

David Cockburn, PhD
Department of Philosophy, Saint David's University College, University of Wales, Lampeter, Wales, UK

Christie Davies, PhD
Department of Sociology, University of Reading, Reading, UK

Shirley Firth, MA
Winchester, Hampshire, UK

Francis X. Grollig, SJ, PhD
Professor, Department of Anthropology, Loyola University, Chicago, IL

Michael Grosso, PhD
Bronx, NY

Harold B. Haley, MD
Associate Chief of Staff for Education, VA Medical Center; Clinical Professor of Surgery, Baylor College of Medicine, Houston, TX

Wei Wei C. Huang, RN, EdD
Associate Professor of Nursing, Bronx Community College of CUNY, Bronx, NY

Jan Knappert, PhD
Department of Religious Studies, University of London, London, UK

Stanley Krippner, PhD
Saybrook Institute, San Francisco, CA

David Lorimer, MEd
Vice-Chairman, International Association for Near Death Studies, Northleach, Gloucestershire, UK

Ahmad Anisuzzaman Muwahidi, PhD
Professor, Department of Philosophy, University of Dhaka, Dhaka, Bangladesh

Marvin Newman, JD
Department of Business Studies, Rollins College, Winter Park, FL

Kofi Asare Opoku, BA (Hons), BD, STM
Associate Professor of Religion and Ethics, Institute of African Studies, University of Ghana, Legon, Ghana

Ven. Michael Perry, DD
Archdeacon of Durham Cathedral, Durham, UK

Jamuna Prashad, PhD
Research Adviser, Foundation for Reincarnation and Spiritual Research, Allahabad, India

Alfred Ribi, MD
Director of The C. G. Jung Institute, Zurich, Switzerland

Gertrude R. Schmeidler, PhD
Professor (Emeritus), Department of Psychology, City College of CUNY, New York, NY

Daya Shanker, PhD
Senior Lawyer, High Court of Allahabad, Allahabad, India

Kwasi Wiredu, PhD
Professor, Department of Philosophy, University of South Florida, Tampa, FL

PREFACE

Men fear death as children fear to go in the dark,
and as the natural fear of children is increased with
tales, so is the other.　　　　　　— *Francis Bacon*
　　　　　　　　　　　　　　　　　　1561-1624

Of all human fears, none has been more enduring, more universal, or more frightening than the fear of death. From ancient times and throughout different cultures, man has attempted to master this eternal fear, but never with success: The land of darkness and the shadow of death are still with us.

It is not surprising, then, that denial of death became our chief comforter. As Samuel Johnson wrote, "The whole of life is but keeping away the thought of death." But denial is only a temporary measure; it ultimately fails, and our fears return. William James, the great American psychologist and philosopher, expressed the futility of trying to deny the reality of death: "Let sanguine healthy-mindedness do its best with its strong power of living in the moment and ignoring and forgetting, still the evil background is there to be thought of, and the skull will grin at the banquet."

In order to stare back at the grinning skull and confront death, as modern society is finally attempting to do, it is essential to develop new insights and attitudes about death while freeing ourselves from the power of the countless tales, myths, and customs that have influenced us over the centuries. Not that these creations of human culture are to be despised or abandoned: They have served us, for good or ill, and they stand as a repository of truths which we must now examine and learn to decipher.

The first step in this educational process is to discuss death freely and openly, removing at least some of its shroud of secrecy and mystery. In recent years considerable progress has been made in this direction, so that death is no longer a taboo subject, nor is it hidden or ignored as in the past. Next, it is important to view death in a global, comprehensive way by integrating the thoughts and attitudes of different cultures and traditions. What unique insights are manifested in the rituals and customs that characterize any given culture? What do the world's various cultural heritages share in common with respect to beliefs and observances surrounding death and dying?

In attempting to gain a new understanding of death such as is possible only with the advent of global communication and travel, we are faced with the challenge of breaching the walls that have hitherto separated not only cultures but also vocations and academic disciplines. No single perspective is broad enough to encompass the meaning of death; no single tradition or discipline, however august or rigorous, is sufficient to illuminate our way through the passages of death and dying. Specialization, however necessary and unavoidable, exacts a price, which in the present case is our fragmentary and disorganized concept of death. Clearly, what is required is an approach that permits exchanges of ideas, a dialogue arising from a cross-fertilization of many disciplines and cultures. Such is the underlying purpose of this book.

Perspectives on Death and Dying: Cross-Cultural and Multi-Disciplinary Views brings together the ideas and experience of a distinguished group of scholars involved with the study of death and death-related subjects. These renowned contributors include anthropologists, psychologists, theologians, philosophers, sociologists, scholars of comparative religion, social workers, and parapsychologists. Their work reflects the views of many societies and cultures, including those of Islam, Africa, India, China, Japan, and the West. It is hoped that by viewing these diverse perspectives side by side for the first time, the reader will gain greater insight into, and understanding of death, and perhaps be able to apply this knowledge to the development of a sustaining personal framework for coping with death and dying.

The editors recognize that a single volume of this type can hardly reveal the secrets of death. But our aim will be realized if, as a result of this introduction of cross-cultural and multi-disciplinary relations to an area from which they have been sadly absent until now, some light may be shed into death's dark corners.

ACKNOWLEDGMENT

The editors wish to acknowledge the support and encouragement of the Foundation of Thanatology and the Institute for the Study of Death in the preparation of this volume. All royalties from the sale of this book are assigned to the Foundation of Thanatology, a tax exempt, not for profit, public scientific and educational foundation.

Thanatology, a new subspecialty of medicine, is involved in scientific and humanistic inquiries and the application of the knowledge derived therefrom to the subjects of the psychological aspects of dying; reactions to loss, death, and grief; and recovery from bereavement.

We are especially grateful for the cooperation of the Institute for the Study of Death, whose initiative led to the publication of this book.

PART 1

*Cross-Cultural
Perspectives*

Mythological Aspects of Death and Dying

Stanley Krippner

Myths are narratives that serve as cultural or personal paradigms: they can explain natural phenomena, guide individuals through life, assign them their place in society, and connect them with the spiritual forces of the universe. Joseph Campbell (1986) describes myths as products of human imagination whose meaning lies not in literal denotions but in their metaphoric and metaphysical connotations. Myths about death and dying vary from culture to culture, but their mutual power to control, socialize, and harmonize human behavior is evident to anyone who examines their stories and symbols.

Westerners view life and death as a straight line that extends through time. According to this belief, the longer the line, the more successfully one can attain longevity. To those believing in this myth, a young person's death is seen not only as a tragedy, but an event that can shake religious faith. As a result, a death of a child demands elaborate rationalizations; the youth was "called by God," "needed in heaven," or "paid a debt incurred by the parents' sins."

On the other hand, most American Indian traditions do not view life in terms of a straight line but as a circle. One cycle is completed when a young person reaches puberty; another cycle is completed when he or she has children. After puberty, the individual expands, serving the community, the earth, and the "Great Spirit." Rites of passage during puberty often included a solitary journey into the wilderness for several days of fasting and prayer. These and other practices were geared to enable young warriors to receive a vision-inspired death chant that they could use throughout their lives to maintain contact with the "Great Spirit" during times of stress and danger; falling from a horse, being attacked by an enemy, or while burning with a fever, the death chant was a constant companion. It was meant to be available in times of need. The death chant united the familiar with the unfamiliar and as a result, it prepared the Indians for death. When they died they did so with great clarity, because they were already conversant with a mythology that integrated living and dying (Levine, 1982, pp. 25–26). As well, their view of life as a circle allowed them to die in wholeness when it was fully completed. As the Ogala Sioux leader Crazy Horse commented, "Today is a good day to die, for all the things of my life are present" (Levine, 1982, p. 5).

LIFE'S FINAL MOMENTS

When the Aztecs sacrificed a prisoner, a rope representing the umbilical cord often was tied around the victim's abdomen symbolizing that once death occurred there would be a rebirth into another world (Huxley, 1974). In the Hindu tradition, to die with God's name on one's lips is a deliberate way of returning to the "Source of Being" until one's next incarnation. When Mahatma Gandhi was struck by an assassin's bullet, he uttered the name "Ram," one of the appellations for God (Levine, 1982, p. 27). Such reverence has marked the deaths of countless Roman Catholics who in their final moments repeated the phrase "Sweet Mother of Heaven." A traditional parting proclamation for Jews is "Hear, O Israel, the Lord our God, the Lord is One."

The final words uttered by those verging on death may influence the beliefs their survivors have about the meaning of life and death. The last words of St. Francis of Assissi were, "Welcome, Sister Death." St. Teresa of Avila proclaimed, "Lord, now is the time to arise and go. . . . My soul shall enjoy the fulfillment of all her desire!" However, other, less serene, characters have also influenced the collective mythology about death. These people have died with expressions of anger, terror, or hopeless resignation. Benito Mussolini even begged his captor for more time — "But, but Mr. Colonel" — before his execution (LeComte, 1960).

Some people face death in ways characteristic of how they lived. For example, when the military hero Ethan Allen was told that the angels were waiting for him, he exploded, "Let 'em wait." George M. Cohan's last words were of his wife ("Look after Agnes"); similarly, Charles II of England spoke of his mistress ("Let not poor Nelly starve"). President Grover Cleveland insisted, "I have tried so hard to do right." Others manage to make a philosophical statement; the Blackfoot Indian Chief Crowfoot stated, "A little while and I will be gone from you, whither I cannot tell. From nowhere we come, into nowhere we go. What is life? It is a flash, a firefly in the night. It is a breath of a buffalo in the winter time. It is as the little shadow that runs across the grass and loses itself in the sunset." Julius Fucik, a Czechoslovakian journalist arrested by the Gestapo in World War II, wrote, before his execution, "Mankind, I love you. Be vigilant!" (Schneidman, 1980). It is said that St. John the Evangelist's dying words were, "Thou hast invited me to Thy table, Lord; and behold I come, thanking thee for having invited me, for Thou knowest that I have desired it with all my heart." Leo Tolstoy was less assured, asking "I do not understand what I have to do." A Nazi soldier wrote to his wife from the Soviet front, "I shall never return. . . . I used to be strong and full of faith; now I am small and without faith. . . . No one can tell me any longer that the men die with the words 'Deutschland' or 'Heil Hitler' on their lips" (Schneidman, 1980). The night before a fatal battle in 1987, a Soviet soldier wrote to his family from the Afghanistan front. His mournful letter predicted his death, and closed with "Damn you, Afghanistan!"

PREPARATION FOR DEATH

There is, perhaps, nothing more profound for a person to contemplate than the basic question of existence — the possibility of taking one's own life. In an instant, one can be freed of all bounds and constraints, casting oneself to an unknown fate. While one of the most troubling aspects of suicide is the total rejection of the society left behind, some cultures have incorporated suicide into their mythologies, so that the sacrificing of one's life becomes an ultimate affirmation of the social codes. Moslem warriors have rushed fearlessly into battle, believing that death in the service of their country was the quickest route to eternal paradise. Shogun warriors in old Japan and kamikaze pilots in the Second World War shared the same mythology; supported by this faith, they gave up their lives with apparent ease. The Tupinamba of Brazil could obtain immortality by dying at the hands of their enemies as cannibalized sacrificial victims (Huxley, 1974, p. 108).

The Greek god Hermes, who as herald and messenger of the gods guided the souls of the dead to their final dwelling place, was noted for being as mischievous as he was clever. Indeed, the Hermetic sciences involve occult study and ingenious practices designed to lead disciples to the discovery of their own immortality. Each day, mythologies about death cast their hues and shadows upon our lives. One of the classic philosophical distinctions between the human species and other forms of life is humanity's awareness of its own mortality, and only because of this, assert some commentators, culture is possible.

When faced with a death for which one is not prepared, instinctual terror may obliterate any previous rationalizations and prior rejections of the dogmas one may previously have been exposed to. Prayers learned and long since abandoned may once again find their way back to one's lips. Basic religious questions regarding man's connection with the cosmos may come streaming in upon the doomed person. The question, "Is this all there is?" may be asked in disillusioned horror. A profound longing to transcend the boundaries of the individual ego may break into consciousness. The world's great spiritual systems have been able to establish a connection with this underlying longing for transcendence. Through human community and shared, established meanings, these spiritual systems provide a bridge between individuals and whatever lies beyond them.

DENYING DEATH

Among the Trukese, a Micronesian society, life ends and death begins at the age of 40. One is not regarded as mature until reaching life's fourth decade; only at that point are people felt to be capable of making decisions wise enough to guide their lives. However, age 40 is also believed to mark the point where physical strength begins to decline. Trukese men cannot fish or paddle the canoe as well as younger people, nor can they climb trees and gather bread-fruit with the agility they had previously. The Trukese are considered a "death-affirming" society because the topic is omnipresent. There are advantages as well as disadvantages to aging, and both are acknowledged. For many primitive societies, death was often accompanied by rejoicing and celebration as tribal members made their transitions into the other world (Kübler-Ross, 1975, p. 28).

America, in contrast, is often seen as a "death-denying" society. People often are reluctant to reveal their age; they spend large sums of money to erase wrinkles and transplant hair. Furthermore, elderly people are frequently shunted to nursing homes to keep them out of sight. The anthropologist Ernest Becker (1973) observed that the fear of death often leads to the denial of death. According to Becker, while children are learning this denial process,

> [They] have their recurrent nightmares, their universal phobias of insects and mean dogs. In their tortured interiors radiate complex symbols of many inadmissible realities — terror of the world, the horror of one's own wishes, the fear of vengeance by parents, the disappearance of things, one's lack of control over anything, really. It is too much for any animal to take, but the child has to take it, and so he wakes up screaming with almost punctual regularity during the period where his weak ego is in the process of consolidating things (pp. 19–20).

Becker believed that as people become aware of their imminent death, they construct a series of defenses to armor themselves against it, against the sudden ways in which terror can strike, and against other potential catastrophes.

Francis Bacon observed, "Man fears death as the child fears to go into the dark." From a psychoanalytic viewpoint, Mary Chadwick (1969) sees the fear of death as the Western individual's fundamental anxiety. The silence about death found in technological societies whose mythology exalts dominance over nature has been compared to the silence about sex that characterized the Victorian era. This death fear, and the denial it leads to, has affected all strata of society. Physicians often conspire with the relatives of a terminally ill patient to keep from mentioning death in the presence of the patient. Even Westerners who are religiously inclined fear death as much as others (Feifel, 1969), unless their religious convictions are unusually deep (Templer, 1973). Yet, until recently, as one psychoanalyst observed, the fear of death and specific anxiety about it has had almost no description in psychiatric literature (Rosenthal, 1969).

A curious example of the way in which Western culture has denied death occurs in the alteration of folk tales over the centuries. In February, 1984, Princeton University held a conference on "Fairy Tales and Society." At the conference, special attention was given to the story "Little Red Riding Hood." In the earliest existing version, the hapless child was told by her mother to take some bread and milk to her grandmother. But the wicked wolf arrived first, devoured the grandmother, and waited for Red Riding Hood. Upon her arrival, the wolf ordered her to strip and throw her clothes on the fire. In some versions, he raped the child before consuming her; in others he ate her up immediately. The moral of the tale appeared to be direct: children should not wander outside the village or trust those they don't know because strangers can be cruel and dangerous ("Sex, Death, and Red Riding Hood," 1984, p. 68).

As the years went by, a hunter was added who cut the wolf's belly open, allowing the girl and her grandmother to escape. The 17th century French author, Charles Perrault, added the red hood; the 19th century German writers Jakob and Wilhelm Grimm eliminated the sex and much of the gore. The Brothers Grimm even had the mother warn Red Riding Hood not to stray from the path, thus setting up the misadventures as resulting, in part, from her own impropriety. Even the red hood, in Perrault's day, symbolized a sinful act, further shifting the blame onto the girl, and modifying the original message of sudden death as a reality in an unpredictable world.

"LEAVE-TAKING"

Another modern route to the denial of death is taken by the construction of elaborate cemeteries, the best known being California's Forest Lawn Memorial Park. Its founder, Hubert Eaton, built the "park" in an effort, he said, "to erase all signs of mourning." Thus, death became "leave-taking" and the corpse ("the loved one") awaited burial in a well-furnished "slumber room" after elaborate cosmetic treatment. Soothing music and inspirational messages stream out of loudspeakers that are hidden in the shrubbery which abounds in each of the different sections of the park: "Lullabyland," "Graceland," and the heart-shaped "Babyland." The lyrics of Tom Paxton's (1976) song ridicule the rather unusual procedures at Forest Lawn:

> Oh, lay me down in Forest Lawn in a silver casket,
> Put golden flowers over my head in a silver basket.
> Let the Drum and Bugle Corps
> Play Taps while cannons roar,
> Let sixteen liveried employees
> Pass out souvenirs from the funeral store.

Evelyn Waugh's (1948) parody of Forest Lawn, *The Loved One*, is also a satirical account of America's denial of death. Indeed, the popularity of Waugh's novella seemed to result in a diminution of using "the loved one" as a euphemism for a dead body (Wass, 1979). The extravagant funerals so common in the United States are excoriated in books such as Ruth Mulvey Harmer's (1983) *The High Cost of Dying* and Jessica Mitford's (1963) *The American Way of Death*. These critiques, and others like them, portrayed the measures we take to make the dead look like a living, but sleeping, person. These books propose that a prettied-up corpse in a ghoulish make-believe sleep is an irreverent, irreligious denial of death's reality. Mitford, for example, describes the merchandise (coffins) of the Practical Burial Company, which offers "warm, luxurious slipper comfort" in patent, calf, tan, or oxblood designs, as well as Courtesy Products' "new Bra-form, Post-Mortem Form Restoration." Florence Gowns, Inc., manufactures a line of "hostess gowns and brunch coats" for the departed, while the "Monaco" coffin with "Sea Mist Polish Finish" and a lining of "600 Aqua Supreme Cheney velvet" is advised for "the bon vivant who dreams of rubbing shoulders with the international smart set."

Some survivors go to the opposite extreme, arranging for immediate disposal of the body by burial or cremation, with little interruption of their day-to-day activities (Herson and Scott, 1979). But this position of noninvolvement can be just as death-denying as the elaborate funeral with the expensive metal casket "hermetically sealed" to prevent "seepage" from disturbing "the loved one's slumber." As a matter of fact, it is often forgotten that metal coffins once served a practical function; they discouraged body-snatching in the late 18th century when the rise in medical study required corpses in quantities that were unavailable through legal channels. At the present time, this concern is not valid, but the return to a plain wood coffin is unacceptable to many people because it reminds them too vividly of the body's eventual decay and decomposition.

BOOKS OF THE DEAD

The contemporary Westerner's denial of death stands in sharp contrast to the various ancient "books of the dead," which offer precise guidelines for the dying. The Egyptian *Rev Nu Pert Em Hru* (or *Chapters of Coming Forth by Day*) dates back to about 1600 B.C. and is a collection of texts that contain formulae (some of them contradictory), prayers, hymns, and descriptions of the "Fields of Peace" in the afterlife. The ancient Egyptians went to extraordinary lengths to express their fascination with death as suggested by their ornate mummies, treasure-filled tombs, and elaborate ceremonies.

One might expect that the ancient Egyptians were a society of morose, dejected people, who spent an inordinate amount of time brooding and preparing for their imminent demise. To the contrary, the Egyptians lived joyously; their land was blessed with abundant, life-giving resources and the fertile Nile Valley. For most of their history, they were at peace because of their geographical isolation from others. Egyptian pharaohs were generally benevolent despots who believed in responsible government. Indeed, as democratic ideas gained ground in Egypt, the funerary texts became available to more people. Interestingly, the fear of death amongst the Egyptians existed precisely because so many of them had so much to lose; this fear led to their elaborate construction of tombs, mummies, and beliefs concerning the afterlife, not as may commonly be assumed, by a suppression of thought about death (Rossiter, 1979).

Quite a different document is the 8th century B.C. *Bardo Thodol* (or *Liberation by Hearing on the After-Death Plane*) (Evans-Wentz, 1957). While the Egyptians had no doubt as to the reality of their world, this Tibetan book of the dead views the whole human experience — both before and after death — as fraught with illusion. This treatise offers guidance at the time of death as well as in the state after death. By following the necessary route indicated in the book, the reader will learn how to transcend those aspects of life that are unimportant because they are merely transitory. Dying is seen as containing the potential of initiation and the power to consciously control the process of death and regeneration. The Tibetan book of the dead teaches those that are dying to face death calmly and with a clear mind so that one will be able to transcend bodily suffering and infirmities with a trained intellect that is directed not so much toward the end of a life, but toward transcendence to a new life.

The *Bardo Thodol* is the reverse of death-denying; indeed, it holds that the unwillingness to die produces unfavorable results. Rather than taking sick people from their homes and postponing the death process medicinally while the mind is numbed by anesthetics, the Oriental sages stressed the importance of mental awareness. When the Tibetan yogi Milarepa was preparing to die, he chose a comfortable cave in which to expire and welcomed death with a song about the inevitability and naturalness of his passing. The *Bardo Thodol* implies a yogic method of liberation from the very life and death cycle itself (Evans-Wentz, 1957). For Milarepa and his fellow yogis, neither the hermetic-ally sealed "Monaco" coffin nor the ancient Egyptian "Fields of Peace" would have held much allure.

Books similar to the *Bardo Thodol* exist in Hindu, Moslem, and Mesoamerican literature, each reflecting a different cultural path. The medieval collection *Ars Moriendi* (or *The Art of Dying*) attempts a similar task. In some of these books, the reader is advised that the states of consciousness reached in a near-death experience can be experienced during life through methods such as meditation or initiation (Grof, 1980). In fact, Timothy Leary, Ralph Metzner, and Richard Alpert (1964) adapted the *Bardo Thodol* for use as a manual to guide neophytes using psychedelic drugs to alter their consciousness. *The American Book of the Dead* presents certain esoteric teachings about death for an American audience (Gold, 1978).

The death-denying mythology in the United States began to shift in the 1970s with the pioneering efforts of dedicated clinicians such as the Swiss-American physician Elizabeth Kübler-Ross (1969, 1975). She courageously con-fronted the issues faced by dying patients in a death-denying culture, ulti-mately providing the entire society with crucial insights about living and dying. Kübler-Ross' work was followed by dozens of sophisticated books that address the issue of dying from a Western psychological viewpoint, such as Fred Cutter's *Coming to Terms with Death* (1974), Stephen Levine's *Who Dies?* and *Healing into Life and Death* (1982, 1987), Edwin Schneidman's *Voices of Death* (1980), and Michael A. Simpson's *The Facts of Death* (1979).

ANNIHILATION VS. TRANSCENDENCE

Ernest Becker's book *The Denial of Death* won the Pulitzer Prize for Nonfiction in May 1974, two months after Becker had died. Becker asserted that the idea of death — and the fear of it — haunts the human being like no other concept. Because humans experience and understand their mortality, they hunger for transcendence. Becker points to ways that this hunger is passionately applied to material realms as people attempt to convert earth into heaven, material goods into gods, and self-preservation into immortality. As the only creatures aware that their lives come to an end, human beings have to devise other ways to guarantee some kind of indefinite duration.

Part of the genius of Becker's contribution is his compelling argument that excess gold, currency, and possessions have come to psychologically symbolize immortality and have become the central mechanisms in the denial of death. The amassing of surplus wealth goes to the very core of human motivation, as does the urge to stand out as a hero, transcend the limitations of the human condition, and achieve victory over finitude. Becker (1975) claims that evil is based on people's attempts to deny their mortality. By believing that they can transcend their place in nature, they often pursue costly, illusory substitutes for immortality, to the detriment of meeting the attainable requirements of life in the earthly sphere.

In assessing Becker's work, Ken Wilber (1981) agrees with his basic thesis but criticizes Becker for not acknowledging, and therefore denying, the existence of a spiritual realm. Through this rejection of transcendent and mystical experiences, Wilber believes Becker to be guilty of a reductionism that denies the highest aspects of human nature. While Becker sees suffering and evil as rooted in humanity's misguided longing to deny its own insignificance, Wilber sees human evil and suffering as due to the failure to attain union with God.

For both scholars, evil is the result of human beings' attempts to deny their own insignificance. Becker thinks such fears as well founded, while Wilbert understands them as the confusion of ego with essence. Wilber states that humans intuit Spirit as their true and prior nature. By attempting to achieve on earth a perfection that can only be found in the transpersonal "beyond," humankind has confused the finite and the infinite, producing a plethora of problems. For Becker, religion is based on the wishful longing for a realm beyond death; for Wilber, religion is based on the longing for an intuited realm that is, indeed, encountered after death.

This fundamental disagreement is important to understand before surveying various cultural and personal myths about life after death. Some religions do not rely on accounts of a literal afterlife or belief in an immortal soul. Others, however, glowingly describe entrance into the infinite as, variously, emerging from darkness into light, the slaying of dragons or the destruction of demons, the glorious opening of the heavenly gates, or the revelation of divine entities (Elliott, Feinstein, and Krippner, 1986).

The theme of Divine Judgment occurs in Judaic, Christian, Moslem, Zoroastrian, and some Mesoamerican traditions. Heavens may consist of celestial cities, paradisical gardens, radiant beings, erotic encounters, angelic music, sensual delights, and/or galactic visitations. Hells may be marked by terrifying monsters, inexorable suffering, instruments of torture, and/or fiery conflagrations. Reincarnation is a tenet that is central to understanding human destiny in Hinduism, Jainism, certain Mesoamerican traditions, and many forms of Buddhism. Some cultural mythologies perceive passageways from one world into the next, vehicles to facilitate the journey, purgatories and other indeterminate states, and unitive bliss where self-identity is lost, and even schools of esoteric wisdom where a soul can develop its spirituality under the guidance of a master instructor.

Among Westerners, adherence to any of these religious belief systems tends to be a matter of choice rather than a cultural imperative. The breakdown of the West's religious mythologies along with the prevailing materialistic worldview has led to a wide variety of secular strategies for finding comfort and death. Any of the following may be more appealing than the annihilation felt at the prospect of dying.

1. We can imbue our time on earth with a richness of meaning that cannot be overshadowed by the certainty that we must someday exit. Corliss Lamont (1970) observed, "we can make our actions count and endow our days with a scope and meaning that the finality of death cannot defeat."

2. We can survive genetically. Within our bodies are the chromosomes inherited from our ancestors, and we can pass them on to our children. Bertrand Russell (1951) reflected that parenthood provides a biological escape from death, "making one's own life part of the whole stream, and not a mere stagnant puddle without any overflow into the future." Many cultures have developed these biological capacities into guiding myths that make rapid repopulation a cultural requirement, such as in Confucianism where lack of progeny was considered the greatest unfilial act (Lifton, 1983).

3. We can live on through the memory of others. We are links in the chain of the progression of humanity. Through not only our children, but through all whom we touch with our presence, our words, and our actions, we are made immortal.

4. We can live on through our lasting works, such as art, music, science, literature, philanthropy, and social innovation. Miguel Serrano (1966) observed that books are made of living material and "continue to cast light through the darkness long after the death of their authors." Others have noted that art, more than any other activity, survives death (Choran, 1974). The positive influences we may effect in human affairs may become living testimonies of our lives.

5. Some see a hope for immortality in the fountain of youth promised by the perfection of organ transplant operations. Corneal transplants are not uncommon, and the years ahead may bring increasing success in kidney, lung, and heart transplants. Malcolm Muggeridge (1970) jokingly observed that this practice may result in "keeping us on the road indefinitely, like vintage cars, by replacing our worn-out parts."

6. We can survive in the cosmic process, carrying our banner for a brief moment in the universal parade of existence. Robert Jay Lifton (1983), in his study of Hiroshima survivors, found that they were helped to regain their own sense of continuity following the atomic blast by reciting the proverb, "The state may collapse, but the mountains and the rivers remain" (p. 22). Herman Melville, in his novel *Moby Dick*, observed, "Immortality is but ubiquity in time."

Carl Jung examined various cultural mythologies and found that they all contained beliefs about life after death. Jung admitted that embracing a personal myth of survival after death was, for him, psychologically hopeful and enriching. Lifton (1983) notes that despite their differences in belief about an afterlife, the common thread in all great religious mythologies is the quest of their hero-founders for spiritual realization, which enabled them to confront and transcend death, thus providing a model for generations of believers.

The lives of Buddha, Christ, Mohammed, Moses, and other religious leaders came to encompass various combinations of spirituality, revelation, and ultimate ethical principles that could divest death of its "sting" of annihilation. Lifton (1983) observed:

> The basic spiritual principle, with or without a concept of afterlife or immortal soul, is the ancient mythological theme of death and rebirth. One is offered the opportunity to be reborn into a timeless realm of ultimate, death-transcending truths. In that realm, one can share the immortality of the deity, obtain membership in a sacred community or a "covenant with God." Or that ultimate realm might take on the more concrete imagery of a "heaven," or of the negative immortality (unending suffering) of hell (pp. 20–21).

Lifton concludes that whatever the imagery, there is at the heart of religious mythology a sense of spiritual power. That power may be understood in a number of ways—dedication, capacity to love, moral determination—but its final meaning is the power over death.

For many people, the need to come to terms with death has been mollified by adopting one of the secular mythologies such as living through one's progeny or through one's actions, creations, or identity with the cosmos. For others, adherence to a religious or philosophical mythology suffices to answer their questions about death and to give them a framework from which to operate. In any event, myths are still needed in the contemporary world. Nothing else commands their explanatory power. And death, perhaps more than any other topic, requires the confrontation and search for meaning that mythology provides.

REFERENCES

Becker, E. 1973. *The Denial of Death*. New York: Free Press.

Becker, E. 1975. *Escape from Evil*. New York: Free Press.

Campell, J. 1986. *The Inner Reaches of Outer Space: Metaphor as Myth and as Religion*. New York: Alfred von der Marck.

Chadwick, M. 1969. Notes upon the Fear of Death. In *Death: Interpretations*. Ed. H.M. Ruitenbeek. New York: Delta.

Choran, J. 1974. *Modern Man and Mortality*. New York: Macmillan.

Cutter, F. 1974. *Coming to Terms with Death*. Chicago: Nelson-Hall.

Elliott, P., Feinstein, D., and Krippner, S. 1986. *Rituals for Living and Dying*. Ashland, OR: Innersource.

Evans-Wentz, W. Y. ed. 1957. *The Tibetan Book of the Dead.* London: Oxford University Press.

Feifel, H. 1979. The Problems of Death. In *Death: Interpretations.* Ed. H.M. Ruitenbeek. New York: Delta.

Gold, E.J. 1978. *American Book of the Dead* (rev. ed.). New York: Doneve Designs.

Grof, S., and Grof, C. 1980. *Beyond Death.* New York: Thames & Hudson.

Harmer, R.M. 1963. *The High Cost of Dying.* New York: Collier.

Herson, M.J., and Scott, R.A. 1979. Memorial Services and Funerals as Options. *Counseling Values.* 23:261–272.

Huxley, F. 1974. *The Way of the Sacred.* Garden City, NY: Doubleday.

Kübler-Ross, E. 1975. *Death: The Final Stage of Growth.* Englewood Cliffs, NJ: Prentice-Hall.

Kübler-Ross, E. 1969. *On Death and Dying.* New York: Macmillan.

Lamont, C. 1950. *The Illusion of Immortality* (2nd ed.). New York: Philosophical Library.

Leary, T., Metzner, R., and Alpert, R. 1974. *The Psychedelic Experience: A Manual Based on the Tibetan Book of the Dead.* New Hyde Park, NY: University Books.

LeComte, E. 1960. *Dictionary of Last Words.* New York: Philosophical Library.

Levine, S. 1987. *Healing into Life and Death.* Garden City, NY: Anchor.

Levine, S. 1982. *Who Dies? An Investigation of Conscious Living and Conscious Dying.* Garden City, NY: Anchor.

Mitford, J. 1963. *The American Way of Death.* New York: Simon & Schuster.

Muggeridge, M. 1970, February 20. Essay. *The Observer.* p. 25.

Paxton, T. 1976. Forest Lawn. In *We Are but a Moment's Sunlight: Understanding Death.* Eds. C.S. Adler, G. Stanford, and S.M. Adler. New York: Pocket.

Rosenthal, H.R. 1969. The Fear of Death as an Indispensable Factor in Psychotherapy. In *Death: Interpretations.* Ed. H.M. Ruitenbeek. New York: Delta.

Rossiter, E. ed. 1979. *The Book of the Dead: Papyri of Any, Hunefer, Anhai.* Freiburg, West Germany: Productions Library.

Russell, B. 1951. *The Autobiography of Bertrand Russell, 1872-1914.* Vol. 1. Boston: Little, Brown.

Sex, Death and Red Riding Hood. 1984, March 19. *Time,* p. 68.

Schneidman, E. 1980. *Voices of Death.* New York: Harper & Row.

Serrano, M. 1966. *C.G. Jung and Hermann Hesse: A Record of Two Friendships.* New York: Schocken.

Templer, D.I. 1973. Death Anxiety in Religiously Very Involved Persons. In *Death Anxiety.* New York: Manuscript Information Corporation.

Wass, H. 1979. *Dying: Facing the Facts.* New York: Hampshire/McGraw Hill.

Waugh, E. 1948. *The Loved One.* New York: Dell.

Wilber, K. 1981. *Up from Eden: A Transpersonal View of Human Evolution.* Garden City, NY: Anchor.

2

African Perspectives on Death and Dying

Kofi Asare Opoku

The African cultural heritage provides enormous resources for the understanding of the phenomenon of life and death. These resources are the considered product of many centuries of experience and mature reflection, and they represent Africa's own insights into the meaning and significance of life and death.

Life and death were created by the Creator, as the Akan talking drums put it in the drum text: "Odomankoma boo'nkwa, boo owto" (The Creator created life and death). Death follows life in an unalterable sequence that is a given condition of human existence.

That death was created by the Creator means that in the African understanding, death is not an intrusion that comes to disrupt or negate the order of life. Simply, at the end of earthly life comes death. Because personhood is conceived of as a process of becoming, a human being is understood to be always in the process of becoming something else. With this dynamic understanding of life, the rituals that are performed at the crisis points in the life of a person—birth, puberty, marriage, and death—are intended to ease the transition from one stage of life to the next. Death, therefore, is one of the rhythms of life, and is firmly integrated into the totality of life. In the outdooring ceremony among the Ga people, for example, the text of the prayer recited by the officiant states, inter alia, "He came with black, may he return with gray." In other words, the newly born baby has come into the world with black hair, and the wish is being expressed that he *returns* with gray hair, a wish for a long life here on earth followed by death.

ORIGIN OF DEATH

Because death is accepted as part of life, Africans have sought throughout the ages in their mythology to explain how death came about (Parrinder, 1967:54–63). These mythological accounts not only tell interesting fables, but also express truths about the human condition. Even though some of the myths tell of a time when human beings did not die but were simply rejuvenated when they grew old (Abramsson, 1951), they all show how death became an inescapable part of the human experience. The most important consideration is not how death entered the world, but the fact of the reality of death, which is in conformity with the human condition. A life without death is clearly contrary to our nature as human beings.

Among the myths of the origin of death are some that express the idea that given a choice between immortality and death, human beings chose death. According to an Asante myth narrated to the present writer by A. C. Denteh, when the early human beings started experiencing death, they pleaded with God to put a stop to death. Their request was granted. For three years no one died; however, strangely enough, no one gave birth to a child during this time. The people could not bear this situation, and again pleaded with God, this time to grant them the ability to have children even if it meant accepting death also. Thus, among the Asante, death and birth are complementary; just as death takes away members from the society, birth compensates for the losses death inflicts on the community.

The truths inherent in these myths notwithstanding, death remains a riddle, and attitudes to it are ambivalent. Even though death is accepted as part of life, it is regarded as impolite to state bluntly that someone is dead. It reflects good breeding and courteous comportment to refer to the death of someone in euphemistic terms. The commonest way is to say that the deceased "has gone home," "joined the ancestors," "did not wake up from his sleep" (as the Akan put it "odae a, wansore"); or that the "person's bed does not suit him" (as the Adangbe put it, "e sa dele") or that the person "has decided to seek a new sleeping place." The deceased may also be said to have "become God's property" or "to have kicked down salt," meaning that the person has stopped eating salt. This explains the practice common in many African societies of presenting the dead with saltless food. Finally, the proper way to refer to the death of a king or a chief is to say that he has "gone to his village."

From these euphemistic expressions about death, it can be seen that death is regarded as a journey to man's original place or home, and not as an end or an annihilation. The deceased goes to join the ancestors, to live in the land of the spirits; as Mbiti (1969:157] expressed it:

> Death is considered of as a departure and not a complete annihilation of a person. He moves on to join the company of the departed, and the only major change is the decay of the physical body, but the spirit moves on to another state of existence.

Therefore, the attitude to the phenomenon of death is positive, because it is comprehensively integrated into the totality of life. Life in the African cultural tradition is so whole that death does not destroy its wholeness. Death becomes, therefore, a prolongation of life. And, instead of a break between life and death, there is continuity between the two (Mulago 1969:138).

This means that the relationship between the living and the "living-dead," as Mbiti aptly describes them, remains unbroken and that the community of the living and the community of the "living-dead" experience a reciprocal permeability, for there is constant interaction between the two communities. This wholeness of life expresses itself in the fact that the African family or community is not made up only of the living but also of the dead, and there is always a supernatural or extrahuman dimension to the family and community.

Those who die do not lose the identity they had when they were living persons. They maintain their status and their social positions as mothers, fathers, sisters, brothers, cousins, aunts, and children as well as kings and queens. Moreover, the obligations they had towards members of their families are maintained after death; thus, there is a symbiotic relationship between the two communities. The living have their part to play in keeping the relationship with the "living-dead" alive, and the latter also have a part to play.

These ideas explain the rituals connected with death, which are symbolic preparations for the deceased to enter the abode of the ancestors. In the Akan traditions, death is a journey; therefore, the person in the throes of death is given cold water to drink to cool his or her heart before the start of the journey. The body is bathed and dressed in a manner befitting a person traveling, in order that he or she may reach the destination properly attired so that the person may be welcomed by the inhabitants of the place. Several personal belongings that the deceased will require are put into the coffin before interment. These include toiletries, clothes, a calabash or drinking cup (so that the person can drink water during the journey), and some money with which the deceased can purchase something on the way.

In other parts of Africa, to emphasize that death is not a complete destruction of the individual and that the person is going to continue living the same kind of life in the land of his or her destination, the corpse is equipped with whatever is needed to continue life in the spirit world. In some farming areas, farm implements, yams, and grain may be put into the grave for the deceased to continue his or her occupation in the land of the ancestors. According to Metuh (1982:143), the dead person among the Ibo of eastern Nigeria, "is given his working tools, his gun, his bag, some cloth and if he is a rich man, coins. . . ."

In the past, wives and servants of kings were killed to accompany them because of the firm belief that the king would continue to live as such and would need his wives and servants. Others voluntarily took their lives in order to accompany the king, as Opoku (1987:13) explains:

> This attitude was held with such utter conviction that little anxiety was shown in the face of death. An authentication of this attitude could be found in Benin where servants and persons especially indulged by the king would compete with each other for the privilege of being buried alive with the body of the king when he died so that they could attend on him in the next world.

Messages are also given to the deceased to take to people on the other side, just as messages are given to a person going on a journey to convey to people at his destination. Giving messages to the dead presupposes the ability of the living to communicate with the dead, and this communication continues well after the corpse has been buried in the grave. Among the important messages given to the deceased is the exhortation to identify themselves at the outskirts of their destination so that their relatives may come and take them home. According to Nketia (1955:44–45), among the Akan, deceased kings and chiefs are told:

> When you reach the outskirts of the town, mention your name so that strong men might carry you shoulder high for you rule two worlds.

The Dangbe of Ghana give herbs peculiar to their ethnic group to the corpse; these herbs identify the deceased with the ethnic group to which he or she belongs upon entering the spirit world (Ayim (1982:25). Tribal marks are also useful means of identification by one's ethnic group in the abode of the dead.

In other parts of Africa, death is considered to be a birth into the world of the living-dead. The Abaluyia of Kenya give concrete proof of this belief by burying their dead completely naked, so that they may be born into the other world just as we are born naked into this world (Mbiti 1969:155).

The occasion of death also provides the opportunity for asking for more life. The messages given to the deceased, as Dickson (1984:194) wrote:

> . . . are illustrative of the African concern for life: they are concerned with health, children, and generally those things which would strengthen the effectiveness of the petitioners as contributors to the maintenance of society's equilibrium.

This is based on the belief that the dead can confer favors on their relatives or kinsmen.

CONTINUATION OF LIFE BEYOND THE GRAVE

The above ideas indicate clearly that there is a widespread notion that death does not lead to the destruction of either the person or the identity of the deceased and that, in the main, death is a journey from this world to another. Death, therefore, becomes a gateway that links the two worlds, and life is constant, before and after the grave. Mbiti (1969:155), wrote:

> The dying person is being cut off from human beings, and yet there must be continuing ties between the living and the departed. Relatives and neighbours come to bid fare-well to the dying man and to mourn his departure, and yet there is continuity through his children and through the rituals which unite the two worlds. Death causes ritual impurity just as it interrupts normal life; but it is not permanent since it is cleansed and normal life is afterwards resumed. The grave

is paradoxically the symbol of separation between the dead and the living, but turning it into the shrine for the living-dead converts it into the point of meeting between the two worlds.

There are two major reasons for the belief in the persistence of life after death and the indestructability of a part of the human personality. The first has to do with the concept of human personality (Opoku (1978:91–140). Each person has a divine spark in him or her that comes from the Creator and links him or her directly to the Creator. This divine spark the Akan call "okra," and it is not subject to the destructive forces of death. This okra is part of "Onyame" (God) in every person, and its departure or return to its source signifies death. Because God does not die, the okra too does not die; hence, the Akan say, "Onyame bewu na mawu" (I shall only die if God dies), or "Onipa wu a, na onwui e" (when a person dies he is not *really* dead). Thus, death does not destroy the okra or divine spark, which continues to live and to be interacted with by members of the family. The okra has an antemundane existence as well as a postmortem existence.

A second reason for the belief in the persistence of life after death stems from the African conception of the relationship between the human being and the surrounding world. A person is not completely detached from the world or from total reality, although a person may be said to be distinct from the surrounding world. But human beings share much with the world around them, and human identity is not asserted by the distinction that is made between humankind and the world, as it is in the West. On the contrary, human beings in Africa are understood to be united with the world around them — earth, water, plants, animals — because the same essential power vital to existence, often called vital force, undulates through them all.

The Fulani creation story, as related by Soyinka (1975:57f), underscores the unity between man and the elements thus:

At the beginning there was a huge drop of milk.
The Doondari (God) came and created the stone.
Then the stone created iron;
And iron created fire;
And fire created water;
And water created air.
Then Doondari descended the second time.
And he took the five elements.
And he shaped them into man.

This essential vital force, a quintessential reality that flows through all beings, is antecedent to the birth of every human being into the world, encompasses human beings throughout life, and remains in existence after death. Human life is therefore part of ongoing reality, and each death is a reassimilation into the reality of the world. As Balandier and Maquet (1974:103) expressed it:

Conceived of in this way, the death of an individual is not an ontological scandal, annihilating a being who is completely self-sufficient and has his own destiny. Rather, it is the progressive reabsorption into the world of one of its manifestations that was always deeply rooted in it . . .

That death does not mark the cessation of life and does not end the human being's self-expression explains the meaning African traditional religion gives to life. Life is not the opposite of death; life is constant because those who die continue to live. The opposite of death is birth, and birth is the one event that links every human being, on the one hand, with all those who have gone before and, on the other, with all those who will come after. A human being is therefore constantly at the center of the human drama, with unbreakable links reaching both to the past and to the future.

The source of the relationship between Africans and their ancestors is based on the fact that the dead continue to live, for there would be no need to communicate with them if they ceased to live after death. The dead do not just fade into nothingness, as Idowu (1973:188) wrote:

They do not for any reason fade into nothing or lapse into any kind of durational retirement. In the invocation of ancestors in certain African localities, the liturgy embraces those remembered and unremembered, those known and unknown. It is often said specifically, "we cannot remember all of you by name, nevertheless we invoke you all." Further, ancestors connected with certain professions like medicine, crafts or priesthood are mentioned as far back as the first one who initiated the practice. . . . During annual festivals, or special rituals, ancestors are traced as far back as the beginning of things.

Nor does the existence of the dead depend on the memory of the living. The dead have an independent existence. They do not continue to live merely because they are remembered by those who are living, for the fact of life and non-life is not dependent on the memory of human beings, for human memory does not create life.

TYPES AND EXPLANATIONS OF DEATH

Generally, there are good and bad deaths in African societies and the manner of death dictates the kind of funeral rites that are performed. A good death, called "Onwu Chi," God's death, by the Ibo (Metuh 1982:142) is a death that comes after a person has attained a ripe old age. A good death, which is also regarded as a natural death, may be the result of what is considered to be a clean disease, for there are bad deaths caused by unclean diseases such as leprosy, epilepsy, dropsy, and the like. Bad deaths may also be due to violent accidents and deaths caused by suicide.

Even though in the normal run of things people have no control over the way and manner of their deaths, the distinction between good and bad deaths is made and ancestorhood is conferred or denied on the basis of the way and manner of one's death. These ideas are dictated by some fundamental beliefs as well as by societal values, and a study of funeral rites in Africa reveals these beliefs and values.

It is believed that people die only to come back. Because society wants to rid itself of what it regards to be evil or bad deaths, people who die bad deaths do not receive full burial rites so that they may not come back to repeat what they did. Those whom society wants to come back receive full burial rites in order to reinforce the values that society holds dear. Ancestorhood also depends on the conduct of people in life. Those who lived lives worthy of emulation, or those who lived exemplary lives, are accorded the status of ancestors, for the dead constitute a source of reference for an ethically accepted life.

Human beings have both a material and immaterial part to their beings, but they are not divided entities and the unity of human personality is a fundamental assumption in African thought. Both parts of the person interact with each other; what happens to the immaterial part of the person affects the material part, and vice versa. Death therefore has both physical and non-physical causes. The physical cause may include old age, disease, accidents, or injuries. However, physical causes alone do not adequately and exhaustively explain the phenomenon of death; thus, the nonphysical causes are used to provide a comprehensive explanation of death. Nonphysical causes include evil spirits, sorcery, witchcraft, and other mysterious forces and summons from the ancestors. That nonphysical causes of death are recognized does not mean that physical explanations are denied. Death is the result of many factors, physical and nonphysical, and these are not necesssarily incompatible or mutually exclusive. A death may be caused by illness, but at the same time it can be the result of the will of a spiritual being. This comprehensive explanation enables people to accept and come to terms with what would otherwise remain inexplicable (Opoku 1987:11).

FUNERAL RITES AND BURIAL RITES

The death of a person is always a community affair, and the entire community is involved in the funeral. An Akan proverb says, "owu antweri obaako mforo" ("the ladder of death is not climbed by only one person"—in other words, death happens to everybody). Therefore, the death of a member of the community is an affair in which not only the deceased's immediate family but the whole community takes part. Death is not looked at as an individual affair. Members of the community help the bereaved family in seeing off the deceased, and through donations, help the bereaved family to defray the expenses of the funeral. The death of a person also gives the community the opportunity to give concrete expression to community solidarity. As Dickson (1986:196) wrote, "Death binds up relationships in society, revitalising the living and underscoring their sense of community." The actions that are taken are community forms of action, and whether the deceased's status was high or low, there is a great deal of community interaction.

The burial rites are performed for the purpose of the interment of the corpse. The rites are dictated not only by the circumstances of the death but also by such considerations as the age, social position, and status of the deceased. Furthermore, the burial rites reflect the society's beliefs about the fate of the dead, particularly concerning the rebirth of the dead. Among the Zulu, for example, the belief in rebirth is reflected in the burying of their dead in a squatting position (symbolizing the position of the embryo in the fetal membrane), and the niche in which the deceased is put is called a "navel" (Opoku 1987:15).

The sex of the deceased often influences the way the corpse is laid in the tomb, because the deceased are believed to wake up to continue their roles. Thus, among the Bono of Ghana, a man is buried facing east so as to rise up and go to the farm, while a woman is laid in the tomb facing west so that she may rise up to start cooking the evening meal.

Funeral rites are performed for the purpose of ensuring that the deceased may be able to join the ancestral spirits. There is widespread belief that the spirit of the deceased cannot go to its destination unless the proper funeral rites are performed, and relatives derive satisfaction from the performance of these funeral rites.

Funeral celebrations vary greatly. Children's funerals are brief and simple, and are usually not characterized by wailing, whereas those of adults are more elaborate. The funeral rites mark the transition of the deceased into ancestorhood, but not all who die attain ancestorhood.

In celebrating funerals, usually a period of mourning is declared in which ordinary activities are suspended; in this way, death is made acceptable to society. Even in the midst of funerals, a strong affirmation of life is seen not only in the dancing, which from the African point of view is a powerful affirmation of life, but also in the festivities that end the period of mourning and clearly indicate the resumption of normal life.

AMBIVALENT ATTITUDE TO DEATH?

Although death is regarded in a positive way as leading into life and the gateway to ancestorhood, the physical separation that it brings about between loved ones or members of the family leads to a negative attitude. Thus:

> Death is a wicked destroyer, a killer and a curse which frustrates human effort. It brings about complete physical separation and constitutes a great loss not only to the immediate family in which it occurs but also to the whole community. . . . Death drives men to sorrow and despair and has no respect for beauty or intelligence. It appears like a monster taking young and old and there is nobody who can intervene when it comes (Opoku 1978:134).

Nevertheless, the physical separation leads to a change of status from a lesser to a higher authority. Death increases one's powers, and the bonds holding the members of the family together are not broken by death, but are maintained despite death, like a bridge over an abyss (Mpolo 1979:136). The reality of life after death, as has been pointed out already, means that in the African tradition, death is not the final end of the person and the abode of the dead to which the deceased go has nothing terminal about it. Although it is patterned after life in this world, its residents do not remain there forever. They are believed to return to this life, and life is viewed as a continuing cyclic process. The dead return to their lineages to be reborn, and the symbolism of death and resurrection pervading many African cultural practices (such as initiation rites, and training for the priesthood), underscores its importance. Relatives of the deceased customarily shave off their hair as a symbol of separation from one of their members. The new hair that grows back indicates the belief that death does not destroy life and that life continues to spring up (Mbiti 1975:115).

The cyclical continuity of life as birth, death, and rebirth is at the heart of African religiosity and amounts to what salvation in African traditional religion consists of: an uninterrupted cycle of life through reincarnation (Metuh 1982:154). This sharply differs from the Hindu cyclic conception of life in which salvation consists in liberation from the recurring cycle of birth, death, and rebirth.

CONCLUSION

According to Metuh (1982:153),

The terms "this life," "next life," "after life," "eternal life" are terms borrowed from European Christian philosophy which are foreign to the African system of thought. Life is one continuous stretch of existence and is not split up into "this life" and "the next life." The concept of time is cyclic, not lineal. What happens after death is not the terminal, definitive stage of man's life, it is only a phase in the continuing round of human existence. . . .The spirit land is not a place of eternal repose and happiness. It is rather a transit camp for those awaiting reincarnation to continue the life cycle.

The originality of African ideas about death, which shows itself in the way in which death is faced, ritualized, and interpreted as a continuation of life, reflects the foundational faith of African people. Life is not restricted to bodily existence, and death therefore does not rob life of meaning; on the contrary, it gives greater depth of meaning to life by prolonging it on the spiritual plane (Opoku 1987). Herein lies a fundamental antidote to the threat of human extinction and the morbid fear of nothingness, which have made life for many a modern person utterly meaningless.

REFERENCES

Abrahamsson, Hans. 1951. *The Origin of Death. Studies in African Mythology.* Studia Ethnographica Upsaliensia, Vol. 3. Uppsala: Almquist and Wiksells.
Ayim, M.N. 1982. *The Concept of Life and Death Among the Dangbe.* Master's Thesis, University of Ghana, Legon.

Balandier, G., and J. Maquet. 1974. *Dictionary of Black African Civilization.* New York: Leon Amiel.

Dickson, K.A. 1984. *Theology in Africa.* London: Darton, Longman and Todd.

Idowu, E.B. 1973. *African Traditional Religion: A Definition.* London: S.C.M.

Mbiti, J.S. 1969. *African Religion and Philosophy.* London: Heinemann Educational Books Ltd.

Mbiti, J.S. 1975. *Introduction to African Religion.* London: Heinemann Eucational Books Ltd.

Metuh, Ikenga E. 1982. *God and Man in African Religion: A Case Study of the Igbo of Nigeria.* London: G. Chapman.

Mpolo, Masamba ma. 1979. Community and Cure: The Therapeutics of the Traditional Religions and the Religion of the Prophets in Africa. In *Christian and Islamic Contributions Towards Establishing Independent States in Africa South of the Sahara.* Papers and proceedings of the Africa Colloquium Bonn-Bad Godesberg, 2–4 May. Eds. Karl-Heinz Bechtold and Ernst J. Tetsch. Tubingen: Laupp and Goebel.

Mulago, Vincent. 1979. Vital Participation: The Cohesive Principle of the Bantu Community. In *Biblical Revelation and African Beliefs.* Eds. K. Dickson and P. Ellingworth. London: Butterworth Press.

Niketia, J.H. 1955. *Funeral Dirges of the Akan.* Achimota.

Opoku, Kofi Asare. 1978. *West African Traditional Religion.* Singapore: Far Eastern Publishers.

Opuku, Kofi Asare. 1987. Death and Immortality in the African Religious Heritage. In *Death and Immortality in the Religions of the World.* Eds. P. Badham and L. Badham. New York: Paragon House.

Parrinder, G. 1967. *African Mythology.* London: Paul Hamlyn.

Soyinka, Wole, ed. 1975. *Poems of Black Africa.* London.

3

Death and the Afterlife in African Culture

Kwasi Wiredu

There is a mildly paradoxical unanimity in African studies about the African belief in and attitude to the afterlife. On the one hand, it is universally noted that Africans generally believe that bodily death is not the end of life but only the inauguration of life in another form. On the other hand, it is equally universally remarked that the African attitude to life is a this-worldly one. The paradox is, in fact, only apparent; but quite some conceptual clarifications are needed to see why.

The crucial conceptual issue concerns the nature of the afterworld. In what sense is it an *other* world? Not all African peoples are given to talking about death and the afterlife,[1] but wherever there are any intimations at all of what life in the *land* of the dead is like, the similarities between that form of life and the *earthly* one are striking. The similarities are indeed so striking that the characterization of this life as "earthly" in contrast to the afterlife is already metaphysically inappropriate. In West Africa, for example, where people are not excessively reticent about eschatology, descriptions of the afterlife generally include explicit indications that the transition from this life to the next is by land travel; of course, if you travel from one part of the earth by land, you can only arrive at another part of the earth. In traditional Africa boundaries are often marked by rivers. Not surprisingly, the high point of the postmortem journey is the crossing of a river. Having crossed the river, one enters the land of the departed and joins the society of the ancestors, a society which replicates the political order of premortem society to the extent that rulers in the one retain their status in the other.

It would be interesting and relevant to speculate who or what this "one" is who is supposed to do the afterlife travelling, but it might be more appropriate to call attention immediately to the this-wordly orientation of the conception of the afterlife. Remaining in West Africa for the time being, it is important to note that the whole point of going on the last journey is to become one of the ancestors. The significance of the ancestors consists simply of keeping watch over the affairs of the living members of their families, helping deserving ones, and punishing the delinquent. If an ancestor is a ruler, the scope of his activities goes beyond his own family to the whole of his town or kingdom. In either case, ancestors see to the good of the living. There is, of course, a reciprocal side to this. Reciprocity is a strong feature of African society; in fact, it is a feature of any moral community. Accordingly, the living feel not only beholden to the ancestors for their help and protection, but are also positively obliged to honor them and render service to them as appropriate.

The ancestors may be honored in two connected ways — one general, the other particular. The first way is simply to live uprightly, which is a source of honor to one's family. On the other hand, bad conduct brings disgrace to the living family and displeasure to the ancestors. The ancestors, in their postmortem condition, are credited with veritable moral perfection and are therefore not accessible to disgrace; however, solely because of their elevated moral status, they are thought to be even more scandalized by wrongdoing than the living elders of the family. Wrongdoing may take three basic forms: trifling with the moral law; falling foul of civil regulations or of community customs and taboos; and failing to take good care of family affairs. The last category may involve specific imperatives or even injunctions. Perhaps a departed member of the family has left his successor a half-completed project together with adequate resources for its completion. Completing it does honor to the dead. Paying debts or caring for his dependents are also opportunities to uphold his honor. Or, specific instructions may have been left before death for certain things to be done. These and similar actions form the second, more particular, way in which the living can do honor to the dead, or perhaps we ought to say the dead-but-living.[2] Because these matters imply definite duties, nonperformance may elicit punishment from an ancestor, which usually takes the form of unaccountable illnesses.[3] Incidentally, these are the form of lapses from right conduct that the ancestors are most apt to punish. However, this restriction does not indicate an abridged interest, on their part, in the general morality of their relatives; it only means that the ethical division of labor provides other sources of sanctions. Nor does the restriction diminish the conviction of the living that right conduct redounds to the credit of their departed relations and, besides, warms their hearts.

Concerning direct services to themselves, the ancestors are remarkably undemanding. Dedicatory drops of ceremonial schnapps or modest servings of food in the right place overnight from time to time seem to be all that is required. Nevertheless, such acts, especially those of libation, are of the last consequence, because through them the living communicate their assurances of respect to the ancestors and solicit their timely assistance in connection with specific enterprises. In this way, an ongoing social relationship is maintained with the departed.

To reopen a question previously raised but not explored, what then must the inhabitants of the land of the dead be like to sustain this social relationship with their mortal brethren? If we recall the land travel, river crossing, and the serving of schnapps and food, it occurs to us that they must be conceived as of a somewhat psychophysical constitution.[4] That they must have some analogue of a body is an inescapable inference from the physicalistic setting of their activities and, in any case, from embodied descriptions of sightings of dead individuals. (Although rare, such sightings are culturally typical.) It is no less apparent that they must have minds, because they are supposed to exercise the function of *assessing* the conduct of their relatives and apportioning blight or blessing as the case may require. After all, for at least some African peoples, such as the Akans of Ghana, mind is not an extensionless substance à la Descartes, but simply the capacity to do just such things.[5] From all of which, it emerges not only that the land of the dead is geographically similar to our own, but also that its population is rather like us.[6] Actually, this is not a surprising idea, for it is a natural outgrowth of a conception of personhood that is entertained among the peoples of West Africa with only variations of detail and, indeed, among most African peoples with only slightly more substantial differences. According to this conception, a human being has two types of constituents. The first is the material body as commonly perceived, which presents no immediate conceptual problems. The second constituent, on the other hand, is not easy to characterize. It is not of identically the same type as the material body, and yet it is not of a diametrically opposed category: it is a cross between the two. This second factor of human personality is taken to be what accounts for our being alive or for our having a particular destiny; it is that whose presence means life and whose departure means death.[7] But it is itself conceived on the model of the living body or, better still, of the living person; so much so, that it is frequently spoken of as a replica of a person and credited with the office of a "guardian angel." The ontologically interesting thing about this kind of being is that although it is conceived of in the *image* of a person, it is exempted from the grosser characteristics of the material body. Thus, it can appear or disappear without regard to speed limits for matter in motion or the laws of impenetrability. Moreover, it is capable of action at a distance in which a living person may be severely affected without perceptible contact. The question of perceivability brings us to an important property of the entities in question: They cannot be seen with the naked eye or heard with the unaided ear, except on rare occasions when they elect to make themselves sensibly accessible to particular persons; otherwise, they can be seen or heard only by people with medicinally heightened powers of sight and hearing.

Even so sketchy a characterization of the second basic constituent of a person in the West African conception should make it clear that to describe it as *spiritual* in the sense of total immateriality would be a substantial oversimplification. There is in the West African conception only a reduced materiality, and the reduction affects not its imagery, but its dynamics. At death it is this quasi-material entity that departs to the world of the dead; thus, it is natural that talk of the afterlife should be replete with a this-worldly imagery. This remark is applicable to the thought not only of the peoples of West Africa but also of many other African peoples, perhaps of most or all African peoples. It certainly explains Okot p'Bitek's insistence, in the specific case of the Central Luo, that the "entities which they believed they encountered at the lineage shrines were not *spirits* but the ancestors *as they were known before death*" (added italics).[6]

Mindful of all the foregoing, we now return to the question in what sense the African world of the dead is an *other* world. The answer must be that it is in no sense another world but rather a part of this world, albeit a conceptually problematic part. The problem is that the attenuations of the materiality of the place of the dead and its residents seem to leave us with a material imagery without a solid anchorage. Nevertheless, this imagery has been marvelously efficacious in motivating conceptions of the cultural unity of the living with the dead in the thought of many African peoples. Given this conceptual framework, it becomes intelligible how this life can be seen as a preparation for an afterlife whose whole significance nevertheless consists in the securing of the welfare of the living. It follows, by an obvious transitivity, that in this way of thinking, whatever the meaning of life is, it is to be defined in terms of the circumstances of this life.

I shall return to this last point later, but it might be helpful to compare briefly some other conceptions of life after death. Proceeding in the order of descending immateriality, we may note Plato's theory of survival after death. What survives physical death is the soul, which, for Plato, is an absolutely immaterial entity.[8] During the life of a mortal, this entity is "imprisoned" in the body, so that death is actually a liberation. When death occurs, the soul reverts to a totally rarefied realm of being containing the immaterial and changeless originals of which the things in this world are imperfect copies. There it becomes again directly conversant with the true realities, which in mortal life it was at best capable only of remembering. This soul is, of course, indestructible, and enjoys both a prenatal and postmortem existence. Although beautiful, this conception offers no possibility of a social interaction between the dead and the living, and it is as far removed from African conceptions as anything can be. Indeed, I doubt that it can be translated into the African language that I know, namely, the Akan language (spoken in parts of Ghana and the Ivory Coast).

Within the Western intellectual tradition, however, there is a conception of immortality in which immaterial and quasi-material factors are intermixed. This is the Christian doctrine of the resurrection of the body at Judgment Day. On this fateful day, mortal remains of dead people, the largest proportion of them long transformed into earth, will be reassembled and reanimated with their corresponding souls. Dead persons will be reconstituted by body and soul being put together again in such a way as to recover their premortem personal identities, with the one pleasant exception that the new bodies will be so vastly improved as not to be susceptible to any physical disabilities or carnal cravings. In this purified form they will live in eternal bliss, that is, if they are accorded salvation through the undeserved grace of God. In the alternative they shall be consigned, presumably in not so perfect bodies, to some extremely inconvenient mode of existence forever. Saint Augustine, for one, was adamant on the justice of such eternal punishment. If it seems harsh, it is only because "in the weakness of our mortal condition there is wanting that highest and purest wisdom by which it can be perceived how great a wickedness was committed in the first transgression."[9]

Three points arise, one of near similarity, two of outright contrast. If we view the resurrected people as whole persons, they are quite similar to the inhabitants of African lands of the dead. The resurrected and saved are like mortal persons in imagery but unlike them in their mode of action. Saint Augustine (op. cit., Bk. xxii: 29–30) actually speaks of them as being "clothed in immortal and spiritual bodies" that "shall live no longer in a fleshy but a spiritual fashion." Saint Augustine remarks furthermore, "What power of movement such bodies shall possess, I have not the audacity to conceive. . . . One thing is certain, the body shall forthwith be wherever the spirit wills, and the spirit shall will nothing which is unbecoming either to the spirit or to the body." The bodies in question are obviously neither purely material nor purely immaterial (which in any case would be self-contradictory) but, in truth, quasi-material. There is, then, some similarity between the African and the traditional Christian images of the dead-but-living. The similarity, however, is only skin deep, for the raised Christian is a combination of an immaterial soul and a quasi-material body whereas the departed African is, by original constitution, a quasi-material being. Nor does the latter have to wait as a split person in some transitional realm with the "Day of Judgment" to attain the wholeness of postmortem personality.

The absence in the eschatology of many African peoples of a day of judgment together with its inexorable sequel, positive or negative, marks a very significant difference with the Christian variety.[10] The Day of Judgment by definition is an apocalyptic watershed, bringing the end of the temporal phase of cosmic history. Thenceforward, this world is no more. Hence the question of the relationship of the inhabitants of this world with those of the next does not arise. This life is not only a preparation for the next, it is also waiting for the next. Moreover, the very meaning of this life consists in the fact that there is a next one. Historically, this point of view has been held widely in the Western world, though not universally or always within the confines of orthodox Christianity. Jacques Choron in his interesting book *Death and Modern Man* (1964) has collected a number of striking expressions of that view from some remarkable men, including the following: "If immortality be untrue, it matters little whether anything else be true or not" (Henry Thomas Buckle, 19th century historian); "If there is no immortality, I shall hurl myself into the sea" (Tennyson); "Without the hope of an afterlife this life is not even worth the effort of getting dressed in the morning" (Bismarck); "Without immortality. . . all the generations of mankind are fighting a forlorn hope. . .our life is blind and our death is fruitless (A.E. Taylor, who was one of the leaders of Plato scholarship in Britain a generation ago); "Without the belief in the existence of the soul and its immortality human existence is 'unnatural' and unbearable" (Dostoyevsky). From a logical point of view, it is difficult to see how the meaning of life can consist in even more life, but the interesting thing for our discussion is that most traditional Africans are likely to find such sentiments extremely surprising. For example, although a Nuer or Dinka elder takes the existence of life after death for granted, he does not set much store by it. According to Evans-Pritchard (1956:154), the Nuer religion "is a this-worldly religion, a religion of abundant life and the fullness of days, and they neither pretend to know, nor...do they care what happens to them after death." In the society of the Nuer, says Evans-Pritchard, either by nature or by convention, "Every man has at least one son and through this son his name is forever a link in a line of descent. This is the only form of immortality Nuer are interested in. They are not interested in the survival of the individual as a ghost, but in the social personality in the name" (p.163). Godfrey Lienhardt (1961:129) makes the same observation in connection with the Dinka; "Children and cattle multiplying and prospering from generation to generation are the ultimate value of Dinka life." Or, as he also notes, "Dinka greatly fear to die without issue in whom the survival of their names — the only kind of immortality they know — will be assured" (p. 319). Thus, to the traditional Dinka, "Notions of individual personal immortality mean little" (p. 319). Lienhardt's wording in these quotations might suggest that Dinka do not believe in the existence of personal survival after death; however, that cannot very well be his intent, for he himself gives accounts of how they try (through various procedures) to establish satisfactory relations with their departed ancestors. The point is simply that even though they do entertain this belief, it is not where they derive their sense of the worthwhileness of life. It is in this that the Nuer and Dinka are typical of Africans generally.

In not being specially thrilled at the possibility of eventually becoming ancestors in the country of the dead, the Dinka and Nuer are very much unlike the Akans of Ghana and the Ivory Coast or the Yoruba of Nigeria and Benin, or the Mende of Sierra Leone. In these regions the ancestors are highly prized and respected, and the notion of one day becoming an ancestor is cherished. Yet, becoming an ancestor, as already pointed out, only enables one to help the living to realize human purposes. To a typical Akan, for example, a life that has meaning is one that makes reasonable achievements[11] in the direction of personal, family, and communal welfare. A life of that sort would be a meaningful one even if there were no belief in an afterlife. In point of fact, one's life after death does not figure in one's destiny. Human destiny begins and ends in this world. To hurl yourself into the sea simply because there is no life after death would strike a traditional Akan as equivalent to madness.

In West Africa, indeed, living a full and meaningful life is a condition for becoming an ancestor.[12] This is probably not universally the case, but in the view of some peoples, such as the Akans of Ghana, a person whose life is cut short by an accident, an "unclean" disease, or any other untoward circumstance does not gain immediate access to the country of the dead; he becomes a neighborhood ghost, an occasional source of frightening apparitions, until he can be born again to try to work out a complete life. This, by the way, is the nearest approximation to purgatory in the Akan system. It is also one of the two forms of limited reincarnation postulated in that system. The second form is supposed to occur when a mother loses a baby, and then has another soon afterwards. In such circumstances, it is assumed that the same person goes back and forth. Aside from those two types of cases, any talk of reincarnation is largely metaphorical. An Akan or Yoruba will speak of the second coming of an ancestor—to be sure there can be multiple comings of the same ancestor—and mean by this mainly that the new addition to the family bears striking physical or psychological resemblance to the ancestor in question. The literal component of meaning would be that the influence of the ancestor himself is at work in the phenomenon.

It is not accidental that in such thought systems, belief in reincarnation is so definitively circumscribed. Because the ancestors are so important in the affairs of the living and because status is enhanced by longevity, it is useful to have permanent ancestors. Any generalized and continuous turnover of ancestors would obviously detract from that scheme. Note again that this concept of immortality is a pragmatic one; it is immortality for the service of mankind. In this way of thinking, a paradisal type of immortality in which people endlessly enjoyed themselves (in however "spiritual" a fashion) without any responsibilities would be viewed as glorified idleness.

The African land of the dead, then, is not heaven in the Christian sense. The life of the ancestors is pictured as one of dignity and serenity rather than of bliss. There are, of course, no temptations or tribulations in that life, but neither are there any excitements. The one preoccupation of that existence is with the good of the living wing of the family and clan. It is upon their ability to achieve this aim that the importance of the ancestors is predicated. Thus, beneficial interaction with the community of the living is the first law of their being.

If we look for a substantially analogous concept of survival after death in Western thought, we will obviously not find it in orthodox Christianity. The likeliest place would be in the theory of the astral body found in the literature of spiritualism. Death here is regarded as the departure of the soul (which is itself a kind of body) from the physical plane to another place of existence, namely, the astral. The soul, in contradistinction from the physical body, is of a highly subtle constitution, but it is still basically corporeal. It is, moreover, of the form of the body, and although the soul is generally not visible to the ordinary eye, "those who have eyes" can see it and even hold converse with it. This gives the departed soul a certain sociability and helpfulness. Thus, it is not unknown for the dead to reveal the whereabouts of lost valuables or to help crime detection with crucial information, according to spiritualist claims. It may be said, accordingly, that in terms of ontological status and social relevance the astral survivor is akin to the inhabitant of the land of the dead as spoken of in African eschatology.

In the Western tradition one can trace the notion of the soul as an astral body to Tertullian, the idiosyncratic, early church father (AD 160–220). He argued that the conclusion that the soul is corporeal (although ethereal) can be inferred from the Christian doctrine of purgatory.[13] What contemporary spiritualism adds to Tertullian's conception is the social dimension. However, this social dimension is unsystematic and desultory in comparison with that of the African idea of ancestors. The African ancestors rule their kin from the grave, so to speak; the same cannot be said of their astral counterparts. Because of their minimal social interactions with the living, the cultural significance of the latter (even among the persuaded) is not as great as that of the former.

What is this cultural significance? We have already mentioned the role of the ancestors in the enforcement of morals.[14] Morals, broadly construed, cover ethical rules proper as well as customs and taboos. It is with respect to their relevance to the last two kinds of rules of conduct rather than the first that the ancestors have their greatest cultural significance. This is not because their status as guardians of the morality of their living relatives — morality being taken in the narrow sense — is not important, even though often restricted. The reason is twofold. First, in the case of morality, narrowly defined, the ancestors can only enforce rules whose basis or validity is independent of their own wishes or decisions, whereas customs and taboos are frequently of their own making; and second, customs and taboos (if available) are more essential to the individuality of a culture than morality. These two considerations each require brief elaboration.

To take the question of morality (in the narrow sense) first: It is often supposed that in Africa morality is determined by the injunctions of the ancestors and other extrahuman powers. This is usually inferred from the very evident influence that beliefs about these beings have on African conduct. If "determine" is interpreted in a causal, psychological sense, the conclusion follows tautologically from the premise, for the claim then amounts simply to the observation that thought of the ancestors, as a matter of psychological fact, does actually cause traditional Africans to behave in certain ways. However, if the alleged determination of morality by the ancestors is taken in a logical sense, the claim is false, or at any rate, not true of all African thought, because at least in the case of the Akans, the justification of moral rules consists solely in considerations concerning the harmonious adjustment of the interests of individuals with those of the community. The will of an ancestor, or a "god," or indeed, of God, may function as an incentive for an action, but never as its justification.[15]

Customs, on the other hand, are frequently held to be justified simply because they were established by our ancestors long ago. Even here it is pertinent to note that the rules concerned are supposed to have been laid down by the ancestors while they lived, so that their interest in them after death is only a continuation of premortem concerns. Furthermore, although the average mind does not look beyond precedence for the justification of customs, the really wise men of the group can point out their rationale. This is probably also true of taboos. On the face of it, a taboo is an arbitrary prohibition based on the will of some nonhuman power and backed by threats of unusual consequences. In fact, on deeper scrutiny, such rules may be found to have some rhyme and even reason. For the purpose of this discussion, the important point is that the reason for a custom or taboo is always pragmatic. A pragmatic reason may justify a practice without making it universally obligatory. By contrast, moral reasons are universal. Because of this universality, moral rules cannot figure in the differentia of a culture: Morality is too essential to human culture to vary from culture to culture. But some things do vary from culture to culture, and custom is certainly one such thing. Because the ancestors, however one looks at the matter, are crucial for the existence in African societies of customs and taboos, their importance in the individuation of African cultures is obvious.

Besides the general relevance of the ancestors to custom and taboo, many African societies observe elaborate and protracted customs relating to the process by which a person becomes an ancestor. Death (unfortunately) is the first necessary condition for ancestorhood. When death happens, people feel an obligation to give the deceased a fitting send-off to the land of the ancestors, and that involves both spontaneous and formalized mourning and various funeral ceremonies. The scale of a funeral process, judged in terms of the intensity of the mourning, the number of persons attending, and the meticulousness of the formalities is taken to reflect the respect in which the deceased is held. On this account, people will go to no end of trouble to ensure grand funeral rites of their deceased relatives. There is much less ado about dead bodies, however, among some ethnic groups in Africa. Among such people the mortal remains of the departed are disposed of with businesslike dispatch. The population of Ghana, for example, includes groups practicing both types of extremes as well as groups with intermediate funeral habits. The peoples of the northern part of Ghana are extremely brisk in their manner of sending off the dead to their new home, while the Akans, among others, devote major effort and time to that procedure. The Yorubas of Nigeria are even more famous for their lavishness of attention and expense, and I have heard it said that the Luo of Kenya are not far behind. Among peoples of such an orientation, funerals are among the most important visible observancs in cultural life. Because people keep on dying, they are, perhaps, the most continual.

Two aspects of the great preoccupation with the mourning of the dead and associated rites among many African peoples are worth noting. On the one hand, the outpourings of feeling on such occasions have resulted in some of the most beautiful traditional poetry in Africa.[16] Moreover, the frequent funeral gatherings offer constant opportunities for the exchange of assurances of sympathy and solidarity and for concrete acts of mutual aid. On the other hand, in recent times the emphasis on funerals has shown a tendency to degenerate into expensive exhibitionism, which, in view of the strong pressures for conformity in African societies, can drive even the reluctant to ruinous funeral expenses. In my opinion, we see here one of the most negative features of contemporary culture in some African countries.

The sense of tragedy in the face of death is, of course, not necessarily any less in communities with brief funeral rites than in those with extensive ones. The fact of death itself strikes many African peoples as something needing explanation beyond physical causes and effects, hence the many myths on the origin of death to be found in the folklore of many African peoples. The basic message of these myths is that the human species brought death upon itself by disobeying God. However, it should be observed that, by and large, what particularly exercises the African mind is not just any death, but only the death of one who has attained adulthood but not a ripe age. Thus, the death in old age of a person who has led a full and productive life is not strictly an occasion for mourning. The Akans would attend the funeral of such a person in white, instead of the customary black, brown, or red. This is taken as a mark of the recognition that the person was blessed by God with a full and completed term of life. In similar circumstances, the Yorubas actually speak of celebration rather than lamentation. The thought seems to be that when one has had ample time to work out one's destiny, it only remains to go and take one's place among the ancestors. On the other hand, for the child who dies, the question of joining the ancestors does not arise, and in many places there is not even the pretense of a funeral. Although a minor is recognized to be a human being entitled, in an even greater degree than an adult, to help, affection, and all due consideration, such an individual nevertheless is not regarded as a full *person* and cannot therefore be a candidate for ancestorhood. Not even death is credited with the power to transform the immaturity of a child into the necessary maturity of an ancestor.

But death in immaturity or, for that matter, at any stage short of ripe age, requires a special explanation. In the *normal* run of things a person should grow up, raise a family, and help his community in all desirable ways before giving up the ghost, or to speak in Akan terms, before giving up the "okra" (which is the Akan name for the life principle). A life cut short, then, indicates an interruption of the normal sequence of events. Nonintelligent matter operates according to regular laws, which, of themselves, cannot account for such departures from normality. Only an intelligent agent or agency can cause such a disruption of the normal flow of affairs as the nipping of a whole life's potential in the bud. This is, in effect, the train of thought that leads the traditional African mind, when there has been a premature death, to inquire not whether some intelligent agency is invovled but which.

For example, suppose a child playing with a loaded gun pulls the trigger accidentally and thereby kills a promising young man. The gross mechanics of the situation do not elude the African mind, but the question remains why this particular man and at this particular juncture of his life? If this question is answerable, it will only be in terms of reasons, purposes, and intentions. The traditional African assumes that it can be answered,[17] because he considers that everything has a sufficient reason[18] either by way of mechanical causation or intelligent (or quasi-intelligent) design. This scenario can be questioned, but that does not belong to our present purpose, which is to depict the reverberations in African culture of the resultant mode of explaining what is taken to be anomalous death.

African ontologies almost always include a supreme being and a whole hierarchy of extrahuman beings and forces, many of whom (or which) are capable of abridging life in certain circumstances. There is, accordingly, a choice of explanations. Perhaps the young man in this example has fallen victim to the envious machinations of a witch. When seriously explored, such a hypothesis can have the profoundest social consequences, because the suspicion would be bound to fall on someone close by, who henceforward becomes a spoken or unspoken enemy. The consequent tensions and dissensions constitute some of the most unhappy aspects of African communal life. However, perhaps the young man may have died as punishment from the ancestors for a grievous sin that he committed. For example, he may have committed adultery with his uncle's wife, than which few greater enormities can be imagined in the family life of a people like the Akans (to name one group). Here too, the wages of sin is death—sometimes.

Other possible explanations exist, as one can easily surmise, but anything beyond tentative suspicion requires extranormal verification. Therefore, the interesting thing to note here is that such modes of explanation inevitably call forth into existence the institution of divination, which is an extremely important component of many African cultures. Premature death, of course, is not the only problem requiring the expertise of diviners; there is no lack of others— sickness, personal adversities, or even communal reverses—but death is the most worrying. Divination occurs on varying scales and in varying degrees of development in probably all African societies. Among the Yorubas, it appears to have advanced almost to the level of a science, complete with a sophisticated mathematical apparatus. Divination seems to take the place of revelation in many African cultures, a fact that accounts for the absence of prophets of God in the corresponding traditional religions. Our ancestors, along with other types of beings, are thought to vouchsafe adequate hints and advice to their people. The proliferation of prophets of God in the charismatic church movement, which has been sweeping across Africa in recent times like wildfire (if we may be excused a rather mundane simile in connection with such a "spiritual" phenomenon), is another contemporary twist to a traditional African cultural trait. African divination seems to have domesticated Christian revelation!

It is apparent from the foregoing discussion that, one way or another, the idea of immortal ancestors dominates African thought about death and the afterlife. Will this belief in the ancestors survive rational investigation in the modern world? The question, perhaps, betrays a rationalistic overoptimism: Whole races do not indulge in intellectual self-examination. Unfortunately, they can be overtaken by intellectual events emanating from abroad. This is exactly what has happened in Africa. Her peoples—or a great proportion of them—have been overtaken by the intellectual packages embedded in Islam and Christianity. Therefore, the question should, perhaps, rather be, "Can the African belief in the ancestors and the associated cultural practices survive the impact of foreign cosmologies?" If such phenomena as religious conversion proceeded in a strictly logical fashion, it might be expected that the belief in question would, for large masses of contemporary Africans, be a thing of the past and that, in consequence, there would be quite radical alterations in their culture. In fact, however, what has often happened has been not alterations but accretions. Christian[19] practices regarding the mourning of the dead, for example, in spite of presupposing a different system of eschatology, have simply been added to traditional ones, thus compounding the extravagance of the funeral process where that tendency exists. This is typical of the general confusion in contemporary African life deriving from the uncritical acceptance of foreign ideas. I might add that there is not necessarily anything wrong with accepting foreign ideas; however, what is regrettable is to take them without critical scrutiny. If the unexamined life is not worth living, then it can be easily appreciated that such an unexamining approach is unlikely to benefit anybody. In Africa today many of the living are dying through the chaos resulting, in practical life, from this intellectual situation. It would be comforting if there was an afterlife of peace and serenity. But unless we are to give into wishful thinking, we must acknowledge that the question of the existence of an afterlife is one requiring both rigorous conceptual analysis and careful evaluation of evidence.

NOTES

1. For example, the Nuer of the Sudan: witness Evans-Pritchard (1956:144): "Death is a subject the Nuer do not care to speak about." See also, as regards the Dinka, Lienhardt (1961:289).

2. Mbiti has made the phrase "the living dead" famous. By this phrase, he means what he calls "the spirits of those who have recently died." But all the ancestors, irrespective of how long ago they departed from this life, are believed to be dead but living.

3. Busia (1951:24) quotes some Ashantis who (believed they) had been punished by their dead relatives for errors.

4. Little (1954:115–6), writing about the Mende of Sierra Leone, remarks that for them "the conditions of this world are apparently continued in the hereafter, and the life led by ancestral spirits seems to be similar in many respects to that of the people of the earth. Some informants described them as cultivating rice-farms, bulding towns, etc. It also seems that the spirits retain an anthropomorphic character and much of their earthly temperament and disposition." Similar accounts of African conceptions of the afterlife abound in the literature.

5. See Wiredu (1983a).

6. The late Okot p'Bitek, one of the most conceptually alert of contemporary African thinkers, wrote, "for the Central Luo the entities which they believed they encountered at the lineage shrine were not spirits but the ancestors as they were known before death; their voices could be 'recognized' as they spoke through the diviner; they 'felt' hungry and cold, and 'understood' and 'enjoyed' jokes and being teased, etc. They were thought of as whole beings, not dismembered parts of man, ie, spirits divorced from bodies" (1971:104). At least one contemporary Luo scholar claims personally to have heard voices from the dead. Gilbert E. M. Ogutu, Lecturer in Religious Studies, University of Nairobi, Kenya, discussing Luo beliefs about death and immortality, asserts, "I have heard the voices of people who died a long time ago as they spoke through the living, stating what they wanted the living to do" (1985:106). The Luo, by the way, are a large ethnic group spreading over territories falling under quite a few present-day African states. To quote Ogotu, "The Luo-speaking people live in the geographical area that covers southern Sudan, south-western Ethiopia, north-eastern Zaire; north-western, northern, and eastern Uganda, western Kenya, and northern Tanzania. . ." (ibid, p. 104).

7. For the Yorubas, the life-giving entity is different from the destiny entity; for the Akans of Ghana both are one, though a distinct apparent entity is postulated by them to account for unique personal presence of each individual. The ontology of all these entities is, however, basically the same. (On the Yoruba, see, for example, Idowu 1962, Chap. 13; on the Akans and West Africans generally, see Opoku 1978, Chap. 5).

8. See, for example, Plato's *Phaedo*. An equally "abstract" conception of postmortem existence is found in the mystically oriented doctrine according to which a human being consists of a body and an immaterial soul that at death is absorbed back into the "universal mind." But this can hardly be called a doctrine of immortality, certainly not one of personal immortality.

9. Saint Augustine, *City of God*, Bk. xxi:15.

10. Some African people appear to envisage some kind of "judgment" after death. However, this does not have the cataclysmic cosmic connotation of the Christian Day of Judgment. Each person or group of persons undergoes "judgment" as they come along, and they then go to hard or comfortable places according as they have been bad or good. Suffering in the former case, however, is not always irreversible. See Awolalu 1979:58–59 on postmortem judgment among the Yoruba. On somewhat similar beliefs among the Dogon of Mali and the LoDagaa of Northern Ghana, see the summary accounts in Ray 1976:141–146. On the LoDogaa the most detailed study is Jack Goody's (1962).

11. The idea of reasonable achievements is intended to be contrasted with the kind of exaggerated notions of achievement that might encourage megalomania—a type of mentality that the Akans sought to forestall with the maxim, "It was given to mortals to achieve something, not everything." ("Onipa be yee bi na wameye nenyinaa".)

12. See, for example, Sarpong 1974:34–36; also Awolalu 1979:54.

13. "But what is that which is removed to Hades after the separation of the body; which is there detained which is reserved until the day of judgment?...[For] whatever is incorporeal is incapable of being kept and guarded in any way; it is also exempt from either punishment or refreshment. That must be a body by which punishment and refreshment can be experienced." (From Tertullian's *De Anima* as excerpted in Flew 1964:92. Incidentally, Tertullian was a North African, but it is not clear that his origins had anything to do with his corporealism, if we may coin a word. Saint Augustine also invites mention here. In his case, what would be surprising would be if his North African origins had anything to do with his eschatology.

14. This role may be observed in perhaps most African societies, but it is apparently not universal in Africa. For example, Krige and Krige (1954:80) say that "Ancestor worship of the Lovendu plays hardly any part...in upholding tribal morality." They even assert, "Ancestors ae capricious" (ibid, p. 63).

15. See Wiredu (1983b).

16. As regards the Akans, J. H. Nketia (1955) has collected a great deal of such poetry. These verses sometimes take a metaphysical turn. A famous example, and perhaps one of the profoundest, is this (in part):

> We have, since we arose from ancient times
> been exposed to incessant suffering.
> The *Ogyapam* tree and its ants are from antiquity
> The Creator created death and death killed him
> Thou Deceased, Condolences, Condolences, Condolences.

(p. 125)

17. A number of scholars and philosophers have noted essentially this point, though with their different slants. See Daryll Forde's general introduction to Forde (1955:xi). Also K. A. Busia (1962:20f), Minkus (1984), or, most philosophically ratiocinative of all, Sodipo (1973).

18. The Principle of Sufficient Reason was one of the cornerstones of Leibniz's philosophy. In his system, every contingent fact is referred to the will of God, but in the African system it appears that the wills of much lesser beings also can constitute sufficient reasons for some occurrences. At all events, the principle itself is undoubtedly a

cornerstone in the traditional philosophies of many African societies. Among the Akans it is formulated as follows: "Biribiara wo ne nkyera se" (literally, "Everything has its explanation").

19. This is less true in the case of Moslem converts in whom conversion appears to be a relatively totalistic condition of mind. Even here, however, coherence has not been achieved between Islamic and indigenous life and thought.

REFERENCES

Saint Augustine. *The City of God.* Many editions.

Awolalu, J. Osmosae. 1979. *Yoruba Beliefs and Sacrificial Rites.* Essex: Longman.

p'Bitek, Okot. 1971. *Religion of the Central Luo.* Nairobi: East African Literature Bureau.

Busia, K. A. 1951. *The Position of the Chief in the Modern Political System of Ashanti.* London: Frank Cass & Co., Ltd.

Busia, K. A. 1962. *The Challenge of Africa.* New York: Frederick A. Praeger, Inc.

Choron, Jacques. 1964. *Death and the Modern Man.* New York: Collier Books.

Evans-Pritchard, E. E. 1956. *Nuer Religion.* Oxford: Clarendon Press.

Forde, Daryll, ed. 1954. *African Worlds: Studies in the Cosmological Ideas and Social Values of African Peoples.* Oxford: Oxford University Press.

Goody, Jack. 1962. *Death, Property and the Ancestors.* Stanford, Calif.: Stanford University Press.

Idowu, E. Bolaji. 1962. *Olodumare: God in Yoruba Belief.* London: Longman's, Green and Co., Ltd.

Krige, J. D., and Krige, E. J. 1954. The Lovendu of the Transvaal. In *African Worlds: Studies in the Cosmological Ideas and Social Values of African Peoples.* Ed. Daryll Forde. Oxford: Oxford University Press.

Lienhardt, R. Godfrey. 1961. *Divinity and Experience* Oxford: Clarendon Press.

Little, Kenneth. 1954. The Mende in Sierra Leone. In *African Worlds.* Ed. Daryll Forde. Oxford: Oxford University Press.

Mbiti, John S. 1969. *African Religions and Philosophy.* London: Heinemann.

Minkus, Heleine K. 1984. Causal Theory in Akwapim Akan Philosophy. In *African Philosophy: An Introduction.* Ed. Richad A. Wright. University Press of America.

Nketia, J. H. 1955. *Funeral Dirges of the Akan People.* Achimota, Ghana.

Ogutu, Gilbert E. M. 1985. The African Perception. In *Immortality and Human Destiny: A Variety of Views.* Ed. Geddes MacGregor. New York: Paragon House.

Opoku, Kofi Asare. 1978. *West African Traditional Religion.* London: F. E. P. International Publishers.

Plato. *Phaedo.* Many editions.

Sarpong, Peter. 1974. *Ghana in Retrospect: Some Aspects of Ghanian Culture.* Tema: Ghana Publishing Corporation.

Sodipo, J. O. 1973. Notes on the concepts of Cause and Chance in Yoruba Traditional Thought. *Second Order: An African Journal of Philosophy,* Vol. 2, No. 2.

Tertullian. *De Anima.* Excerpted in *Body, Mind and Death.* Ed. Anthony Flew. New York: MacMillan Publishing Co., 1964.

Wiredu, Kwasi. 1983a. The Akan Concept of Mind. *The Ibadan Journal of Humanistic Studies.* Also in *Contemporary Philosophy, Vol. 5: African Philosophy,* Ed. Guttorm Floistad. Netherlands: Martinus Nijhoff, 1987.

Wiredu, Kwasi. 1983b. Morality and Religion in Akan Thought. In *Philosophy and Culture.* Eds. H. Odera Oruka and D. A. Masolo. Nairobi, Kenya.

4

Islamic Perspectives on Death and Dying

Ahmad Anisuzzaman Muwahidi

"Humankind is mortal": thus goes the old saying. But is it old in the sense that we have now overcome death? No, it is not. Is it therefore the case that in our age human beings are born, age, and grow old, but do not die? No. In spite of spectacular developments in medical technology and the discovery of many "lifesaving" drugs, doctors have not managed to save us from death. Then in what sense is the saying old? It is old in the sense that since humankind's creation, the human being has experienced death, not personal death, of course, but the deaths of other people. The phenomenon of death extends to other living beings as well, but here we shall confine our discussion to the deaths of human beings alone.

Just as the birth of someone, especially in one's own family, has been an occasion for happiness and joy, so a death has likewise been a time of loss and intense grief. But however grievous the event of death may be, it has always been a part of the human predicament, which is what is encapsulated in the saying quoted above. The saying tries to do two things. First, to console the bereaved one with the reminder that death is inevitable and that it happens to everyone, a fact based on our common everyday experience. Secondly, it suggests that human life is finite. We should, therefore, be realistic and accept the fact that like all other living beings our lives start with birth and end with death. Hence we should not imagine or expect that our lives extend beyond the grave and look forward to that postmortem life, rather, we should rest contented (however difficult it may often be to do so) with the finiteness of our existence and should plan our future accordingly. In this chapter we shall see that among other things, Islam challenges this view of human nature and destiny and presents a genuinely optimistic view of the human being's creation and destination.

I am extremely grateful to Robert Edwards for his generous help in carefully looking through several drafts of this paper and suggesting numerous corrections and improvements. I am also grateful to Ian Seymour, Bryn Browne, Michael Doughlan, and David Cockburn for their sincere help and Janie Hartwell for kindly typing the article.

METHODOLOGY OF TREATMENT

The approach to the problems of death and dying depends on the area and nature of one's interest within the great corpus of Islamic tradition. Accordingly, it is no wonder that on the details of this issue different views obtain among different Muslim communities and schools of thought. In fact it is rather natural that the end product should display different features in consistency with and depending on the methodology, the data collected, and the way in which the collected data are used and interpreted. Thus, there could be various approaches to the issue under discussion: psycho-sociological, philosophico-cultural, anthropologico-theological, and so on. Needless to say, we each according to our own interest and approach build our own edifice with those "blocks" of information that ae relevant to it. Obviously, such a construction is accomplished often at the cost of ignoring or at least under-rating some otherwise important aspects of genuine Islamic pareschatology and eschatology.

In the span of an article it is not possible to treat, and thereby do justice to all the aspects of the topic. Instead, I will present an outline of what Islam says on the vital question of death and dying. I shall base my contentions on the Quran and the sayings of the prophet of Islam, and shall exclude those elements that were added to or were subsequently merged with the original body of belief and practice. Therefore, although I am fully aware of the importance of the other approaches within their spheres, I think that the kind of interest we have could best be served by what I have called the "anthro-pologico-theological" approach. My mode of presentation shall be more descriptive than analytical and critical.

THE ISLAMIC VIEW OF THE HUMAN BEING:
BALANCED AND HUMANE

Islam has presented an optimistic view of human life and destiny. This is not to say that no other religion or system of thought has anything optimistic to offer — any hope to give — amidst this apparent dissolution of man's body at death. My statement is not meant to distort an obvious fact of history (Travis 1980; Dahl 1962; Penelhum 1973; Badham 1976).[1] What I mean to claim is that Islam has presented a truly balanced, humane, and realistic view of the human being's destiny couched in the natural and befitting language of hope and security. Without presenting details, let me state how Islam protects human-kind from gross materialistic reductionism on the one hand and over-spiritualism, immaterialism, and deificationism on the other.

We know that there are two mutually exclusive and extreme but strongly represented views of human origin and destiny. One, based on our apparent observation, holds that we are born at a particular point of time and then live for some time and eventually die, never to rise again. According to this view, human life begins at birth and finishes at death. This is the inescapable destiny of the human being *qua* the human being (Lange 1957; Radhakrish, and Raju 1966; Anisuzzaman [in preparation]. This view, I suggest, is not a new one and it is not peculiar to the so-called scientific understanding of the human being's life, and the world, as many people now wrongly believe. In fact, this view is as old as the human race itself, as the history of the many confrontations of the prophets and preachers of all revealed and theistic religions with the atheists and agnostics shows.

The other view is more philosophical in origin, nature, and import. According to this view, in the ultimate analysis, the words "human being" as applied to an embodied living physical being are a misnomer. This view maintains that a human being is not, in fact, a material being, essentially an embodied one. The human being is essentially a spiritual, an immaterial, a nonspatial and hence invisible being. The essential human being is uncreated and hence eternal — that is without a beginning at a particular point of time — and essentially immortal as well (Plato 1972; Grube 1935; The Gita 2:20; Bhaktivedanta Swami 1982).[2]

In contrast to these two mutually exclusive and extreme views, Islam presents a balanced view of the human being's creation, nature, and destiny. We have noted that the first view is based on ordinary observation. A view of the human being's future beyond death, if built upon such a foundation, naturally cannot transcend the frontiers of apparent death. It sees death but cannot go beyond it. Therefore, it is no wonder that the propounders of and adherents to this view would hold that death means the total annihilation of the person. Needless to say, this is a dismal and extremely pessimistic view of human existence. It wholly ignores other sources of knowledge and disregards the inherent and eternal human urge for survival. This view takes note only of the physical and apparent aspect of human nature, potential, and ability, and totally denies the spiritual dimension of human nature. It tries to reduce the mental to the physical or at least subordinates and underrates the importance that the mental has in a person's life. Thus, this view tends to create a deep feeling of total loss and a sense of absolute despair, and eventually makes existence in this world without real purpose and devoid of any profound meaning and value. It is like recognizing only the minute, visible part of a huge iceberg and failing to assess the size and importance of the part hidden underwater. We are aware of the inevitable consequence of such an assertion of the physical and visible only and the unwitting or arrogant denial of the invisible, psychological, and spiritual. In other words, the human being under the spell of this gross, materialistic, and reductionist view is either haunted by the constant thought of inescapable destruction and eternal doom and is thereby led to an unbearable pessimism, frustration, and anguish or else becomes extremely light-minded and ends up as an egoistic hedonist. The history of human culture and society bears testimony to this contention (Jameelah 1975; Klemke 1981). The problems of the one-sided, materialistic view of human nature and destiny will not be discussed here. But, it is useful to remind ourselves of the reason for Islam rejecting such a narrow, pessimistic, and dismal picture of human destiny.

On the other hand, the second view that the essential human being is inherently immortal and eternal leaves no room for real human choice and deliberate action in the determination of a person's destiny. This view, in fact, denies the person's very humanity. Here we do not acquire genuine immortality by our voluntary choice of good deeds and by developing a wholesome personality; instead, immortality lies in our very constitution and nature, and eventually our individuality is lost in the so-called Cosmic, Universal, or World Soul (of God or the Absolute). This view also denies God's power regarding the human being's future life by maintaining that the supposed soul follows its own course of evolution, progressing or regressing quite independently of God.

This view has many drastic consequences. I shall mention only two here, to indicate why Islam also rejects this apparently "too optimistic" and "over-spiritualistic" view of the human being. However, first it seems necessary to state two different interpretations of this view. According to the first interpretation, individual souls are divine sparks originating or emanating from the eternal Soul of God. They are destined to be reunited and eventually dissolved in God as they had been before (Behari 1982; Plotinus n.d.).

The second interpretation maintains that the notion of an individual soul arises out of illusion (maya) and ignorance (avidya). Because of the human being's attachment to the material world and the objects therein, a false notion of individual self or ego emerges. Through rigorous asceticism and meditation a person can be detached from the material world, and thus can come out of illusion and ignorance as it becomes evident that there is only one Absolute Soul (or Reality) and no finite individual soul (or existence) (Radhakrishnan 1972).

My first objection is that both these interpretations are eventually self-defeating. In maintaining that human beings are purely "spiritual" entities, this view takes from them everything that would make them worthy of the name "human." The implication is that the human being qua the human being ceases to exist and the question of the person's eventual survival does not arise. The person is finally lost in the infinite existence of God. We shall come to this point later.

The second objection is that in giving excessive emphasis to the wrongly understood import of the term "spiritual," this view grievously underrates the "material." If this attitude is followed to its logical conclusion, then the material world eventually turns out to be intrinsically evil and profane. This is wrong and against the inherent goodness of God's creation of the physical world. Matter and the physical world are not bad in themselves; in fact, the material world is a necessary instrument for the individual's spiritual development and, provided that a correct use is made of it, this is a great gift from God (Genesis I:1-3; Montefiore 1975; Quran 7:72; 57:27; 2:201; 5:87).[3]

I have said that because, according to the second view, the human being is intrinsically immortal, it does not leave any room for a person to choose immortality by voluntarily performing good deeds and by having an acceptable attitude to God and His creation. Defenders of this view, however, have tried to safeguard it from this criticism. They maintain that this is not a difficulty with this view but a strong point. To explain the human being's freedom and thereby accommodate the notion of human responsibility they bring in the "Law of Karma" (Radhakrishnan 1972:245–249; 354–355). This is not the place to consider the plausibility or validity of the law of karma, but two brief responses can be made. First, however, cautious the attempts may be to render intelligible the notion of human responsibility with the help of the law of karma, the fundamental point remains that here actions only decide the nature of a future existence and the place in which it will take place and not the ultimate destiny of the human being. That is to say, the person does not *acquire* immortality; it is already there. Second, detached and disillusioned actions *(nishkama karma)* eventually lead to the annihilation of the individual soul (the person). So, actions performed strictly in accordance with the law of karma turn out ultimately to be self-defeating practices.

On the other hand, if the hope of an everlasting life is based not on the inherent nature of an immaterial soul but on the decision, will, and mercy of an Almighty God, then the human being spontaneously feels the urge for good and wholesome deeds because only through good deeds and unconditional self-surrender to an absolute dependence on God can the favor of a new and blissful life in an everlasting world be won. Understood in this way, belief in a life beyond death does justice to both God's omnipotent creativity and never-failing promise as well as to the human being's own conscious choice and deliberate effort. The Quran seems clearly to uphold this view of human future life. This will become obvious from the subsequent discussion. The Quranic stand is clear both on human creation and postmortem life. The Quran in numerous verses states that the human being is not eternal and has not emanated from the Being of God. The person has been created *ex nihilo* at a particular point of time, lives for some period and eventually dies. The person after death becomes a nonentity again from which, through His blessings and by an act of sovereign will, God recreates that individual. Thus, the life after death is not inherently present in human nature which, as it were, follows its own course of fruition, but is exclusively dependent on God's will and omnipotence. God, however, has promised that He will re-create human beings after death and will give them a form of existence fully commensurate with their bodily acts, psychological states, and spiritual achievements. Thus, by stating that we do not end forever with death but are created again to have an everlasting life, the Quran has kindled a light of hope and desire in the darkness that surrounds us at death. At the same time, by connecting the mode and nature of the promised future life with our own deeds here, it has made us fully responsible agents in the making of our own destinies and in selecting our own destinations.

Let us now refer to some verses of the Quran and the sayings of the prophet of Islam to vindicate the points that we are trying to make and see how these relate to our specific issue of death and dying.

The Human Being Is a Created Being

The Quran states that the person has been created (Quran 7:11; 96:1-2).[4] The person is not eternal (Quran 76:1). There was a time when there was no human existence and a time is coming when all human beings will be dead and none will remain alive (Quran 3:185). Only God is eternal (Quran 2:255). He is the first and the last (Quran 57:3).

The Human Being Is Not a Partner of God

The Quran (59:22–24; 112:1–4) states that God is one and alone. He has no partner in any of His actions or attributes (Quran 4:36). Everything beside His exalted Being is His creation and no more than a servant (Quran 3:83; 4:173; 19:93). Like all other creation, the human being also owes existence to Almighty God and like them constantly depends on Him for the continuance of existence and survival (Quran 67:15–16); and like them the human being is equally subject to death (Quran 3:185). Even the heavens and the earth are also destined to be destroyed (Quran 99:1–23; 101:5). Thus, Islam is very emphatic in its opposition to humanity's claim to inherent immortality.

Although Mortal, the Human Being Will Be Raised Again

According to Islam, although not essentially immortal, the human being will be re-created by God after death (Quran 2:2–8; 19:66–68). So, practically speaking, death does not finally extinguish the person. God has promised to give human beings everlasting life and He does not fail in His promise (Quran 3:194; 21:104). In fact, all human actions and psychophysical states are being recorded and preserved (Quran 19:79; 80:15; 82:10–12), and in the world to come people will be judged accordingly (Quran 2:284; 99:7–8). Those who do good deeds have nothing to fear there (Quran 2:277; 3:130–143). But those who have a record of evil deeds and who transgress and violate the commandments of God will have their due punishment (Quran 3:176–78).

Individual Responsibility

A sense of individual responsibility is crucial for doing good deeds, for having a feeling of security against undue fear for the burden of others, and indeed for a fair judgment to be passed on one's ultimate destiny. Unlike many religions where one is supposed to bear the burden of others or of one's own supposed previous births and forms of existence of which one has no present knowledge, Islam lays exclusive emphasis on one's own deeds here and now in the determination of one's final destiny and destination. The Quran states that one will not be held responsible for the deeds of others (Quran 2:286; 4:111; 6:69, 165).[5] One is the maker of one's own destiny (Quran 8:51–3; 53:39). Sex, color, language, race, and so forth are not for discrimination but for identification (Quran 49:13). None of a person's actions will go in vain (Quran 3:115, 195; 39:69–70). God has no special relation with any nation or person in a way that is not based on righteousness and piety (Quran 2:80, 111–112; 65–66). He requires no middleman between Him and another person (Quran 2:48; 19:87). He sees and knows everything and hears everybody (Quran 2:96, 181; 4:58; 12:34; 25:20; 4:11). What He requires are good deeds, profound belief in Himself, unconditional submission to His commands, and explicit trust in and reliance on His promises (Quran 2:177; 3:114; 13:19–24). Thus, wholesome actions and acceptable *belief-states*[6] are very important in Islam, and provide the foundation for a blissful life in the world to come. This world is seen as a region of actions (Quran 67:2), a place for developing wholesome belief-states. Death brings an end to that opportunity (Quran 63:10–11). Therefore, one's life in this world is very important. All of one's actions (except some that have recurring effects on the lives of others and on the course of history) are stopped at death. A person however, continues to be rewarded or punished for such a recurring action even after death as long as the chain of the work continues to exist (Quran 4:85; Nawawi 1986; Vol. II, 489; Tabrizi 1976; Vol. I, 146). Thus, for some people a link with those actions that they initiated in this world remains even after their deaths. Hence, Islam urges people to do good work that will have this recurring effect and not to open the door of an evil work with recurring effect.

With the above ideas in mind let us now turn for further clarification very briefly once again specifically to the human being's creation and relate the result to human destiny and the phenomena of death and dying.

The Human Being's Creation and Position

As noted above, although Islam maintains that God has created everything and that all things are at the level of His servants, human beings have something special. God has created them specially and blessed them with many gifts and potential qualities (Quran 17:70; 38:75; 55:1–4; 90:8–10). Thus, Islam holds that human beings are not the result of an accident or unplanned conglomeration of certain kinds of physical particles, nor that they are essentially one with the Being or attributes of God, nor that they share in any way in His essential functions (Quran 18:51-52; 08:27). However, human beings are the representatives *(Khalifah)* of God on earth who can reflect the attributes of God in their deeds and personalities or by misusing their autonomous power of freedom of choice and action, may choose not to reflect the attributes of God and can give way to the unbridled fulfillment of their own selfish desires and passions (Quran 95:4–6).

Thus, the Quran states that human life is very important, meaningful, purposeful, and valuable. According to it human life *(Ruh)* is a special kind of divine command *(Amr)*, which is given effect when a suitable body is made ready to receive that order. Similarly, death is just a withdrawal of that command (Quran 3:6, 145, 156; 17:85; 39:42).

Being Mindful of Death

Islam stresses that as a divine command the event of death is highly significant in a human being's life. Hence one important feature of the teachings of Islam is that it has enjoined upon believers that they should remember the fact of death and be aware of the kind of change it is going to bring about. It also urges them to prepare accordingly for postmortem existence. We should note in this connection the contrast between the Islamic and contemporary Western attitudes to death and dying. Increasingly in the West (Aries 1974; Elias 1985), everything is done to distract attention from death and dying, and a negative, escapist, and opportunist ethos is thus created. Islam, on the other hand, urges believers to have a positive attitude to death and to be sympathetic to dying persons. In the West, many people seem to think that with the exception of those who are personally or professionally involved in caring for the old, the crippled, and the dying, it is not fitting for others to be concerned with these people or this aspect of human life. Islam opposes this attitude, and holds that a genuine appreciation of these people is very important for the wholesome growth and development of a genuinely human personality. It states that visiting the dying and the dead in their graves and remembering death — which is the separator of people from all their worldly bonds and the equalizer of all human beings — help one to be free from excessive attraction to the material world and from all the evils that emerge from such an undue attachment. These actions develop within people a feeling of self-satisfaction and contentment over whatever material things they have and encourage them to do such things as benefit both themselves as well as others (Gazzali 1982: Vol. IV, 469–472; Nawawi 1986: Vol. I, 332–335).

Signs of Good and Bad Deaths and Modes of Death

There is no uniform rule for all or any standard sign that, without qualification or consideration of the context and background of the person dying, would be said to indicate either a good or a bad death. Different states obtain for different people. And in fact the Quran does not mention any such signs, nor are these available in the authentic sayings of the prophet of Islam. Al-Gazzali, of course, mentions some marks of good and bad deaths and relates them to a saying of the prophet, but they are not decisive in any way and, therefore, nothing precisely can be predicted about the fate or destiny of the deceased on the basis of those signs.[7] Thus, though normally an honest person is expected to die a good death and a bad person is expected to have a painful and bad death, it could be otherwise; and an honest person might have a painful, even violent, death. On the other hand, a bad person might have a quiet, calm, and peaceful death. Therefore, it is maintained that pareschatological and eschatological events are exclusively in the hands of God (Tabrizi 1976: Vol. I, 57). He may decide to give a comfortable death to a dishonest person and painful death preceded by a prolonged illness and agony to an honest person. Of course, this does not mean that God's decision is capricious or arbitrary. On the contrary, it is guided by His infinite wisdom and justice (Quran 1:3; 45:2–6; 62:13; 95:8).

Thus, no one can guarantee the success or failure of another in postmortem life from observation of the circumstances of the other's death. The person's actions while alive are very important. Of course, according to Islam, good deeds if not accompanied by an acceptable set of beliefs do not merit any positive reward in the hereafter (Quran 5:15; 18:103–106). Hence, an acceptable belief-state at the time of one's death (*Khatima bi-al-Khair*) is crucial for a blissful life in the hereafter (Muslim 1986: Vol. I, pp. 139–40; Nawawi 1977: 36–37).

Sudden and Violent Death

It is an obvious fact of experience that although everybody prefers a calm and quiet end, many meet a sudden and at times painful and violent death. The Islamic view of such deaths is that there is nothing intrinsically good or bad about them. If one is good, then one should not worry about these. The prophet is reported to have said, "Sudden death is a solace to a believer and a grief to a non-believer" (Gazzali 1982:474). Thus, to be killed in a holy war (*Jihad*), to be drowned in water, to die in childbirth, or to die of some fatal disease gives one the coveted status of a martyr (*shahid*) (Nawawi 1986: Vol. II, 645–646).

It is strongly believed that though under normal conditions death is painful (Gazzali 1982:472–477), martyrs do not feel the pain of death, even if they are attacked brutally. Their profound faith makes them oblivious to apparent pain and even to torture (Nawawi 1986: Vol. II, 636). For this reason sincere believers have never been afraid of death; they have not aspired after a comfortable death nor have they worried about an apparently painful death.

Duties Prior to Death

Islam enjoins certain duties on both the dying and on those who are near and around them.

Duties and Responsibilities of Dying

As we have said, Islam expects everyone to remember death and to prepare and remain ready for it. This becomes more important if somebody can anticipate that death is imminent. In such a condition one is asked to make good one's deficiencies in ritual worship, prayer, and other religious obligations and responsibilities. One is required to ask forgiveness of all and is encouraged to forgive others as well. One is required to pay off all one's debts, but if that is not possible arrangements must be made so that they can be paid. One must ask one's heirs and descendents to pay the debts if they cannot be paid from one's own property. Under the Islamic law the heirs and descendents are obliged to take this responsibility. If one is unable to make any arrangement for paying one's debts, one must ask one's creditor(s) for forgiveness. But, if it proves difficult for a creditor to renounce a claim or if a creditor is unwilling to renounce it, then the relatives and Muslim society as a whole must negotiate with the creditor, and society is enjoined to pay the debts of an insolvent person. A dying person has another important responsibility: to make a will. At this time no arbitrary gift or endowment beyond one third of the total estate can be made, however. One is then asked to remove the unwanted hairs from one's body and to trim the rest, to cut one's nails, to clean one's teeth, to wash, to wear clean clothes, to sprinkle some nonalcoholic perfume over one's body and garments, to recite the Quran, to remember God and ask His forgiveness, to be satisfied with His decree and absolutely to depend on His mercy and forgiveness (Quran 2:160, 180, 240, 280; 3:122; 4:33; Malik 1981: 330; Nawawi 1986: Vol. I, 333; Kaysi 1986: 159–160).

Duties and Responsibilities of Those Around the Dying

The first duty of persons near the dying person is to help the dying to do all the above things. Next they are asked to forgive the dying person, to read the Quran beside that person, to invoke blessings upon all previous prophets and especially upon the prophet of Islam and to ask forgiveness for all, particularly for the person who is dying (Kaysi 1986: 175–182).

It is also maintained that the Devil (Satan) tries to mislead one at the time of one's death. So Islam urges that those around the dying should continue loudly to recite the *Kalima* (profession of faith) till the person expires. They should also keep ready some water or nonalcoholic drinks in case the dying person should need it (Nawawi 1986: Vol II, 474).

Duties of the Living Towards a Dead Person

The duty of the living is to wash the body and give it the ritual bathing (except in the case of those martyred in Jihad, who are to be buried in those clothes in which they have been martyred), to dress it in the prescribed funeral dress (if available), to scent the body and dress with nonalcoholic perfume and camphor, to offer the funeral prayer, and to bury the body as soon as possible. Islam discourages delay in burying the dead. The property of the dead is to be distributed in accordance with the law of inheritance (*Faraidh*) in the Quran (4:11–12, 33, 177; Doi 1984; 271–345). All these acts — bathing and washing the deceased, dressing and perfuming the body, offering the funeral prayer, carrying the bier, digging the grave, burying the body and finally occasionally visiting the grave and making supplication for the dead person — have great merits in Islam because they remind one of one's own death and thereby expedite one's preparation for death and the afterlife (Bukhari 1984: Vol. I, 40; Malik 1981: 208-9; Nawawi 1986: Vol. II, 465–488; Tabrizi 1976: 84–90).

Prohibition of Crying and Wailing

Islam prohibits crying and wailing, tearing of clothes, or wearing any specific dress signifying or indicating mourning, especially by women (Nawawi 1986: Vol. I, 805). Because, as we have seen, death is not an end of a person's career but the gateway to a fuller life, Islam of course, allows, rather recommends, the expression of sincere feelings for the dead and the shedding of tears as these express genuine humanity. It condemns lack of sympathy and feeling on the part of the living towards the dead as this is indicative of hard-heartedness (Nawawi 1986: Vol. I, 31–32; Vol. II, 477–478).

Desire of Death

We have noted that Islam is a religion of action and on the corpus of a person's actions is built that person's future life. The temporal life being the sole region of action that is brought to an end by death, Islam strongly prohibits suicide (Quran 4:66; Bukhari 1984: Vol. II, 251–252; Muslim 1986: 62–65; Ezzeddin and Johnson-Davis 1980: 112). Therefore, under normal circumstances it prohibits one from desiring death. But if circumstances become such that it seems impossible to do any good work and that there is every possibility that if one lives longer, one will be gradually led to evil, then one is permitted, even encouraged, to desire and pray for death (Nawawi 1986: Vol. I, 337).

Euthanasia

Islam does not permit euthanasia in any circumstances, because it deprives the person of the right to life and the possibility of action. In Islam human life is so important and valuable that one is instructed to perserve, sustain, and defend it in all just ways. This is also because, as we have noted, human life is a great gift of God and His special command. One is not the owner of one's life. So one can neither kill oneself nor take the life of another. As the creator and sustainer, God is the real owner of a person's life. He alone has discretion over human life, and He has made it clear where killing is allowed (Quran 2:178–179, 191; 4:89, 91–93; 47:4; Nawawi 1977:58).

At times God inflicts pain and suffering upon one for one's eventual benefit. Therefore, it is obvious that euthanasia cannot be permitted even in cases of acute pain and suffering. Nor can anyone in such a predicament ask to be killed or to be allowed to die by the withdrawal of proper care of medication. Of course, in such difficult circumstances one may pray for an early end of one's life, or one can request others as well to pray for oneself, and these other people can also pray for one's early death (Quran 2:155; 47:31; Nawawi 1986: Vol. I, 39, 337).

Nature of Postmortem Existence and What Happens After Death

Now we shall very briefly state the nature of death itself, what happens at the time of one's dying and what follows after that, and the existence one is supposed to have after death.

We have noted that according to the Quran, life is a divine command and death is the withdrawal of it. It is withdrawn by the instrumentality of angels, the chief of whom is called *Azrail* (peace be upon them). Usually this involves some amount of both physical and psychological pain. Physical pain may be expressed in the form of a disease or other suffering, violent death, and the like, or this pain may be the sort of natural feeling owing to the separation of life from the body, or it may simply be due to the end of life itself. Psychological anguish is caused by the thought and feeling of separation from everything with which one is directly attached in this world. Thus, people who are more attached to this world get more pain, and people who are less attached, less pain. One can lessen or overcome such mental anguish to the extent one is mentally detached from this world. Mental anguish can also be avoided by a profound belief in the life to come where everything will be justly and in a wholesome manner compensated by God (Quran 3:235, 161; 4–77; 6:61–93; Gazzali 1982: 475–481).[8]

What Happens at the Time of One's Dying

As said above, the angel of death comes and causes one to die by withdrawing or putting an end to one's life. Here the coming of the angel need not always be understood in the sense that he travels the world visiting every dying individual in person. In fact, usually the angel remains in his abode and effects death from there in the form of some apparent causes. Thus, people identify the cause of death with a disease, an accident, the failure of the heart, and the like, and from observing the circumstances of death, they do not not have enough evidence to refer it to an angelic agency and so to God (Quran 2:285). Hence, according to Islam the whole chain of events and phenomena surrounding death and life after death as described are beyond the observation and experience of other living human beings. For them, these are indeed matters of the Unseen World (*ghaiyib*) and of belief (Quran 2:2–5). At the time of death God orders the angel of death to subject a dying person to those conditions which He chooses fit for that person. Hence, Muslims try to please God and not any other forces of nature, including the angels, in the form of offering prayer to them and worshipping them. In fact, such prayer and worship are considered unforgivable sins (Quran 3:80, 4:97; 6:61; 34: 40–41).

What Happens After One Has Died

People after death are instantaneously created and raised again in an interim world (*Barzakh*) in similar bodies with memory and psychological characteristics fully restored (Quran 2:15; 23:100; 40:46; 50:4; Nawawi 1986: Vol. I; 267). They then face a preliminary test conducted by two angels, *Nakir* and *Munkar* (peace be upon them), who question them about their beliefs and way of life. Those who fail the test are tormented until the final judgment. Those who succeed in the test may have different life situations. Some simply sleep up to the day of judgment. Others enjoy a blissful life and await the final judgment. Before the final judgment and resurrection, the heavens and the earth and everything in between them are destroyed and kept in that state for a stipulated period, after which God re-creates them in a suitable form (Quran 83:3–6; 9:101; Tabrizi 1976: Vol. I, 86–89; Gazzoli 1982: 506–510).

Resurrection and the Final Judgment

At a suitable point of time after God has remodelled the heavens and the earth He gathers all human beings together in the great plain for the ensuing final judgment. At God's order all human beings from the beginning to the end assemble there. God judges them and decides who goes to heaven and who to hell.

Nature of Resurrection Life

The Quran presents a concrete picture of both heaven and hell in which human life is fully embodied and in many ways like ours in this world. (Quran 76:11–22; 78:21–36; 84:18–36, 88:2–16; Bukhari 1984: Vol. VIII, 354–387). Some people think that this picture is too crude and to a large extent sensual. So they speak of a purely spiritual existence in the postmortem life (Ali n.d.).[9] We have noted that apparently this looks reasonable and not unattractive. However, close consideration betrays its inherent weakness and self-contradictory features. We have noted the self-defeating aspects of an over-spiritualistic view of the human being. If an entity is to be and remain as a human being, it must need a human body and the acknowledged human attributes, abilities, qualities, and characteristics, whether the place be here or hereafter. Of course, a person need not have all those incidental qualities and features that at times we have found in that person in this world. Thus people need not be ill, mained, jealous, or the like in the resurrection world. I think we intuitively understand what is necessary for humanity and what is not. This is an obvious point and needs no further elaboration. But surprisingly, many people under the spell of an apparent attraction for the over-spiritualistic view of human nature forget this obvious fact. They do not take seriously, for example, the question of how one would look if one did not have a body — could that sort of existence (if at all possible) be a perfect or even human existence at all in the sense we understand it? If not, what other sense could we attach to a bodiless thing and at the same time insist that it is still a human being? To pursue the point, is it human life if the beings in question cannot eat, drink or relish other gifts of God or enjoy the company of their fellow beings? Again, is a heaven acceptable to us as human beings if we are transformed into light and lost in God? Could such an existence (even if granted) be called a genuine human existence? The answers are obvious. This sort of existence cannot be called human existence and is indeed suicidal for humanity. Further, what sense can we give to the claim that the postmortem person will not be lost in God but will always enjoy the pleasure of being in the presence of God without accepting the fact that that person has a body? The retention of individuality in the absence of a body is obviously unintelligible because without spatial dimension things cannot be individuated. The claim that the memory of the past and the dispositions arising out of the former bodily contact ensure this individuality is not intelligible and hence not tenable, for under this description it is not clear how memory or previous dispositions inhere in something which itself is not substantial. The discussion could be followed and elaborated but we think that the fundamental point that life after death cannot be that of a disembodied and immaterial entity has been made sufficiently clear (Cook 1969: 117–151).

Hence, in Islam heaven is a place where human body, mind, and soul are harmoniously integrated to give full expression to human beings' sublime feelings towards God as well as to enable them to relish and enjoy all the good that their fellow human beings and other creations and gifts of God can give them. On the other hand, life in hell also is fully embodied but utterly frustrated and disastrous (Quran 55:41–78. 56: 11–56; 69: 19–37; Bukhari 1984: Vol. VIII 362–374; Nawawi 1986: Vol. II, 919–928).

RECAPITULATION AND CONCLUSION

We have seen that Islam recognizes and gives proper importance to the obvious fact that the human being dies and that after death the human body dissolves and disintegrates. The Islamic view of human destiny does not end there, however, and accordingly it does not deny any hope for future life. Nor does it accept the over-spiritualistic view of the human being which of course ensures immortality but at the cost of losing humanity. In fact, the Quran strikes a balance between these extreme and one-sided views and reconciles the opposing claims of total annihilation and inherent human immortality. It also denies the claim that the postmortem life is a sort of disembodied and shadowy existence, which is the logical consequence of the self-refuting view that the essential person is an immaterial and immortal entity. Islam maintains that the promised future existence is a much fuller and more complete human life. It is a composite and fully integrated life of the body, mind, and soul. It is a perfect human existence with all glory and splendor, if one has conducted a good life; otherwise, the afterlife is an everlasting disaster.

So it is obvious that there is nothing frightening in death for those who conduct their lives in a wholesome manner, as is expected of them by the creator who has given them their temporal lives and on whose decision depends their future lives. For this reason, good Muslims have throughout the ages remembered death and accordingly tried to prepare themselves for it.

A profound belief in an everlasting life based on the promise of God has ensured the meaning and purpose of human life. Muslims, therefore, have become neither frivolous nor the victims of despair. It is true that a sense of inadequacy in performing good deeds has been a cause of fear of death for many Muslims, but a sincere belief in God's mercy and compassion also equally has kindled the light of hope for forgiveness, helping them eventually to overcome the fear of dying and death by ensuring an everlasting blissful life after death.

NOTES

1. Some hope is obviously present in the Judeo-Christian tradition. However, contradictory claims by different theologians are making it increasingly difficult to opt for any particular interpretation as the only Biblical view of human destiny. This becomes even more difficult when we come to the question of the nature and form of postmortem human existence. Nevertheless, I am convinced that in general terms the Biblical view is optimistic and that according to it the human being is not finished once and for all at death. There are numerous works on Christian understanding and hope for a future life and the nature of that life. Travis (1980), Dahl (1962), Penelhum (1973), and Badham (1976) are representative accounts of and useful references to the diverse views obtaining in the Biblical tradition.

2. Although rooted in the remote past, this view is clearly and systematically stated in the writings of Plato (Plato, tr. Hackworth 1972; Grube 1925) in the West, and many subsequent thinkers. In the East, The Gita (2:20) upholds this view very strongly. It has been defended by many philosophers and theologians (Bhaktivedanta 1982).

3. The Biblical account of creation maintains that the physical world and its contents are good because after the end of each stage "God saw that it was good" and after creating everything "God saw everything he had made, behold, it was very good" (Genesis I:1–31; Montefiore 1975). The Quran also holds a similar view. In fact, the Quran encourages people to pray for what is good in the world, urges them to remember their share here, and disapproves of shunning the gifts of God (7:72; 57:27; 2:201; 5:87).

4. Numerous passages in the Quran are relevant to the points made, but for easy reading I refer only to one or two verses among them.

5. When I say that the Quran denies that one is responsible for the deeds of others, I mean that it denies a sort of preordained, transcendental, or hereditary responsibility that one is supposed to bear because of the mere fact of one's birth as a human being, or the fact that one belongs to a particular family, race, or linguistic community. According to this view such a burden is one from which one cannot free oneself by one's own individual efforts. An instance of what I call a sort of preordained or transcendental responsibility is the doctrine of "original sin" in some forms of Christianity. Another is that of hereditary responsibility, which is the punishment of children for an offense of their parents or vice versa, or of a member of a race or nation merely for belonging to that race or nation (as was the case in pre-Islamic Arabia and many other places, and still is in some modified forms in many parts of the world). An instance of hereditary privileges (that is, privileges not acquired by merits of one's own) is the social and spiritual advantages that one enjoys by being a member of the royal or priestly family (*Brahman*, for example). Similarly, the fact that others are deprived of these opportunities merely because they are born into "lowly families" (*sudra, chamar:* untouchables in India) illustrates how some people are made to suffer or denied their legitimate rights through no fault of their own.

The Quran does not, however, deny that there is a very important sense in which one is responsible for others. As a social being, the individual, to a considerable extent, is indeed responsible for others. In fact, according to the Quran, a Muslim cannot be an idle spectator of his/her surroundings nor an unconcerned and self-centered participant.

The Muslim is, instead, an enthusiastic activist whose assigned aim in life is mainly to attempt to transform the moral, religious and human conditions of the world to conform to divine guidance. A person who fails in making this effort must be held responsible. Hence one cannot say, for example, "I am not concerned with what other people do. It is their affair!" On the contrary, as the viceregent of God one must resist the forces of evil and strive to establish obedience to God, truth, and justice, both as an individual and with other people. In this sense, therefore, one is responsible for the deeds of others, and if one fails in making the necessary efforts to dissuade or restrain others from pursuing their evil courses and they continue to do "evils" one will be accountable to God and have a share in their misdeeds. On the other hand, if one encourages others to do what is required and expected of them by God, one will have a commensurate reward from God and a share in their good deeds (The Quran, 3:104,110,114; 5:2; 9:71; 103:1–3; Also cf. Imam Abu Zakariya Yahya bin Saraf an-Nawawi, *Riyadh-us-saleheen*, tr. S. M. Madi Abbasi, New Delhi: Kitab Bhavan, 1986, Vol. 1, pp. 121, saying 174, p. 128, saying 187, pp. 131–134, sayings 193–197).

6. I have used the words "deeds" and "actions" predominantly to refer to moral, religious, and humanitarian actions or deeds. As regards a person's other amoral actions, they are more amenable to specific laws of nature established by God than to direct divine appreciation and judgment (Quran, 3:140). Similarly, by "acceptable belief-state" I have meant that to be acceptable to God one must believe in One God, accept His guidance sent through the prophet of the time, and submit to divine decree (Quran 3:64; 4:64; Also cf. Shaikh Wali-ud-din Muhammad b. 'Abdullah al-Khaib al-'Umari al-Tabrizi, *Mishkat-ul-Masabih*, tr. Abdul Hameed Siddiqui, Lahore: Islamic Publications Ltd., 1976, Vol. I p. 57, saying 83). According to the Quran, God does not punish any nations unless a prophet is sent to them. Hence He has sent messengers to all people of all ages in different lands (Quran, 10:47). This process of divine guidance by means of prophets, the Quran claims, has culminated in the mission of Muhammad (Peace and blessings of Almighty God be upon him: 5:3), the seal of the prophetic line (33:40). Hence after his coming all people are required to accept him as the greatest blessings of God to them and to follow his instructions and guidance faithfully (Quran, 2:107; 34:28; 7:158; 59:7; also see Imam Muslim, *Sahih Muslim*, tr. Abdul Hamid Siddiqi, New Delhi: Kitab Bhavan, 1986, Vol. I, pp. 8–17, sayings 11–35).

7. The saying which Gazzali relates to the prophet is this: "Look to the dying man with his three conditions. When perspiration comes out on his forehead, when his eyes shed tears and when his lips become dry, the blessings of God are poured upon him. When his throat gives out gurgling sounds, his colour becomes red, his lips become mud-coloured, the punishment of God befalls on [sic] him" (1982: pp. 478–479).

8. For a detailed description of the angel of death and the phenomenon of death, see Khawaja Muhammad Islam (1976:82–102). Although this book is not authentic, it gives a vivid description of the topic under discussion.

9. Abdullah Yusuf Ali (n.d.) among some other thinkers tries to present and explain the Quranic picture of life after death in purely spiritual terms.

REFERENCES

Ali, A. Y. n.d. *The Holy Quran: Translation and Commentary*. Brentwod, Md.: Amana Corp.

Anisuzzaman (forthcoming). A Critical Account of the Various Materialistic Notions of the Self. In *Philosophy and Progress*. Dhaka University.

Aries, P., tr. P. M. Ranum. 1974. *Western Attitudes Toward Death*, pp. 85–107. Baltimore: Johns Hopkins Univ. Press.

Badham, P. 1976. *Christian Beliefs About Life After Death*, pp. 47–94. London: SCM Press.

Behari, B. 1982. *Sufis, Mystics and Yogis of India*, pp. 75ff. Bombay: Bharatiya Vidya Bhavan.

Bhaktivedanta, A. C. 1982. *Coming Back*, pp. (i)ff. London: Bhaktivedanta Book Trust.

Bukhari, I., tr. M. M. Khan. 1984. *Sahih al-Bukhari*. New Delhi: Kitab Bhavan.

Cook, J. W. 1969. Human Beings. In *Studies in the Philosophy of Wittgenstein*. Ed. P. Winch. London: Routledge and Kegan Paul.

Dahl, M. E. 1962. *The Resurrection of the Body*, pp. 11–84. London: SCM Press.

Doi, A. R. 1984. *Shariah: The Islamic Law*. London: Ta Ha Publications.

Elias, N., tr. E. Jephcott. 1985. *The Loneliness of the Dying*, especially pp. 29, 43–91. Oxford: Blackwell.

Ezzeddin, I., and Davis D. Johnson, 1980. *Forty Hadith Qudsi*. Beirut: Dar-Al-Koran Al-Karim.

Gazzali, I., tr. A. M. F. Karim. 1982. *Ihya Ulum-Id-Din*. New Delhi: Khitan Bhavan.

Grube, G. M. A. 1935. *Plato's Thought*, pp. 120–149. London: Methuen.

Islam, K. M. 1976. *The Spectacle of Death*. Lahore; Urdu Bazar: Tablighi Kutub Khana.

Jameelah, M. 1975. *Islam and Modernism*, pp. 16–24. Lahore: Urdu Bazar, Sant Nagar, Mohammad Yusuf Khan.

Kaysi, M. I. 1986. *Morals and Manners in Islam*. Leicester: The Islamic Foundation.

Klemke, E. D., ed. 1981. *The Meaning of Life*, pp. 55–173. Oxford: Oxford University Press.

Lange, F. A. 1957. *The History of Materialism and Criticism of Its Present Importance*, especially pp. 1–36. London: Routledge and Kegan Paul.

Malik, I., tr. M. Rahimuddin, 1981. *Muwatta*. New Delhi: Kitab Bhavan.

Montefiore, H., ed. 1975. *Man and Nature*, pp. 56–61. London: Collins.

Muslim, I., tr. A. H. Siddiqui. 1986. *Sahih Muslim*. New Delhi: Kitab Bhavan.

an-Nawawi, I., tr. S. M. Madni Abbasi. 1986. *Riyadh-us-saleheen*, Vol. I, pp. 121, 12, 131–134. New Delhi: Kitab Bhavan.

an-Nawawi, I., tr. E. Ibrahim and D. Johnson-Davis, 1977. *Forty Hadith*. Damascus: The Holy Quran Publishing House.

Plato, tr. R. Hackforth. 1972. *Phaedo*, especially pp. 158–60. Cambridge: Cambridge University Press.

Penelhum, T. 1973. *Immortality*, pp. 51–99. Belmont, CA: Wadsworth Publishing.

Plotinus, tr. S. Mackenna. n.d. *The Enneads*, 3rd ed., The Fourth Enneads, pp. 338–368. London: Faber.

Radhakrishnan, S. 1972. *Indian Philosophy*, Vol. I, pp. 184–186, 245–249, 354–355, 415–417, 594–595; Vol. II, pp. 565–578. London: Allen & Unwin.

Radhakrishnan, S., and Raju, P. I., eds. 1966. *The Concept of Man*, pp. 476ff. London: Allen & Unwin.

Tabrizi, A., tr. A. H. Siddiqui. 1976. Mishkat-ul-Masabih. Lahore: Islamic Publications Ltd.

Travis, S. H. 1980. *Christian Hope and the Future of Man*, pp. 93–117. Leicester: Inter-Varsity Press.

5

The Concept of Death and the Afterlife in Islam

Jan Knappert

In this presentation I endeavor to summarize the Islamic beliefs and doctrines about the transition of the human soul from this world to the next. It is no doubt considered as the most vital subject for study and meditation in the entire world of Islam. Indeed, as the Islamic writers say: Dying is a very difficult work. They proceed to give precise prescriptions about a person's duties and behavior in order to smooth his passage from this life.

Western readers will note that the central character in this paper is always the man. Although I am well aware of this problem, my work is only to translate and summarize. The student of another religion, in publishing the results of his or her studies, should be heard but not seen. Since all the texts I consulted speak about what happens to a man, that is what I repeat. The Koran itself gives the example. For instance in Chapter 4, where marriage impediments are discussed, the holy book addresses men only: "Forbidden to you are your mothers and daughters, your sisters, your aunts paternal and maternal, your brother's daughters, your sister's daughters, your mothers who have given suck to you, your suckling sisters, your wives' mothers, your step-daughters who are in your care . . ." (Arberry 1964, p. 75). The famous passage 4:34 admonishes women to obey their husbands: "Men are the managers of the affairs of women. . . Righteous women are therefore obedient . . ." (op. cit. p. 77). It follows that women must do as they are told by their husbands; Islamic law and duty-lore have been composed for men and address men, except in special cases such as the rules of behavior for menstruating women (Koran 65:4). Even that passage is really for men.

Islam is a completely man-centered religion; women take no decision except to obey. When I suggested once to my most liberal and learned Islamic teacher, Yusuf Khamisa, an Indian, that women were equal to men, he just laughed. Those who pretend otherwise are either ignorant or insincere. The following tale illustrates this attitude: Once upon a time a Houri (a type of angel) looked down on a devout Muslim who was being nagged by his wife. "Poor woman," thought the Houri to herself, "She does not know that in a short time she will be a widow." Being a widow in Islam is a hard life. I can only translate and summarize what I have found in the sources or have been told by Muslim scholars.

A woman will be required to do research in the women's quarters regarding the question: what do women think about this life and the afterlife?

The word Allah, "God," is masculine in Arabic, Urdu and Hausa; Persian, Turkish, Malay, and Swahili do not distinguish genders. God himself, according to the scholars of Islam, is neither male nor female. God has no human body, so that it is impossible to state that God is a man or a woman. God is unique and incomparable. In English we use the pronoun "He" to refer to God, usually without prejudice.

It is a difficult task for students of the religions and cultures of Oriental and African peoples to describe the thoughts of those peoples in English without making them sound harsh and crude, or, on the other hand, without diluting so much of the original intention of the Oriental writers that its true meaning is lost. We shall never understand those peoples with whom we have to share this planet, if we hide ourselves because of the enormous differences in thinking that exist between Occidentals and Orientals. Far from wishing to underline the differences, I have always endeavored to seek clear understanding and empathy with all nations. That should not, however, make us blind to their real other-ness.

The belief that every human being has an immortal soul (Arabic, *nafs*) is shared by Islam and Christianity.

What happens to this soul during and after the hour of death, that is, its parting from the body with which it was born, is quite well known in Islam, for two reasons. Firstly, the scholars of the Islamic countries have reflected a great deal about death and the afterlife because they took the admonitions of the Prophet Muhammad seriously. The Koran, which is regarded by Muslims as the literal word of God, frequently refers to what will happen to the souls in the Other World, and every verse of the Koran has been the subject of elaborate treaties of exegesis for fellow scholars as well as for the broad (illiterate) masses of the people of Islam.

These tracts are written in all the languages of Islam: Arabic, Hausa, Malay, Persian, Swahili, Turkish, Urdu, and others. Many of these booklets are printed and can be bought in the little bookshops of the Middle East, Indonesia, West Africa, and elsewhere. As in Christian Europe, the best literary sermons of the great preachers of Islam have been collected and printed, mainly in Arabic, and these are also available for study and reflection.

I have searched numerous bookshops from Morocco to Pakistan and questioned many local Islamic scholars on the subject of life after death. The present essay is the fruit of these studies in a very condensed form; the complete studies could fill a book!

The first point about which all Islamic scholars agree is the unexpectedness of death and the unpredictability of its hour. Death may come literally at any time, they all assure us. Therefore, they advise us to be ready for death at any moment of day or night, for the suddenness of death will give us no time to prepare for it.

Westerners do not appreciate that as a result of this preparedness, the relations Muslims have with their own lives are very different from those in a Western, secularized, urban society. Westerners prepare for old age. They will take out insurance or invest in a pension fund. They look forward to retiring at 65 and taking up a hobby such as gardening, which may mean planting rose bushes that will flower after years. Westerners plan to live long, and most of them live past 75.

The Prophet Muhammad died at 63 and that is considered by many Muslims as a blessed age to die. Their attitude to life is one of readiness to say goodbye to it at any time, and at very short notice. Why invest in a pension? Would that not be defying God? One of the common themes of Islamic legends is that of King Shaddad of Ad, who built a city of gold and diamonds for himself to live in. "It will be as good as Paradise," he boasted. When the city was completed and the king climbed the steps to its shining gate, there was a gentleman waiting for him. It was God's messenger announcing death without delay. The tale of Alexander the Great is found in all the storybooks: how he conquered the world and then died suddenly at 33.

The only investment for the future that is encouraged in Islam is building a mosque. Thus numerous mosques can be found, many now standing in the desert where there were once flourishing cities. This theme is yet another used to inculcate the brevity of life.

On this motif numerous poems have been written in all the Islamic languages by mystic poets, beginning with the description of some ruin, usually the palace of an ancient emperor, thus:

Where Sulaymán once ruled, inspiring awe and fear
the dove by day, the owl at night is all I hear.
Fear no king, is the moral of this; fear God's decree alone.

Muslim scholars therefore advise their followers to invest not for later in this life, but in the other life. This is done by means of sadaka, or charity, money given to the poor, the sick, the widows and orphans (since the sudden death of husbands and fathers leaves many people without protection, that is, without a pension!), the pilgrims, the fighters in the holy war, and students and scholars, such as the writers and preachers themseles. Students are young people who prepare themselves to become scholars in order to teach the Koran and its laws to the people. The pilgrims are all those who are on their way to visit the holy city of Mecca, which is a God-pleasing duty once in a life.

A holy war is a war against heretics, such as the Iranians are now waging against the Iraqis. Even more, it is a war against any non-Muslims, such as the Palestinians are now waging against the Israelis, the northern Sudanese against the southerners, the Islamic Eritreans against the Marxist Ethiopians, and the extremely devout Afghans against the "God-denying atheists." It is the duty of all Muslims to help those fighters who are sacrificing their lives for the sake of God in their heroic struggle. All the money that a Muslim will spend on these good causes, will buy him "a palace in paradise" as all the texts assure us. Giving money to the poor will buy a "silver horse to carry the soul straight into Paradise across the narrow bridge that spans the fire of Hell." We must conclude that charity in Islam is thus intended to allay the fears of punishment in the next world, rather than for its own sake. The fighters in the holy war, too, will reap immediate benefits: as soon as they die they will rise up and enter Paradise unhindered, without delay. The Islamic guidebooks for a pious life urges a man to give away all his money in this fashion so that he has nothing to carry on the way to heaven: "If you leave anything behind, it will only be a reason for quarrelling among your heirs, it will arouse their greed and tempt them to sin. Poverty is better. The Lord will provide."

While the Muslim awaits death, he should spend his days in prayer, for since death can come at any moment, it will be infinitely easier and less painful if the Announcer of Death finds the believer absorbed in prayer. We shall see presently why it makes so much difference. Poverty and sickness should be borne in patience and silence; they are only so many tests sent to us by God. Lamenting one's fate is in reality complaining about the suffering God sends us, that is, accusing God. Of course, no one can take God to task. God is always right; no matter what happens, it is God's will, and therefore a good thing.

Death comes *ghaflan*, as all the texts confirm, "when you are not paying attention." The suddenness of death in Islamic countries is the result of numerous diseases, too many to list here. Most are parasite-borne diseases caused by unhygienic living conditions, malnutrition and anemia (especially in women at childbirth), poverty and hunger, which are in turn caused by overgrazing of the pastures, desertification, insufficient preparation of the fields for agriculture, early aging as a result of hard work, and so on. Most of these problems could be solved if people would only invest in the future, but this is precisely where the vicious circle of this sad philosophy of life closes. Wherever some of these problems are solved, such as providing piped, healthy water in Iran, or providing American grain in Egypt, the population quadruples in one generation, so that there is as much hunger as before. Obviously it is God who makes the Americans send grain, which proves that no one need worry over the future: He will provide. This closes the cheerful loop of the circle of faith without care.

If a man is very ill and his relatives believe that death is approaching, they are advised to keep him company, "for death is a lonely business." That is very true and very beautiful. The only people who may die together are warriors on the battlefield. For most people the great crossing has to be faced alone.

The relatives should take turns in sitting at their kinsman's bedside, and pray with him. They should repeat: "There is no god but God and Muhammad is the Prophet of God," many times, until the dying person repeats the phrase. After that no more should be said, for reasons that will become clear presently. The dying man must not be permitted to blather or rave, for that is talk inspired by the devil and will lead away from the path to heaven. Only prayers and repeating God's names is advisable, for God will hear His name wherever it is pronounced.

It is possible that in the mist of death people have seen apparitions which they later, if they recovered, related to others. Most of these visions are frightening, but all the writers agree that this fright is the effect of a bad con- science. Good people have nothing to fear and will see nothing frightening.

Suddenly a man will appear to the sick man, who will ask him suspiciously: "Who are you?" In his anxiety he may cry for help, but his loved ones will be unable to help him: he is beyond help, he has already left them, like a boat leaving the shore. Helplessly floating away from all that he knows and loves, he will hear his visitor say: "I am the angel of death, God sent me to you. Your end has come." At once, he will start separating the soul.

The word "angel" is here used in its original meaning of God's messenger. The Arabic word *malak* comes from Hebrew *mal'akh* "messenger," from which the Greek *angelos* is a translation. Thus an angel may not look nice and friendly at all; he may look hideous.

The Islamic writers describe in detail what happens when a man meets his Death. First they tell us what happens to a sinner. Death will look to him like a black monster, ugly and terrifying. Growling angrily, displeased that God has sent him to a sinner, Death will at once start pulling the soul out of the body. He does this by taking hold of the soul in the mouth. This is no doubt a relic of the concept of death as the breath that flows away. In many languages the word for soul meant originally "breath." The last breath is often depicted (for example, in ancient Egypt) as a bird or insect, such as a butterfly, flying out of the mouth. We are not told how Death can grasp a man's spirit.

We are told, however, that a sinner is strongly attached to this life and, therefore, to his body. The soul is difficult to part from the body, as the angel pulls it without delay or mercy. This is an awfully painful process, only because the man did not prepare himself for death. He cries out in fear and pain, but no one comes to help him, for God's decree is inescapable.

It is first in the toes and the fingertips that the soul becomes detached from the body, so that they become white when a person is dying. This point has been confirmed by physicians. Gradually the soul is dragged out of the body, and at last it comes out, hovering like a bat flying from its cave at night.

The experience of a good soul is entirely different. When the Angel of Death approaches him, he does indeed look like an angel, beautiful, handsome, dressed in white, the color of the soul's purity, and shining with the light of Paradise. Death is not harsh but modest, asking timidly: "Our Lord sends you greetings and asks you if it is convenient that I take you with me now? But perhaps you still have business to do? God invites you to come and see Him." Of course the good soul begs this angel: "Quickly accompany me to His presence. All these years I have wanted nothing more. I have been waiting for your arrival with impatience. Why did you stay away so long? What else do I have to do here on earth except praying? No business keeps me here, I am ready to depart." Indeed, many years of fasting have made the soul as light as a bird, and continuous prayer has made it pure and luminous. Out of its own free will it flies out to meet its death, the good messenger of our Lord. He carries it safely to its detination.

Who is the Angel of Death? His name is Izrail, although that name does not occur in the Koran which only refers to the Angel of Death (32:11) who, it says, will take care of us after death. When God had created Adam's soul, He wanted clay to make Adam's body. He commanded Jibril (Gabriel) to go and fetch it, but the archangel came back saying that Earth had refused to give a piece of herself for the creation of a being that would disobey the Creator. None of the other angels succeeded either, until God sent Izrail, who went down and simply tore out a piece of earth without listening to her cries, for to him nothing mattered more than to obey God's command immediately. It is for this reason that God appointed him Soulsnatcher, Lifetaker, because of his *Qillatu'r-Rahma*, his smallness of mercy. Death must obey God's will at any time; immediately and without personal thoughts. There is only one way in which a man can postpone his death, that is by constantly pronouncing the holy names of God. No angel may stop the flow of God's names. The angel will return to God and ask Him what to do. God will give him an apple from Paradise. As soon as the pious man smells the apple from paradise he will be so overcome by the desire to see its beauty that his soul will voluntarily surrender itself to death and fly up to Heaven with him. For the devout, this earthly life has no attraction. They yearn for eternity.

What happens after the bad man's soul has been pulled out like a weed from the earth, and the good man's soul has come out by itself, flowing easily like water out of a waterskin? The good soul is taken up to heaven to meet its maker, but only for a brief moment of joy. Then it is taken down to earth again and placed in the grave near its body but no longer in it. The bad soul remains in the house, "fluttering about like a bat." It can witness its relatives beginning their bickering over the inheritance, it can hear them utter blasphemous language about the deceased himself, who is still lying above earth. That is the beginning of the sinner's punishment, for the dead can do nothing to prevent the living from sinning or committing stupidities. Suddenly the dead man will see who really loved him and who deceived him, who respected him and who hated him.

In Islamic countries, interment takes place on the day of death, if possible, so that most deceased are buried within 24 hours. Doctors are seldom present to sign death certificates and most people could not afford a doctor anyway, in rural areas. All the same, it has happened that a dead person woke up before his grave was closed above him, "and lived to see the sun rise."

In Islamic countries all but the rich are familiar with death. Infant mortality may be as high as fifty percent and mothers often die in childbirth owing to lack of hygiene. Miscarriages are not normally recorded, nor are stillbirths, as they are infected with misfortune. Many babies die, too, so that in Iran a woman visiting a friend in childbed may say: "You have seen its face, May you never see it die." Another common saying is "As soon as he can walk you know he will help you in old age." Toddlers too, often die, and when asked of what cause, the mother will say phlegmatically: *ishâl* "diarrhea," which may mean dysentery or even cholera, which is endemic in Egypt and is invariably brought home by all the pilgrims after they return from Mecca. This explains the Islamic peoples' familiarity with death, and its sudden appearance, which is comparable to Europe 150 years ago.

Early in the morning the corpsewasher is invited to come and wash the body (*ghusl*), not for hygienic purposes but because prayers will be recited for the deceased, and to that end he has to be ritually pure, just as the living have to perform the ablution before beginning their prayers. Prayer purifies the soul and the more a man prays the more his soul will shine.

After being washed, the body is wrapped in a shroud (*kafan*) and carried to the cemetery; this latter ceremony is laden with emotion so that women are, in many countries, not allowed to be present as they are supposed to be too prone to emotions. Prayers are recited all the way to the burial place by the local scholar, who will be well paid for it. If the burial occurs the morning after death, a *khatma* will be read. This is a recital of the entire Koran by a teacher and his class, up to 30 people, which is considered particularly meritorious for the deceased. Otherwise, Chapter 6 may be read, and the *Burda*, a pious hymn. Other people may attend the funeral without being any relation to the deceased. They may be blind beggars who will recite special prayers for the soul of the deceased, for some alms. Carrying the bier (*jenaza*) is also very meritorious, so that the bearers are frequently relieved by other bearers. The more people attend, the more saintly was the deceased. Traffic has to stop, bystanders must recite prayers, such as "God is Great, He has power over all things, Praise be to God the Lord of the Universe, there is no God but He. O God, increase our faith and submission. There is no protection except with God. Every one of His creatures will taste death."

Women must be careful not to weep or to praise the deceased excessively since that would increase his punishment, if not true. Every tear that falls on the grave will become a flame that will torture his soul. The reason for this belief is the knowledge that God has decreed all that happens to us, so that complaining would be rebellion against God, which is the most dreadful of all sins.

Graveyards may never be touched, let alone moved or abolished. The dead must be left there until Resurrection. Each grave has the name of its inhabitant on it, so that the awakening angel will know who lies in it. The Wahhabis, however, object to any name or tombstone because, they say, before Judgment there will be a great storm in which all traces of human works will be obliterated: there will be no more cities, towers, or castles, no monuments or inscriptions. Even rocks and mountains will be levelled, the rivers will dry up, and seas and lakes will be filled. The earth will be one vast plain where the sandstorm will rage. Then, when His time comes, God will restore every atom of our bodies. He knows all our names. He will give every soul its body. After that we shall all rise from our graves when the trumpet sounds for the third time. The trumpet-angel is already waiting. Thus, according to the Wahhabis, there is no need for names on graves. They will disappear during the great Destruction of Doomsday when all vanity will fall into dust. It would also show lack of faith in God's omniscience if we think we have to remind Him of our names.

All believers are terrified at the thought of that last day, "When the stars will come spiralling down, when mountains will be set in motion" (Koran 81:1–3), when the risen will search frantically for their loved ones, for the holy prophet, and for the Bridge to Paradise. Therefore, they want to be buried near the grave of the Prophet who will lead them into Paradise.

These long dissertations about the Last Day are necessary to explain people's anxiety about the correct position of the grave and the body in it. A deep pit is dug with a cavity in one side for the body to rest in. Boards or flat stones are placed over the body in such a way that no earth will fall on it when the pit is filled in later. The body is laid in it in such a way that it will face Mecca when it rises from the grave. It would seem logical then, to lay it on its back with its feet towards Mecca, so that when the dead man gets up he would automatically face Mecca. That, however, is not allowed: no one may sleep with his feet towads the holy city. Therefore the body is placed with the face turned to the right, facing Mecca. Some authorities say it has to be placed on the right side, but I do not think that follows from the texts. Only the face has to look to the right. All this is very important because it is believed that Judgment will actually take place in or near Mecca so that many pilgrims actually hope they will die during their pilgrimage in Mecca and be buried there. Others want to be buried near Medina where their Prophet awaits resurrection. He will rise first, at the second sounding of the trumpet, and all his faithful followers will follow his banner into Paradise, by God's special command.

When the body has been laid in the grave, before the earth is filled in, a *faqih* (scholar) will come forward to function as the *mulaqqin*, the instructor of the dead. This happens in Egypt but is frowned upon in West and North Africa. The *mulaqqin* will speak into the grave: "If they ask you who is your God, speak: There is no god but God; if they ask you who is your prophet, speak: Muhammad is the Prophet of God; if they ask you: What is your religion, speak: Islam is my religion; if they ask you: What is your direction, speak: The Kaaba in Mecca is my direction. (*Quibla* refers to the direction towards which a Muslim has to perform his prayers. Every mosque is so positioned that the worshippers will face Mecca when they begin to pray.) If they ask you, what is your book, speak: "The Koran is my book." (The Christians' book is the Gospel, the Jews' book is the Torah.)

When the grave has been closed, bread and money will be distributed, and, for a rich man, even a buffalo may be slaughtered as *kafara*, expiation, to expunge his sins from record.

Inside the grave, the soul has to stay with the body until the day of resurrection. It is separated from the body but it can feel everything that happens to the body, pains and joys. If the deceased was a sinner, the earth will cry out: "Lord! Why has Thou decided to use me to contain this foul sinner?" It will weigh down heavily on the body and squeeze the corpse. That explains why so much care is taken to prevent the earth from actually touching the body. If, however, the deceased has been good, the earth will make itself spacious to accommodate him.

There, lying in his grave, the dead man will be very lonely. His relatives and loved ones have gone away to quarrel over his possessions. His wives will want to remarry after a period of 130 days, as the law prescribes. His children will now do whatever they wish, without paternal admonitions. They will go and squander the estate that it took him a lifetime to build up. They will sell his land and his slaves to have a good time, and there is nothing he can do. His daughters can walk the street; he should have married them off as early as possible. There he lies, helpless, fretting over what he should have done before.

He has yet more reasons to be worried. Any moment there may arrive two messengers from God, the Angels of His Inquisition. Their names are Munkar and Nakir, both of which mean "Unknown." If he has been a sinner, they will have a terrible aspect. They will look black and horrifying, like monsters with fiery eyes. They will start torturing him at once, and, though dead, his body will feel the torture. They will beat him with iron rods and singe his flesh with redhot staves, tearing pieces of flesh out with glowing tongs. After a minute the dead flesh will grow back as it was before, Meanwhile they will interrogate him, as predicted: "Who is your God? Who is your Prophet?" He will reply patiently: "There is no god but God and Muhammad is the Prophet of God." After this they will leave him in peace. This explains why it is so vital to teach the dead man these words, and why, before his death, he has to be made to repeat these words if he does not do so already. Indeed, many people, when lying down, before going to sleep, will repeat these words in Arabic: La ilaha illa Allahu, There is no god but God. It is hoped that after endless repetition the tongue will be so used to these words that even after death in the grave it will still continues La ilaha illa Allahu. And wherever His name is pronounced, He will hear it. In this way the tongue will save its master, when it is well trained. Imagine what will happen if a man used his tongue to repeat blasphemous language or to swear! The tongue is there for prayer, for praising the Lord. For any other words it should be used sparingly, for it will be asked on the Day of Judgment: What did your master use you for? It will answer truthfully either, he made me recite the Koran, or he made me call after sinful women, shout abuse at religious men.

If, however, the deceased has been good, Munkar and Nakir will look what they are: shining angels from heaven in clean white robes with bright smiling faces. They will speak softly and ask politely if the deceased, whose name they know, will answer some questions. The good man does not mind: he knows all the answers; he has never had time to sin; he was too busy worshipping the Lord, which is a full-time occupation. He has given away his money to charity so that all his sins have been "wiped out" from the record, for that is what money is for. If he was a saint, if he spent all his time in the mosque, except when his parents needed him, if his prayers have been so numerous that his soul is completely purified, if he has thrown his forehead on his prayermat so often that it became sore, this sore spot will become luminous after death and emit light in the dark grave. Munkar and Nakir, seeing this light, will treat him with exceptional courtesy. They may even bring a letter in God's own hand-writing, inviting the soul to come to heaven at once to rejoice in the contem-plation of the divine proximity. There is no greater joy.

But even if the deceased has to spend the rest of time (until Doomsday, the end of time) in his grave, it will have a window through which he can see Paradise, so that its aromatic breeze will waft the fragrance of its many flowers into the spacious grave. An angel will come and keep the good man company. Thus, the centuries will pass by rapidly.

If the man died in the holy war, fighting the unbelievers, sacrificing his life "on the path of God," then he will not have to wait at all. An angel will come down in the shape of a bird of Paradise (sic), embrace the soul of the fallen hero, and carry him upwards to heaven where he will stay forever, rejoicing with his comrades, enjoying heavenly food and wine from the grapes of heaven that make no one drunk. No wonder that many men rush to the front hoping to die as saints.

These are, very briefly, the current ideas in Islam concerning death and what happens after. The theme of Doomsday Resurrection, and Judgment, followed by the sending of the bad souls to hell to be tortured for all eternity, and of the good souls to Paradise, and what they will see there, is material for a separate article or even a book. It has been summarized in Knappert (1985, p.461 ff).

If the reader thinks that these ideas are complicated, the truth is that I have drastically condensed and simplified the contents of numerous small and big books written by Islamic scholars for their own students. These books go into great detail such as which punishment is meted out for which sin, how exactly the dead body must be washed and wrapped in the shroud, and what the shroud should be made of (white cotton is the best). The translations of the prayers for the dead would fill another book, as they have to be said after one day, after 40 days and again after a year; they may last a whole night. Let no son neglect the prayers for his parents, for they will come out of their graves and haunt him in visible form at night, begging for the prayers he owes them, for they are being tortured until the expiatory prayers are performed. The food of the dead is prayer. Strong good souls may be asked for favors, so that people can be seen praying near the graves of the saints, hoping those saintly spirits will intercede with God on their behalf. In this way, an entire cult of the saints developed in Morocco, Algeria, Iran and elsewhere, but it is strongly con-demned in Saudi Arabia, illustrating that this subject should be treated country by country, because the differences are enormous. In Pakistan the dead saint may even expel evil spirits from women! I hope that I have given just a few glimpses of Islamic beliefs about the afterlife.

REFERENCES
(Only works in European languages are listed here)

Arberry, A. J. 1964. *The Koran Interpreted.* Oxford: Oxford University Press.

Attema, D. S. 1942. *De Mohammedaansche Opvatting en Omtrent de Jongste Dag en Zijn Voortekenen.* Amsterdam: Hoord-Hollandsche Uitgeversmaatschappij.

Bagdadee, H. E. 1969. *Belief and Islam.* Istanbul: Hikmet Gazetecilik TAN Matbaasi Ltd STI.

Cerulli, E. 1949. *Il Libro della Scala.* Roma: Città del Vaticano.

Corbin, H. 1964. *Histoire de la Philosophie Islamique.* Paris: Gallimard.

Dammann, E. 1940. *Dichtungen in der Lamu Mundart des Suaheli.* Universität Hamburg: Friedrich de Gruyter.

Encyclopaedia of Islam, Vol. IV. 1974. Leiden: E. J. Brill, s. v. Izrail.

Gibb, E. J. W. 1958. *A History of Ottoman Poetry,* Vol. I. London: Luzac.

Horton, M. 1917–18. *Die Religiose Gedankenwelt des Volkes im Heutigen Islam,* 2 Vols. Halle A. S.: Max Niemeyer.

Hughes, T. 1964. *Dictionary of Islam.* Lahore: Premier Book House.

Jaffur Shurreef, tr. Herklots, G. A. n.d. *Qanoon-e-Islam, or the Customs of the Moosulmans in India.* London: Curzon Press.

Klein. 1971. *The Relgion of Islam,* p. 80 ff. New York: Curzon Press.

Knappert, J. 1971. *Swahili Islamic Poetry* I–III. Leiden: E. J. Brill.

Knappert, J. 1967. *Traditional Swahili Poetry.* Leiden: E. J. Brill.

Knappert, J. 1985. *Islamic Legends* I–II. Leiden: E. J. Brill.

Lane, E. 1963. *The Manners and Customs of the Modern Egyptians,* Chap. 28. London: Everyman's Library.

Lane, E. 1971. *Arabian Society in the Middle Ages.* London: Curzon Press.

Macdonald, D. B. 1965. *The Religious Attitude and Life in Islam.* Beyrouth: Khayat's Oriental Reprints.

Munajat-e-Nakbul, Holy Prayers from Quran and Hadis. 1932. Durban: The Young Men's Muslim Association.

Padwick, C. 1961. *Muslim Devotions.* London: S.P.C.K.

Peermahommad Ebrahim Trust. 1971. *Doa'* (Prayers), Vol. II–III. Qureshi Art Press: Nizamabad, Karachi.

Rippin, A. and Knappert, J. eds. 1987. *Textual Sources for the Study of Islam.* Manchester: Manchester University Press.

Rizvi, S. S. A. 1968. *Elements of Islamic Studies,* pp. 72–73. Dar es Salaam. Bilal Mission of Tanzania.

6

The Good Death: Approaches to Death, Dying, and Bereavement Among British Hindus

Shirley Firth

Britain is a multicultural society that includes large numbers of Hindus. An advantage of living in a multicultural society is that the interaction between one's own culture and others forces a reappraisal of beliefs, values, and cultural norms that are normally taken for granted or avoided. In Western culture, death has become a taboo subject in ordinary conversation, and often causes so much embarrassment that friends and neighbors will cross the street to avoid speaking to a bereaved person. As a result of scientific advances that prolong life, serious illness tends to be "more lonely, mechanical and dehumanized," which Elisabeth Kübler-Ross suggests may be our way of denying "the impending death which is so frightening and discomforting to us that we displace all our knowledge onto machines" (1970:3). Apart from accidents, death usually occurs in hospitals. Because of good preventive medicine, premature death, particularly of children, may be thought to be avoidable. When it does occur, therefore, there may be little previous experience to enable the individual and family to deal with it. However, the problem is more than one of scientific knowledge; it is also a question of living in a wealthy, success-oriented post-Christian society in which the rewards for efforts are in the here and now, so that many people do not have a belief system or philosophy that enables them to face the enigma of death. As Schiller said in his *Humanism:*

> Whether science decided for immortality or annihilation, the blissful ignorance that enabled one to ignore the subject in everyday life would be gone for ever. Hence an uncertainty to which we have grown adapated is instinctively or deliberately preferred to a knowledge that would involve the readjustment of ingrained habits (Lorimer 1984:4).

Nevertheless, as a result of the pioneer work of Doctors Elisabeth Kübler-Ross, Cicely Saunders, and others into the care of the dying and bereaved, it is recognized that we have to reexamine our attitudes to death and dying. Cross-cultural perspectives can help us to do this by challenging established modes of thought and practice and providing reminders that aspects of traditional life in any community may provide a stable framework in which to deal with such crises as death. They also throw light on the processes of social change, particularly in a culture forced to come to terms with a new setting at the risk of losing the very stability that provides its continuity and strength. This chapter examines how a Hindu community in Britain deals with death and bereavement. Hindus have very clear ideas about how people ought to die. The ideal of the Good Death is not unlike the approach recommended by Kübler-Ross, based on her own experiences of rural Switzerland, where people died in their own homes, having said goodbye to the family and dealt with their "unfinished business," serene in the belief that they were moving on to another life. Yet this is rare and often difficult to put into practice in Britain. An examination of Hindu approaches is of value in understanding the mechanisms by which people cope with death, and stimulates the reappraisal of our own values and beliefs about death, and our own practical ways of dealing with it.

HINDUS IN BRITAIN

Hindus who settle in Britain come from East Africa and India — mainly from the Punjab and Gujarat — bringing with them their culture, religious beliefs and practices, and family structure, as far as these can be maintained. Living in a host community with very different culture, belief systems, and family patterns can create tension and force adaptation and change, particularly in situations of illness and death, because it may not be possible to follow traditional procedures. This problem is more acute for those coming from rural India; those from urban India and East Africa are more likely, for example, to have experienced modern hospitals with intensive care units. Lack of fluency in English, or of good interpreters, can create further problems for people at moments of crisis. Ignorance on the part of medical or social work professionals about religious beliefs and cultural outlook can exacerbate an already frightening situation. After a death, there are major changes to adjust to. Cremations cannot be performed within 24 hours as in India or East Africa because of the need for postmortems, lack of space in the crematorium, and because relatives may have to be summoned from long distances to attend. Hindus' beliefs about the progress and ultimate fate of the soul appear to depend upon immediate cremation and the performance of the correct rituals by suitable Brahmin priests at the end of the mourning period; in turn these acts will affect the future well-being of the eldest son or chief mourner and his family. It is not always possible to obtain an experienced *mahapatra* or *mahabrahmin* (funeral priest), and some priests will not perform funeral rites. Experienced members of the family, caste, and community give guidelines for procedures, and provide powerful support. If, however, the individuals or families are isolated from their relatives or the caste community for some reason, and cannot obtain a priest, anxiety or guilt may result because of the discrepancy between what they feel ought to be done and what is possible. Young Hindus may feel alienated from the traditional ways, especially if the world they experience at school or work is very different from the one at home. If they are not familiar with religious language and teaching, and if they distance themselves from the religious practices in the home (often solely in the hands of the mother), they may be particularly bewildered when disaster strikes.

Nevertheless, despite these problems, the great strengths in the Asian community become particularly obvious at times of bereavement. A process of adjustment is taking place as the community becomes established; as one Gujarati put it, "There is one truth for India and another for Britain." From the point of view of death studies, there is a great deal to be learned from the concept of "The Good Death," which provides a philosophical approach to dying, and from the religious and cultural mechanisms for coping with bereavement, which allow for stages in the mourning process and legitimate the changes in roles and status resulting from a death in the family. Clearly, a study of another culture raises questions of how far the assumptions, psychological categories, and terminology used in "Western" studies are relevant or appropriate. At cognitive and doctrinal levels immediate and obvious differences occur, involving, for example, such concepts as *karma, samsāra, and mōksha* and beliefs about the process of death itself and the imme- diate fate of the soul following death. It is not clear whether it is correct to call the 12- or 13-day period following a Hindu death a "mourning" period, although it is called *shok* or sorrow, when pollution and danger from the wandering spirit, *prêta*, are also of major concern. Obviously mourning and "grief work" are being done, as understood in bereavement literature, but the stages of grief as described by Murray-Parkes, Elisabeth Kübler-Ross, and others may prove to be too culture specific to be appropriate, although the evidence so far indicates they are relevant.

My research, in progress at the time of writing, is exploring the above issues in a small Hindu community in Southampton, drawing on psychology, anthropology, and religious studies, looking at the way beliefs and attitudes to death and bereavement are reflected in caste and family traditions, in the changes that have taken place or are perceived to have taken place, and the extent to which the maintenance or loss of these beliefs and attitudes has affected the process of adjustment to bereavement. In addition to information derived from interviews with Hindus in Southampton, some material was obtained from relatives or from individuals of the same caste and sectarian background of Gujarati and Punjabi informants during a three-month field trip to India in 1986. This material has been included because it throws light on particular attitudes. While in India I also visited Varanasi and Hardwar, which are both very sacred places on the river Ganges; people come here to die (to die in Varanasi [Kashi] enables one to go straight to heaven). Hindus from Britain return to one or both these places with the ashes of their relatives and have the *shrāddha* ceremonies performed here themselves or on their behalf by other friends and relatives.

There are about 2,000 Hindus in Southampton, according to statistics of the Commission for Racial Equality. The majority are Gujarati business castes (Patels, Lohanas, Banias, Darjis, Sonis, etc.) who have come from East Africa; a smaller but influential group of Punjabi Hindus are mainly Khatri and Brahmin, with some Sonis and others, many of whom have come from India. The Hindu community has one of the few intentionally built temples in the country, completed three years ago. Although there was considerable unity in building it, subsequent power struggles for control appear to have some basis in regional affiliation, although people assured me it is due to personal power politics (Knott 1981). In terms of religious and sectarian affiliation, the Gujaratis mainly belong to two Vaishnava bhakti sects. The Pushtimarg sect follows the teachings of Vallabhacharya, or Swami Narayan, with intense devotion to the living Swami, believed to be an avatar of Sāhajanand Swami, the 19th century founder and himself an avatar of Vishnu. Many of the Punjabis are followers of Arya Samāj, while others call themselves Sanātan Dharm.[1] However, worship, which in India is largely domestic,[2] has acquired a congregational aspect here. There seems to be a blending of traditions, so that an Arya Samāji *havan* will be followed by a Sanatani *arti* (prayers with a lighted lamp in front of the images of the gods, which are banned by orthodox Arya Samājis), and a Sanatani family may conclude the funeral service with a *havan* in the home in lieu of the *piṇḍa* ceremonies on the 10th to 12th days. The latter will then be arranged in India by relatives there.

THE GOOD DEATH

Hindu informants express a very clear concept of the good death. Life should be lived in such a way that death does not take one unawares:

> So you're getting ready. It's like if you start getting ready for a holiday a long time before the holiday. . . this journey we start renouncing our things. . . in the world and people around you — you have less and less attachment towards the family, towards belongings, and more and more you do *dhān seva* (religious giving). We have to be dead and living, not living dead. People who worry about death are living dead because they are so worried thinking about it. People who are not thinking about it, who are all ready for it, will never ever die. . . the body dies, the soul just takes over the next form unless your soul is fortunate to reach Him (Punj. Br.).

If one is prepared and not attached to life, then relinquishing it is easier:

> My mother never said, "I want to live, I want to live." She said everything was well settled, the children were settled. She was a very religious person — at night she used to sing *bhajans* (hymns) and she said, "If anything happens now I'll not be worried, I'll go in peace." That way her death was a very good death. She (realized) that everyone has to go. She was very peaceful. (Guj. Patel)

Ideally, a person dies in old age, having lived to see his/her son's son's son. The person should have dealt with all his/her unfinished business, seen to the marriages of unmarried daughters or granddaughters, and said goodbye to members of the family.

> My father had a hernia at 60. He was a very holy soul. Three days before he knew he was going to die, so he called all the family members to come "so we can all live together." They put Ganga water in his mouth and when he died his forehead was bright. He said he was happy because all his family were there. (Guj. Br.)

Death should be entered voluntarily and peacefully; in a sense, it should be "willed," so spiritual preparation is important. One should die with the name of God on the lips and in the heart, and many informants have described the death of a parent or grandparent who died chanting "Ram, Ram." If the person is unable to do so because she/he is in pain or unconscious, relatives should do this for him or her, or chant "om" or the Gayatri Mantra, or read Chapter 15 of the Bhagavad Gita or some other holy book. This is to make sure that the person dies with the mind fixed on God:

> If you have committed minor karmas and at the time your thoughts are filled with God, if you say God's name (at death) then you will obviously go to heaven, because God is there. If someone is about to die and you think he is going to go, its important that you make him repeat God's name or you read any sloks (verses) from the Gita or whatever to make his mind concentrate on God (Guj. Patel).

It is important to die on the earth. In India, the dying person is taken outside to a courtyard when possible, although in a home for the dying in Varanasi the person was placed on the floor. Here it is desirable to die on the floor, with the head to the north.[1] Various reasons are given for this, the most common being that there should be no physical constraints or boundaries, and the body should be aligned to the magnetic currents of the earth. It is considered very inauspicious to sleep in this position normally. Several Gujarati informants in India also referred to Yama's messengers or Rama and Sita coming from the South, where Yama is considered to dwell, to collect the soul. At the point of death, tulsi leaf and Gangajal (Ganges water) should be put in the person's mouth, and if it has not already been done, the body should be placed on the floor and a diva should be lighted to show the way to the soul.

> My mother — she was like a saint and she died in just five minutes. She was 103 and she can put thread into needle, she walks without stick, she never holds stick. Without stick she was walking at the end and she asked for bed on the floor. After that there was no one to give her a light — mostly when people die we give a diva like a candle — we give into her hand. You know flour — we make that like chapatti flour and we make diva from that and put some ghee on top of that

and give to her on her hand which is going to die to show him or her a way to God. . . . [then] my sister's son. . .came there. He said, "What's happening, Bibi?" She said, "O thank God you came here. Come and give me *diva* on my hand," and my sister started crying and she said, "Don't cry, I'm going to God. Let me go first. Don't stop my way.". . .He did everything, [then] she said, "Put my head in your lap, I want to go to God. (Punj. Br.)

A sudden, or premature death is a bad death, although even here, if the death is painless and the person has died with "Ram Ram" on the lips it may be regarded as a good death. A 72-year-old man went to his doctor's office to collect some medicine, and he had a heart attack there. The doctor, who was a Hindu, told him to say "Ram Ram" as he was dying, and subsequently the family took great comfort in the fact that he had died a "good death." Violent death and suicide are particularly bad,[3] and the latter will not have a cremation but will have an earth or water burial, since the proper *agni sanskār* (fire ceremony) cannot be done. The signs of a bad death include vomit or excreta. It is also bad to die during the *panchaka* or dark days of the moon, and six inauspicious months of the year, and if this happens remedial ceremonies have to be undertaken.

HOSPITAL DEATHS

Clearly, if people die suddenly, or in a hospital, it may be very difficult to give the dying person the support and help required to "die his own death." Patients who have climbed out of bed to lie on the floor have been put back by uncomprehending nurses, and intensive care units or general wards do not lend themselves to numbers of relatives standing around and chanting. There is often an understandable reluctance on the part of medical staff to say someone is dying. This problem is increasingly being faced by medical professionals in training courses on death and bereavement and applies to patients in all communities. If the patient's family has difficulty communicating because of language misunderstandings, and if the medical staff does not understand the particular requirements of Hindus, this compounds their problems.

Mostly the person is sent home in India rather than dying in hospital, they say the last few minutes that are left you can take the person home. But then, people who are very scientific, they still have hopes and they say they would rather leave him here and let him die in your care. . . . Here . . . a lot of people die in hospital and they (don't) put the bodies on the floor . . . and a lot of us families are very shy to follow very strictly — we feel out of place, like a Muslim praying towards Mecca on the factory floor. In hospitals, when someone is near to death then he must have his next of kin with him. . . . When people know that he is near to death we start reciting the *Gita*, religious books. The only people who can do it is their own. The nurses won't do it, the doctors won't do it, they don't know, so obviously we must be told [that the person is dying] rather than keeping the news away and only being told after the death has happened. I know it's not easy to say, look, he is going to die. It's easier to say, "He's alright, nothing to worry about," and all of a sudden you go back next time, to visit, or you're given telephone call to say, "Sorry, we couldn't save him." There are rituals preferably to be done before a person dies.... If the family are there...(you adjust gradually) because when you are reciting the Gitã...you still have hope...and you slowly believe that this soul is going to depart from you....

A 15-year-old girl whose father died in the hospital expressed her rage and frustration over her father's death. It seemed clear to her and to her mother that his condition was deteriorating, but the staff either ignored their complaints about his condition or assured them he was going to recover:

They kept assuring us and we took their word for it, but to us he seemed to be getting worse, but they know more than us, so we accepted it that he was improving but it didn't seem to us to be true...he was very restless that day, vomiting...and he was putting his blanket over his head—it's a bad sign for us if somebody covers his whole face and...so my mum went to the doctor and after a whole lot of persistence and persuading he came eventually...and half an hour later we were told he had pneumonia and they said they'd have to put him into intensive care.... And then there was another bad sign—you know after somebody dies they bring all the flowers to the hospital, the wreaths and everything...and all these flowers came in front of my father's room....Then we went home and I kept on saying, "Is there anything to worry about?" and they said, "Nothing, we'll take care of him, pneumonia is nothing nowadays," and at 3:00 a.m. there was a phone call...and this doctor said, "Your father has passed away." If he had known he would have had everything done [He left no will]. He always told us, "I'm not scared of dying. I'm not worried at all, as long as I know what is happening.... He would have prayed...in his last time, but really he would have worried about us...he would have had a bit of strength, at least my family's with me at my last time. We think he lost [hope], he couldn't just take it any longer, all these tubes around him, helpless, he was like a little child in jail.... If we had the slightest idea we would have sat in the waiting room all night....My uncles believe that if we'd been with him, he would have been stronger and maybe he would have survived. I said [to the nurse] "Did my father say anything at the end?" and she said, "Oh, do you expect people when they die to say things? In your religion?" and I said, "I just want to know what his last words were," and she said "Oh, I didn't know that you'd have expected him to say anything," as if it was something really strange and out of this world that a person dying would say anything.

The mother of the girl was a well-educated, but shy, woman whose spoken English was very good but accented. Her comprehension of the situation was consistently underestimated by the medical staff, who assumed the daughter, who was very intelligent and lively, was much older. Once the father was in intensive care the mother was kept out and never saw her husband alive again, and her daughter was asked to interpret for the nurses, although her father spoke and understood English perfectly. The family was left feeling very angry because the husband's deterioration was obvious to them and they felt they had been fobbed off with lies and evasion. Subsequent complaints via the Commission for Racial Equality met with little response from the hospital and the consultant told them that patients with the father's condition often did die. The girl felt that the offhandedness of the staff had a racist dimension, "because we are black." Fortunately, not all Hindus have such experiences, but they are not uncommon, and the issues raised by this kind of situation need examining with some urgency. Obviously there are considerable practical difficulties in allowing numbers of relatives into a ward at all hours of the day and night, especially if there is a need to chant mantras or sing hymns, and any emotional reactions are distressing for staff as well as patients. However, it is in the interests of staff, patients, and the families to communicate openly and with care and compassion and to provide the best environment possible for terminal care without leaving a residue of unnecessary bitterness and anger.

FUNERALS

In India, the body would be washed and dressed in the home immediately after death prior to being carried on a stretcher to the cremation ground. This is done the same day as the death up to sunset; an evening death will be cremated the following day. Although there are now electric crematoria in many urban areas, my informants in India regarded the traditional open pyre as preferable, although, even when the electric one was used, traditional ceremonies could be performed outside it on a raised platform up to the time the body went into the oven. In Southampton the cremation takes place several days after the death, and in the meantime the body is kept in the funeral home. When Indians first arrived, bodies were washed immediately after death, as they would be in India. A young Gujarati went to wash his brother's body at the hospital mortuary with the help of an uncle. Because it was a sudden death, there had been a postmortem, so as soon as they were allowed to go they went to the mortuary and were appalled to find another opened body on a slab, inadequately concealed behind a screen:

> It was a terrifying experience and it was just one room and there was another dead body there which was just opened and all they had there was just a screen and everytime I was going around (to dress my brother) I was looking at two bodies.... My uncle helped me a lot and I had to do it because the other people who should have offered didn't because they were scared.

The washing and dressing is now done immediately before the funeral. The director of the most popular funeral home does his best to meet the needs of the Asians in the community — Muslims, Hindus, and Sikhs — but sometimes gets into difficulties. Bearing in mind the Muslim abhorrence of a non-Muslim touching a body, he tends to leave bodies alone for relatives to deal with. However, in the case of the man whose death is described above, many tubes remained in place when the body left the hospital, and the relatives were appalled at having to remove them. There are caste and family traditions concerning the washing and dressing procedures, and older relatives will be consulted. Local people of the same caste and sex will also give assistance and advice. In India the body of a man will be dressed in a dhoti; here it will be dressed in the clothes he normally wears, preferably new clothes. A woman will be dressed in the type of clothes she normally wears, although if she predeceases her husband she will wear her wedding sari or suit, or clothes in bridal colors. The body is then placed in a coffin instead of tied on a bier, and taken by hearse to the family home. If the home is very small, the coffin may have to be taken in through a window. A priest who is willing to take funerals will have been called if he can be found; if not, a local elderly Brahmin woman from a priestly family who knows the mantras may be called upon to chant some mantras instead. A number of the priests who come are not trained in taking funerals and may "invent" the appropriate Sanskrit readings. As the body enters and the lid is removed the *Gayātri Mantra* or some other mantra is chanted, and Chapter 15 of the *Gītā* or other scriptural passages will be read. In India *piṇḍas* (balls of rice or wheat) may be offered both in the home and at the pyre; in Britain I have only observed this done twice, when a wheat *piṇḍa* was made and placed on the coffin. Various substances, such as *ghī* (melted butter), *tulsi* (a sacred leaf, of the basil family), a coin ("to pay the ferryman crossing the river of death"), and *Gangajal* are placed in the mouth, and a mixture of herbs, *ghī*, flowers, coconuts, spices, and *Gangajal* placed on the body prior to the family and friends circumambulating the body and touching the feet. The exact procedures are based on caste and family traditions. If there isn't a senior member of the family to direct affairs, a phone call may be made to a senior relative in India to clarify what should be done, how many circumambulations should be made, and what substances should be used. The coffin is then closed and taken to the crematorium. In a number of Gujarati castes, women don't go to the crematorium, but Punjabi women will go. At all times the coffin will be carried by members of the family and close friends who have an obligation to "give a shoulder." At the crematorium there is a short service and eulogy prior to the removal of the body. The eldest son or chief mourner goes below to press the button to start the fire, although some wish to push the body in physically. Double-decker buses are hired to take the large numbers of relatives, friends, and members of the community to the crematorium. After the service, mourners and friends return to the deceased's home and sit with the family quietly and then drift away. In many Punjabi families, however, the pundit returns to the house for an Arya Samaji *havan*, the Vedic fire ceremony, followed by the *pagri* ceremony (not observed by Gujaratis), which is regarded as the conclusion of *sok*, even if fewer than the normal 10 or 13 days have passed. It is often done this way because it is difficult to get a priest again and because, if many people have come from abroad or from other parts of Britain, it is convenient to condense the ceremonies into one. However, one family, who had a funeral for an elderly mother on the eighth day after the death and said that was the end of all the ceremonies, suddenly had cold feet on the 13th day and arranged for another *havan*. Some

Shaivite Brahmins would go straight to a temple after a cremation in India; in Britain, because the temple is dedicated to Rādha-Krishna, and the Vaishnavas have stricter views on purity, they cannot do it, in spite of there being a "photo" of Shiva's consort, Sheriwallimāta, in the temple.

THE MOURNING PERIOD

In India the period of mourning or *shok* begins immediately after death and lasts between 10 and 13 days. However, for the immediate family, and particularly for widows, mourning continues in various forms for up to a year, depending on family traditions. In Britain, for reasons given below, it is often shortened. The furniture is removed from the living room, white sheets spread on the floor, and friends and neighbors drop in throughout the day to listen, condole, and participate in the readings and singing of hymns. It is regarded as obligatory by all the community to pay their respects and *afsos* (regrets). The visitors will recall the dead person, get the mourners to describe the details of the death over and over again, and recount their own experiences of loss and bereavement. Alternating with this are readings from the *Gītā* or, with Punjabi Hindus, a long poem written by an East African Arya Samaji, called *Amrit Varsh*. In one instance, a group of women came for two hours every afternoon to visit a Khatri widow, and chanted the poem together, whereas she read two chapters of the *Gītā* to herself every day until the funeral. She found this alternation extremely therapeutic, because the visitors gave her an opportunity to talk about her husband and his death as much as she needed; others shared their experiences of bereavement with her and wept with her, and the readings gave her a great deal of sustenance because they reminded her that this was God's will and death was not the end of life. She said that in East Africa people would only have come at specific times and allowed the family to eat and take rests in peace, but that the constant stream of visitors prevented her from ever taking a break, which was a strain at the time but appreciated later. A Sikh neighbor and other friends provided food during the early days and after the funeral.

In India, pollution lasts for 10 days after death in most of the Hindu castes represented in this study. Traditionally there are many proscriptions, which include sleeping on the floor, not eating sweet food or offering any food or drink to guests, and men do not shave until the *piṇḍa* ceremony on the 10th day. In Vaishnava families *murtī pūja* (worshipping images) is not done, and, as has been mentioned, one cannot go to the temple. During this period the "ghost," or *prêt* is wandering around, and is tempted by unresolved attachments to cling to the family:

> When a young man dies his soul and the wanting of his wife and the wanting of his children, his wishes, or the things he wanted to do or needed to be in the family (cause the soul to be) bewildered and (hang) around the family without the physical body. (Darji)

For this reason it is necessary to provide food in the form of *pinda* and water for 10 days to enable it to form a new body. On the 12th day, at the *sapindikarana* ceremony, it is merged with the *pitṛs* or ancestors. These ceremonies are often being abbreviated or abandoned. Many people I spoke to in India performed the 10 daily *pinḍa* ceremonies in one single ceremony of 10 *pinḍas*, and sometimes the ceremony was brought forward for convenience. The ceremonies have to be performed by specialist priests, called *acharājs* or *māhabrāhmins*, who do not only know the requisite procedures, but are able to receive the gifts given after death on behalf of the dead person. These gifts consist of all the things she/he would require in daily use and include bedding and a bed, clothing, shoes, and food. A "pure" Brahmin is not supposed to receive them because with the gifts comes the burden of the sin of the deceased person; only hereditary specialists who perform the requisite *pūja* can bear this burden. In Britian, it is difficult to find such specialists. If a family pundit comes to take the funeral, as at the funerals I attended, he is not able to accept these gifts. In none of these funerals was the *sapindikarana* performed, but money was sent to India with instructions to have the ceremonies performed there. In many instances money was also sent to provide gifts to the poor instead of making gifts to Brahmins. However, Gujarati mahabrahmins are more readily available in Britain, and will come on the 10th or 12th day. Following the ceremony the tail of a cow or calf (ideally this should be live if available, but in Britain—as sometimes is the case in India—a silver calf is substituted) is bathed in milk and water and then given to the Brahmin since the *ātma* can catch hold of it to cross the river of death. The ashes are tradi- tionally collected on the third day, and should be disposed of in a river or the sea; when possible, they are taken to the Ganges at Varanasi or Hardwar. Some Hindus in Britain dispose of ashes in a river or the sea, but some water author- ities have objected on the grounds that this would be polluting. Sometimes ashes are also mailed to Varanas where specialist priests perform the correct ceremonies. There is an annual ceremony, called shrāddha, in which further offerings are made to the deceased relatives, or *pitṛs* both in the form of *pinḍas* and in gifts to the Brahmins, which maintain a continuous link between the living and the dead and gain merit and good *karma* for both.

BELIEFS AND EXPLANATIONS

Reference has already been made to the belief that the deceased has to grow a new body in order to go to *pitṛ lok*, the place of the fathers, and the annual *shrāddha* is based on the assumption that the deceased is there. However, in practice, people believe one of three things: the soul is in one of the heavens (or hells, though this has never been mentioned), either as a temporary reward (or punishment) prior to rebirth; or in a state of eternal bliss with God (usually Vishnu or Krishna), or has achieved *moksha*, liberation, conceived as unity with the Absolute and dissolution of personality; or has been reborn. According to Dr. Sudhir Kakar, in a personal interview, these beliefs provide useful choices

— if one does not like a deceased relative, one can think of him or her as being reborn as a vulture! A number of informants have spoken about dreams of the deceased. One lost a baby girl and her sister had a dream in which the child said, "My mother has given me everything except bananas. If you will give me bananas I'll come again." They went to the temple of the mother goddess and offered bananas, and within a month she was pregnant again with her eldest son. She also dreamed her best friend's husband would come again in the child soon to be born to her daughter-in-law. However, only one informant, a lecturer in India, referred to the possibility that people might meet in heaven. A devout follower of Swami Narayan, she believed her mother was with Swamiji in *Akshardham*, heaven, and now that her father had died they were together: "Now he is also with my mother, maybe there is no relationship between those souls which are there as husband and wife and father or mother. . . but all of them are in the same place and very happy. . . and when you think like that you get a little peace of mind."

The destination of the soul depends on karma. Although karma is often spoken of as absolutely deterministic, many of the ceremonies before and after death suggest that other factors may be at work, just as dying in Varanasi (Kashi) is supposed to take you straight to heaven. (You have, of course, to have good karma to be there in the first place.) Karma is the usual explanation for premature or untimely death. The death of a child is conceived of as either the parent's or child's karma, or both: "The child has a certain period fixed with you. [Understanding this] helps the parents to come to terms with the death. . . the only way you can explain to the mother is that this child was only going to live with you for five years, and you have to accept it, because now the child has gone for its betterment." The level of acceptance of this doctrine may be related to the level of a person's education and devotion. Several educated informants were bewildered and puzzled by a painful or apparently unnecessary death of a good person. Both the informant whose husband died in the hospital (mentioned earlier) and an academic referred to anger against God, but this is very uncommon in the evidence so far: "My sister suddenly expired at the age of 21 when she was doing her MBBS. My father's reaction was complete anger at her death; he was blaming God. She was going to be a doctor and suddenly she expired, so. . . why has God done this?" (Gujarati lecturer).

Adjustment

Several young informants have expressed difficulty coping with the expectation of their relatives or visitors to cry "on demand." The daughter of one deceased man found the procedure very difficult:

> At the beginning I didn't like it because they'd come and my mum would start crying and I'd hate that, but when the scripture readings started, every time a new person would come they'd start crying. I hated it and I felt as if they were making my mum ill as well. . . but afterwards when I got used to it, you know, the same people kept coming, then that was O.K.

Another young girl said, "They used to cry loudly, so loudly, but what they were doing really was impressing everybody around them that they were feeling the grief, but what you really feel inside is something different." A Darji girl found it difficult to mourn a grandmother who died in East Africa because she had not known her. She offered the visitors who came to pay their condolences cups of tea and could not understand their shock until it was explained that the house was polluted, and no food or drink would be accepted. When the father of a close friend died, she didn't know how to help her or what to say until she read the *Gita* and suddenly felt that now she was not afraid of death any more, and she would be able to tell people not to be afraid because the soul didn't die, it just "changed its station."

Young people who do not know what should be done and fail to arrange for the correct ceremonies for relatives may experience profound guilt subsequently when they find out what should have been done. One informant arranged for the funeral of a brother who had died suddenly in the United States in accordance with the recommendations of the funeral director there. Later, when his uncle helped him to arrange the funeral of his father and when he realized what he should have done for his brother, he felt very distressed and guilty at his failure to have done it properly.

One of the questions raised initially was the appropriateness of English concepts, such as guilt, to the Hindu context. The fact that my informants who have used the word are educated in the English language makes it difficult to judge how far they have been influenced by English usage. However, it appears that it is valid, in the sense of remorse, if stripped of its Western theological connotations, although in the example above the doctor also felt culpable. The Swami Narayan lecturer, quoted elsewhere, described her guilt at refusing her mother mango juice (on doctor's orders) just before she died. This is "something I can't get over, when you are alone and when you think, you remember everything as if it just happened. . .why did we refuse this?" She subsequently took remedial action by providing a feast of mango juice to the monastery but continued to feel unhappy. Educated informants in India also recognized delayed grief, denial, and displaced anger in other people but said it was particularly difficult in India to acknowledge anger towards, for example, parents, because "your upbringing doesn't allow this," even if a parent or mother-in-law has treated you badly: "Even for a child, when you are being brought up, if you don't love your parents, you don't express it, you are made to feel guilty. How can I possibly not love my parents? Children are made to feel they've got to love their parents. People don't acknowledge [anger and dislike], not that it's not present." Although it was regarded as healthy and normal to express emotion, it had become unfashionable in urban India. "We laugh quite openly, we don't cry, it's just not done. . .we don't seem to mind shouting at people when we get angry. . .but we do seem to be inhibited with our tears and sorrow. In the village, people are very open about expressing grief" (Gujarati lecturer). Another spoke of her mother's failure to come to terms with the death of her terminally ill son. She herself had been orphaned young, so "she didn't want to show her emotions to anybody and she kept everything to herself . . . and pretended that nothing had happened, so that inhibition must have killed her inside . . . her health deteriorated and she had many tantrums and all the hopes were focused on me, so that was a great burden on me."

The psychological concomitants of pollution warrant further exploration. It has been suggested that it may be a metaphor for anger, but, of course, death is also profoundly mystifying and fearful, the fear of ghosts real, and the sudden departure of a familiar figure needs to be dealt with in a satisfying way. The process of "building a new body" during the period of liminality would, it seem, help in the process of healing the psychological gap between the person's death and the re-establishment of normal life, as well as ensuring that the ghost had been adequately disposed of.

WIDOWS

The change of status for widows is marked less dramatically in Britain than in India where there is still sometimes head shaving. However, Gujarati widows will break their bangles on the coffin, and wear white or light colors thereafter; Punjabi widows have their change acknowledged during the *pagri* ceremony where the eldest son, indicating that from now on he is head of the household and will look after his mother, gives her a sari and gold bangles to symbolize his new status. Widows in Britain may feel the restrictions imposed by other members of the community are unnecessary, but are afraid to risk the disapproval of the community by breaking them. If the widow is young, rumors and gossip can spread rapidly through the area, particularly because some families regard a young widow as unlucky and may blame her for the death of her husband. One young widow who continued to wear colored saris and make up, and resumed a normal social life, was very much criticized. However, those Indians who do not belong to one of the tightly knit caste or sectarian groups in the community can feel their isolation acutely at the time of bereavement. There may also be problems over changing expectations of roles. A widowed mother, for example, may want to live with a son who has married a Westernized woman and established a nuclear family, and finds problems with different attitudes to the role of wife and mother. These changing expectations can create considerable marital and family tension, with pressure from outside to conform to tradition and live as one family, as well as guilt on the part of the son, who feels torn between the expectations of the two women and the rest of the Hindu community.

Despite some of the problems mentioned, it is at the time of death that communal solidarity is at its strongest, and members from all communities support one another. Despite the pressures of visitors during the mourning period, the support is perceived to be of very real help and comfort. The insistence on weeping, in terms of recent bereavement studies, is a very valuable expression of grief, and the alternation between talking about the dead person, weeping, and scripture readings provides a gradual period of adjustment to his/her absence. The changes in role and status, which are particularly acute for a widow, are marked by ongoing ceremonies, such as the *pagri* ceremony handing authority over to the eldest son, and, should she wish, by ongoing rituals with gifts for Brahmins and clearly marked stages for up to a year. The performance of the *havan*, for Punjabis, which is a group activity, with individual books provided for participants, seems to be replacing the *piṇḍa* ceremony. The latter, which is restricted to the chief mourner, the immediate family, and the requisite number of Brahmins, tends to be performed on the family's behalf in India, or at a later date when it is possible to go there.

CHANGES

The implications of these changes for belief, and vice versa, as well as those mentioned at the beginning, have to be explored further. The conviction that "the peace of the departed soul depends on the family. . . if we don't help the soul through the passage by doing all these rituals, then obviously it's still in the atmosphere, like ghosts and all these *bhut prêts*. . . these are the souls that have not been done properly at the time of cremation," has serious implications for belief and practice. However, very few of my British Hindu informants mentioned such a belief or gave more complex details about the soul hanging around after death or the need to provide nourishment to enable it to grow a new body. They said instead the ceremonies were *"ātma ki shānti ke liye,"* for the peace of the soul. This may indicate that they do not know or that it was not important. Priests in India told me that the immediate cremation, with the *kapal krya*, or skull-breaking ceremony, were vital for releasing the airs left in the body and enabling the soul "to know that it is dead." For someone with this belief the delayed cremation could also be a problem, though none of the British informants have mentioned it. However, qualified and learned Brahmins are not readily available, either as teachers of the Sanskritic tradition or as practitioners. The Hinduism that evolves in Britain, therefore, may have much less dependency on Brahmins, with a corresponding adapatation of belief. Such a change seems to be borne out both by the fact that many people, both in India and in Britain, give gifts to the poor in lieu of the Brahmins, and by the strong sectarian groups with devotion to a guru or swami. At the same time, the feeling that certain things have to be done and can only be done in India means that the umbilical cord is still very strong. The role of the Brahmins is also changing, because many family pundits are being called upon to take funeral ceremonies, which they have previously never done, so that the rituals themselves are evolving.

CONCLUSION

Hindu beliefs are, of course, of great interest in their own right, but it is also very important that we understand the religion and way of life of a large community in our midst. Since Hindus are themselves going through a process of change — not unique, of course to Britain, but exacerbated by aspects of life in an alien environment — it is important to understand what these changes are and how far they affect the community, particularly with regard to the way they deal with death and bereavement, so that the caring professions can approach them with understanding and sympathy. Death is a threat to any society. As Peter Berger says, it "presents society with a formidable problem not only because of its obvious threat to the continuity of human relationships; but because it threatens the basic assumptions of order on which society rests (1969:23). If those basic assumptions are being challenged anyway, both from within and through interaction with the host community, then it is all the more threatening; on the other hand, the new community may be creating what Frank Reynolds and Earl Waugh call a "new language" to cope with the situation:

> Where on the one hand accepted and conventional activities offer the support of society's forms in the face of death, on the other their very regularity and inflexibility may contribute to a collapse under the absurdity of death's presence. The immediate result of this explosive new element in life is the birth in effect of a new "language." Though not necessarily verbal it is a genuine attempt to cope with and give expression to a violent new challenge. . . .The way is opened for articulating emerging experiences in consort with other moods and attitudes, and individuals wander down many paths trying to make sense of the con-junction of themselves and that peculiar occurrence at that particular time (Reynolds and Waugh 1977:1).

Hindus, in attempting to come to terms with this challenge, can also provide a challenge to the host community. The model of the Good Death reminds us that such a notion is not an alien one, but also belongs to the religious traditions of the West, which in turn may need to be re-examined in the light of new experiences and new conditions. It is also useful to examine, in a cross-cultural perspective, the religious and therapeutic value of rituals, both at death and for a period of mourning, which provide legitimate ways of expressing grief and give shape and meaning to the period of transition between life with a person and the resumption of life without, and to the changes of role and status for the survivors with massive community support. These factors, which provide cohesiveness and strength to individuals and to the Hindu community as a whole, are also undergoing rapid change. Some of them are in danger of being lost, not least because of external pressures and lack of understanding. It is here that the hospice movement and the growth of studies into death and bereavement have generated a deep interest in finding out more about the processes surrounding death, which, it is hoped, will encourage further exploration and greater understanding of Hinduism. It is important to find some sort of meaning in death, to find some sort of explanation that is cognitively as well as emotionally satisfying. The concept of Good Death appears to do this.

GLOSSARY

Darji: tailor caste

dīva: a light or lamp burning ghee

havan: Vedic fire ceremony, which is the focal point of worship for followers of the Arya Samaj sect

Khatri: a Punjabi business caste

mokshā: liberation, enlightenment

pagri: a turban, which is given to the eldest son by his wife's family, after his father's death, as a sign that he is now head of the family. Some Punjabi families give these to all the sons.

samsara: the continuing cycle of death and rebirth

NOTES

Some informants who were quoted at length preferred that their caste, region and affiliation were not mentioned, since this might lead to identification. In respect for their privacy, all mention of caste and region have been deleted.

1. Arya Samaj: a 19th Century Hindu reform movement that sought to return to the pure teaching of the Vedas and abolish image worship and caste practices. It is popular among Punjabi Hindus. Sanatan Dharm: The eternal religion, used to describe nonsectarian Hinduism.

2. The temples in India do not have congregational worship on a regular basis. People go singly or as families to worship one or several particular deities, and groups will gather for festivals and special occasions, or in the case of sects such as Swami Narayan or Pushtimarg, to hear their Swami or Guru. In Britain, Sunday has become a day of regular worship for the whole community, and when not dominated by one group, the services have tended to become fairly eclectic.

3. The exceptions to the prohibition of suicide are religious deaths by ascetics, and *sati,* the burning of widows. The term *sati* means "a good woman." Violent death is also regarded as bad; however, informants said that the death of Gandhi by violence was a good death because he died with the name of God on his lips.

REFERENCES

Berger, P. 1969. *The Social Reality of Religion,* p. 23. London: Faber and Faber.

Knott, K. 1981. *Hinduism in England: The Hindu Population in Leeds,* p. 16. University of Leeds Department of Sociology Religious Research Papers.

Kübler-Ross, E. 1970. *On Death and Dying,* p. 3. London: Tavistock.

Lorimer, D. 1984. *Survival,* p. 4. London: Routledge and Kegan Paul.

Reynolds, E., and Waugh, F.E. 1977. *Religious Encounters with Death: Insights from the History and Anthropology of Religion,* p. 1. University Park and London: Pennsylvania State University Press.

ADDITIONAL BIBLIOGRAPHY

Huntington, R., and Metcalf, P. 1979. *Celebrations of Death: The Anthropology of Mortuary Ritual.* Cambridge: Cambridge University Press.

Kaker, S., 1978. *The Inner World: A Psychoanalytic Study of Childhood and Society in India.* Delhi: Oxford University Press.

Kane, P.V. 1941; 1953. *History of Dharmashastra,* Vols. 2 and 5. Poona: Bhandarkar Oriental Research Institute.

Knipe, D.M. 1977. "Sapindikarana: The Hindu Rite of Entry into Heaven." In Reynolds, E. and Waugh, F.E. (eds). *op. cit.*

Kübler-Ross, E. 1975. *Death: The Final Stage of Growth.* London: Prentice Hall.

Monier-Williams. 1884. *Brahmanism and Hinduism.* London: John Murray.

O'Dea, T., and O'Dea Aviad, J. 1983. *The Sociology of Religion.* Englewood Cliffs, NJ: Prentice Hall.

Parkes, C.M. 1986. *Bereavement: Studies of Grief in Adult Life,* 2nd ed. Harmondsworh, Middlesex: Penguin Books.

Pandey, R. B. 1969. *The Hindu Samskaras: Socio-religious Study of the Hindu Sacraments.* Delhi and Varanasi: Motilal Banarasidass.

Parry, J. 1982. "Sacrificial Death and the Necrophagous Ascetic." In Block, M. and Parry, J. (eds). *Death and the Regeneration of Life.* Cambridge: Cambridge University Press.

Parry, J. 1981. Death and Cosmogony in Kashi. *Contributions to Indian Sociology* 15:337–365.

Raphael, B. 1984. *The Anatomy of Bereavement: A Handbook for the Caring Professions.* London: Hutchison.

Rosenblatt, P.C., Walsh, R.P., and Jackson, D.A. 1976. *Grief and Mourning in Cross-cultural Perspective.* New York: HRAF Press.

Stedeford, A. 1984. *Facing Death: Patients, Families and Professionals.* London: William Heinemann Medical Books.

Stevenson, S. 1920. *Rites of the Twice-Born.* London: Oxford University Press.

Van Gennep, A. 1960. *The Rites of Passage* (trans. Vizedom, M.B. and Caffee, G.L.) Chicago: University of Chicago Press.

7

The Hindu Concept of Death

Jamuna Prasad

Every human being has the awareness and knowledge that death is inevitable. But when and where death will occur is a great secret. Once this awareness about death arises, the person starts searching for the meaning of death. Death is decidedly a grief-inducing element within the experience of our human family. Various religious and philosophical traditions of the world have distinct concepts regarding death. In this chapter the Hindu view of death is presented.

The Hindus believe that birth and death are the jugglery of *Maya*. There is birth for the body alone. Five elements — earth, water, fire, air, and ether — combine to form the body, while the *Atman* is birthless and deathless. These elements are dissolved after death and go back to their sources. In reality, no one is born and no one dies. Death is only the casting off of the physical body, a deep slumber or sleep. It is like the separation of the soul from the physical body.

Swami Shivanand in his book *What Becomes of the Soul After Death* (1979) writes:

> He who is born begins to die. He who dies begins to live. Birth and death are merely doors of entry and exit on the stage of this world. In reality no one comes, no one goes. Brahma or the External alone exists.

Head and Cranston in their book *Reincarnation: The Phoenix Fire Mystery* (1977) have pointed out that in the East the life of a person is like a pilgrimage, not merely from the cradle to the grave, but also through the vast period of time stretching from the beginning to the end of this period of evolution until he or she unites with God.

The Vedas and the oldest Hindu scriptures speak of the elements of reincarnation. Eminent philosopher and scholar Dr. S. Radhakrishnan, in his *Commentary on the Bhagwat Gita* writes that

> The passage of the soul from the body, its dwelling in other forms of existence, its return to human form, the determination of future existence by the principle of Karma are all mentioned in the Vedas.

The Vedas clearly show that the ancient Hindu culture believed in the immortality of the soul. In Bhagavad Gita, Chapter II, Shlokas 23–24, it is said that: "The soul of man is indestructible, is cannot be pierced by sword, fire cannot burn it, air cannot dry it, water cannot moisten it." After reading Gita, Ralph Wado Emerson wrote a poem entitled *Brahma*, a verse from which is quoted below. It sets forth the Hindu concept of death as viewed by Emerson:

> If the red slayer thinks he slays,
> Or if the slain thinks he is slain,
> They know not well the subtle ways
> I keep, and pass, and turn again.

Swami Abhedanand (1973) in his book *Reincarnation* has affirmed that the ancient Hindus believed in a heaven which they called the *Brahmhalok* or the kingdom of Bramha, the creator and the father of the Universe. Then gradually, as the idea of right and wrong became strong in their minds. the Hindus started believing that those who performed good and virtuous deeds in this life, with the hope of getting a reward, go to the realm of the fathers, that is, the *Pitraloka*, and stay there as long as the results of their good works have not been accomplished. After reaping the fruits of all their good and virtuous works, they are bound to return to the earth, according to the desires and actions of their past births. But those who do good works, not for the purpose of getting any reward, nor seeking anything in return, and who live the life of purity and righteousness, will go to the *Brahmaloka*, the realm of Lord Bramha. There they will stay in all glory until the end of a cycle of evolution.

The Bhagavad Gita, popularly known as "The Song of the Divine", is, according to the Hindus, the most cherished work in all the world's religious literature. This book is an appropriate gateway into the distinctive understanding of death found in the Hindu traditions. In the great battle of Mahabharta, the warrior Arjun lost his equipoise, became indecisive, and refused to fight and kill his own kith and kin in the battlefield. Lord Krishna imparted wisdom unto Arjun and revealed the greatest philosophy of life and death. The Lord said that there was never a time when we did not exist, neither Arjun nor his kith and kin. That which is nonexistent can never come into being, and which is can never cease to be. The innermost reality is the *Atman*, which is both changeless and eternal. How can it die with the death of the body?

According to the *Upanishads*, *Atman* is the bridge between the eternal and the temporal. Over that bridge, there crosses neither day nor night, nor old age, nor death, nor sorrow. *Atman* is real, true, and has continuity. The self is illusory.

Hindus believe in the transmigration of the soul, in accordance with *Karma*, and that one must do everything possible to attain emancipation. Transmigration means not just another birth; it means another death also. The doctrine of *Karma* plays an important role in the second birth. James Carse in his book *Death and Existence* (1980) has said that the Karmic burden is the existence one has from the beginning of life. That burden is removed by the full expression of the self. In *Chhandogya Upanishad*, Chapter V, Shloka 107 we find the preachings of God that

Those whose conduct during the previous life has been good presently obtain good birth, such as the birth of a *Brahmin*, a *Kshetriya*, or a *Vaish*; those whose conduct has been bad presently obtain some evil birth such as that of a dog or a pig.

The Smritis say that the soul is born with residual *Karma*.

According to Hindu philosophy, the concept of Brahma is synonymous with *Virata*, viz, an ocean of energy eulogized as *Shakti*, out of which the soul emerges as the Brahma so ordains. After casting off the mortal body on completion of its earthly sojourn, it aspires to merge again with Brahma and, if it is successful, it is liberated from the cycle of birth and rebirth and attains salvation or Moksha, failing which it takes another body and is reborn.

In the doctrine of *Karma* our deeds play an important role. Human beings are rewarded or punished for the deeds performed in their past lives. For this purpose, human beings are born again and again. Then the question arises of how the soul merges with the ocean of energy. *The Bhagavad Gita* says that deeds performed selflessly without any motive or expectation of return but by considerations of duty alone, that is, actions performed *Nishkam*, gradually lead people to a stage when they will not be born again but will be merged with *Brahma*, the Almighty, and be freed from this world and finally attain *Nirvana*, as pointed out by Lord Buddha.

The doctrine of *Karma* determines the chain of rebirth. It is in the process of evolution that we learn to distinguish between *Sakama* and *Nishkam Karma* and try to achieve the cherished ideal of performing duty selflessly, without any expectation of return which finally leads to the attainment of *Moksha*.

As regards the fear of death, Becker in his book *The Denial of Death* (1973) writes that fear responses usually derive from some threat to survival and that of all things that move people the principal mover is fear of death. Threat of death haunts the human mind more than anything else.

No doubt death is considered inevitable by all. But why do the Hindus who believe in life after death reveal death anxiety? What is the cause for this? The two factors that have been identified as affecting this in all religious people, whether they believe in death being the end of life or a doorway to another life, are as follows:

One is the process of dying, including all the suffering and pain through which a person has to pass in order to die; and the other is the separation anxiety, that is, the fear of parting forever from near and dear ones.

The philosopher Jacques Choran (1963) in his book *Modern Man and Mortality* delineated three components to the fear of death: the fear of dying, the fear of what happens after death, and the fear of ceasing to be. On the basis of psychological scrutiny of these dimensions of death, James B. McCarthy in *Death and Anxiety* (1980) pointed out that

The fear of dying and ceasing to be, involved myriad factors extending from a fear of pain, suffering, helplessness, dependency, and loss of control of one's physical and mental abilities at one end of a continuum, to fear of abandonment and of being separated from loved ones, and loss of one's own love for others at the other end.

Fear of death according to R. Schulz (1978) has elements of both physical and psychological suffering. These elements may arise because of the deterioration of the body that is sometimes a consequence of a fatal disease, such as cancer. An individual who has lived an active and vital life can be flabbergasted by such events and may get frightened. Fear of separation may arise because near and dear relations will be lost.

Philosophers R. Kastenbaum and R. Aisenberg, in their book *The Psychology of Death* (1974) have discussed the unwelcoming prospects of suffering in relation to one's fear of death. Dying becomes an aversive event because of the physical suffering attached to it.

In the words of Dorothy Rowe (1982), people build comfortable surroundings; they work in this environment regularly, but they always run the risk that these comforts may disappear at any time, and punishment may begin. Pain and suffering may have to be faced, which may ultimately lead to death. Hence, the fear attached to death is basically the apprehension regarding the suffering of life.

The *Reig-Veda* (1.25.1,2) shows sin to be the violation of divine law with death as the penalty: "Whatever law of thine, O God, O, Varuna, as we are men, day after day we violate, give us not as prey to death to be destroyed by thee in wrath!"

Actually death is not a punishment. It is part of the sequence of life; it is the end of the present life and the beginning of the next life. In spite of the fact that Hindus believe in reincarnation, they perceive the encounter with death as an unpleasant experience that provides a massive shift in the way one lives in the world. It destroys the physicality of an individual. Moos (1977) points out that the stark irrefutable reality of death makes this confrontation a unique challenge.

When individuals become aware that they are about to die, they feel helpless and perceive the abandonment of their hopes and dreams and the necessary parting from cherished family and friends by being cut off by a force over which they have no control. The nature of this personal challenge is determined by several factors, including the characteristics of the disease involved and the degree of discomfort, disfigurement, and deterioration. Fear of all kinds, such as of the unknown, of being abandoned or rejected by loved ones, of physical degeneration, of dependency, of pain, crowd into the mind of the person who is facing death in the near future.

The suffering of the dying, in the opinion of James B. McCarthy (1980), is augmented by the helplessness they feel in combating physical illness and in not being in control of the time and circumstances of their deaths. The fear of helplessness also plays an important role in the fear of death. The fear of death is also interlocked with the fears of separation and abandonment.

Dr. A. Kashyap in her doctoral thesis has expressed the view that the fears related to death are not diminished by belief in an afterlife. Rather, it is the intensified fear of death that increases belief in an afterlife. An individual who is beset with fear and anxiety may espouse cosmological beliefs as an anxiety-reducing defense mechanism. The greater the fears, the more firmly he or she would embrace the protective beliefs. The findings of I. L. Alexander and A. M. Adlerstein (M58) as well as those of M. O. Sarchuk and S. Tatz (1973) also suggest that subjects escape death anxiety by espousing the satisfying concept of an afterlife.

Although the Hindus believe in the continuity of life after death, they are not able to overcome the fear of death. The possible reason for this may be their inability to see that continuity. Some of the Hindu sages and seers claim that by practising *Sadhana* or *Yoga* one can acquire powers to see one's past and foresee one's future, that is, one can become *Trikaldarshi*. If one can achieve such powers, one's ability to see the continuity of life will certainly lessen one's fear of death. It must, however, be emphasized that in order to acquire such powers one has to practice the highest ideals of righteousness with complete devotion, dediction, and surrender to Brahma, the mighty creator and protector of this universe.

REFERENCES

Swami Abhedanand. 1973. *Reincarnation.* Calcutta: Ramkrishna Vedanta Math.

Alexander, I. E., and Adlerstein, A. M., 1958. Affective Responses to the Concept of Death in a Population of Children and Early Adolescents. *Journal of Genetic Psychology* 93:167–177.

Becker, E. 1973. *The Denial of Death.* New York: Free Press.

Carse, J. 1980. *Death and Existence.* New York: John Wiley & Sons.

Choran, J. 1963. *Modern Man and Mortality.* New York: MacMillan.

Head, J., and Cranston, S. L. 1977. *Reincarnation: The Phoenix Fire Mystery.* New York: Julian Press/Crown Publishers.

Kashyap, A. 1973. "A Study of Certain Determiners of Perception of Threat." Unpublished doctoral thesis.

Kastenbaum, R., and Aisenberg, R. 1974. *The Psychology of Death:* London: Gerald Duckworth & Co. Ltd.

McCarthy, J. B. 1980. *Death and Anxiety: The Loss of Self.* New York: Gardner Press Inc.

Moos, R. H. 1977. *Coping with Physical Illness.* New York: Plenum Medical Book Company.

Osarchuk, M., and Tatz, S. 1973. Effect of Induced Fear of Death on Belief in After Life. *Journal of Personality and Social Psychology* 27:256–260.

Radhakrishnan, S. 1977. *Commentry on the Bhagwat Gita,* 6th ed. Bombay: Blackie and Sons.

Radhakrishnan, S. (1927) 1940. *Indian Philosophy.* Bombay: Blackie and Sons.

Rowe D. 1982. *The Construction of Life and Death.* New York: John Wiley & Sons.

Schulz, R. 1978. *The Psychology of Death, Dying and Bereavement.* Reading, Mass.: Addison-Wesley.

Swami Shivanand. 1979. *What Becomes of the Soul After Death.* Theri Garwhal, U.P. India: The Divine Life Society.

Yalom, I. D. 1980. *Existential Psychotherapy.* New York: Basic Books, Inc.

8

Upanishadic Eschatology: The Other Side of Death

William A. Borman

> asato ma sat gamaya
> tamaso ma jyotir gamaya
> mrtyur ma amrtam gamaya
> (Brhadaranyaka Up., "Br." 1:3:28)

> From the Unreal, lead me to the Real
> From Darkness, lead me to Light
> From Death, lead me to Immortality.

This invocation sums up the purpose and the substance of the Upanishads.

The purpose of the Upanishads is to lead one from the transient and the ephemeral, whose nature is desire, action, and suffering, to the Changeless, the One without a second, the Eternal, whose nature is Infinite Peace *(shanti)* and Bliss *(ananda, sukham).*

The former is called *samsara* (Maitri Up., "Mai." 4:34). The latter is called Brahman. Between *samsara*, the phenomenal universe, and Brahman, the Noumenal Existence, Atman (Self), is, as it were, a bridge. Identifying Itself with phenomena It knows Itself as, and acts as if It were one self among many, as an "I." Identifying Itself with Brahman, It knows Itself as the One Self of all subjects, the "I AM."

The Upanishadic search into Ultimate Reality, finds It to be non-dual, One without a second *(advdaita, ekam sat)* (Katha Up., "Ka." 2:2:9–10; Aitareya Up., "Ai." 1:1:1:; Mandukya Up., "Man." 7). There is a massive Unity behind, pervading and constituting all the infinite multiplicity. Brahman is the substratum out of which all the universes and their inhabitants evolve, by which they are sustained, and into which they are withdrawn at the end of each cosmic evolutionary cycle (Taittiriya Up., "Tai." 3:1).

The chief aim of the Upanishads is to demonstrate the identity of Atman (Self), with Brahman (the Absolute), and to show the means by which the votary of understanding may realize this identity directly, thus to realize his own Immortality.

The votary who wishes such understanding and realization finds himself in a condition of pointless activity: dreamlike, meaningless, unreal; a condition of ignorance and obscurity, darkness and numbness. He is nagged by a deep Dread, believing that Death is the only definite result of all the ceaseless, meaningless, beating, proliferating phenomenal whirl *(samsara)* that confronts him. The Upanishads address the student so distressed, and attempt to answer his invocation.

The Human Condition of identification with phenomenal transiency implies such an existential characterization of reality (Mai. 1:2–7). The root of this existential outlook is the Dread of Death engendered by one's self-identification with what is ever passing into nonexistence. The Path from Death to Immortality is the Upanishadic teaching.

THE UPANISHADIC TEXTS: BACKGROUND AND OVERVIEW

"Upanishad" (upa-ni-sad), means "sitting (sad) very near (upa +ni)." The student sits very near the Teacher, anxious to be instructed by him about the nature of the Highest good, the Highest Goal in Life, and the means to attain it. (See Ranade, 1968; Dasgupta, 1961, 1965 and Nikhilananda, 1949, 1952, 1956, 1959.)

"Upanishad" primarily refers to this Knowledge. Secondarily, "Upanishad" refers to the texts that have recorded this Knowledge. Thus, the Upanishadic texts are not systematic treatises of science or philosophy. They are pedagogic tools. But they are scientific and philosophical. They record the instructor's experimental inquiry into Atman and Brahman, his direct experience of them, reflections on the Life leading towards them (Chhandogya Up., "Ch." 6:7, 6:12–13; Br. 2:15–17), and they record how this Knowledge was conveyed to the student.

The Upanishads are not religious texts in the ordinary sense of the word. This cannot be stressed too much. The Upanishads do not rest on authority, but on reason and experience.

BRAHMAN AND ATMAN; MOKSHA AND IMMORTALITY

The Upanishads are concerned primarily with the fourth value of life, moksha, or Liberation from the Human Condition of meaningless suffering and subjection. Moksha denotes Freedom from re-birth in the cycles of samsara.

Achievement and enjoyment of the three prior values of life — wealth, pleasure, virtue — depend on desire, action, and enjoyment of the fruits of action. Upon realization of Atman, of Brahman, all desires are achieved, all knowledge realized. All satisfactions are enjoyed simultaneously. Desire is, as it were, transformed. There is no longer anything outside of Self-consciousness to hanker after or long for that is not already possessed.

Thus, the Upanishads occupy a unique place in the classical literature. They map the Path to the Highest Good, the fullest expansion of Consciousness (jnanam, Tai 2:1(3); prajnanam, Ai. 3:1:2–3; vijnanam, Br. 3:9:28) and Being-Infinity (anantam, Tai 2:1(3); ch. 7:23–25), Non-dual Unity of Being (Sat or Satyam, Tai 2:1(3); Ch. 7:3:5), and Bliss (ananda, Br. 3:9:28; Ch. 7:3:5). This Highest Good is one with Immortality (Prashna Up., "Pr." 6:5). It is Immortal because it is without parts, without members, one without second. The identity of "I" with Atman, with Brahman, with All, is fundamental to the

Upanishads.

The Brhadaranyaka Upanishad repeatedly notes (*e.g.*, Br. 4:4:19) that in Brahman there is no difference, and he who sees difference in the Non-dual Reality, goes from Death to Death (Ka. 2:1:10–11). In one mass of Consciousness-Being there can be no change within, no decrease, no injury, no separation, no Death. The Infinite is the Unlimited. This consummation is Bliss itself, unending.

Where there is limitation (*alpa*, the small, the limited), where there is differentiation and awareness of something other than the Infinite, there can be no significant or lasting Happiness (Ch. 7:23–25). Division and otherness frustrate possession and enjoyment, and therefore happiness. Where there is no limitation, there alone can there be Bliss.

The Upanishadic Seers report that the very nature of Brahman is Bliss (Tai. 3:6, 3:10:5, 2:8–9). Brahman is defined as the Sukritum, Him-Made-All-of-Happiness Who is the *rasa* (the flavor) in all Existence. Any joy is from that Flavor of the Infinite (see Nikhilananda 1952:II:55–56). The flavor in all is that Bliss (Tai. 2:7). The Brhadaranyaka states that all creatures live on one particle of this Bliss (Br. 4:3:32).

The Tibetan Book of the Dead (see Evans-Wentz 1957), and *The Egyptian Book of the Dead* (see Budge 1895;1967), glimpse these heights, but only the Upanishads singularly sustain this highest standpoint and widest perspective, while elaborating the wealth of practical detail and lesser significances of *samsara*, the mundane rounds of life.

MICROCOSMIC–MACROCOSMIC IDENTITY: THE MANY-FACETED UNITY OF EXISTENCE

A fundamental discovery of the Upanishadic Seers is the identity of the microcosm and macrocosm. This identity corresponds to the identity between Atman and Brahman.

One finds throughout the Upanishads the formula "As here, so there" (Ka. 2:1:10).

By means of this formula, a cumulative sense of the mutual identity of all phenomena is gradually established in discursive and reflective consciousness, sometimes by scientific correlations, sometimes by mythic or poetic ones. An intuitive sense of the metaphorical character of the entirety of the phenomenal existence is created, which then symbolizes the metaphysical or ontological unity that stands behind it, and out of which it has all arisen — the Brahman, or Atman.

It is essential to understand this microcosm–macrocosm relationship in order to explain the relation of the *jivatman*, (embodied Soul), to its bodies, to the *jagat* (Cosmos, World; Ishavasya Upanishad, "Ish." 1), and to the Brahman: the phenomenal identity of the *jiva*, how it is ensconced there, and how it utilizes the various bodies or *koshas* (sheathes; Tai 2:1–6; 3:2–6) for subjective experience, enjoyment of the fruits of action, and as vehicles for deepening and widening its self-consciousness and the range of experiences and enjoyments possible to it.

The identity of microcosm and macrocosm, of the Soul and ensouled environment (see Ramadanda, *Evolutionary Spiritualism*, "ES":1965:36–49), is the means of its traversing the cycles of life and death through transmigration, and of its mounting evolution towards realizing its identity with Brahman, the consummation which the various classical philosophies interpret variously.

The fact of this microcosm–macrocosm identity is explained by the original self-bifurcation of the Non-Dual Brahman and subsequent parallel evolution of the cosmos and the beings inhabiting it.

A logical or scientific understanding of this original bifurcation is beyond the capability of intellect and the senses (Ka. 1:2:7; Tai. 2:4; Kena Upanishad, "Ke." 1:3, 2:3; Mund 3:1:8, 3:2:3). Once positing a fundamental duality, however, all further evolution may be scientifically and logically reconstructed.

A constant philosophical examination of the categories underlying the symbolical, mythological, poetical, and metaphorical texts is required to reach the scientific and practical content. This is especially so in understanding the relationship of microcosm to macrosocm and of *jiva*, to Atman, Soul.

DEATH AND ESCHATOLOGY; IMMORTALITY AND TRANSMIGRATION

The main feature of the Upanishadic eschatology, is, in fact, not transmigration, but Immortality.

What is of utmost importance for the Upanishads is not the constitution of the *jivatman* or its various passages through life and the worlds after Death, but its Original, Primordial, Native Immortality: the facts of the identity of Self and Brahman, of subjective "I" and Atman, and that there is no Death for it. That Atman is Immortal. That Nature is beyond words, beyond description or explanation. All the texts are merely the symbol of and means for realizing That; they are material for self-reflection, for self-examination that will lead one back to one's Reality as Atman, as Brahman, and which will encourage one towards activity and meditation, *upasana* and *dhyana*, that are geared to that realization.

Thus, the key to understanding the Upanishadic Philosophy of Death, is that Death is no termination. "Death," as ordinarily used, is an emotive term that denotes one phase in a never-ending series of transitions that have Immortality as their underlying ground and ultimate outcome. The various states differ only in the possession of Self-awareness or its lack.

JIVA, CONDUCT AND GROWTH

Chhandogya 3:134:1, says the *jiva* consists of nothing but Will, and as one Wills, so does one become after leaving this embodiment. The Upanishad admonishes one to carefully form his Will. Chhandogya 3:14:4, says that if indeed one forms his Will to reach Brahman, then on his parting with such *shraddha* (faith), he will doubtless reach the Brahman.

This latter passage explains the importance of the thoughts, will, and consciousness at the moment of death in the determination of future lives.

Brhadaranyaka 4:4:3–4 says that just as a leech coming to the end of a blade of grass takes hold of another blade and draws itself together on the second before letting go of the first, so the *jiva* moves on when taking a new body. There is continuity and consciousness through the transition. The postmortem movement is not random.

The next passage, Brhadaranyaka 4:4:5, says just as a goldsmith fashions a newer, more beautiful form with the old gold, so the *jiva*, after leaving the body, forms a new body suited to the World it is going to.

In explanation, the Brhadaranyaka continues (4:4:5), the self is in fact Brahman, which is identified with all the positive and negative aspects of consciousness, and that as one acts, so does one become. "By doing straight actions *(sadhukari)*, one becomes straight; by doing evil (sinful) actions *(papakari)*, one becomes evil (sinful); by means of good action *(punyena)*, one becomes good; by mean of evil *(papena)* one becomes evil" (my trans.). It is said that one is verily *kamamaya* (made of desire). As one desires, so is one's resolution, will, and determination; as one determines, such are one's *karmas* (actions); and, as are one's *karmas*, so is one's *abhisampadyate* (evolution).

DIRECTION OF THE TRANSMIGRATION

Two crucial elements are introduced here: Desire and Evolution.

First, it is desire that gives direction and unity to the seeming aggregate that we have found to be the *jiva*. Will may finally move one to action, but it seems desire invariably is found to direct the will.

Spiritual evolution is a further element, which is introduced with the words *"adhisampadyate," "vrnoti,"* and *"parinama."* These all indicate something developmental, which the word "evolution" is an attempt to capture. This was stated explicitly where the *jiva* was likened to a goldsmith who creates ever newer and more beautiful forms.

It seems the rounds of transmigration are not merely random, according to desire. There is, evidently, a deeper principle of direction and accumulation at work also, independently of the individual desire, that may determine this or that exact course between the Worlds, and to the next embodiment. Indeed, the subtle body and new identity are made of a consciousness formed by past work and experience *(purvaprajna)*, and according to the next body's needs.

All of these works, knowledges, and experiences go with one at death. This is how the thoughts at the moment of death, the consciousness at that moment, sum up and represent the totality of one's life experience, and determine the next embodiment that would be appropriate to continuation of that experience and evolution. Thus, each transition is leechlike: the new consciousness is suited to and a continuation of the previous, yet, as the goldsmith works, it is a newer and better body, suitable to a bigger, wider, more refined consciousness; a subtle body is built suited to that consciousness.

One's desire may determine one's will and acts, but that desire itself is informed by an ever-growing knowledge gained by the previous cycles of desire, will, action, results, experience. This knowledge is a constituent of the essential identity, stored, as it were, in one's deepest inner structures. This accumulated identity is an asset or capital for the growth of the *jiva*.

Thus, there is a mounting up of consciousness, will, desire, strength, and knowledge with each cycle. With each cycle comes a newer, more beautiful form, and more subtle, more refined will, thought, and feeling capabilities.

LORDSHIP OF BRAHMAN

There is one further element in the Upanishadic scheme of eschatology and evolution of consciousness.

Shetashvatara 5:1–6 says that Brahman has become all this. In becoming all this, he has become the Controller, the Inner Guide within all, within each created being.

The Shvetashvatara continues (5:7–13), it is Brahman as Lord who has entered all wombs and according to their nature rules every *jiva*, and brings each being to its own perfection (*svabhava* and *parinama*). He establishes the working of the various modes of Nature, and acts according to the *gunas* (constituting qualities) of Nature, reaping fruits according to those *gunas* and the *jiva's karmas*. And so He travels the paths of *samsara* as the *jiva* itself.

SUPERMORALISM OF THE UPANISHADS

It is important to note that when desire and attachment are not present, action has no binding power and formative power. This becomes the doctrine of *akamakarmayoga–sadhana* (discipline) of desireless action of the Bhagavad Gita. Shvetashvatara 2:7 notes that on attaining *samadhi* (absorption of consciousness in the Eternal Brahman), works no longer bind one. This absorption is accomplished only upon extinction of all desires. Thus, the Upanishads describe a supermoralism with regard to the Realized Being (the Sage and Seer), who is one with Atman and Brahman.

NEW ESCHATOLOGICAL INVESTIGATIONS AND CONCLUSIONS

This study has brought into prominence the concept of evolution in the Upanishadic teachings. It is only the rise of evolutionism in Western sciences and the evolutionary spiritualisms of Aurobindo and Ramananda in this century that has highlighted these aspects of the Upanishads.

Ramananda

The scientific and philosophical outlooks that have provided the thread for this study derive primarily from the writings of Ramananda, and secondarily from Aurobindo and Krishna Prem.

First, Ramananda greatly extends the analysis of the *jivatman*, the doctrines of *karma* and reincarnation, the evolutionary *raison d'etre* of these, and the Supreme Brahman as Lord presiding over and guiding the entire process, as well as creating, sustaining and reabsorbing it all. In line with the Upanishads, Ramananda (*As I Understand*, 1965:22–23) takes his stand on reason and experience, so his analyses are philosophical and scientific.

Thus, in every question of interpretation and meaning, the effort must be to get at the scientific and philosophical basis of any statement, admonition, or instruction.

In the descriptions given by Brhadaranyaka 6:2:16 and Chhandogya 5:10:5–6, of the return of the *jiva* from the spheres of the Moon, the Soul was said to become like clouds, mist, rain, food, semen, and then fetus, and living *jiva*.

This is clearly a mythological description. To accept this literally would be to contradict the most basic philosophical principles and scientific analyses of the Upanishads, that is, that the *jiva* is fundamentally consciousness, and the subtle body is not of the same category as the physical. Even deeper than this and the conscious self-identity by *manas* and *buddhi* with knowledge and the residue of past actions, experience, and enjoyments is the causal body (*karana sharira*; and perhaps the *alayavijnana*, storehouse consciousness, or *vijnanatman*, Artman-made-of-knowledge, see Raju, 1985: 299n62;n75;403), which by means of these residues determines what elements will be acceptable to constitute the new embodiment. All of these are of an entirely different category than the physical mechanisms described there.

Hence, the various stages in these descriptions must be only pedagogic devices to aid the unrealized student to visualize the process of transmigration and to understand the inevitability of the rounds of existence that he has been instructed to look beyond and urged to leave behind.

Though Desire, *Karmas*, and the Cosmic Rta (Order) are factors in this spiritual evolution, the overarching factor and final support is Lord's Awareness, Will, Omniscience, and Love.

Second, the Upanishads speak very often of a return to animal bodies and to the womb as sources of severe suffering. This seems inconsistent with a modern scientific and philosophical reading. Experience, knowledge, and capacities to enjoy (*vasana*), are all cumulative. Since they constitute the identity of the transmigrating soul, and have their root in Atman and Brahman, they do not diminish simply with a redirection or narrowing of the focus of the *jivatman*. Rather, they are the functional and growing basis upon which the *jiva's* new desires, new *sankalpa* (determinative will), new actions, new experiences, new growth, and further embodiments are built.

Ramananda points out that both the subtle and gross structures of lower forms of life would not be capable of being operated by a higher mental and causal body that is geared to totally different modes of existence and totally different needs of evolution. The less sensitive animal would not experience the pain as the exemplary punishment for which one was consigned to a lower life. Such a lower life would not then serve the moral purposes supposed in the traditional reading.

Reason and science do not bear out certain traditional understandings of the Upanishadic teachings. Ramananda merely states in a footnote that reason fails to testify to the veracity of statements (Evolutionary Outlook, "EO":1965:62n) that assert that temporary residence in the womb is a painful experience and hence can be taken as a punishment to be severely avoided.

Analysis of the *jiva* is clarified and enlarged by Ramananda in light of his evolutionary and scientific understanding of the Upanishads and Upanishadic eschatology.

In the Upanishads, Atman has been identified as Consciousness, and the *jivatman* has been analyzed as having the character of both the *buddhi* and the *atman*, of *volition* and *ahankara* (Shv. 5:8): as being in some way a reflection of Atman, the Great Brahman in its relation to the cosmos. But, again, explanation of that relation in the Upanishads is primarily couched in mythological and metaphorical or poetic terms, as in the discussion of the Purusha in the Aitareya (1:1–3).

Ramananda writes (ES pp. 20–24, 42–48, 108–109 and 114) that if the microcosm mirrors the macrocosm, and the nature of the macrocosm is Consciousness, then the microcosmic *jivatman* must also have Consciousness as its essential nature. As the Brahman has two aspects, Saguna (with qualities) and Nirguna (without qualities), Becoming and Being, in a Transcendental Unity, so must the individual Soul, *jivatman*, be a unit of both Being and Becoming in a Transcendental Unity.

Ramananda calls this Unit (Soul, or Monad), Consciousness-Energy. As this Unit has emerged from that Brahman, so its inevitale course through evolution is its return to that Brahman (ES pp. 108–109 and 114). The Soul is that Brahman, in small.

Since consciousness may be analyzed into the three aspects of cognition, conation, and affection, so the evolving unit of consciousness-energy, the *jivatman*, also has three aspects of consciousness: cognition, conation, and affection.

As the Great Atman, the Great Brahman, has these in superlative, denoted by *Sat* (Absolute Existence), *Chit* (Absolute Consciousnes), and *Ananda* (Absolute Bliss), so this microcosmic Monad must be evolving towards realization of that Absolute through its experiences of cognition, conation, and affection, of being, knowing, acting, and enjoying the identity of Atman and Brahman, whose realization is the consummation of all the Upanishadic inquiries.

Thus, every action and every thought may be analyzed and evaluated for its capability to evolve, that is, to expand, deepen, refine, and lift these three aspects of the evolving consciousness-energy. This analysis provides the thread for developing *sadhanas* (spiritual practice) geared to modern life, shorn of mythological and pedagogical readings, shorn of traditional values that may not apply as once they seemed to.

Dr. Raymond Moody

Finally, one may look to the contemporary studies of Dr. Raymond Moody for aid in understanding certain aspects of the Upanishads on a more scientific basis.

On the other hand, Upanishadic Eschatology may prove useful in clarifying and substantiating or confirming the scientific work being done by Moody in the after-life experience (see also Dr. Ian Stevenson, *Twenty Cases Suggestive of Reincarnation;* more a forensic than phenomenological study, however).

Moody, in *Life After Life*, has given a concise classic study of the after-death experience.

Moody gives about fifteen elements in an ideal model (Moody, 1976:21–25) that most of the cases largely conform to, both in detail of report and structure of the narrative. Thus, there is a prima facie presumption that these cases are reporting a similar experience. Wherever possible, and in the large majority of cases, there has been independent corroboration of reports such as out-of-body viewings.

Dr. Elisabeth Kübler-Ross, the noted investigator of *On Death and Dying* (see Kübler-Ross, 1969), wrote the preface (Moody, 1976/1975) to Dr. Moody's book, stating that his results largely confirmed her own findings.

A statistical study, *At The Hour Of Death*, was published by Karlis Osis and Erlendur Haraldsson, again confirming and expanding upon the work of Moody and Kübler-Ross.

Dr. Moody reports profound changes in understanding and outlook on death by persons who have had these experiences, and even by those who have been close to persons who have had the experiences. He notes also the profound change in their *outlook on life*, both quantitatively and qualitatively different from those reporting marginally similar experience, the etiology of which could be traced to merely psychological, physiological, or pharmacological causes.

All alternative explanations, whether biological, pharmacological, or mechanical, are just that: "alternates" offered because of an *ab initio* refusal to accept the initial reports at their face value on their own terms. The alternative explanations are given on no basis of evidence and speak to no real issues of science. They are offered only as "possibles," "mights," and "maybes." This is very weak formulating of scientific hypotheses. Some different philosophical and scientific game is going on here, not the procedure by which a scientist would normally address a problem.

The Upanishads, and spiritual philosophy and science in general, provide an answer in this area. In fact, the issues are metaphysical (and neither merely linguistic).

Objective science, as developed in the West, is oriented towards investigating the object and reading out the subject. As seen above, however, the route to the Atman, which is the route to the Brahman, is through the subject, through the "I," through the Experiencer of the experiencing. Any scheme of investigation, any investigative instrumentation, any explanatory conceptual apparatus that systematically reads out the subject, cannot possibly be called upon to give a scientific account of that subject.

At The Hour of Death, by Osis and Haraldsson, presents cross-cultural results, involving over a thousand after-death experiences, all reported through trained physicians and corroborated wherever possible.

Osis and Haraldsson also checked for various sociological determinants, psychological categories, and other phenomena besides those of the near-death experience. They began as skeptics, but ended up convinced that the hypothesis of the after-death experience was substantively confirmed over the negative hypothesis that these were purely subjective and psychologically induced phenomena.

Finally, Moody notes that to help the dying person keep in mind the stages through which his Soul will go, and to help those around him hold back from interfering with the Soul's after-death movement, *The Tibetan Book of the Dead* (Moody, 1976:120) "contains a lengthy description of the various stages through which the Soul goes after physical death. The correspondence between the early stages of death which it relates and those which have been recounted to me by those who have come near to death, is nothing short of fantastic."

Moody recounts the same radical change in consciousness, even finding itself outside of the physical body, watching the preparation for the funeral just as his subjects watched the attempts at resuscitation of the body; the confusion and self-questioning of the dead person as to what his state is; a certain regret; depression; lingering near familiar places and people; a strange new non-material and "shining" body; ability to penetrate solid walls and rocks without resistance; instantaneous travel; new dimensions and clarity of thought and perception; great lucidity and keeness; meeting of other similar beings; and the meeting of a clear pure light; feelings of deep peace and contentment; and the mirroring of one's entire life as an object lesson with no judgment but only the feelings of loving acceptance and interest to learn the lessons presented there, without lying to oneself or to other beings.

Moody notes that the *Bardo Thodol (The Tibetan Book of the Dead)* goes far beyond the experiences of his subjects into the later stages of death. As far as his reports do go, however, the similarity is extraordinary, especially considering the distance in time and difference in culture between the Tibetans to whom the book was addressed and the twentieth century Americans who were his subjects. This alone ought to provide some pause to those who would quickly offer alternative explanations. (For similar vivid near-death and out-of-body experiences in the native American tradition, see Neihardt, *Black Elk Speaks,* 1961(32): esp. 20–27; 228–233.)

Krishna Prem's study of the Kathopanishad is also an eschatological work. The Kathopanishad is an after-death dialogue about higher spiritual principles and experience. Where there is a reference to funeral ceremonies, he writes (Prem, 1955:163):

The *shraddha* ceremonies were not always the mere formalities that they usually are nowadays. Those who had knowledge were able to assist the departed soul on its journey through the inner worlds and in such a connection, this text, when transmitted from the mind of the "living reader" to that of the still present though invisible "dead," would, like the ancient, Egyptian Book of the Dead and the Bardo Thodol, still used in Tibet, serve to guide the soul on its wanderings, and enable it to make the utmost use of the strange circumstances in which it found itself after the loss of its body.

The entire Upanishads may be thought of as such an after-death guide. All of their instructions are geared to making the eschatological rounds the vehicle for one's self-conscious spiritual evolution to that Ultimate Realization of oneself as Atman and Brahman. As the *Bardo Thodol* and *The Egyptian Book of the Dead*, however, talk about far deeper or more distant ranges of that Path than recounted in the "near-death" experience, so the Upanishads talk about super-dimensions and the extreme depths of the *samsara* in which these near-death experiences involve only the merest surface of the eschatological or non-physical world-realities.

Moody's work may, however, be of some assistance in interpreting certain passages of the Upanishads where other than scientific or philosophical motives have determined the choice of mythological or metaphorical description.

One can immediately note Moody's reports of the great difficulty his subjects had in describing the subtle bodies they found themselves inhabiting and the new sensory experience had through these (Moody, 1976:51–53). The "ineffable" character (Moody, 1976:25–26), nearly universally ascribed to these experiences, underline our caution against drawing literal inferences from any of the Upanishadic descriptions of the other worlds or of the Soul's subtle material and sensory passage through them. Assimilation of these experiences to the rain-food cycle (Br. 6:2:16 and Ch. 5:10:5–6) must indicate something much subtler than mere involvement in these material forms.

Moody's work is fresh and nonpolemical, and the descriptions not tradition-bound. Once freed of the materialist bias and conservativism, these modern reports may be brought in to aid the interpretation of the classical texts from many traditions where mere scholarly acumen, technique, and logic cannot possibly be sufficient, and where personal spiritual discipline, exercise, and experiences are lacking.

As the above abundantly attests, these texts are not books of logic or speculation, but are like guides, maps, or charts that must be read for factual correlations and practical assistance. Where the guide books are authentic, the common core should be accessible by some sort of triangulation over the dominant landmarks. The meeting of Ancient and Modern, just as of East and West, cannot but be richly fruitful, where it is a meeting for truth sought in the light of love.

REFERENCES

Aschner, Naomi L. 1979. "A Study of Adhyatmik Sadhan, A Modern Indian Spiritual Manual" Ph.D. diss. Faculty of Philosophy, Columbia University. (Presents complete translations of many key chapters, as well as comprehensive and detailed renderings of the entirety of the two volumes of Ramananda's *Adhyatmik Sadhana*. It also gives a detailed analysis of and comparison with traditional *sadhanas* in terms of both new elements and continuities.)

Aurobindo. See Ghose, Shri Aurobindo.

Black Elk. See Neihardt.

Budge, E.A. Wallis. 1967. *The Egyptian Book of the Dead.* New York: Dover Publications. (Orig. 1895 British Museum.)

Dasgupta, Surama. 1961, 1965. *Development of Moral Philosophy in India.* New York: Frederick Unger.

Evans-Wentz, W.Y. (Ed.). 1957. *The Tibetan Book of the Dead.* New York: Oxford University Press.

Ghose, Shri Aurobindo. 1972. *The Upanishads*, 1st ed. Pondicherry: Shri Aurobindo Ashram, Birth Centenary Library.

Kübler-Ross, Elisabeth, M.D. 1975. *Death: The Final Stage of Growth.* Englewood Cliffs, N.J.: Prentice-Hall.

——— 1969. *On Death and Dying.* New York: Macmillan.

——— 1974. *Questions and Answers on Death and Dying.* New York: Macmillan.

Mahadevan, T.M.P. 1952. The Upanishads: *History of Philosophy, Eastern and Western*, Vol. 1, Ed. S. Radhakrishnan. London: George Allen & Unwin, Ltd.

Moody, Raymond A., Jr. 1976. *Life After Life:* The Investigation of a Phenomenon — Survival of Bodily Death. New York: Bantam Books, 1976 (Orig. Mockingbird Books, 1975.)

——— 1977. *Reflections on Life After Life.* Atlantic: Mockingbird Books.

Neihardt, John G. (Flaming Rainbow). *Black Elk Speaks:* Being the Life Story of a Holy Man of the Oglala Sioux — as told through John G. Neihardt (Flaming Rainbow).

Nikhilananda, Swami. *The Upanishads.* Vols. I–IV. New York: Bonanza Books, Vol. I, 1949; Vol. II, 1952; Vol. III, 1956; Vol. IV, 1959.

Osis, Karlis, and Haraldsson, Erlendur. 1977. *At The Hour of Death.* New York: Avon Books.

Prem, Shri Krishna. 1955. *The Yoga of the Kathopanishad.* London: John M. Watkins.

Raju, P.T. 1985. *Structural Depths of Indian Thought.* Albany: State Uniersity of New York Press. (Orig., New Delhi: South Asia Publications Pvt. Ltd.,)

Ramananda, Swami. 1965. *As I Understand* 2nd ed. Bisalpur: Sadhana Karyalaya, Sahu Kashinath Mittal.

——— 1965. *Evolutionary Outlook on Life.* Bisalpur: Sadhana Karyalaya, Sahu Kashinath Mittal.

——— 1965. *Evolutionary Spiritualism.* Bisalpur: Sadhana Karyalaya, Sahu Kashinath Mittal.

Ranade, R.D. 1968. *A Constructive Survey of Upanishadic Philosophy* 2nd ed. Bombay: Bharatiya Vidya Bhavan.

Sarter, Barbara. 1987. Life threatening illness and the inner self. Delivered at the Conference on Allied Health Sciences and Life-Threatening Illness, Foundation of Thanatology, New York. (Abstract 29, in Archives of the Foundation of Thanatology, Vol. 13, No. 2.)

Stevenson, Ian. 1974. *Twenty Cases Suggestive of Reincarnation.* Charlottesville: University Press of Virginia.

9

Conquering Death

Daya Shanker

Humans desire to live forever in the world. No one wants to die; moreover, all are terribly afraid of death. Death is painful, and its causes are many. Humans are ever in the jaws of death, which comes suddenly, when we are not prepared to face it.

The very idea of conquering death thrills the human heart. We live in the age of science, which has changed the face of the planet. Science has conquered the forces of nature, and has harnessed them into the service of humans. We have landed on the moon. We can extract and control energy and power from the sun. The sun, the moon, the oceans, and the winds are all at our command. We have developed weapons that could destroy mankind, and not leave a trace of life on earth. Through science we have also minimized human suffering and disease. We have given eyes to the blind, ears to the deaf, tongue to the mute, and legs to the lame. We can produce life, and preserve the body for centuries to come. But can we conquer death? Could we imagine a world without death? Is victory over death possible for us? These questions have baffled mankind for ages. All philosophy springs from the phenomenon of death.

From time immemorial, the inevitable reality of death has reigned victorious over mankind. Although we know well that evading death is not possible, we try to postpone death. Our efforts have been at least to have peaceful death, if moksha was not easily attainable in one single life. Mankind has been victorious over everything material in this world; why, then, have we not been victorious over death?

Let us first ask what death is. According to the Hindu scripture, *Yoga-Vasishtha*, the diseases of the body cause its *nadis* (veins) to lose their vigor and thus become unable to expand and contract to exhale or inhale air. Consequently, the respiration stops, the creature becomes senseless, and is dead. The *pranas* of the individuals with the *diva* (soul) within come out of the body and roam in the air. The mere cessation of breathing, pulse, heartbeat, or all three is not a sign of actual death. In cases of suspended animation, respiration or heartbeat may stop for several days, and revive thereafter. There are reports of Hatha Yogis being put in a box and buried underground for weeks at a time. They may suspend respiration for this period, but when taken out, they revive. The states of Samadhi, trance, catalepsy, and ecstasy also resemble death. Yogis in Samadhi stop heartbeat, pulse, and respiration, but they are revived immediately when they come down to physical consciousness. Shall we call it death, and call the revival victory over death? Certainly not, because it is neither death nor victory over death. Unless the soul leaves the body, it is not death.

The physical body is composed of *panch-mahabhutas* (five elements): earth, water, fire, air, and ether. When these elements are dissolved and when the soul is parted, death has occurred. The union of soul with body is called birth, and its separation from the body is certainly death. Swami Shivanand, in his book *What Becomes of the Soul After Death*, writes that according to Indian philosophy, there is a subtle body *(sukshma sarira)* within the physical body. When the physical body perishes, this subtle body does not perish. It moves to heaven, to enjoy the fruits of its good actions done on earth. This subtle body perishes only when the soul attains the final emancipation. It attains the eternal. It merges into the Brahma, and is not reborn. Shall we call it conquering death?

Indian philosophy holds that in death, the organs withdraw completely into the heart. Every organ at the time of death unites with the subtle body. Then consciousness is lost forever. The dead cannot see, hear, speak, sense odors, or walk. The dying man carries with him the five *jyana indriyas*, five *karma indriyas* and the five *pranas, buddhi, chitta, mind, ahankara*, the soul with its Karmas, good and evil, which all comprise the *linga-sarira*. This all determines the person's next life.

According to Judeo-Christian tradition, upon thinking of the inevitability of death, Job exclaimed, "If a man die, shall he live again?"

In *Kathopnishad*, Lord Yama, the god of death, revealed to Nachiketas the eternal and divine mystery of what happens to the soul after death. Some souls attain to other bodies, while some fall to a vegetable state in accordance with their knowledge and actions *(gyan* and *karma)*. The knower is never born or dies; it is not from anywhere, and it does not become anything. Unborn, eternal, immemorial, this ancient is not slain when the body is slain. The body is the chariot, the Self is the lord of the chariot, the soul is the charioteer, emotions are the reins, the bodily powers are the horses, and the external world is their field. He who is unwise restrains not emotions and is ever impure; such a person returns to the world of birth and death. He whose charioteer is wisdom, who firmly grasps the reins (emotions), indeed gains the end of the Path, the supreme resting place of the emanating power, the Brahma.

Nachiketas' three questions having been fully answered, he knew death, and became a passionless dweller in the Eternal. He became deathless. He conquered death. Thus, all those who know the self and its union with Eternal Brahma shall conquer death.

The great German philosopher G. W. F. Hegel, in his book *The Philosophy of History*, writes that, "While death is the issue of life, life is also the issue of death. Change while it imports dissolution, involves at the same time the rise of a new life." Death is not the end of life, but the beginning of another life. He who dies begins to live. As a matter of fact, it may be said that no one comes and no one goes. It is Brahma, or the Eternal, alone that exists. Is the rising of a new man after death called victory over death?

Joseph Head and S. L. Cranston in their book, *Reincarnation: The Phoenix Fire Mystery*, say, "Though all dies, and even gods die, yet all death is but a Phoenix fire death, and new birth into the greater and better. . . ."

The Taoist philosopher Chuang-Tzu is of the opinion that

> There was a beginning. There was a beginning before that beginning. There was a beginning previous to that beginning. Death and life are not far apart. Their origin goes back into infinity, and if we look for their end, it proceeds without termination. Life is the follower of death, and death is the predecessor of life. What we can point to are the faggots that have been consumed, but the fire is transmitted elsewhere.

Similar is the view of the German poet J. W. von Goethe who asserted that, "I am certain that I have been here, as I am now a thousand times before, and I hope to return a thousand times."

The Hindu Smriti says that human beings are engaged in the works prescribed for them. They enjoy the fruits of their works in this world, and after death are born again, owing to the unenjoyed portion of their rewards of karma. It may be said that the soul is born with residual karma. The Hindus believe in the doctrine of reincarnation in accordance with their karma. Karma and rebirth are the two great pillars of Hinduism, Buddhism, and Jainism.

Lord Krishna said in the great Hindu Scripture and will of the divine named Gita, Chapter II, Shloka 22, "As a man, casting off worn-out garments, taketh new ones, so the dweller in the body, casting off worn-out bodies, entereth into others that are new."

Gautam Buddha answered the question, "Does a man die altogether at death?" as follows, "No. For what dies is what belongs to this world of form and illusions."

We read in *Rig-Veda* (1,25. 1,2) that sin is the violation of divine law and death is its penalty. It says, "Whatever law of thine, O, God, O, Varuna, as we are men, day after day we violate, give us not, as prey to death, to be destroyed by thee in wrath." *Rig Veda* further depicts that the first man to die was Yama, and the first woman was Yami. "For God's sake Yama chose death to be his portion. He chose not, for men's good a life eternal" (R.V. 10,13,4). The god created a longing and desire in Yama and Yami to procreate. The Lord said unto Yama, "Remembering the earth and days to follow, obtain a son, the issue of his father. Yes, this the immortals seek of thee with longing, progeny of the sole existing mortal" (R.V. 10,1,3).

We find in the Bible also that it was God's will for the first human pair (Adam and Eve) to be fruitful and become many and fill the earth (Genesis 1:28). He further said to Adam,

Because you listened to your wife's voice, and took to eating from the tree concerning which I gave you this command, "You must not eat from it," cursed is the ground on your account. In pain you will eat its produce all the days of your life. In the sweat of your face you eat bread until you return to the ground, for out of it you were taken. For dust you are and to dust you will return.

We further read in the Bible that, through one man sin entered into the world, and death through sin, and thus death spread to all men because they had all sinned, and death is the wages for our sins. It is thus apparent that according to the Bible also disobedience to God is sin, and death is a punishment for disobedience to God, which *Rig-Veda* had enunciated.

Man has cravings and desires throughout life. They are bound to create lust and greed, which lead to impurity. He has some *ahankara, krodha,* ego, pride, and anger as well, which make him have strong likes and dislikes. With wealth and luxuries, and with the limited knowledge, or ignorance, and human instincts, he is bound to commit sins. During a lifetime he has pleasures, pain, sorrow, fear, anger, and sufferings. He is also the slave of fate and circumstances. He is *alpajyani, alpa-shaktiman,* and *parichchinna.* That is, he is endowed with limited knowledge, limited power, and is finite. Death relieves him of all his sins. Desire, anger, vanity, and lust *(kama, krodha, mad,* and *lobha)* all vanish with death. He becomes pure. It is a bliss in disguise. It gives him peace and solace. Death is not evil. It is a natural phenomenon for every human being. Upon death the soul is reflected Chaitanya. It proceeds to heaven. It is gifted with a subtle astral body. The soul merges with the Supreme Soul, the Param-Brahma, who is omniscient, omnipotent, the embodiment of knowledge and bliss, and is infinite. It is not then reborn. It becomes self-luminous and illumines everything. It is formless, all-pervading, timeless, and spaceless. There is neither day nor night. It is indivisible, and does not decay. The soul becomes eternal and immortal.

In Shlokas 14, 15, and 16 of Chapter 8 of *Bhagwad Gita,* Lord Krishna said,

Whoever constantly thinks of me intensely and with one-pointed mind, to such steadfast Yogis, I am easily attainable and having thus reached Me and merged in Me, they are not born again in the fleeting world of woe and misery. O, Arjuna son of Kunti, while all the worlds created by Brahma and limited by time and have their moment of dissolution, on reaching, Me, there is not rebirth. He gets Nirvana.

The Bible says, "Be Ye therefore perfect, even as your father which is in Heaven is perfect."

The Buddhist scriptures prescribe that, "Those who do not care for happiness of desires and cast them off, they soon depart and attain Nirvana. They are not subjected to transmigration."

Sir Edwin Arnold in his translation of Bhagwad Gita wrote that in the words of Lord Krishna

The wise in heart mourn not for those that live, nor those that die. Never the spirit was born, the spirit shall cease to be never. Never was time it was not. End and beginning are dreams. Death hath not touched it at all, dead though the house of it seems! Nay, as when one layeth his worn-out robes away, and taking new ones sayeth, "These will I wear today!" So putteth by the spirit lightly its garb of flesh, and passeth to inherit a residence afresh.

In *Bruno's Trial Before the Inquisition*, Giordano Bruno said,

I have held and hold souls to be immortal. Speaking as a catholic, they do not pass from body to body, but go to Paradise, Purgatory or Hell. But I have reasoned deeply, and, speaking as a philosopher, since the soul is not found without body, and yet is not body, it may be in one body or in another, and pass from body to body. From spirit, the life of the Universe, proceeds the life and soul of everything that has soul and life.

Ralph Waldo Emerson in his book *Nominalist and Realist* has very rightly written that,

It is the secret of the world that all things subsist and do not die, but only retire a little from sight and afterwards return again. Nothing is dead; men feign themselves dead, and endure mock funerals and mournful obituaries, and there they stand looking out of the window, sound and well, in some new strange disguise. Jesus is not dead; he is very well alive, nor John, nor Paul, nor Mahomed, nor Aristotle; at times we believe we have seen them all, and could easily tell the names under which they go.

In the Tibetan Buddhist scripture *Book of the Golden Precepts* under the title "The Voice of the Silence," the precepts say,

Search the eternal and the changeless SELF. The self of matter and the self of spirit can never meet. One of the twain must disappear. There is no place for both. In order to become the knower of the universal SELF, thou has first of SELF to be the knower. . . . All is impermanent in man except the pure bright essence of Alaya — the universal SELF. Man is its crystal ray, a beam of light immaculate within, a form of clay material upon the lower surface. The shadows (or bodies) lie and vanish, that which in thee shall live forever, that which in thee knows, for it is knowledge, is not of fleeting time; it is the man that was, that is, and will be, for whom the hour shall never strike.

The great American theosophist and Sanskrit scholar Charles Johnston translated the great Hindu scripture called *Brihad Aranyaka Upanishad*. In his book *Selections from the Upanishads and the Tao Te King*, while dealing with states of sleep, dreams, and waking in the cycle of reincarnation, Johnston writes about the visit of the sage Yajnavalkya to the Kingdom of King Janak. The king puts many questions to the sage about life, death, and the spirit of man. Janak asks, "When the sun and the moon are set, the fire sinks down, and the voice is stilled, Yajnavalkya, what is then the light of the spirit of Man?" The sage Yajnavalka replied, "The soul then becomes his light." Janak further inquired, "What is the soul?" The sage replied,

It is the consciousness in the life-powers. It is the light within the heart. . . . The spirit of man has two dwelling places: both this world and the other world. The spirit of man wanders through both the worlds, yet remains unchanged. . .when the body is in deepest slumber, the state called Sushupti, the soul of the man, leaving the bodily world, is completely free, soaring upwards and downwards, laughing and rejoicing with fair beauties, clothed in radiance, returns again by the same path hurrying back to his former dwelling place in the world of waking. . . . Through his past works he shall return once more to birth, entering whatever form his heart is set on. According as were his works and walks in another life, so he becomes. He that does righteously becomes righteous. He becomes holy through holy works. He that does evil becomes evil. Man verily is formed of desire, as his desire is, so is his will; as his will is, so he works; and whatever work he does, in the likeness of it he grows. The mighty awakened soul unborn grows not old, nor dies, for the soul is immortal and fearless. The soul is the fearless Eternal. He grows on with the Eternal.

Once Lord Buddha asked one of his disciples, Sariputta, "Well Monk, does not life burden you, and don't you like to be released by death? Or does living fascinate you, because there is a noble mission to fulfill?" The disciple Sariputta answered, "Venerable Teacher, I desire not life, I desire not death. I wait until my hour shall come, like a servant that waits for his wages." Life is thus a fulfillment of the will of God. The individual soul is nothing but a reflection of the Pram Brahma, the Supreme Soul.

One who has self-consciousness and has known the SELF, and has also realized the identity of his inner Being with the Param-Brahma is a Jnyani. Jnyani has no cravings, no desires, and is free from all sins. He attains absolute existence. He is timeless. He lives forever. Death shall never come to him. He has conquered death.

More than five thousand years ago, India enjoyed a golden era when science, technology, astronomy, and spiritualism were at a peak. During this time, the Hindus reported many such instances of man conquering death or having command over death. According to the great epic *Maha Bharatha*, Bhishma Pitamah had the blessings of the Lord, and had death at his command. After being hit with the poisonous arrows of the great warrior Arjun, no one could survive; all victims met death instantaneously. However, Bhishma kept his death at bay for 53 days. He left his body and met the Eternal Soul only when he so desired. The great saint Markandeya also conquered death through the worship of Lord Shiva.

Savitri was a pious woman. By her purity of heart, and faithful worship, she attained the blessings of God, and thus revived her dead husband Satyavana.

Jeemutwahan was the prince of the Kingdom of Vidyadhars, called Naganand. He was a great believer in nonviolence and self-sacrifice, pure of heart and mind, and merciful. He was killed by the bird Garud, but was brought back to life by the prayers of his wife, Malayawati, and blessed with goddess Jauri, wife of Lord Shiva. He then ruled his kingdom for a very long time.

According to the Christian faith, the ultimate fate of the righteous is eternal life. In Zoroastrianism, Mohammedanism, and Christianity there is a belief that the body and the soul shall be raised from the grave after the judgment. They will be renewed and revived. Jesus Christ also tasted suffering and death. Moreover, this death was not an ordinary death, but a great sacrifice. As a reward, God restored his Son to spirit life. The Bible says, "Even Christ died once for all time concerning sins, a righteous person for unrighteous ones, that he might lead you to God, he being put to death in the flesh, but being made alive in the spirit" (1 Peter 3:18).

Jesus Christ was victorious over death through his resurrection. God's kingdom, through Christ, will accomplish a resurrection of billions of dead humans as foretold in the Bible: The Sea gave up those dead in it, and death and Hades gave up those dead in them, and they were judged individually according to their deeds" (Revelation 20:13). The life force will be infused in each organism. After death, man will live again on this earth; death shall not be his end. Death shall be put under the feet of Christ, and will never be allowed to dominate God's creation and human beings.

Certainly, victory over death is possible for those who are righteous, pure, and wise, and who meditate on the immortal, changeless self. For this we shall have to worship God, help and serve the poor, do meditation, and attain self-realization. The knowledge of self destroys all fear of death. By knowing God alone, one conquers Death. There is no other way to Salvation (Yajurveda 21–282).

Thus, I say with force that man has the will and the capacity to conquer death. Although it may not be possible scientifically, it is certainly and surely possible through spiritualism.

10

Rebirth and Afterlife in Buddhism

Carl B. Becker

More people inhabit Asia than all the rest of the world put together, and the scope and diversity of their linguistic and religious traditions defies simplistic exposition. Strictly speaking, all of the world's great religious traditions — Judeo-Christian, Islamic, Hindu, Buddhist, Confucian, and Taoist, among others — have originated in Asia. These and many less-known traditions have not only existed side by side, but have influenced each other and branched into numerous sects and independent religions. It would be unreasonable if not impossible to try to catalogue all of their various attitudes towards death and the hereafter in a single presentation. Therefore, this article will focus on the most international and philosophical of the East Asian traditions mentioned above, namely Buddhism, and review the fundamental ideas about survival, rebirth, and the nature of the afterlife found therein.

REBIRTH IN EARLY BUDDHISM

From its earliest beginnings, the philosophy of Buddhism has paid considerable attention to the issues of death and afterlife. A profound recognition of impermanence, suffering, and death is central to the philosophy of Buddhism. According to the traditional biography of Gautama Siddhartha, it was the sight of an old man, a sick man, a dead man, and a holy man which led him to renounce his palace and wordly possessions and seek a solution to the problem of suffering. The impermanence of life became a model for his understanding of the impermanence of all things; the suffering of disease and death became expanded into the Buddha's teaching that all is ultimately suffering (*dukkha*). The idea that life continues after death is fundamental to Buddhist thought, and is usually expressed in the idea of rebirth in human or animal bodies. *For if there were no rebirth—if death were the ultimate end of all experiences—then suicide could be seen as an easy solution to an existence conceived as inherently more painful than pleasurable.* Moreover, if this existence were thought to be the only one that a given man might experience, one might be more easily encouraged to make the most hedonistic use of these few short years, rather than seeking to overcome personal desires and transcend materialism. It is precisely this Buddhist view — that this life is but one of millions of continuous lives of suffering, destined to continue indefinitely until the cycle is stopped — that necessitates a path of selflessness and discipline leading to enlightenment and freedom. Thus, not only death but the conviction of survival is essential to the Buddhist philosophy. For various cultural as well as philosophical reasons, many of the countries that have adopted Buddhism have paid much attention to its death-related ceremonies and rituals. In China and Japan, the elaborate ritual of Buddhist funerals, and the practice of warriors meditating on corpses and graveyards, has given Buddhism the epithet of a "religion for the dead" (cf. Amore, 1974, p. 134). In several respects, the issues of death and survival are more important to Buddhism than to the Judeo-Christian philosophical traditions.

Broadly speaking, Buddhists believe that there are two significantly different possibilities after death: either some aspect of the person's psychophysical influence will be reborn in a new body or he will achieve a state called *nirvana*, which is above and beyond the realms of death and rebirth. There has been substantial debate about what is reborn, and about how the state called nirvana should be interpreted.

Culturally speaking, Buddhism has been modified by each of the countries it has entered or influenced, but the most important divisions are probably the southern Theravada school (represented by the Pali *Nikayas*), the Sino-Japanese Mahayana, and the Tibetan Tantric. In general, we might classify these three divisions as follows: the Theravadins believed that "salvation" is to be achieved through self-culture and meditative disciplines; the Mahayanists believed in salvation through the grace and power of god-like Bodhisattvas; and the Tantric practitioners sought salvation through magical practices or rituals. This article focuses on the concerns of the Theravadins, who probably best represent the classical and paradigmatic Buddhist worldview.

The Context of Early Buddhism

Even prior to the Buddha, numerous schools of Indian philosophy already held dogmatic views about the nature of man, the self, and survival of death. The earliest *Vedas*, or sacred writings of the Brahmins, use the word *atman* (Sanskrit; Pali, *atta*), which refers to the animating force, life, breath, or soul, and is analogous to the Greek term *psyche*. Eventually, many schools came to think of *atman* as an unchanging and eternal core of man's being, the seat of consciousness that survives bodily death. This *atman* is said to be reborn through numerous existences (human, subhuman, or divine). It was to be ultimately liberated from this cycle of rebirths by intellectually and meditatively realizing its oneness with *Braham*, Absolute Reality, of which the *atman* was essentially a tiny part (De Silva, 1975, p. 20).

By the time of the Buddha (560–480? B.C.) many theories had arisen as to the nature, origin, and fate of the *atman* (these are discussed and refuted in the

Brahmajala Sutra; see note on *Anquttara*). The major contenders in the debate seem to be the *eternalists* and the *nihilists*. The eternalists held that the soul was separable from the body at death like a sword from its scabbard or the pith from a blade of grass. Radhakrishan (1939, p. 83) summarizes this view:

> If there is one doctrine more than any other which is characteristic of Hindu thought, it is the belief that there is an interior depth to the human soul which, in its essence, is uncreated and deathless and absolutely real.

At the same time, however, schools of nihilists and materialists held either that there was no soul at all, or that it was dissolved into various component elements at death. These views were not merely differences in metaphysical speculation, but they resulted in drastically different ethics and lifestyles. The materialists, fearing no postmortem reward or punishment for present deeds, tended to advocate either hedonism or passive inaction. Eternalists, on the other hand, often stressed respect for living beings and ethical self-discipline to the extent of self-mortification *(atta-kilamathanu-yoga).* Thus, the Buddha arrived on a scene already dominated by highly sophisticated philosophies of the soul and life after death.

The Theory of No-Soul

After a long course of ascetic austerities and meditations, Gautama Buddha came to see that all phenomenal elements are constantly changing and impermanent *(anicca).* Not only are men not inhabited by an unchanging essence or soul, but furthermore there is nothing in man that can properly be identified with a soul at all; this is the theory of *anatta,* or no-soul. Based on this analysis, the Buddha saw suffering *(dukkha)* to be a pervasive characteristic of material existence, and ascribed this suffering to man's desire for unattainable permanence and a false clinging to a mistaken notion of individual self-importance. Early Buddhists used several arguments to demonstrate this ultimate unreality of an *atta* or permanent unchanging self.

The most widely quoted of the arguments against the soul appear in the questions of King Milinda (Greek: Menander), in which the king and Nagasena discuss the concept of the self; although postdating the Buddha himself, they are representative of Theravada thought on the issue. In these illustrative but typically very repetitive conversations, Nagasena asks the king whether a chariot can be equated to its yoke, axle, wheels, body, or flagstaffs. Of course the king denies that a chariot is equivalent to any of its components taken alone, but he defends his use of the word "chariot" as an appellation or designation of the composite entity. The conclusion to be drawn is that the word "chariot" refers to nothing other than the aggregate of these material elements, and that there is no innate "chariot-ness" within it (De Bary, 1969, pp. 30–32). Just as the chariot can be analyzed into its material components, with no residue of "chariot-ness" left over, the Buddhists teach that man can be analyzed into five essential aggregates, which exhaustively describe the human being and eliminate the need for any underlying soul. These five aggregates (panca-kkhanda) are not limited to material elements, but include sensory and psychological components.

Since a person cannot be identified with any of the khandas taken alone, and the khandas taken together exhaust the description of the person, the Buddhists conclude that there is no remaining self or atta, outside of the interdependent complex just described.

With human essence, self, or soul (atta) thus analyzed out of the picture, the question of what happens to man after death becomes even more serious. Superficially, it might seem that when the body disintegrates at death, all of the other khandas, which are mutually interdependent on bodily processes, must also cease and disperse. But we have already observed that the idea of rebirth is indispensable to the coherence of the Buddhist philosophy. In fact, the Buddha taught that the karma (action, especially mental volitions) of the dying man had a cause-effect relation, and in that sense a continuity, with the birth of new beings. He used the term rebirth, as opposed to reincarnation, which might imply that a single soul were reincarnated in several consecutive bodies. Rebirth, on the other hand, suggests a causal continuity, but not personal identity, between one birth and the next.

Buddhists hold that this teaching was not merely a crude attempt to reconcile traditional Hindu concepts of karma and reincarnation with an ethical theory that de-emphasized the centrality of the self (Jayatilleke, 1974, p. 134). Rather, they say that these conclusions were based upon the direct paranormal knowledge of the Buddha, attained through years of meditation. These extra-sensory capacities, common to many meditative traditions, enabled the Buddha a clear recollection of his previous lives (pubbe-nivasa-nussatina, retrocognition) and a direct vision of the death and rebirth of beings (cutapapatanana) (Upadhyaya, 1971, p. 368).

Even in his own day, Buddha was frequently misinterpreted by rivals as denying the doctrines of karma and rebirth. The Buddha, when questioned, explicity denied this interpetation. Another philosophical reconstruction would assert that the karmic effects of actions influence other future generations, but not the reborn individual.

> [Buddha's] later followers endeavored to reconcile his twofold doctrine of no-permanent-soul and the moral responsibility of the individual. . . . In the Hindu view, the same individual acts and suffers in different lives; the usual modern Buddhist view is the same; but the strict original Buddhist view is altruistic, the actor being one, and the ultimate sufferer or beneficiary another individual. (Jennings, 1947, p. xxxxvii; emphasis ours)

This is an ingenious attempt to make the idea of karma more palatable to modern behaviorists, but it flies in the face of the letter and the spirit of early Buddhist teachings. Since a permanent underlying self is denied, it is true that there is no absolute identity between the original actor and the later recipient of the fruits of that karma—just as I am not the same person now that I was when I started studying Buddhism. But the causal connection between my earlier studies and my present views and experiences is unmistakable. Buddha's theory of karma is not humanistically reducible to biological and sociological influences continuing after death. Nor is death the end of the road for the individual, or else suicide would relieve us of the suffering of existence. Man dies and is reborn. The corpse and the new baby are causally conditioned and interconnected, but not identical.

Analogical Treatments

Numerous analogies in the early texts help to explain the importance of continuity over strict identity in the causal process. Nagasena gives the case of the man who steals mangoes, and later pleads that the mangoes which he stole were different from the ones which the owner planted. King Milinda agrees that although the stolen mangoes are not identical with the ones planted, they are nevertheless causally conditioned; neither the same nor totally unrelated, they are different parts of a single causal sequence. If a fire were to spread from a neglected campfire to an adjacent field, the burning field could be called neither the same fire nor a different fire from the campfire. Similarly, the curds that form today from yesterday's milk, or the verse that the student repeats after learning from his teacher, are neither absolutely identical to nor different from the original milk or original poem. There is merely a causal sequence of events that enables us to identify one with the other, or to say that one has given rise to the other. Rebirth is taken as another case of this same sort of process (Trenckner, 1962, pp. 46–48).

Clearly the sort of identity that humans have thoughout their lives is a continuity of constantly changing mental and physical conditions, only identifiable with previous states through its spatiotemporal and causal contiguity. Opposing the Hindu analogies of the soul as an inchworm moving (relatively unchanged) from one leaf to another, the Buddhists pefer the analogue of the flame passing from wick to wick—a process lacking any permanent shape or substrate. It would appear that in answer to the question "What is reborn?" we should accept the Buddha's answer that there is no permanent thing or stuff which flits from body to body, but rather than when the five *khandas* are dissolved at death, the four nonmaterial *khandas* continue, like a causal current or stream of existence-energy *(bhava-sota)* to influence another material substrate—a fetus in a receptive womb (Jayatilleke, 1974, p. 119).

Intermediate States

However accurate this characterization may be, it is very difficult to depict to ourselves just how this immaterial causal current operates. Skeptics might argue that analogies of flames and curds are appropriate to the case of identity between a boy in 1950 and the man he became in 1990, where a continuous material substrate and memory are available. But it is precisely the lack of such a material substrate between the dying man and the newborn baby that renders these analogies inadequate. Even in Buddha's day, there were strong movements to reinstate the *atta*, or one of the *kkandas*, or a subtly material self, as the stuff that went from point A to point B (i.e., the corpse to the fetus). One of the most eligible candidates for the "entity which is reborn" was the *vinnana*, the *khanda* most closely connected with consciousness. Pande lists several texts that support this view, suggesting that the idea of a transmigrating *vinnana* is pre-Buddhist. This *vinnana* resembles the *atta* (Skt.: *atman*) of some Hindu *Upanishads*, with the important difference that it is not taken to be something permanent, but rather as an ever-changing complex (Pande, 1974, pp. 493–495). Later Buddhists seized on the Buddha's use of the term *gandhabba*, the mental complex essential to the birth of a baby, as the stuff which is reborn, or they confused the psychic body *(manomayam kayam)* admitted by Buddhist meditation theory, with that which is reborn. The *vajjiputtakas* came to be known also as *puggalavadins*, because they proposed that there was a *puggala* or self, neither identical to nor differnt from the *khandas*, and that it was this *puggala* which was reborn. They claimed that Buddha's teaching of anatta did not mean that there was no self whatsoever, but simply that there was no eternal and unchanging self (Pande, p. 490, n. 223). Buddhaghosa (1931) criticizes the *puggalavadins* from the standpoint of the *Abhidhamma* school, centuries later, but then he proceeds to substitute the term bhavanga, or "existence factor" in exactly the same role. Asanga, in the *Yogacarabhumi*, discusses an intermediate state between the death of the former person and the birth of the latter (Wayman, 1974, p. 238):

> There is synonymous terminology. The term "intermediate state" is used because it manifests in the interval between the death state and the birth state. The term *gandharva* is used. . . the term *manomaya* is used. . . the term "resultant" *(abhinirvrtti)* is used because it is productive in the direction of birth.

Such a proliferation of the terms used to refer to the entity that is reborn, and such theorizing about the intermediate states between death and rebirth, are contrary to the teachings and antispeculative attitude of the Buddha. However, they demonstrate the difficulties of even the most outstanding classical commentators in making sense of rebirth as an energy transfer across distances without a substrate.

Hindus like Radhakrishnan and Westerners like Grimm have suggested that the Buddha developed the *anatta* theory for ethical reasons, but that he actually believed in a sort of *atta* being reborn in successive bodies (cf. Upadhyaya, 1971, pp. 302–304). The cultures of China, Japan, and Tibet, lacking both the vocabulary and the sophisticated philosophical tradition of the Buddha, adopted even more concrete ideas of transmigrating souls. However, early Buddhism taught an instantaneous rebirth of thought complexes, neither identical with nor different from the dying person, and not definable in terms of a single permanent underlyng substance. Since there is no single element or substrate that is reborn, if we wish a more detailed description of rebirth, we must inquire not about the object or stuff that is reborn, but rather about the process and the factors that influence it.

The Determinants of Rebirth

The belief in rebirth in new bodies was quite widespread even prior to the Buddha's time, with protracted debate about its implications. Some people contended that, in accordance with the law of Karma, those who had done a preponderance of good deeds would be reborn in happy states, and those who had done a preponderance of evil would be reborn in evil states. Others, while admitting the concept of rebirth, denied the effect of karma in placing a soul in a new womb; they gave counterexamples of good men who had purportedly been reborn in evil circumstances, and evil men who were reborn in happy situations. The Buddha discusses each of these views with Ananda in the *Mahakamma-vibhanga sutta* (*Greater Analysis of Deeds Sutra*). In each of many similar sections, the Buddha asserts first of all that there are such things as good and evil deeds, and that we should not allow ethical distinctions to become blurred. Then he proceeds to support the idea of karma even further by declaring that all deeds will ultimately produce their effects, good for good and evil for evil. Both views — that good and evil lives inevitably produce good and evil rebirths, respectively, and the converse, that there is no correlation between actions and rebirths — are condemned as the result of overgeneralization from too limited an understanding, perhaps from psychic visualization of too limited a sample. The Buddha suggests that some deeds (*karmas*) are operative and others inoperative. However, the total balance sheet of good and evil deeds performed during a given lifetime is summarized in the state of mind held by the dying person. This is fully in accord with the Buddha's teaching that there are no underlying substances but only sequences of thought processes, and that the transition from death to rebirth is but another instant in the continuity of such psychophysical processes. The *Mahakamma Sutra* explains:

> At the time of dying a right view was adopted and firmly held by him; because of this, at the breaking up of the body after dying, he arises in a good bourn, a heaven world. . .or at the time of dying a false view was adopted and firmly held by him; because of this, on the breaking up of the body after dying he arises in sorrowful ways.

The Buddha is not saying that these firmly held views at death are the exclusive determinants of rebirth. He is suggesting that both previous deeds and the last-held thought complexes may influence rebirth, in accord with his avoidance of strict determinism and indeterminism. Historically and philosophically, this teaching is important because it opens the door to future schools of Buddhism, which increasingly emphasize the holding of right views at the moment of death, and which consider this to be more important than living a moral life in determining one's future rebirth.

A somewhat clearer version of the nature of the transference of energies at death is gained by placing it within the Buddhist view of conception. In the Buddhist view, sexual intercourse alone is inadequate to give rise to a conscious human being. For conception to take place, there must be present not only the male sperm and the female ovum, but also karmic energy (sometimes also called *gandhabba*) from a third source. According to Nyanatiloka (1955, p. 2):

> Father and mother only provide the necessary physical material for the formula-
> tion of the embryonic body. . . .The dying individual with his whole being
> convulsively clinging to life, at the very moment of his death, sends forth karmic
> energy which, like a flash of lightning, hits at a new mother's womb ready for
> conception. Thus, through the impinging of karmic energies on ovum and sperm
> there arises, just like a precipitate, the so-called primary cell.

The analogy of lightning here may be illustrative. We know that light is generally given off by physical objects glowing, burning, or reflecting other light, and we know that sounds are generally produced by collision or friction between two objects. And yet, on careful analysis, the lightning is seen to be neither a physical object nor the collision of physical objects, yet it produces light and thunder. In fact, by the time that the light and sound reach our senses, the atmospheric processes that gave rise to the phenomenon we name lightning are already stabilized and the infinitesimal electrical particles involved are already absorbed in a new state in which they are no longer identifiable. Lightning is a visible manifestation of the imperceivably rapid movement of imperceivably small particles. In rebirth, the Buddhists would say, the character of the person born demonstrates that there had been, prior to his birth, the influence of these life-clinging karmic forces, imperceivable except through their effects.

The Buddha sought to avoid speculative and doctrinal extremes in any direction. He said that his understanding of rebirth was gained not from metaphysical speculation or Hindu mythology, but from direct (paranormal) perception of the workings of the universe.

Philosophical Difficulties with the Buddhist Concept of Rebirth

There are at least three obvious philosophical difficulties in the Buddhist case for rebirth: (1) the problem of the spatiotemporal gap between the dying man and the newly conceived fetus; (2) the problem of population increase in the number of living beings; and (3) the problem of evidence for or against the rebirth theory. Let us examine the Buddhist resolutions to each of these issues.

Spatiotemporal Gaps

The Buddha's descriptive analogies of rebirth are very effective in explaining the senses in which the person born is neither identical to nor different from the person who had just died. But in each of them (mango, flame, wave, child becoming a man, etc.) there is a spatiotemporal continuity from one state to the next, which enables us to identify the latter with the former as part of the same larger process or pattern. In the case of death and rebirth, however, there is no visible continuity between individual A_1 on his deathbed and fetus A_2 which receives the karmic lifeclinging impulse at A_1's death. There is at least a spatial gap between the location of the final thoughts and volitions of the dying man and the arising of the first rudimentary consciousness in the infant or fetus. Although no precise way exists of determining whether there is such a temporal gap or not, the gap between the season of the greatest number of deaths (winter) and the season of the greatest number of births (spring) would seem to suggest a gap between the last thoughts of dying man and the first thoughts of newborn babes. Moreover, there is a vast difference between the complexity of verbal and intellectual thought patterns possessed by the majority of old men at their deaths, and the manifestly nonverbal and undiscriminating thought structures of all newborn infants. Thus the continuum of death and rebirth observed paranormally by the Buddha might seem to be contradicted. To make sense of the Buddhist theory, then, we must approach it not only objectively, but from within the philosophical view of reality that the Buddhists held. A return to the Buddhist perspectives on *khandas* and *kamma* will help us resovle these apparent dilemmas.

In the Buddhist view of the person, only the first of the *khandas* is grossly material; the rest are fundamentally psychological characteristics, nonetheless ontologically real for all their being immaterial.

The Buddhists admit that all material elements return to dust at death, and therefore we are wrong to seek any *physical* traces linking a dying man with a newborn babe. The nonmaterial *khandas*, however, are not limited to spatial dimensions, which implies that a dream or a thought cannot be located spatially within a cranium. Moreover, telepathy, clairvoyance, and "out-of-body" travel are accepted within the Buddhist worldview as natural results of long ascetic and meditative practice. Practice of such powers *(siddhis)* is condemned by the Buddha as being unconducive to enlightenment, and likely to distract the practitioner from more spiritual goals. While modern Westerners would consider telepathy to be an inexplicable example of causation at a distance, early Buddhists could easily accept this phenomenon of one well-trained mind reading the thoughts of another, or transmitting its thoughts to one not physically present.

If we grant that thoughts cannot themselves be spatially located (although associated with a specific person), and that they can be sensed or transmitted psychically by individuals who are physically separated, then we have also conceded that causation at a distance is possible in the realm of psychological phenomena. This is precisely what the Buddhist rebirth theory contends: that psychological factors continue to influence one being or another uninterruptedly. More specifically, the dying man's wish for life naturally becomes associated with that baby whose psychophysical makeup is most receptive to precisely those psychic complexes. We may or may not choose to reject the theory of rebirth on other grounds, but any *a priori* dismissal on the basis of spatial gaps alone is thus eliminated by this analysis. The problem of temporal continuity need not arise at all if we accept the early Buddhist tradition completely. But if it is held that the problem of temporal continuity does arise, or that it is another aspect of the spatiotemporal causality problem, it might be answered in any of several ways.

First, along the analogy of the nonspatial character of consciousness outlined above, it might be argued that consciousness is essentially nontemporal, as demonstrated by our abilities to remember past situations vividly or to foresee future situations clairvoyantly. Thus, it might be argued, psychic components (khandas) neither exist nor cease to exist when dissociated from their cranial counterparts; they simply are not amenable to temporal measurements until they are again affiliated with neural, physiological structures existing within this temporal continuum.

Another approach would be to argue that there are formless realms where old thoughts, actions, and desires (kamma) await fruition. Such a postulate is sometimes taken as a prerequisite for the acceptance of a nondeistic karma theory. If it is admitted that all thoughts and deeds are "stored" in some not merely physiological sense, until the situation is right for their fruition as moral reward or recompense, then there need be no additional difficulty in admitting that the consciousness complex or karmic energy of a dying individual might be similarly "stored" temporarily until the optimally suited conditions for its rebirth matured. However, the mechanism of such a "storage" process, either for karma or for individuals, remains inexplicable.

A third approach would be to suggest that consciousness is reborn, immediately, not necessarily in a human realm, but perhaps as a god, spirit, animal, or other creature whose birth passes unnoticed. This possibility will be discussed more seriously below. The important conclusion to be recognized here is that, if any of the above perspectives are admitted as possible, then the period between death and rebirth can be accounted for, and the problem of spatiotemporal continuity no longer stands as an objection to the theory of rebirth.

Overpopulation

The problem of overpopulation is often raised against the doctrine of rebirth or reincarnation. Simply stated, it observes that there are more people on planet earth now than a millenium ago, and asks where all the souls of the new people came from. The argument itself rests on several assumptions that do not apply to the Buddhist theory, but let us reason our way through them.

In the first place, Buddhism believes neither in a temporal nor eternal soul, as has been emphasized above. Therefore, we should not imagine a condition of millions of disembodied souls "waiting around" in ethereal heavens for embodiment. Rather, both mind and body are evolved from material and psychological components. It is completely within the realm of reason that psychic complexes have evolved with ever-increasing complexity to suit their material bases, over the course of millions of years. It is possible that some dying people's thoughts influence more than one fetal organism at a time. Alternatively, it is possible that beings elsewhere in the universe, on other planets, or in spirit realms are reborn as men. Finally, the increasingly animal tendencies of mankind, if they are such, might be taken as an indication that an ever-increasing number of animal souls are finding expression in human minds and bodies these days.

While these responses are largely speculative, the important point is that the Buddha recognized many levels of existence of beings not recognized by most modern Westerners. Although these resemble those ⁴of the pre-Buddhist Upanishadic tradition, the Buddha denies that he has merely copied a prior mythology. In numerous contexts and on many different occasions, he refers to his own interactions with gods and spirits, made possible by his paranormal powers. If there indeed exist such invisible beings, then a population count of visible beings alone is inadequate to invalidate the theory of rebirth.

The Buddhist view of the universe is more comprehensive than that normally held by modern materialists. We already observed how the Buddhist analysis of human personality into *khandas* gives equal ontological footing to psychological and physiological components of persons. In its broadest categories, the Buddhist universe may be divided into the realms of things immaterial and formless (*arupadhatu*), those with form but only subtle matter (*rupadhatu*), and the physical/sensual realm of form and gross matter (*kamadhatu*). It is thought that rebirth can take place in realms of hell, ghosts, titans (*asuras*), animals, men, and gods (Story, 1975, pp. 65f.) Just as there are many classes of men and animals within the visible material realms, so there are many classes of gods, spirits, and demons in the invisible realms. But it is generally held that only on the human level can man's karma (thought and action) influence his destiny; the other levels are essentially expiatory or compensatory, places where the merit or demerit of prior lives is rewarded or punished. Neither heaven nor hell are taken to be eternal in the Christian sense. Gods and demons are also subject to causal laws and to the cycle of death and rebirth, although their lives are held to be longer than human lives. These other realms (*lokas*) are not necessarily seen as physically above or below this one, but as inter-penetrating it; sometimes they are conceived as generated by consciousness in an idealist fashion (Amore, 1974, p. 124). There is one question as to whether the Buddha really believed all of the mythology behind the doctrines of heavens and hells, or merely taught it as a moral goad for the common people in his audience. It is clear, however, that the Buddha believed in the existence of (and claimed to have interacted with) invisible gods and spirits, and that he saw people born into higher or lower realms of existence depending on their karma and mental states (Jayatilleke, 1974, pp 135, 143).

Against rebirth, Westerners generally adduce the fact that very few children seem to remember their previous lives. On the other side, the Buddhists might argue that even a few documentable cases might indicate the plausibility of the rebirth theory, for what is expected is not perfect memory by everyone of former lives, but simply some indications of influence. It is important to note that the rebirth theory is not logically self-contradictory nor poses the sort of insurmountable philosophical difficulties that confront the purely materialistic theory of the resurrection. For this early Buddhist formulation to work, however, it demands acceptance of at least (1) causality at a distance, (2) the existence of psychic powers not dependent on physical bodies, and probably (3) the existence of some realms other than the visible material one.

If these Buddhist premises are granted, then the Buddhist theory of rebirth based on psychic continuity and influence can be rendered coherent and in that sense tenable. The question of whether rebirth theory in fact accounts better for observed data than other theories then becomes an empirical one, which we shall consider shortly. There may be many psychological reasons for personally preferring or averring from the theory of karma and rebirth (e.g., the oft-cited allegation that it leads to a philosophy of resignation and stagnation), but these feelings clearly have no bearing on what is actually the nature of reality.

NIRVANA: THE ALTERNATIVE TO REBIRTH

The Buddha did not envision rebirth in a happy heaven as the ultimate goal of life. The heavenly realms, although pleasant, are causally conditioned and therefore impermanent, producing additional suffering in their demise. The common majority of suffering humanity might well wish to escape its suffering even temporarily through a heavenly rebirth. But a more enlightened perspective would suggest that the entire cycle of birth, death, rebirth, and change is inextricably interlaced with suffering. In that case, the ultimate goal to be sought is not a temporary stay in heaven but a permanent release from the entire cycle of birth and death. In early Buddhism, such a release can only be obtained from right practice and thought while in the human realm; even the gods and demons must become human (and male) before such freedom can be realized (Jennings, 1947, p. xliii). Therefore, although the human realm experiences more suffering than the heavenly realms, it is privileged above all others in its access to this soteriological option: the complete escape from the wheel of rebirth.

This escape, or freedom, is generally known as *nirvana* (Pali: nibbana). Its etymological roots suggest the meaning of "blowing out" or extinction (cf. Upadhyaya, 1971, pp. 337, 341). It is often analogized to the blowing out or extinguishing of a fire (the passions). It might seem that if all existence is suffering, then the only escape from suffering is in nonexistence. Such reasoning has led many western interpreters to conclude that nirvana is simply the utter extinction of personality, although the Buddha sometimes explained it in more palatable terms so as not to shock his listeners. Since nirvana is the final goal of Buddhist life and teaching, it is essential that we come to terms with this question: does nirvana actually imply annihilation, or some form of survival after death?

The early Buddhist scriptures are far from unambiguous about the meaning of nirvana. Their allusions to it tend to be more allegorical than literally descriptive. Problems of interpretation are intensified when we try to translate the words and concepts of nirvana into English, in a dramatically different culture and age. We may take four views as representative of the major schools of thought: (1) nirvana as annihilation; (2) nirvana as eternal life; (3) nirvana as an ethical state in this world; and (4) nirvana as a transcendent, ineffable state in which time and person are superceded.

Among the first modern interpreters of Buddhism to the West was Eugene Burnouf, who translated the Lotus Sutra and other Pali and Tibetan works into French in the mid-19th century. Burnouf's view of nirvana is typified by his translation of a passage in the *Avadanasatakam* (1876, p. 525):

> Until finally, Vipasyin, the completely perfect Buddha, after having performed the totality of obligations of a Buddha, was like a fire of which the fuel is consumed, entirely annihilated in the element of nirvana in which nothing remains of that which constitutes existence.

This analogy of extinguishing a fire or lamp becomes archetypical for annihilationist interpreters, its conclusions based primarily on etymological grounds.

Even within the Buddha's lifetime, his opponents were quick to accuse him of teaching a nihilistic philosophy with the goal of self-annihilation. The Buddha was equally insistent in countering these charges, for there had been annihilationist philosophers before him, and he scrupulously avoided their paths. Refuting the annihilationist misinterpretations, he addressed his monks:

> [I] am accused wrongly, vainly, falsely, and inappropriately by some ascetics and Brahmins: "A denier is the ascetic Gautama; he teaches the destruction, annihilation, and perishing of the being that now exists. . ." These ascetics wrongly, vainly, falsely, and inappropriately accuse me of being what I am not, O Monks, and of saying what I do not say. (Grimm, 1958, p. 5)

There are even passages that would indicate the Buddha took a much more positive, even eternalistic view of the nature of man.

> I did exist in the past, not that I did not; I will exist in the future, not that I will not; and I do exist in the present, not that I do not. (Jayatilleke, 1974, p. 200)

Perhaps it was a more serious encounter with passages like these that caused Western interpreters to rethink their original annihilationist interpretations. LaVallee Poussin came to believe that there are states of blessedness and existence beyond the power of language to depict or mind to imagine until actually experienced. He advocated that Westerners continue to think of nirvana as a kind of annihilation, because Western thought patterns will not enable us to conceive of blessedness or existence apart from mental and physical objects, which are not present in nirvana. To avoid building mythical "castles in the air," which would not correctly describe the reality of nirvana, the Buddha remained silent, but this silence should not be taken to imply that nirvana were not a real state. If LaVallee Poussin is correct in this interpretation, it goes a long way towards explaining both the reticence of the Buddha to verbalize his understanding of nirvana, and the difficulty of Westerners to see nirvana as anything other than annihilation.

While there are many arguments that the Buddha did not believe in a nirvana of annihilation, the arguments that he did believe in the eternal bliss of a soul in nirvana can be summarized into three types: (1) Buddhist borrowing from Samkhya or Brahmanism; (2) the theory that anatta applies only to the khandas and that a soul might exist outside of them; and (3) the positive metaphors and adjectives used to describe nirvana. However, none of these arguments is very strong, and they often amount to little more than a rationalization for the conviction that a great world religion could not be nihilistic. There are dangers in both the annihilationist and eternalist viewpoints, as K. N. Upadhyaya appropriately comments on the views of Grimm, Kieth, and Radhakrishnan (1971), p. 38):

> All this clearly shows that these scholars, while countering the annihilationist view of Nibbana, are carried away by their own arguments to the opposite extreme of eternalism. It is indeed, very difficult to steer clear of these two opposite views. . . .

It seems that the Buddha had tried to avoid both extremes, and one way to follow him in this is a humanistic agnosticism.

When questioned as to whether the saint exists after death, the Buddha remained silent. There is widespread agreement on one point: the reason for the Buddha's silence on this question was that he felt that such speculation or knowledge did not lead to spiritual or moral advancement. The man in this world is analogized to a man wounded by an arrow, who can waste no time in asking the shape and origin of the arrow and the man who shot it. Rather, he must exert all his energy towards removing the arrow, the immediate cause of his suffering. Similarly, the Buddha taught a way towards the relief of the suffering of this immediate material existence, and not a system of metaphysics. The circle of birth, death, and rebirth can be broken if desires and cravings are eliminated.

The entire teaching of *anatta* was more to encourage a selfless moral life than to provoke discussions on the nature of a soul. These considerations lead many Buddhist scholars to the conclusion that nirvana refers not to any ontological state, nor to a view of existence or nonexistence after death, but rather to an ethical state here and now. This conclusion does seem to have the happy advantages of not reading too much into the Buddha's silence, and not leading to invidious comparisons of Buddhism with other religions.

Japanese Mahayana Buddhists also tend to emphasize the ethical implications of nirvana in this life, which they prefer to term *satori*, or "enlightenment."

In Mahayana Buddhism, the ethical state of the enlightened person is not merely one of apathy or of total detachments; it is one of action and compassion as well. It closely follows the Bhagavad Gita's model of selfless action (*niskamkarma*) and makes way for the model of the Bodhisattva: the compassionate enlightened being who returns to this suffering world to save and help unenlightened sentient beings. Yamakami explains (1912, p. 33):

> In its negative aspect, Nirvana is the extinction of the three-fold fires of lust, malice, and folly. . . . In its positive aspect, Nirvana consists in the practice of the three cardinal virtues of generosity, love, and wisdom.

D. T. Suzuki denies that non-Buddhists are even qualified to deal with the problem of nirvana, but his own interpretation appears very similar to Yamakami's. For Suzuki (1963, p. 51), nirvana is destruction

> of the notion of ego-substance and of all the desires that arise from this erroneous conception. But this represents the negative side of the doctrine, and its positive side consists in universal love or sympathy (*karuna*) for all beings.

Many scholars of stature have thus interpreted nirvana as a state purely limited to the world of living men, with little or no reference to existence after death. Some interpret nirvana as mere detachment from worldly desires; others add the requirement of positive ethical action within the world. Although this may seem to be a more noncommittal, and hence safer, approach than the extremes of nihilism or eternalism, it still tends either to one side or the other. If the entire message of the Buddha were simply that men should be moral and not concern themselves with the afterlife, then no matter how profound this philosophical attitude, it lacks the conviction of one who has seen that men are reborn repeatedly into lives of suffering and that all karma must bear its fruit. If being detached or compassionate alone is enough to eliminate suffering and karma, we should expect some further description of how such actions or attitudes stop the cycles of birth, death, and rebirth, which are the bottom line of Buddhist philosophy.

Early Buddhism has reference to two types of nirvana: *upadhisesa* ("with substrate") and *nirupadhisesa* ("without substrate"). The former is the state of the saint still living in the world; the latter is the state of the saint after death. Even if we admitted that the "ethical state" interpretation adequately explained the meaning of "extinction" (in terms of extinction of desires while the body still lives), we would still be left with the troubling question of what is meant by a bodiless ethical state, the second kind of nirvana discussed! Surely it makes no sense to speak of postmortem apathy, detachment, or compassion, of a being that ceases to exist after death! Moreover, we have already seen that the Budha repudiated nihilism and affirmed that he would continue to exist. We also know that nirvana refers not to a personal, body-dependent existence after death, for the body and khandas are held to separate. And Buddhism clearly repudiates the notion of permanent or unchanging entites, including souls, in this material phenomenal universe. To paraphrase Conan Doyle's famous observation, when all else is ruled impossible, the improbable must remain the fact. So it seems with early Buddhism: both eternalism and annihilationism have been ruled impossible, and nirvana must mean something more than an ethical state, because there is a type of nirvana after the body is dead and inactive. Thus, however distasteful to Western language-bound thought patterns, the only alternative seems to be that there is a state which language does not adequately describe, and yet is one which the Buddha and Arhats experienced before and after death. This state, although difficult to characterize or talk about, is not nothing, it is *nirvana*.

The analogies of a flame passing from wick to wick and ultimately extinguished, or of different water always flowing through the "same"river, are often used to describe the ever changing nature of the phenomenal world, and the similarity-in-difference of the man who is reborn with the man who has died. However, extinction of the flame is not the only analogy for nirvana. Another important one is that of the small flame swallowed up in a larger one. As King Milinda learns from monk Nagasena (De Bary, 1969, p. 30):

> "Reverend Nagasena," said the King, "does the Buddha still exist?"
> "Yes, your majesty, he does."
> "Then is it possible to point out the Buddha as being here or there?". . . .
> "If a great fire were blazing, would it be possible to point to a flame which had gone out and say that it was here or there?"

Thus, there is a sense in which the individual flame is no longer identifiable, no longer individual, no longer limited to a single wick. It is not therefore utterly destroyed, but rather expanded by losing its prior individuality. Like raindrops in the ocean, they do not lose all existence whatsoever, but rather lose the prior limitations and characteristics of their separateness.

"[Nirvana] takes away the sting of death and leads to immortality in the sense of the "Upasama" [merging] of the individual in a higher reality, like that of a burning flame in its source" (Pande, 1974, p. 504). Narasu (1907, pp. 224f.) also insisted that "the denial of a separate self, an *atman*, does not obliterate the personality of a man, but liberates the individual from an error. . . ." This may seem like a very foreign concept to individualistically indoctrinated Westerners. There is a famous passage in the eighth Udana in which the Buddha asserts that there *is* a state which is unborn and uncompound (cf. Woodward's trans., 1948, II, p. 98). From this reference also, we may conclude that nirvana *is*, that the Buddha who has attained nirvana *is*, and that this teaching is not merely a sugarcoating for a doctrine of annihilationism. Why, then, was the Buddha so adamantly silent about the nature of this state? Pande (1974, p. 510) suggests that

> One describes it best by preserving silence, for to say anything about it would be to make it relational and finite. . . Buddha adhered to this position so rigorously that his silence has become enigmatic.

Thomas concludes that the Buddha had reached the realization of a state about which neither existence nor nonexistence as we know it could be asserted. LaVallee Poussin agrees that Western langauge lacks the subtlety needed to convey the nature of nirvanic states. If Conze is correct that only mystical knowledge is possible of nirvana, then it is understandable that the Buddha should desire to avoid easily misinterpreted metaphors. Jayatilleke (1974, p. 122) reasons that

> The person who has attained the goal is beyond measure (*na pamanam atthi*). Elsewhere, it is said that he does not come within time, being beyond time (*kappam neti akappiyo*) or that he does not come within reckoning (*na upeti sankham*). In other words, we do not have the concepts or words to describe adequately the state of the emancipated person.

It is just this inaccessibility to verbal description that has rendered nirvana such a difficult concept for language-bound Western philosophers. The negative adjectives so often applied to nirvana should not be taken as evidence of Buddhist nihilism. Instead, like the *via negativa* of the medieval Christian descriptions of the mystic Holy, they deny that nirvana has anything in common with the mundane or conceptual. Upadhyaya (1971, p. 343) explains

> They by denying everything mundane and conceptual to Nibbana suggest its supramundane and non-conceptual nature in the best possible way, though the positive expressions are also useful in so far as they assert the reality of Nibbana and allay the fears of the nihilistic conception.

With typical Buddhist logic, we are left with the following conclusion: Nirvana neither exists nor does not exist, i.e., it is neither within the realm of existence as we know it, nor is it an illusion. The saint is not reborn, nor does he die, nor is it proper to use any ordinary adjectives about the ineffable state he experiences. His old personality does not continue, and yet the person is not utterly annihilated. Such a state of nibbana is achievable, and it is a viable alternative to rebirth after death. To accept that there are states of being beyond the phenomenal, not even amenable to description in everyday discourse, may require a radical change of worldview of Westerners lacking in mystical experience. Yet this idea — that there are blissful and otherwise indescribable nirvanic states — seems to be the clearest conclusion we can reach concerning what the Buddha experienced and was trying to communicate. Thus, Buddhism presents us with two alternatives to the Western ideas of survival in heavenly realms: (1) a "rebirth" of mental processes and characteristics into another human (and possibly nonhuman) body; (2) an achievement of a transcendent bodiless state defying further referential description, but characterizable by peace, bliss, and absence of change and desire. This view of the nature of life and the inevitability of rebirth became popular throughout South and East Asia and remains dominant there today.

REFERENCES

Amore, R. C. 1974. The Heterodox Philosophical Systems. In *Death in Eastern Thought.* Ed. F. H. Holck, pp. 114–162. Nashville: Abingdon Press.

Anguttara Nikaya (Gradual Sayings). Unless otherwise specified, all scriptural references will be taken from the Pali Text Society editions. Ed. Thomas or C.A.F. Rhys-Davids. London: Luzac or Oxford University Press.

Buddhaghosa. 1931. *The Path of Purity (Visuddhimagga).* London: Pali Text Society.

Burnouf, E. 1876. *L'introduction a L'histoire du Buddhisme Indien.* Paris: Maisonneuve et Cie.

Colebroke, H. T. 1873. *Miscellaneous Essays.* Ed. E. B. Cowell. London: Trubner & Co.

Conze, E. 1951. *Buddhism: Its Essence and Development.* Oxford: Bruno Cassirer.

DeBary, T., ed. 1969. *The Buddhist Tradition.* New York: Modern Library.

DeSilva, L. A. 1975. *The Problems of the Self in Buddhism and Christianity.* Colombo: Study Centre for Religion and Society.

Grimm, G. 1958, *The Doctrine of the Buddha.* Berlin: Akademie Verlag.

Jayatilleke, K. N. 1974. *The Message of the Buddha.* New York: The Free Press.

Jennings, J. G. 1947. *The Vedantic Buddhism of the Buddha.* Delhi: Motilal Banarsidas.

Kalupahana, D. J. 1975. *Buddhist Philosophy: A Historical Analysis.* Honolulu: University Press of Hawaii.

LaVallee Poussin, L. 1908. *Bouddhisme: Opinions sur l'histoire de la dogmatique.* Paris: Gabriel Beauchesne et Cie.

Law, B. C. 1973. *Heaven and Hell in Buddhist Perspective.* Varanasi: Bhartiya Publishers.

Nyantiloka Mahathera. 1955. *Karma and Rebirth.* Colombo: Buddhist Publication Soceity.

Narasu, L. 1907. *The Essence of Buddhism.* Bombay: Thacker & Co.

Pande, G. C. 1974. *Studies in the Origins of Buddhism.* Delhi: Motilal Banarsidas.

Radhakrishnan, S. 1939. *Eastern Religions and Western Thought.* London: Oxford University Press.

Rhys-Davids, T. W. 1921. Nirvana. In *The Pali Text Society's Pali-English Dictionary,* 326a. London: Luzac & Co.

Sarathchandra, E. R. 1958. *The Buddhist Psychology of Perception.* Colombo: University Press.

Story, F. 1975. *Rebirth as Doctrine and Experience.* Kandy; Buddhist Publications Society.

Suzuki, D. T. 1963. *Outlines of Mahayana Buddhism.* New York: Schocken Books.

Trenckner, V., ed. 1962. *Milindapanho.* London: Luzac & Co.

Upadhyaya, K. N. 1971. *Early Buddhism and the Bhagavad Gita.* Delhi: Motilal Banarsidas.

Wayman, A. 1974. The Intermediate State Dispute. In *Buddhist Studies in Honor of I. B. Horner.* Dordrecht: D. Reidel.

Woodward, F. L., trans. 1948. *Minor Anthologies of the Pali Canon.* Esp. *Udana VIII,* Vol. 2. London: Oxford University Press.

Yamakami, S. 1912. *Systems of Buddhistic Thought.* Calcutta: University of Calcutta Press.

11

Chinese Perspectives on Death and Dying

Wei Wei C. Huang

In the past 20 years, information about death and dying has proliferated rapidly. However, literature concerning attitudes toward death and care of dying patients having different cultural and ethnic backgrounds is scarce. The United States is a nation of nations; ethnicity and diversity are the very essence of America's uniqueness. Hence, it is important for health professionals to understand the role culture plays in forming one's attitudes toward death so that patient care may be individualized. This chapter examines Chinese people's attitudes toward death from several perspectives in the hope that health professionals will be more sensitive to the cultural aspects of patient care.

There is a common belief in China that birth, aging, illness, and death are the four phases of human life. They progress from one to the next, and each should be graciously accepted. A dying patient is often portrayed as lying in bed, smiling, and surrounded by relatives and close friends. Yet, fear of death and avoidance of the topic are prevalent among Chinese.

At a young age, a child is taught to be very careful with words that are remotely associated with the "misfortune" of death. The word "death" and its synonyms are strictly forbidden on happy occasions, especially during holidays. Uneasiness about death often is reflected in an emphasis on longevity and everlasting life. "Wishing you live as long as the South Mountain" is the expression most frequently used to congratulate an elder on his birthday. "Mountain," in China, symbolizes strength and permanence. Political leaders long to be hailed, "Long live our great leader!" In daily life, the Chinese character for "Long Life" 壽 appears on almost everything, including jewelry, clothing, and furniture. It would be a terrible faux pas to give a clock as a gift, simply because the pronunciation of the word "clock" is the same as that of the word "ending." Recently, many people in Taiwan decided to avoid using the number "four" because the number has a pronunciation similar to the word "death." Such a phenomenon prompted the editor of a famous newspaper to appeal to the public not to be so superstitious. He contends that the number "four" has always been considered a lucky number in China.

What causes such a discrepancy between what is written about Chinese people's attitudes toward death and what is practiced by them in real life? The question may be answered by examining the influence of Confucianism, Taoism, Buddhism, and superstition on forming their attitudes.

The Chinese have always been interested in issues of life and death. "Life and death are among the most popular problems with which traditional Chinese thought has been grappling unceasingly ever since the time of Confucius, and to which various kinds of answers have been given" (Yu, 1962, p. 24). However, the emphasis seems to have been laid more on the issue of life than on that of death. This emphasis on life as opposed to death by Chinese people can be found in the words of Confucius himself (555–479 B.C.). When one of his disciples asked, "What is death?" Confucius answered, "If we do not know about life, how can we know about death?" (Chan, 1963, p. 498). Confucianism centers on cultivating virtues of filial piety, righteousness, benevolence, conscientiousness, and altruism, while leaving such matters as life and death to heaven's will or fate.

Although Confucius rarely spoke of death, his teaching has had a profound influence on attitudes toward death in China. First of all, his emphasis on filial piety forms the foundation of ancestor worship, which leads people to believe that they will be remembered after death by their descendants and that their spirits will be nourished and appeased by such offerings as food, paper houses, and paper money. This lessens the fear of death for many people. In addition, the rules of funeral rites are spelled out in one of the Five Classics of Confucian literature, Li Chi (the Book of Rites). These rules, together with many customs and superstitions that have been added since the time of Confucius, have been followed for more than 2,000 years by the Chinese people.

Another dominant school of thought is Taoism, which also exerts a strong influence on Chinese attitudes toward life and death. "Tao" means "the Way," that is, the way the universe works and how it keeps a proper balance in all its relationships and activities. Taoism advocates returning to nature and letting nature run its course; it emphasizes simplicity, romanticism, and freedom of action or inaction following one's own spontaneous nature. As to the question of life and death, Taoists believe in the cultivation and prolongation of life by following the laws of nature, but see death as a natural development of life that should be accepted as a matter of course. They assert that life is the concentration of ch'i, or vital force, in the body. When there is ch'i, there is life; when the chi'i is exhausted, the person dies. Therefore, learning to increase ch'i in the body is essential to attaining longevity.

Despite their philosophical differences, both schools hold the Chinese classic I Ching (Book of Changes) in the highest esteem and deeply believe in its yin-yang theory. The essence of the yin-yang theory is that the universe is made up of two forces, yin and yang, which exist in everything. The yin force is associated with earth, darkness, female, cold, and death, whereas the yang force is associated with heaven, light, male, heat, and life. These two forces are in a constant state of change; they interact with each other on a continuum to achieve balance and harmony. A disturbance in the balance of these two forces results in disorder and chaos. According to *I Ching*, this principle of yin and yang applies to everything—from rotation of day and night to the management of government. The human body is seen as the universe in miniature; an imbalance of yin and yang leads to disease and death. So far as the question of human existence is concerned, this school of thought asserts that a person should strive to achieve balance between yin and yang, but accept death when it comes. This resignation to fate and acceptance of death may be called the Chinese people's "naturalistic view" of death.

Why, then, do Chinese fear the topic of death? The answer seems to lie in what may be called their "superstitious view" of death (Yu, 1962). As mentioned earlier, Taoists believe in cultivation and prolongation of life. Unfortunately, their love of nature and life was later misunderstood and distorted by some people. As a result, many superstitions and magical practices were added to the philosophy, and Taoism gradually evolved into a kind of religious cult. At first, people engaged in all sorts of activities, such as exercise, special diets, drugs, regulation of breathing, and different forms of sexual behavior in the hope that they would live longer. Later, this desire for longevity turned into a longing for "no death." According to Yu, the idea of "no death" became so popular in the Han Dynasty (206 B.C.–A.D. 220) that many people were sent to sea by the Emperor to search for "drugs of no death." The term "no death" was lavishly used to name many things. There were "no-death people," "no-death country," "no-death mountain," "no-death tree," and "no-death water." Eventually a new immortality cult evolved from this wordly desire for longevity. The followers of this cult wished to become immortals who would live in some faraway paradise. As a result, the Chinese people began to regard death as something bad that should be avoided.

In a different direction, the concept of immortality of the soul (the spirit of the dead) has an even greater impact on Chinese people's fear of death. The popular belief is that after death man turns into a Kuei, or ghost. While it is believed that all ghosts are powerful and that one should try to please them, many are believed to be so ugly and wicked that one should guard against them. Chinese often use the phrase "full of ghosts' ideas" to describe a cunning person. This researcher remembers some of the advice she received in her childhood: "Don't answer anyone's calling unless you can see the person and know who this person is!" or "Don't go near water after dark because water ghosts may drag you down with them!" Even today, many Chinese believe that ghosts can assume a human form and do harm to people. This fear of ghosts also undoubtedly contributes to Chinese people's anxiety about death.

In about A.D. 65, Buddhism was introduced to China from India. It spread rapidly and soon became firmly established. The Buddhist concept of rebirth, or reincarnation, and its systems of heaven and hell definitely reinforced the "superstitious view" of death among Chinese people. Buddhists believe that while the spirits of truly pure, good, and righteous persons go to the "Western Heaven" to live happily ever after, the rest will go to hell to be tortured before their reincarnation. Since no one wants to go to hell and no one is sure that he/she will not be sent to hell after death, the best way is to avoid death and live forever.

In summary, for a long period Chinese people viewed death as a natural event in life. They loved and treasured life, yet accepted death as man's final destination. Nevertheless, this "naturalistic view" of death was gradually replaced by beliefs in immortality, ghosts, and heaven and hell. Thus, death became associated with pain and horror. The impact of this "superstitious view" of death is so strong and widespread that today it is a dominant factor in the attitude toward death for Chinese in all walks of life. In the experience of this author, many Chinese hold the "superstitious view" when they are not facing death, but take the "naturalistic view" when death is at their doorstep.

Death is a human experience. No one's emotions are left untouched by a terminal illness or the death of a loved one. Many of the fears about death (physical pain and disfigurement, separation from loved ones, and abandonment by those who are in charge of care) and the needs of dying patients (physical comfort and grooming, realistic hope, and empathy) are universal (Simmons and Given, 1972; Kübler-Ross, 1969, 1975; Hampe, 1975; Freihofer and Filton, 1976; Paige, 1980). Nevertheless, a person's true feelings toward death can only be understood within the overall pattern of the person's life. As health professionals, our unfamiliarity with behavior, language, and custom, and lack of knowledge about a particular culture may drive us to seek refuge from our fears and anxieties by leaving those patients and their families in darkness and despair. Health professionals must develop their cultural sensitivity and assess such factors as ethnicity, language, family constellation, health and illness beliefs, and diet and nutritional preferences while planning care for their patients (Louie, 1984).

It is only through the identification of differences that the uniqueness of each person can be recognized, and individual needs of patients met. It is only through the identification of similarities that a common ground for humanity, understanding, and mutual respect among different cultures can be found, and the dream that "All men are brothers," as a Chinese saying goes, can become a reality.

REFERENCES

Chan, W. T. 1963. *A Sourcebook in Chinese Philosophy.* Princeton, NJ: Princeton University Press.

Day, C. B. 1978. *The Philosophers of China: Classical and Contemporary.* Secaucus, NJ: The Citadel Press.

Freihofer, P. and G. Felton. 1976. Nursing behaviors in bereavement: an exploratory study. *Nursing Research*, 25(5):332–337.

Hampe, S. O. 1975. Needs of the grieving spouse in a hospital setting. *Nursing Research.* 1975. 24(2):113–119.

Huang, W. W. 1983. Attitudes toward death among nurses, physicians, elementary school teachers, and professors in Taiwan, Republic of China. Ed.D. diss. Teachers College, Columbia University.

Kübler-Ross, E. 1969. *On Death and Dying.* New York: Macmillan.

Kübler-Ross, E. 1975. *Death: The Final Stage of Growth.* Englewood Cliffs, NJ: Prentice-Hall.

Lee, J. Y. 1975. *Death and Beyond in the Eastern Perspective: A Study Based on the Bardo Thodol and the I Ching.* New York: Gordon & Breach.

Yin, Y. T. 1939. *My Country and my People.* New York: John Day.

Louie, K. B. 1984. Cultural issues in psychiatric nursing. In *The American Handbook of Psychiatric Nursing.* ed. S. Lego. Philadelphia: J. B. Lippincott.

Paige, S. D. 1980. Alone into the alone. A phenomenological study of the experience of dying. Doctoral diss. Boston University. University Microfilms No. 80-24, 234.

Simmons, S., and B. Givens. 1972. Nursing care of the terminal patient. *Omega.* 3(3):217–225.

Yu, Y. S. 1962. Views of life and death in later Han China: A.D. 25–220. Ph.D. diss. Harvard University.

12

Death in the Maya Cosmos

Harold B. Haley and Francis X. Grollig

Records of the Maya exist from at least 2,000 B.C. to the present day. They lived in Southeast Mexico, Belize, Guatemala, Northwestern Honduras, and Northern El Salvador. Past and present, they speak many related languages; however, some of them are not mutually understandable in the past or now. The Maya were part of a general Mesoamerican culture with a considerable number of features distinct to the Maya.

Most of the literature about the Maya concerns those living in the so-called "Classic Period," which was approximately A.D. 200 to 700. In recent and current times, the very early Maya, back to 2000 B.C., have been studied in both Belize and the Yucatan. The "Pre-Classic Period" — roughly 300 B.C. to A.D. 200 — has been the subject of much recent archeological work and subsequent interpretation at the sites of Tikal, Uaxactun, and Kaminaluyu in Guatemala, and Cerros in Belize. Recent major works have been published about the "Early Classic Period," centering around A.D. 400, and the "Post-Classic Period" (Hellmuth, 1987; Sabloff and Andrews, 1986). We are therefore rapidly gaining knowledge of the Maya throughout the entire Pre-conquest period. In addition, the cultural anthropology, linguistics, and activities of modern-day Maya throughout the regions described are under study. Nevertheless, this chapter will refer primarily to the Classic Maya, with other time references indicated when appropriate.

The Maya were and are sophisticated people. They had a hieroglyph writing system, a highly developed calendar, were knowledgeable in astronomy (particularly the sun, Venus, and many different stars and their relationships to time), a good mathematics system (they discovered and used the concept of "0" before the Europeans did), many different superb art styles (including much beauty, imagery, and symbolism), and very important, a well-considered cosmology and religious system that was developed over time.

Politically, the Maya existed in independent cities and city-states. They were never a centrally controlled people, as later large empires were in Preconquest America. Their belief systems in religion were held across many language and political boundaries. Local variations are not well known.

The death beliefs of the Maya were part of their overall belief in religious systems. These can be looked at as part of the Mesoamerican culture, the generalized Maya belief systems, and local variations.

Beliefs, concepts, and practices concerning the Maya were and are an important part of their living. The literature contains a considerable number of fragmented studies, most of them interspersed in larger papers or chapters covering many subjects. In this chapter we will bring together data and thought on many facets of death in the Maya. For some topics we will present what appears to be an accepted current state of general knowledge or understanding. For other topics we will state positions that we currently hold. The following topics will be examined: sources of data and concepts, Maya beliefs, political aspects of Maya beliefs, ancestors and ancestor worship, the underworld, functions of Maya pyramid temples, necropoli, elders, euthanasia, and areas where research is needed.

When one speaks of beliefs or attitudes of a group of people such as the Maya, Aztec, or the people of Bombay, what are we really talking about? There is no single set of beliefs held by all of the people in any community or any culture. Presumably, this was as true in the past as it is today. The records available to us about the Maya are primarily of the elite in certain areas. We do not know how much difference occurred between areas. Within the same area there would be wide differences. A Central American village today can have active, as well as nominal, Roman Catholics. An increasing number of persons are also claiming allegiance to various protestant groups, from liberal to fundamental. In addition, some still believe in the old gods. It is said that there is a percentage of Satan worshippers. Finally, a significant number would not believe in any of the above. Human nature not having changed much, the same would probably have been true a thousand years ago. It is also difficult to establish when events occurred, because the Classic Maya flourished over a period of possibly 700 years. Surely there would have been some changes during that time. In this chapter we will discuss those beliefs we know, which, in most cases, represent the elite. The descendants of the people we are considering live today in isolated areas and often in a culture of poverty. In the past, these same groups did not live in cultures of poverty, yet there were probably wide ranges of belief then just as there are today.

Death beliefs are part of an overall religious belief system. Religious beliefs of the Maya are represented, and must be looked at, in three ways: (1) Maya representations of general Mesoamerican concepts and gods including rain, death, agricultural, sun, Venus, and underworld. The Maya and their beliefs about death, ancestors, underworld, etc., came centuries before the Aztecs, but both relate to other general Mesoamerican concepts; (2) Those adaptations that appear to be Maya and different from other Mesoamerican. Included here are animism (Maya identification with earth, water, caves, animals, plants), legends exemplified by *Popol Vuh*, humanness and personalism of religious artistic expression, and individualization of ancestors; and (3) Local belief systems. The Maya never had persistent centralized governments and therefore must have had considerable local variation in beliefs. Differing burial practices are one evidence of this.

The study of any belief system of the Maya uses several kinds of materials. Some data is obtained from records of precontact time, including archaeological materials, four Maya Codices, any other pre-Columbian writings or presumably authentic Post-conquest recollection of previous beliefs, and interpretation of ceramics, stelae, wall panels, lintels, and other art forms. The difficulty with these materials is that one interprets them from personal viewpoints and not within the context of the people who created them.

Shortly after the conquest many samples of oral tradition or material from earlier Maya writings were converted into Spanish, and have become important sources of history of the Maya. Many have been authenticated historically by archeological findings, which suggest that their general validity is probably good. The best known translation is *Popol Vuh*, a history of the highland Maya in Guatemala (Edmonson, 1971; Tedlock, 1985). There is a series of 14 others, the *Chilam Balam*, from various specific locations, and the history of these locations. Another source is *The Annals of Cakichels*. Within all of these documents are records of some customs and beliefs in specific areas. A major example of universal beliefs is the lowland Peten pots illustrating highland Quiche myths of the Popol Vuh.

Mural paintings have been found on walls in a number of sites. Bonampak in the Usamacinta Valley, Tancah and Tulum in Quintana Roo on the far eastern coast of Mexico, Chacmultun in the Yucatan, Cacaxtla in Central Mexico, and Santa Rita in Belize all show strong Maya influences. There are death scenes in some of these paintings, but, in general, they are not a very important source.

Pottery, or ceramics, presents a very important source of material about who the Maya were, what they believed in, and how they lived. Michael Coe has insisted for years that the Classic Maya pottery basically shows scenes referring to the underworld and death (Coe, 1975). This points out that much of our knowledge of the Maya is not only based on the elite, but also on bural materials and funeral practices. This narrows that part of the total culture of which we have knowledge and understanding.

The second source of material is the conquest-era recordings of various Spanish persons working with the Maya people. For this topic, there has been much reliance on the materials from Bishop Landa as translated either by Tozzer (1941) or Landa (1937). Some of the statements made by Landa's informants lack face validity. They do not appear to be consistent with other information concerning the Maya and also tend to suggest that these informants were either Christianized or were telling Bishop Landa what they thought he wanted to hear.

A third source, which offers fascinating information that is difficult to interpret or apply, relates to the customs, practices, and beliefs of the modern Maya. There are many difficulties in using these data as an index to what the Classic Maya thought. To begin with, there is the thousand-year lapse of time. In addition, the modern Maya are isolated and tend not to be part of the mainstream of the large countries of which they are a part. Their viewpoint tends to be local, that is, of their own village. They also are working in a culture of poverty as opposed to a full social spectrum, which included the grandeur of the Classic Maya. Another factor is that the many excellent anthropological studies of Maya villages show many local variations in beliefs and practices. This naturally raises the question of whether or not the same local variation occurred in Classic Maya days as it does today. A guess would be that it probably did. It was probably true then, but the paucity of actual data does not give the proof needed.

MAYA BELIEF SYSTEM, INCLUDING BELIEFS ABOUT DEATH

The overall cosmology or belief system of the Maya incorporates religious beliefs and beliefs about death. Many of the beliefs are pan-Mesoamerican and also occur across long periods of time. We will try to identify those concepts that are Maya, particularly Classic Maya, across both time and distance. The term "Maya" is probably localized to individual places and times to fit the needs, understandings, self-images, and political relationships of local people, customs, geography, and resources. This means trying to think conceptually about how many different Maya there were. In addition, consideration must be given to those central Mexican intrusions (Teotihuacan, Toltec, etc.) that can be identified. Maya death beliefs appear to relate to religious beliefs, but also to the day-to-day living in which deaths of animals, plants, and humans were all regularly seen.

People do have some control over their own activities, but have little or no control over external factors. Natural disasters, such as storms, volcanic eruptions, or earthquakes, cannot be controlled by humans. Neither can the external forces exerted by rulers, large organized groups, and other viable pressure sources. Many events are explainable by these contacts. Yet many community beliefs are based on beliefs of individuals. This leads to thinking in the realm of religion. Where did human beings come from? If we were created, a creator is implied and raises a question of continuing influence and power of the creator. The concept of supernatural beings, that is, people who are not subject to the same laws and limitations of life and activity as are mortals, begins to emerge. Does the universe influence supernaturals and naturals? Do the supernaturals influence the universe and humans? Can the supernaturals affect rainfall, temperature, fertility (of humans and of agriculture), plagues and other illnesses, and thus affect factors that greatly influence the way humans live? If such supernaturals exist, who are they and where did they come from?

This idea of the supernatural leads to one of the most important concepts of mortals, one that causes the exercise of religious practices and raises the question "How can humans influence the supernaturals and the cosmos as a whole?" Of all of the events in human life, death is one of the most important and probably the one over which mortals have the least control. This, therefore, is a strong stimulus for humans to search for the meaning of death, why it occurs, what happens later, and how they can exert control over the supernaturals or any other factors that affect all these aspects of death.

In the last decade, many writings have emphasized the Mayan preoccupation with death. In the decade before, many writings emphasized the Mayan preoccupation with time. As one visits Mayan sites of various sizes in various locations, one is impressed with other aspects. Agriculture was obviously one of the great concerns because mortals have to eat. The larger the Mayan site, the more one is impressed with major architecture of all kinds. Some structures are shelters only, but many serve other functions and suggest a variety of activities. Time and death certainly are part of these activities, but the whole general aspect of living, including religion, government, political organizations, entertainment, and all group activities of mortals provide another area of Mayan preoccupation. Which of these receives the most emphasis? Or does a preoccupation become primarily a question of the viewpoint of the observer?

When trying to find relationships among these various concepts, one becomes aware ideas of cyclicity, dualism, and continuity of life appear to be of great importance of the Maya. Cyclicity and dualism may be two separate concepts, or they may be different ways of looking at the same concept. In the Maya world, as well as our own, mortals live with many cycles. The cycle of day and night is the most obvious. The general cycle of the year is another. Obviously related to both of these is the sun. The Maya early recognized the Venus cycle. The simple human need of survival forces the recognition of agricultural cycles. This would easily lead to the next intellectual step of death and rebirth as a cycle. Many of these cycles seem to be built on rhythmic alternation of opposites, such as day/night, young/old, and so forth.

There are other aspects of dualism besides the calendric. These include health/illness, good/bad, male/female, and so on. One could then take the position that the Maya were extremely conscious of the cyclicity and dualism of life and that time and death were part of this larger conception. All of this then folds into the continuity of life as manifested in the noncyclical Maya long-count calender. This cyclicity and dualism may be the reason that the Maya seemed to fear death less than modern persons. Schele and Miller (1986) describe this as follows.

> For the Maya, the anticipation of death must have been sharp. Life expectancy was shorter than it is today, infant mortality was higher, and everyone, elite as well as commoner, lived with warfare and sacrificial ritual as ever-present realities. The immediacy of death lead the Maya to dedicate much of the ritual and art to the defeat of death's final grip on their lives. Depictions on objects of all types treat the whole process of death, from the soul's entrance into the Maya Hell called Xibalba, to a final apotheosis or rebirth. We will see that much of the mythology in funerary art describes death as a journey whose challenges were known. Death's special imagery is found on coffins, wall paintings, pottery jades, and other objects that accompany the dead into their graves and guided them in their confrontation with the Lords of Death.

The death/rebirth concept was possibly best expressed in the Tomb of Pacal, which is in the shape of the uterus, suggesting a spiritual rebirth, according to Ruz (1970): "Dr. Franz Termer as well as the author are of the opinion that the cavity was made in this strange shape as a stylized representation of the womb. Burial in such a cavity would be a return to the mother by association of the concepts of mother and earth, sources of life." Ruz also makes a point that the Maya, unlike the Mexicans, seemed less obsessed in their art with real human death, but that this is compensated for by a greater presence of death in abstract form, especially in symbols that appear frequently.

One of the ways of looking at the Maya cosmos is that mortals live in a unity of time. The Maya of any era lived under the influence of gods and ancestors from the past and in anticipation of becoming ancestors in the future. The same gods existed in the past, affect things in the present, and will be in the future. These gods, in each phase, may be the same or may be in different manifestations. Likewise, mortals existed before in previous lives, live today, and will exist in the future, perhaps as ancestors.

The other part of the Maya cosmos is the unity of the universe. In the unity of the universe, the earth, air, water, plants, animals, and heavenly bodies were alive. These aspects of life were not just alive, but interacted. This is best shown in the concepts and representations of the underworld where all of these are shown (often symbolically) and interact with each other. The cyclicity of time, earth, and other aspects of living are then all parts of this larger unity of the cosmos.

A final consideration is made to the many bridges between humans and other times and other live media. The Hero Twins are a bridge between the middleworld and the underworlds. Priests and shamans, kings and autosacrifice were bridges with the ancestors. Ancestors were perhaps bridges to the gods, or were gods themselves. These bridges are included in the overall cosmology or belief systems within the Maya culture. They are an integral part of the religious beliefs and, as stated before, a part of the death beliefs.

POLITICAL ASPECT OF DEATH BELIEFS

The art, architecture, and legends of the Maya are primarily of the elite people. Studies of tombs, cemeteries, and other burials clearly show stratification of society very early in Maya times. Common people were frequently buried unaccompanied in the ground, whereas great rulers had tombs and were accompanied by people and gods. There were many stages between these two extremes, again as described by Ruz (1983):

In the funeral rituals, the chronicles reveal a differentiation in the treatment which is given to the corpse, according to the social category of the individual: incineration for the lords and important people whose ashes were kept in earthenware urns or in wooden statues; and simple graves, below or in back of the hut for the common people. Archaeology has succeeded in defining an entire scale of values for the different kinds of burials, in accordance with the level which the deceased occupied in society: a simple burial in an open grave in the ground, a grave lined on the inside with stone slabs and closed with a stone and a chamber with walls and a domed roof. The grave can be found below the floor of a hut, inside a civil or religious structure, inside a platform or in the interior of a mound built with funeral ends; some were decorated with mural paintings. The burial could be individual or communal, and in the latter case it is easy to recognize the remains which correspond to the principal personage and those of his companions, the victims sacrificed to attend him in the beyond. The number and quality of the objects deposited as offerings vary also according to the same scale. The maximum funeral construction that we know in all the American continent is beyond any doubt the impressive crypt constructed on the inside of the Temple of Inscriptions in Palenque which contains a colossal sarcophagus of stone covered with low reliefs which provide indications of the lord buried there. The richness of the architectonic unit, of the grave and offerings, throw light on the political, social and religious importance that he would have had.

All of this points to the stratification of society. Leaders must have people to lead. Those people must be given motivation, stimuli, or if necessary, coercion to be followers of the leaders. Persuasion can take many forms. Force is one, but there are others. Political beliefs should be important. Religious beliefs appear to be important. The Maya political leaders used religious belief as a political force. At given times and places, we are not certain how organized, structured, or formalized the Maya beliefs and practices were. One does not know how much the religion, beliefs, and practices resulted from motives and methods of individual people (often rulers) or particular cult groups. How much of religion was a metaphysical belief system and how much of it was an instrument of self-justification, political opportunity, or an organizer of group efforts poses interesting questions.

The ancient Maya were at least as skilled as we are at psychology and politics. The uses of religion by Pacal, Chan Bahlum, and Kan Xul (Robertson, 1978) would be valuable to Papa Doc and Baby Doc or, for that matter, to the leader of Singapore who is now trying to bring his son along as a successor.

Every Maya site from which we have appropriate material identifies and shows the lineal and family relationships, accomplishments, and some of the rulers. The rulers are frequently shown in religious contexts. "Priests" are shadow figures not presented in specific identifications. The relationship appears to be rulers and gods, best identified as ancestors. The priest is one of the helper levels rather than the controlling factor. This supports the proposal that religion in all its pomp and circumstance was an appeal to the Maya heart and soul, which for the Maya was primarily a political expression.

ANCESTORS AND ANCESTOR WORSHIP

Ancestor worship was evident in Pre-Classic, Classic, and Late Classic times, as well as at the Conquest and in the present. Ancestors are found in many places. In the highlands they are resident in sacred mountains; in all areas they may be found in temples, in houses, under floors, and in the heavens.

As part of the Maya cosmos where all factors are alive and interact, ancestors are alike and are in communication with mortals in the Middleworld. Ancestors set standards of morality, give guidance, and punish infraction by bringing illness, which may be mild or severe depending on the infraction.

There appear to be four kinds of ancestors: old ancestor gods, lineage patron gods, recently deceased leaders, and recently deceased commoners. The old ancestor gods are accepted by the community and have general powers and influence. These frequently are the Maya equivalents of general Mesoamerican deities. Lineage patron gods are chosen by a ruling family as "their" god. The Palenque Triad, especially God K, is a good example. Another example is the Jaguar God of the Underworld as a lineage patron god at Tikal. The recent leaders or elite are cremated after death. Their ashes are placed in urns, in skulls, or in sacred locations and are idolized, at least by the elite and possibly by commoners. The hieroglyphic stairway (Structure 26) at Copan has five large seated figures representing early kings who are now revered ancestors. At Tikal on early stelae the ancestor was usually depicted as a face gazing down from above, providing a kind of a pedigree for the ruler. R. E. W. Adams (1977) describes "royal cults" as the practice of regarding the elite as semi-divine who survive physical death and continue to influence this world from the afterlife. These local ancestral gods are specific for a given locale. There is no information about how Copan ex-ruler ancestral gods were regarded at Tikal. Finally, commoners who die become ancestors, and are accepted as supernaturals by the family with power and influence on families and individual family members. There are altars and shrines to these family ancestors in private homes. Unknown is the definition of which commoners become ancestors. Is it only male heads of families? Can wives, single persons, or children who die become ancestors?

The deification of ancestors was common. This seems to have been a heavily political position. The "royal cults" again appear to be of political use in the belief system. Freidel and Schele (1983) point out that the Maya elite asserted that they were the direct descendents of the Hero Twins, while commoners were lateral lined. Again, this is a political issue of the elite asserting, "We are leaders because we are divine and we are different from you."

People communicated with the ancestors in a number of ways. They did so directly. They communicated through priests or shamans. They did so through their leaders. One way of communicating was in hallucinatory rituals or rites calling forth a Visual Serpent from whose mouth a person, probably an ancestor, is emerging. We need to know more about the uses of each of these and the actual meaning and beliefs related to each. Ancestor worship appears to be prevalent through the Maya, but is not universal in all Mesoamerican society.

The Underworld Relation to Other Worlds

How many worlds were there? The Maya appear to have had an Upperworld (the heavens), a Middleworld (human world), and an Underworld. Not much thought has been given to the Upperworld, other than references to thirteen levels. Was there geography? Were there a number of Upperworlds? Was there a physical heaven? Was there a spiritual or supernatural heaven occupied by many different parties? If so, would there have been heavens for the old ancestor gods who moved around pretty freely? Some suggest that another place for more current ancestors may be in the Northern Heavens, perhaps around the North Star (Schele and Miller, 1986). What kind of space are the family ancestors in? Are they also inhabiting the Middleworld or do they have a corner of the Upperworld? Is the Upperworld made up of the sun, the moon, Venus, and all the other named and characterized heavenly bodies plus those that are not named and characterized? The imagination can float rather freely in considertion of possibilities of Upperworlds.

Because of the legends and representations in art, there are more specifics to think about in the Underworld. Our feeling is that there was one functioning Maya Underworld, but that more data are needed. One reason for confusion probably comes from the difficulty in determining whether or not the "Nine Lords of the Night" are the same as the gods or lords of the Underworld. The meaning of "Lords" is vague. There are many more than nine gods of the Underworld; some are well defined but are defined differently in different sources. Many are undefined. One funereal pot shows fourteen figures that probably are "gods." Some authorities recognize hundreds of supernaturals. We do not know if these are discrete individuals or different manifestations of a supernatural concept. For example, is there a concept of an animal god with many representations, including mythical composite animals, as well as clearly identified realistic animals? Some of the questions would be, Is Itzamna a god of the Upperworld who is the same god in the Underworld, or is Itzamna a vague creature called the "Old God"? Is he God L, God N, God D, God A? Are Gods L and N the same as Gods One Death and Seven Death as described in *Popol Vuh*? Is there a hierarchy of gods in the Underworld, and how does this relate to the concept of Nine Levels and Nine Gods? Again we think that there is one functioning Underworld. The nine levels appear to be significant, but are not interpretable with present data. The nine levels may be a concept carried from the Maya to Central Mexico. Hellmuth (1987) states:

> I believe a model of nine trials, nine hazards, or nine stages of situations is more
> likely than nine steps or later. Nine places, perhaps, but in the Maya situation
> it is not possible to offer scientific, pictorial, linguistic, epigraphic, ethnohistoric,
> or ethnographic evidence for an Aztec model. Chilam Balam is not acceptable
> for Pre-Toltec Period for Southern Low Land.

The situation is complicated by other ways in which the number "nine" enters the picture. The Temple of the Inscriptions at Palenque, Temple I at Tikal, Temple A-III at Rio Azul, the Castillo at Chichen Itza, and Structure 16 at Copan each have nine tiers. If each temple exists primarily as a ruler's tomb and that ruler is a god, then the question is whether or not each of the nine tiers represents a level of the Underworld that the ruler goes through. This is possible, and is an interesting concept; however, it is not definitive.

The Underworld Itself

"What is the Underworld?" is a question that needs much data and thought. It may have a geography. There may be different locations in the Underworld. Each may have different resident gods, ancestors, dead people wandering around, and various real and mythical animals, birds, and plants. There appear to be at least three broad kinds of underworlds. There are the After-Life areas, which we assume to be underworlds, but presumably could be upperworlds where people who died special deaths go. "Special" means those who died in battle, in childbirth, by drowning or lightning, and by suicide. There are presumably other special categories that we have not identified. It is important to emphasize here that these categories depend on the manner of death or the occupation at the time of death. The quality of living and style of living do not appear to affect this.

A second category of individuals, who may have had special treatment, are the rulers. There are some suggestions that rulers, immediately after death, go to the heavens as ancestor gods. There are other strong suggestions that rulers go to Xibalba and must go through the trials and obstacles encountered by the Hero Twins as described in the *Popol Vuh*. Some would successfully overcome the trials, would climb the World Tree, and be freed into the heavens, probably the Northern Heavens, as new ancestral gods who would live forever and become old ancestral gods. This does not imply, however, that everyone overcomes the obstacles and trials. Does this mean that those who do not overcome the trials stay in the Underworld forever? Can they make new efforts to overcome the trials and therefore leave to become ancestors? This then leads to the consideration of who else besides the rulers can accomplish this. Or do the ruler's wife and children, when they die, go to Xibalba and encounter the same trials and have the same alternatives? Are there other people who go through this chain of experience? Are these the ones we are calling the "elite"? Are the "elite" the prime ministers, the lawyers, the money changers, the artists, and other parts of the ruler's entourage? Are the ruler's cousins, distant relatives, and illegitimate offspring also included in the entourage?

The third category are the commoners. When they die, there is a suggestion that they wander in the labyrinth of Xibalba. At times they are in contact with the gods, and after four years may leave the Underworld and become family ancestors. Commoners are not well represented in art, architecture, and legend, therefore, not much information is available.

It is most important to emphasize here that the Underworld may be a dismal, unpleasant place where unpleasant things can happen. This appears to be the nature of the place. What happens in this area does not clearly seem to result from how one lived in the Middleworld. It may result from one's occupation, one's status in life, or what one was doing at the time of death; however, it doesn't appear to relate to whether one is "good" or "bad." Stated another way, the Christian concept of "hell" is different from the Maya concept of Xibalba.

With so much fascinating interpretative work having been done in the last few years concerning the nature and meaning of the Underworld (by Coe, Schele, Quirarte, Robicsek, Hellmuth, Miller, and many others) and some very rich recent publications in this area, we do not plan to go into similar discussions. However, the need for allegorical thinking about these materials should be emphasized. For example, in the Popol Vuh the Hero Twins destroy each other and later are restored. This is alleged to so excite the gods One Death and Seven Death, Lords of the Underworld, that they ask the Hero Twins to do the same with them. In the legend, the Hero Twins do kill One Death and Seven Death, cut up their bodies, but then do not restore them to life. The Hero Twins are then free to leave the Underworld and ascend to the Upperworld. This is a delightful legend and is pictured in story and on pottery. Presumably, Lords of the Underworld would be too smart actually to make themselves this vulnerable. An allegorical explanation is that physical death of the Underworld gods is not actually needed. By being clever and tricking the Lords, the Hero Twins degrade and symbolically "kill" the Lords. This is an example for the Maya to do things cleverly, symbolically, and indirectly rather than by direct confrontation.

There is a somewhat similar ancient Greek myth about two good witches and an old king who had two wicked daughters. The witches killed a sheep, cut it up, and then boiled it. From the boiling water a young, fine lamb emerged. The daughters enticed the king to submit to the same procedure. He did, only to die. Then there is the story of St. Patrick who talked the Irish snake into entering a box. The good saint then quickly locked and threw the box into the ocean.

THE FUNCTIONS OF THE MAYA PYRAMID TEMPLES

Recently there has been some debate whether the primary function of the pyramid was that of a temple, and then because it was there, burials occurred. The opposing view was that the structures were primarily built as burial places for rulers. At present, it would seem that the Maya pyramid temples served many different functions, probably simultaneously but with different emphases at different times and as constructed by different people.

Some of the possible, or real functions, would include the following:

1. A tomb for the ruler and others that the builder thought appropriate
2. A portal to the Underworld for the person whose tomb it was
3. A site to be used for the deification and worship of ancestors
4. A setting and a format for people to communicate with their ancestors, divine or not
5. A site for rites, rituals, and religious events
6. A site for political activities

7. A site for propaganda
8. A way of organizing people's labor in construction and possibly their loyalties and beliefs in making this the center of some other aspects of their lives
9. A way to implement the self-agrandizement of rulers or cults
10. A place involving life, death, politics, social activity, and entertainment
11. A part of a large complex including its associated plaza and nearby structures
12. A way of using the sky, clouds, trees, and all of nature as a backdrop for their theater of life
13. All of the above

The same structure was probably used in different ways over different times. The various temples that were built by rulers to memorialize themselves or their parents or spouses probably had that as a significant concept for some period of time. The significance, then, decreased with each katun as new rulers (gods) built their own memorials. As each site grew, different temples were each dedicated to a different ex-ruler who was now an ancestral god. Through this growth, the significance of each ex-ruler must have diminished, but the status of the whole lineage may have been strengthened. After a while, whose temple it was may or may not be important. A named memorial continues to have functions and changing functions over time, even though the intent and even the memory of the original naming may have been left behind.

NECROPOLI

At the Mesa Redonda de Palenque in 1973, there were suggestions that some peripheral Maya sites should be considered Necropoli. Various arguments have been presented for Palenque, Copan, Tulum, and others to be considered as Necropoli. We agree with the opposing concept presented by Foncerrado de Molina (1974). Jaina is an isolated area with several large pryamids and many elaborate burials, probably of people brought from a distance to be buried there (Pina Chan, 1968). These may very well have been both primary and secondary burials. Necropolis is defined in the dictionary as "city of the dead." A second definition was cemetery, especially a large elaborate cemetery or an ancient city. A "city of the dead" indicates that the area of the burials would have been a special site in which death and the remains of those who had died were a purpose in themselves. Such may have been the case at Jaina (Corson, 1976).

Most Maya sites in which appropriate excavations have been carried out have shown large numbers of burials. Many exhibit organized planned ways of burying people. There are definite elaborate burials for the elite. From this it could be concluded that every Maya town had cemeteries as any other town does. These cemeteries were divided into different social levels. This seems to reiterate that the concept of a unique place for the dead probably does not apply to many Maya locations.

ELDERS AND EUTHANASIA

Not much data is found on the role of elders in Maya society. Landa (1937) describes this ritual:

> They sought among them an old woman, the most decrepit and advanced in years they could find, and they took her out to the country, the whole town accompanying her, and they looked for a crossroad or meeting place of many roads and seated her there, and hemmed in and surrounded by all, in loud voices and all at once each one confessed and publicly told his sins and guilts. And when that shouted and tumultuous confession was finished, the priest drew near with a great stone and struck the poor old woman so many blows on the head that he killed her, and when she was dead the whole town and all the confessants approached and covered her with stone in a moment, erecting and raising over her a great tomb, and with this the sacrifice and confession came to an end and they returned to their own houses completely convinced that now all their sins were taken away and that the town remained purified and clean on account of that sacrifice and the poor woman bore the sins of all on her shoulders to represent them there to their gods to appease their anger (page 226).

Landa (Tozzer), on page 20, footnote 123, states "Avendano tells us, as quoted by Roys (1933, 178) that they (the Itzas) have the custom of beheading the older men when they reach the age of 50 so that they shall not learn to be wizards and to kill except the priests of their idols, for whom they have great respect."

In the Maya representation of gods there are many representations of what is known as the "old god." Many different gods are presented as old gods. Many other figures are shown who may not be gods, but have old faces.

None of these scattered data are definitive. Certainly the fact that people grow old is recognized. Gods may be old. The oldest woman found was used as the scapegoat for society. The Avendano quote suggests a worry about unusual powers of elderly men. None of this is definitive.

No good records of euthanasia are found. Presumably this concept was not present in the Maya society.

AREAS OF NEEDED RESEARCH

The concepts discussed in this chapter are all tenuous. More information, more data, and better interpretations are needed. Some topics present themselves with particular needs.

In recent years the Underworld has received a tremendous amount of attention, primarily based on funerary pottery and the interpretation of Popol Vuh (Robicsek and Hales, 1981). We have probably gone almost as far as we can with the available data. That data is still sketchy and further information will be most welcome.

An important specific aspect of this is more precise identification and understanding of the gods of the Maya, including the death gods. A current analysis of some important classic Maya gods is found in a recent provocative book (Schele and Miller, 1986). A recent dissertation further defines Maya gods.

The pictorial material should be looked at again, looking for individuals who can be identified as priests, shamans, or other "religious" leaders.

Data concerning the role of elderly people are very sketchy. Again, more insight will depend on more literature and materials.

Women seem to have almost no place in the representation of religious belief systems. The *Dresden Codex* shows the goddess, Ixchel, in many settings. There are women on many of the pots, in the murals, and on stelae, but their roles have not been studied.

The meanings and roles of the ball game in politics, religion, and death is an area of slowly increasing understanding. More is needed.

Most of present thinking is monolithic. We speak of the Maya, or of rulers, or of people in a particular site, such as Piedras Negras, Tikal, and so on. Detailed study should give us more individualization of who these people were, what they did, and what they thought. Did the Maya have any Aknatens? Were there rebels? Were there great innovators? What were the roles of individual leaders?

Much more thought needs to be given to possible Maya intrusions into Central Mexico. Xochicalco and Cacaxtla both show that the Maya did have presence and presumably influence in other areas. Did general Mesoamerican gods begin with early Maya and conceptually migrate to Central Mexico, or vice versa? So far, not much study has been given to Maya concepts in the religious systems in Central Mexico.

CONCLUSIONS

This chapter presents many concepts relating to different aspects of the Maya beliefs about death. The principal concepts are as follows.

(1) Humans live in a unity of time. The Maya lived under the influence of gods and ancestors from the past and in anticipation of becoming ancestors in the future. Time is both cyclical and linear.

(2) Unlike other Mesoamerican people, the Maya occupy the cosmos including the earth, air, water, plants, animals, and heavenly bodies. All of these interact in the Upperworld, Middleworld, and Underworld.

(3) Maya religious beliefs are primarily political. They are developed and used by the elite for purposes of establishing and maintaining their own positions and for controlling and organizing common people. Theology, philosophy, and cosmology exist to advance the political power of the leaders.

(4) Ancestors are extremely important in the Maya world. There appear to be four kinds of ancestors: the old ancestral gods, many of them Maya representations of general Mesoamerican gods; old gods adopted as lineage patron gods by local dynasties; recent leaders who upon death become local ancestral gods; and individual persons who upon death become family ancestors.

(5) The Maya had an Upperworld, a Middleworld, and an Underworld. The number of Underworlds, number of levels of Underworlds, and the actual functions of the Underworld are all speculative questions; at present, however, there appears to be one functioning Underworld, possibly with different geographical locations and occupied by many different kinds of beings.

(6) The Maya Underworld is not the Christian Hell. Location in the underworld appears to be a function of occupation or manner of death and not a function of how one lived in the human (middle) world. The Underworld is not a place of specific punishment. Rather, it appears to be a place of challenge. In addition, there appear to be different Underworlds for different people. Those who die in given situation, those who are rulers, and those who are commoners may have different afterlives.

(7) None of the data reviewed give any evidence for the concept of euthanasia in Maya society.

REFERENCES

Adams, R. E. W. 1977. *Prehistoric America.* Boston: Little, Brown & Co.

Coe, Michael D. 1975. Death and the Ancient Maya. In *Death and the Afterlife in Pre-Columbian America.* Ed. E. P. Benson. Washington, D.C.: Dumbarton Oaks.

Corson, Christopher. 1976. *Maya Anthropomorphic Figurines from Jaina Island, Campeche.* Ramona, California: Ballera Press.

Edmonson, Munro S. 1971. *The Book of Counsel: The Popol Vuh of the Quiche Maya of Guatemala.* New Orleans: Tulane University.

Friedel, David, and Schele, Linda. 1983. *Symbol and Power: A History of the Lowland Maya Cosmogram.* Princeton Conference.

Hellmuth, Nicholas. 1987. *Monsters and Men in Maya Art.* Graz: Adeva.

Landa, D. 1937. *Yucatan Before and After the Conquest.* Trans. W. Gates. Baltimore: May Society.

Molina, Foncerrado de. 1974. Reflexiones en torno a Palenque como Necropolis. In *Primera Mesa Redonda de Palenque Part II.* Ed. M. G. Robertson. Pebble Beach, California: Robert Louis Stevenson School.

Pina Chan, Roman. 1968. *Jaina La Casa En El Agua.* Mexico: Inah.

Robertson, M.G. 1978. An Iconograph Approach to the Identity of the Figures on the Piers of the Temple of Inscriptions, Palenque. In *Tercera Mesa Redonda De Palenque, Volume IV.* Eds. M. G. Robertson and D. C. Jeffers. Palenque: Pre-Columbian Art Research Center.

Robicsek, F., and Hales, D. M. 1981. *The Maya Book of the Dead.* Charlottesville, Virginia: University of Virginia. (Rollout photograph by Justin Kerr, Vessel 30, page 25.)

Ruz-Lhullier, Alberto. 1970. *The Civilization of the Ancient Maya.* Mexico: INAH.

Ruz-Lhuillier, Alberto. 1983. *The Mayas.* Mexico: Fund. Cult., San Jeronimo Lidice.

Sabloff, J. A., and Andrews V. E. W. 1986. *Late Lowland Maya Civilization.* University of New Mexico.

Schele, L., and Miller, M. E. 1986. *Blood of Kings.* Fort Worth: Kimbell Art Museum.

Tedlock, Dennis. 1985. *Popol Vuh (The Mayan Book of the Dawn of Life).* New York: Simon and Schuster.

Tozzer, A. M. 1941. *Landa's Relacion De Las Cosas De Yucatan.* Ed. A. M. Tozzer. Cambridge, Mass.: Peabody Museum.

PART 2

Multi-Disciplinary Perspectives

13

The Ethics of Certain Death:
Suicide, Execution, and Euthanasia

Christie Davies

Nothing is more certain and nothing more uncertain than death. Each human being knows that he or she will die eventually, but not how or when. However, it is possible to make statistical calculations of two kinds about death. One can enter into a computer personal characteristics such as age, sex, occupation, income, ancestry, weight, cigarette consumption, and so forth, and be given a rough estimate as to his or her life expectancy. Also, people suffering from a particular illness may be told that they have only so many months to live, even though this too is a statement of probabilities; many people have lived for decades despite such a prediction.

The causes of death of a particular individual can be both random and unplanned. This is true even of most deaths brought about by a human agency. For example, in war when armies clash or planes bomb a city, the aim is generally to kill enemy soldiers or civilians as a group, not particular individuals. Bullets and bombs do not have anyone's name on them, whatever the superstitious may believe. Snipers may deliberately pick out officers as targets rather than enlisted men, but usually any officer will suffice: they are shooting at a category, not at an identified individual. Those in charge of long-range artillery or aerial bombing are even less concerned with specific individuals as opposed to aggregates.

Furthermore, informal rules are often observed in the middle of a battle concerning the non-killing of particular individuals at the mercy of the elements and rendered temporarily unable to fight. If a ship is sunk or an airplane is shot down, those responsible for the act may refrain from shooting the sailors struggling to escape from the wreck or the aircrew who have bailed out even though these men are often highly trained and skilled (who cannot necessarily be assumed to have surrendered) and can be of great value to the enemy. The greatest oddity, though, is the taboo against assassination, not just of politicians and military leaders — which might be attributed to the operation of an informal "top-people's labor union" — but even of particularly skilled officers. In World War II, when Britain was being bombed by the Luftwaffe from bases near the French coast, with casualties, substantial material damage, and even potential defeat, a senior officer in the Commandos suggested to an even more senior RAF officer that an attack should be made on a Luftwaffe base, known to have previously mounted particularly effective and deadly attacks on British cities. The Commandos would land silently, overpower the guards, sneak up on the known Luftwaffe aces in their billets and cut their throats. The scheme was rejected as being assassination and, therefore, impermissible. Attacks were later made on U-boat bases on the French Atlantic coast. However, to the surprise of the German submariners, these attacks were never on the U-boat commanders or personnel, nor on the commander-in-chief's chateau at Kernevel, even though it was close to the sea[1] and easy to attack!

At the other extreme of human conflict is the case of a duel between two people, where clearly there is a risk of one person killing the other. The key word here is "risk," for a duel, by definition, must offer some chance of success to the weaker party so that the outcome is not certain in advance; the rules of duelling ensure this. Either, or both, or neither of the participants may be killed in a duel. Duelling is stupid, morally wrong, and unjust, and the rulers of a centralized state, wishing to preserve their monopoly of violence and of the institutional resolution of conflicts, may make the killing of a man in a duel a capital offense. But in the eyes of those who uphold the duelling code, the uncertainty of the outcome of a duel distinguishes this form of killing from murder as just.[2]

Premeditated murder is a clear instance of a lawless termination of a person's life at a time decided by the murderer. In most modern western societies such an act produces an intense sense of moral outrage, indignant repudiation, and demands punishment rather than compensation—a sharp contrast to the public reaction to death in "normal" warfare or death as a result of gross human negligence. I have inserted the word "normal" to stress that even in wartime there are rules protecting innocent individuals from being selectively, but arbitrarily killed under the guise or in the confusion of wars between nation-states. The punishment of war criminals is based, at least in theory, on this principle.

There remain several controversial acts involving the deliberate taking of human life, which creates problems when we try to fit them into the simple moral dichotomy outlined so far—i.e. suicide, execution, and euthanasia. My aim here is to examine critically some of the curious moral arguments and decisions in relation to these difficult issues with the intention of introducing a little doubt and rationality.

Western societies have undergone a gradual weakening of the traditional moral condemnation of suicide; consequently, society generally tends to feel pity and sympathy for the person who has died, rather than moral horror and outrage. Indeed, those who maintain the old view may be regarded as callous reactionaries. Suicide has since been redefined as a medical or psychiatric problem, rather than a moral one. In some ways there is a degree of benign humbug involved, for many of those who commit suicide are sane individuals who have made a rational choice. The verdict "the deceased took his or her own life while the balance of mind was disturbed" is often reached on flimsy evidence or by circular reasoning, and the more-or-less compulsory psychiatric treatment of those who try but fail is not necessarily justified, although it may be a reasonable general precaution.

The more interesting contemporary moral issues relating to suicide arise when others are involved. (Euthanasia will be discussed separately later.) Here I wish to look at the cases where suicide impinges on other forms of deliberate killing involving the use of state power.

The use of capital punishment by the state is in itself a source of moral controversy. For reasons of retribution, deterrence, or incapacitation, the state decrees that persons convicted of a capital crime have the right to have a definite date fixed for their death. Whatever the moral and practical justifications for capital punishment may be, the official determination of a person's time of death is one that has long excited horror and provoked the genius of writers as diverse as Dickens, Camus,[3] Dostoyevsky, and Stendhal.[4]

In his novel of the French revolution *A Tale of Two Cities*, where a man awaits the guillotine, Dickens describes the horror with which time passes:

> Another pause of oblivion and he [Darnay] awoke in the sombre morning unconscious where he was or what had happened until it flashed upon his mind, "this is the day of my death!".... The hours went on as he walked to and fro, and the clocks struck the numbers he would never hear again. Nine gone for ever, ten gone for ever, eleven gone for ever, twelve coming on to pass away.... Twelve gone for ever.[5]

Dostoyevsky, who had had direct experience of being sentenced to death for a political offense, shows the torment of certainty of death even more sharply:

> The chief and the worst pain is perhaps not inflicted by wounds, but by your certain knowledge that in an hour, in ten minutes, in half a minute, now, this moment, your soul will fly out of your body, and that you will be a human being no longer and that that's certain - the main thing is that it is *certain*.... A man who is murdered by brigands is killed at night in a forest or somewhere else and up to the last minute he still hopes that he will be saved. There have been instances where a man whose throat had already been cut, was still hoping, or running away or begging for his life to be spared. But here all this last hope which makes it ten times easier to die, is taken away *for certain*; here you have been sentenced to death and the whole terrible agony lies in the fact that you will most certainly not escape and there is no agony greater than that. Take a soldier and put him in front of a cannon in battle and fire at him and he will still hope, but read the same soldier his death sentence *for certain* and he will go mad or burst out crying. Who says that human nature is capable of bearing this without madness?[6]

Later Dostoyevsky refers to the despair that was one part of the most significant death sentence in history:

And when the sixth hour was come there was darkness over the whole land until the ninth hour.

And at the ninth hour Jesus cried with a loud voice, saying Eloi! Eloi! lama sabachthani? which is being interpreted, My God! My God! why has thou forsaken me? (Mark 15, 33–4, see also Matthew 27, 45–6)[7]

It is not surprising that an awareness of the torment undergone by those awaiting execution has provoked the suggestions that condemned persons should be allowed, if they so wish, to commit suicide. Their fate is the same, i.e., death shortly after the passing of sentence, but it is more humane to allow them to choose the method and exact timing of their death. In Greek and Roman antiquity "imposed suicide" was a privilege often extended to favored classes of offenders who would otherwise have been executed.[8] However, the British Royal Commission on Capital Punishment of 1953 was for a curious mixture of reasons,[9] unwilling to consider this possibility, as indicated by the following excerpt from their report:

We ought to mention here a suggestion — though only to dismiss it — that the prisoner should be offered some lethal dose the night before his execution and allowed to escape the gallows by drinking it if he so chooses. The suggestion is prompted by feelings of humanity, but the objections to it are manifest. The purpose of capital punishment is not just to rid the community of an unwanted member; it is to mark the community's denunciation of the gravest of all crimes by subjecting the perpetrator, in due form of law, to the severest of all punishments. Moreover, so long as suicide is condemned in England by the law as a crime and by the Church as a sin, the proposal could be represented as one to make murderers into a privileged class in whom alone this act was condoned. The Archbishop of Canterbury said:

". . . I think if society demands this penalty, it must itself inflict it, and quite clearly inflict it itself, and not invite the victim to do it for himself. I think that even in those grave and serious conditions a man should stand for his own responsibilities and meet them, and at that point it is not wise to invite him — I even think it would not be kind to invite him — to seek his own way out. . . . It is always a sin to commit suicide; to take one's own life is always a form of self-murder. . . . It is a dilemma that he should not be faced with."[10]

Behind these moral statements lurks the issue of power. Even under these fateful circumstances suicides are seen as defying society by choosing when to die, as "allowed to escape" from the power of the state to make and carry out that decision for them. That this is the case may be seen from the incredible lengths to which those guarding persons condemned to death go in order to frustrate any attempt at suicide.[11] Prisoners are deprived of any article of clothing — ties, belts, laces — that could be used to commit suicide, and are watched continuously. If they manage to evade their guardians as Dr. Crippen did when he broke the lens in his eyeglasses and slashed open a bloodvessel, then they are remorselessly resuscitated.

The fact that questions of power are at stake is particularly well shown by a number of incidents occurring at the time of the trials of war criminals at the end of World War II. General Hideki Tojo, a wartime premier of Japan, knowing he would be put on trial after Japan's surrender, carefully planned his suicide by getting a doctor to mark the position of his heart on his chest with the ink used for brushwork calligraphy. He told his wife "My life doesn't matter. A military man has always to be ready to die".[12] When the American military police came to arrest him, Tojo shot himself. The Americans hastened to fetch a doctor, an officer of the arresting party declaring, "We want this bastard alive." The Japanese doctor, or rather the interpreter, was told: "Tell him he's under orders to save the guy's life." The doctor declared that Tojo's condition was hopeless. An American army doctor then arrived and, ignoring both the Japanese doctor's opinion and the patient's plea that he be allowed to die, gave Tojo a transfusion of American blood.[13] Only his prompt and skillful care kept Tojo alive so that he could stand trial. After his trial, conviction and death sentence, he was watched and searched incessantly and even his dentures and spectacles were confiscated.[14]

Behind these extraordinary precautions lay the frustration experienced by the Allied authorities in Germany where, of the National Socialist leaders who would have been tried for war crimes, Hitler and Goebbels had committed suicide before the final surrender, and Himmler on being captured. Rudolf Hess had tried to stab himself with a bread-knife while detained in a Welsh lunatic asylum, and Dr. Robert Ley had strangled himself with the hem of a bath towel made into a noose.[15] Marshal Hermann Goering stood trial and was condemned to death, but took poison and died about an hour before he was due to be executed[16] in defiance both of the strict security precautions, which even forced prisoners to sleep with the light on (though dimmed) and their heads and hands visible at all times,[17] and of a sermon by one of the chaplains on the sin of self-destruction. Goering had been frequently searched when at Nuremburg, and a vial of poison had been taken from a tin of coffee in his possession when he had surrendered. At the time an official investigation exonerated the prison staff,[18] but recently it has been revealed that the cyanide pill he used was smuggled in for him by an American officer he had bribed and that the American board of enquiry had suppressed the truth as being too shamful to reveal.[19] Like all the National Socialists on death row, Goering had repeatedly tried to discover the exact time of his execution. Subject to the fears of men who know that a fixed date and procedure has been set for their death, Goering nevertheless wanted to postpone his suicide until the last possible moment. The American Lutheran Chaplain Rev. Henry Gerecke afterwards spoke of Goering's air of secret triumph during his last days: "It was as if he were saying: 'Go ahead fellows: do with me what you like. I'll fix you in the end. Self-execution by potassium cyanide was his crowning achievement.'"[20]

Here in these extreme circumstances it is possible to see the enormous symbolic significance that may be placed on the question of *who* puts someone to death when the time of a person's death has been decided. Even though the condemned prisoner cannot escape dying within a time limit set by those in authority, it is still a triumph for the prisoner and a disgrace for the authorities if suicide replaces execution. Such a suicide is an act of defiance against those in power, against society and its rules and procedures. Indeed, it is the only choice that condemned persons can make when all else — in this world, at least — is decided for them.

In another quite different context we can see interesting cultural differences in the way different societies view the right of the state to demand or at least request that an individual face certain death not as a penalty but as a duty. In Western societies members of the armed forces, whether conscripts or volunteers, are expected to risk their lives in wartime and indeed even to undertake missions where their chance of survival is very small. Nonetheless there is in principle at least some chance that any particular individual will survive and a refusal to plan military operations such that any one person will be killed for certain, even if the alternative is that a larger number of men are placed at considerable risk and more casualties sustained overall. Perhaps a hypothetical example will make this clear.

An air force commander is told that it is vital to knock out a distant and heavily defended target. The calculation is made that it will probably take 240 bombs to do the job. Each plane carries 20 bombs and a crew of five who have only a one in four chance of surviving the operation and getting back alive. This means that 12 missions must be flown and that 45 of the 60 crew members involved will be killed. A statistician now calculates that if each plane carried only enough fuel for a one-way trip, then 30 bombs could be carried per plane, only eight missions would be needed, and only 40 members would be killed. However, it would be 40 out of 40, i.e., there would be a zero chance of surviving the mission.

My argument is that a commander brought up in the Western ethical tradition would pick the former option even though it is more costly in lives. It is this belief that it is wrong to send someone to absolutely certain death, however desperate the situation that has led Westerners to regard the Japanese kamikaze tactics of World War II or Shi'ite "suicide" attacks[21] with such bewilderment and horror. The distinction has been well put by Jean Baechler:

> One must admit that their (kamikaze, etc) behaviour shocks us and we are tempted to describe them as inhuman. However, there is hardly any significant difference between crashing one's plane into an enemy ship and accepting an assignment to fight a rear-guard action. One can however, distinguish two differences. The first concerns the difference in nature — from the psychological point of view — between a certainty and an infinitely high probability. The kamikaze is sure he will perish, while the rear-guard retains an infinitesimally small chance of coming through alive. On the other hand there is an infinite distance, and in any case an ungraspable one, between the action of an individual kamikaze and the outcome of the war, whereas the action of a rear-guard patrol is directly at the service of an immediate and tangible end (to allow a strategic withdrawal, to hold up the enemy for a while, etc.). In the first case the sacrifice

is for a somewhat abstract beneficiary; in the second, the individual who undertakes the sacrifice and the person who benefits from it are almost on the same plane.[22]

The kamikazes were a widespread phenomenon on air and land as well as at sea, and in all cases a deliberate means to an end and not a mere fanatical gesture. They represented a last desperate attempt to surmount America's overwhelming superiority in armaments during the Pacific war. Thus Japanese infantrymen charged American tanks with land-mines or other explosives strapped to their backs,[23] a tactic that had previously been used in the Japanese attack on the Russian fortifications at Port Arthur in the Russo-Japanese War of 1904–1905.[24] The Americans were forced to equip their tanks with flame-throwers in order to prevent such attackers getting too close.[25] Japanese fighters rammed B-24 bombers in the air at the Battle of Saipan and rammed the B-20s sent to bomb Japan itself, a tactic which understandably alarmed the attackers.[26] Manned torpedos were designed and suicide torpedo boats prepared for defense against invasion.[27] The most well-known tactic, that of crashing a plane loaded with explosives into a ship, was highly effective and more American ships including carriers were sunk or damaged in three months than in all previous Japanese operations including Pearl Harbor.[28] Given the volume and accuracy of the anti-aircraft gunnery of the American navy and the need to employ new half-trained pilots because of past losses, the use of the kamikazes was a highly rational tactic if Japan was to avoid total defeat.[29] To a large extent the men involved were volunteers (albeit under considerable social pressure), though some of the later army (as distinct from navy) pilots were given no choice.[30] It was a tactic as much suggested from below as imposed from above, and many of the senior officers who had to send the kamikazes into action did so with reluctance[31] and only after they were convinced that such a tactic would be effective.[32] In the case of the human torpedos, the Admirals insisted that they be fitted with an escape hatch like an ejector seat even though the men would probably be killed by the shock wave anyway.[33] The kamikazes were an essentially instrumental phenomenon in contrast to, say, the Western captain who deliberately chooses to go down with his ship and thus in many cases deprives his navy of a highly skilled and trained officer as well as a ship.[34]

Even though Westerners have come to understand the logic, the rationality of the kamikaze, they still balk at the idea of an individual choosing or being sent to certain destruction in the service of the nation. Baechler cites a French expert on military aviation as having advocated the use of kamikaze tactics in 1914 as a logical solution to a particular military problem,[35] but there is no evidence that his view was systematically put into practice. On September 1, 1914 just after the outbreak of World War I the British cabinet minister Charles Hobhouse recorded in his diary:

We are told to expect Zeppelins over London at any night. W.S.C. [Winston

Churchill] has sent 100 aeroplanes to Dunkirk to watch for them. In the last resort
the officers in charge of aeroplanes will charge the Zeppelins, but in view of the
certain death have arranged to draw lots for the task.[36]

What is interesting about the response of the British officers is that when
death was certain in a particular encounter they did not call for volunteers or
give orders to selected individuals to sacrifice themselves, but reintroduced an
element of chance by arranging to draw lots. They did not in any way shirk
the danger (which was equivalent to ramming a B-29 bombing Japan) but they
preserved the Western moral rule that no one person be singled out for *certain*
death even *sed miles sed pro patria*. Individuals did of course sacrifice their lives
for King and Country, but they did so in the knowledge that the central moral
principle of the collectivity they served was one that valued each individual.
There was no equivalent of the Japanese view that each individual owed an
infinite debt to Japan and the Emperor, or the Shinto belief that the spirits of
the kamikazes or others killed in the line of duty were instantly transported
to and installed in the Yasukuni shrine in Tokyo where all Japan would pay
homage to them.[37] For Westerners even defeat can be honorable and the
Japanese view that suicide is preferable to surrender is abhorrent, because it
implies that the value of the individual is to be measured in terms of honorific
service to the state. General Hideki Tojo's instruction for the military, "Do not
live in shame as a prisoner. Die and leave no ignominious crime behind you,"[38]
which meant wounded men blew themselves up[39] rather than be captured, that
shipwrecked men deliberately drowned rather than be rescued by the enemy[40]
is alien to those Western religious and secular traditions that emphasized the
unique value of each individual and his or her right to self-determination.

The contrast is an important one in relation to the final case to be discussed,
namely euthanasia. In its simplest form euthanasia merely amounts to a form
of assisted suicide. Many people choose to terminate their lives because of
incurable pain, because of declining mental and physical powers leading to progressive erosion of their independence or even the central meaning of their
lives, because of the fear of the descent into total senility. For all these reasons
the probability of a person committing suicide rises with age (though roughly
in line with other causes of death).[41] Sometimes, though, the personal decline
from which they wish to escape also prevents them having access to the means
of committing suicide, and they ask someone else to provide these. In other
circumstances they may negotiate with their doctor to obtain a quicker and less
painful death, to enter the blurred area where euthanasia blends with the relief
of pain. A degree of mercy killing is probably quite widespread both in
Western Europe and North America, but is rarely open to public scrutiny or
controversy. Even if a legal prosecution does occur, provided the perpetrator's
motives are acceptable, juries try not to convict and sentences are low.[42] In the
Netherlands alone, euthanasia, though not specifically permitted by law, is
carried out openly and with the de facto consent of the courts after a formal
discussion of each case. The number of patients involved is relatively small and

is falling as better ways of alleviating pain become available. The numbers could, though, increase if individuals (fearing senility or idiocy rather than pain) were to seek a promise of euthanasia in advance of their loss of faculties by writing a "living will" while they were still able to give informed consent. Having seen the state to which others have been reduced by accident, disease, or extreme age, they might seek a guarantee that their own life not be prolonged in such circumstances either for their own sake or to save their relatives and close friends needless suffering.

Both the advocates of euthanasia and those operating the relatively open and permissive Dutch system have been the subject of a good deal of abusive moral indignation. At the 1987 International Conference on Death and Dying held at St. David's University College of Wales, Lampeter, a critic of the Dutch classed them with Nazi Germany as being the only two modern societies to approve euthanasia. This particular type of argument is very common in oral controversy and polemic; indeed, whatever its intellectual origins it has become part of the folklore of those who are strongly opposed to euthanasia and especially of concerned and committed Roman Catholics. It is an argument that has a strong and a weak form, both of which ignore the question of the power of the state and the demands made by society on the individual, which is central to the analysis advanced here.

The strong form of the argument asserts or at least implies that the contemporary Netherlanders in permitting euthanasia and also in practice allowing abortion on demand have sunk to the moral level of Nazi Germany in their disregard for the sanctity of human life. What is omitted from the argument is that euthanasia in the Netherlands takes place with the informed consent of the person concerned; indeed, it is he or she who initiates the process. The only beneficiaries are the person choosing euthanasia and those close to them who are spared a good deal of anguish. The same point may be made about many other parallel controversial cases in Western societies, as when the life support machine of someone who is brain dead is switched off or doctors deliberately refrain from medical or surgical intervention to preserve the life of the severely handicapped newly born.[43]

By contrast, euthanasia in National Socialist Germany was compulsory and the consent of the person and their next of kin was not necessary. Between 1939 and 1941 a minimum of 50,000 feeble-minded and insane people were "humanely" gassed, particularly in Hadamar near Limburg where the local children knew and joked about it and the old folk feared it would be their turn next to go *"durch den kamin"* (up the chimney).[44] The purpose of the exercise was to eliminate the "useless eaters," i.e., those who failed to advance and in a very minor way indirectly hindered the aims and particularly the military ambitions of the state. There was a good deal of angry and effective protest[45] from the moral spokesmen of the German people who both earlier and later failed to speak out against the Holocaust and other genocidal acts, the treatment of slave laborers who were worked to death, or the murder of P.O.W.'s and the political opponents of the regime.

The euthanasia program was but a small part of a general policy of enhancing the collective powers of the state and of the German nation that the rulers of the Reich claimed to represent, in total disregard of the rights, wishes, and happiness of the individual. As part of exactly the same policy, abortion was strictly forbidden in Nazi Germany and abortionists were liable to receive 6 to 15 years imprisonment in a concentration camp, whereas under the Weimar Republic a fine of 40 marks was the maximum penalty.[46] Capital punishment was freely employed in pursuit of the same collective ends. By contrast in the Netherlands there is abortion on demand because, as in the case of euthanasia, the laws prohibiting it have fallen into disuse and in 1870 the Dutch were one of the earliest nations in Europe to abolish capital punishment.[47] Even before that there had only been two executions in the period 1850–1870, both in the year 1860.[48] The contrast between the Dutch regard for the individual and his or her suffering and welfare and the Nazi view that the state should have almost limitless power to kill could hardly be stronger.

The weaker version of the thesis linking euthanasia in the Netherlands today to the horrors of the National Socialist era is based on the oblique and saponaceous argument of the "slippery slope." Those who permit euthanasia (or even abortion) today are in this view undermining the fundamental respect for the sanctity of life which is all that prevents us from slithering down into a trough where no one's right to life will be respected if their existence inconveniences society. It is a crude analogy not easily subject to any empirical test. If the moral slope on which we stand is in fact gentle and the coefficient of friction high, we may not be at risk of sliding downhill. Indeed those obsessed with analogies drawn from objects resting on inclined planes would do well to remember that bodies with a high center of gravity and a narrow base are apt to topple before they slide. Also it is by no means clear that the refusal to tolerate suffering, which is the basis of our contemporary willingness to contemplate euthanasia, is a force that has led on balance to a greater willingness to take human life. In England at the beginning of the nineteenth century young children were executed for minor offenses against property, and during World War I hundreds of British soldiers were shot for desertion or cowardice.[49] Today this degree of harshness is unthinkable, and the Dutch (who seem a rather less punitive people than the British) abolished capital punishment a century in advance of Britain.

A society's view of human life is a composite aggregate of many slopes of different kinds with movements up and sideways as well as down. To see the Netherlands or other Western democratic countries that are inclined to tolerate euthanasia as at serious risk of degenerating into a state of tyrannical or chaotic disregard for the life of their individual citizens simply because they no longer respect the shibboleths of a nastier past era is absurd. In a world where, for the citizens of most countries, life is cheap and insecure, Batavia is a haven of safety and respect for the individual.

The slippery-slope argument is sometimes backed up by a recital of the myth that the Nazis first cautiously introduced euthanasia and then when they saw that this departure from traditional ethics was accepted without serious criticism by the citizens of the Reich, felt that they could take the further nasty step to the final solution of the Jewish problem together with the slaughter of Gypsies, Slavs, and other people defined as subhuman or even dangerous vermin. The main flaw in this argument is that its factual premises are incorrect. Many people in Germany, notably the Bishop of Limberg and the Bishop of Munster, *did* speak out against the killing of lunatics and the feeble-minded and they did so with effect.[50] Reitlinger comments, "It is probably that on no question was Hitler's personal dictatorship more severely challenged than this one."[51] In consequence despite the euthanasia program, the feeble minded probably stood as good a chance[52] of survival as their fellow Germans because they were not conscripted into the armed forces, were evacuated from large cities to protect them from the bombing,[53] and were unlikely to be involved in the plots against Hitler. By contrast no one of any significance spoke out on behalf of the Jews or stressed their common humanity.[54] Perhaps there were those who would have done so but were not allowed to or were too afraid.

Even so, the contrast between the loud and effective moral indignation aroused by the gassing of a limited number of the incurably insane and feeble minded and the silent indifference with which the gassing of several million Jews was greeted is overwhelming. Some of the most determined German and Axis opponents of euthanasia slid down the slippery slope to the moral abyss of the Holocaust, and others must have run down it enthusiastically. When it came to the crunch, their much vaunted absolute morality and supposed moral courage did not inspire them to make a decisive and effective moral protest when it was most needed. In consequence those who utter the same moral squawks today lack any kind of credibility. By contrast, the Dutch who now allow euthanasia went on strike during the Nazi occupation of their country in order to protest strongly against the persecution of their Jewish fellow-citizens, and only the threat of a second Rötterdämmerung silenced them. The same universal compassion for the suffering of other individuals that has led them to adopt euthanasia today enabled them to see the force of a point ironically perhaps best put by Shylock:

> Hath not a Jew eyes? hath not a Jew hands, organs, dimensions, senses, affec-
> tions, passions, fed with the same food, hurt with the same weapons, subject to
> the same diseases, healed by the same means, warmed and cooled by the same
> winter and summer, as a Christian is?[55]

The moral is that Jews, like the members of all religions, nations, or social classes, are full human beings. None of us, though, have a guarantee that we will remain so in terms of Shylock's definition. Age, accident, or infirmity can deprive us of these qualities essential to being truly human. What the great persecutors of history such as the National Socialists, the Bolsheviks, Pol Pot, the Maoists, the Ustashi, the Inquisition, the witch-finders, have in common is not that they are in favor of euthanasia, but rather their callous indifference to the fate of those whom their vicious ideologies define not as a mere useless tumor in the body of society but as an essentially malignant growth.

Once again the central issue neglected by the moralizers is that of the power and constitution of the state. In the Netherlands the state has refrained from prohibiting voluntary euthanasia, an action that is totally different in kind from the use of state power to impose euthanasia on selected groups of people in order to free resources for conquest, i.e., to subtitute guns for the butter of the useless eaters. This distinction is parallel to the difference between the permissive view of abortion taken in the Netherlands, the United States, or Britain and the use of compulsory abortion in contemporary China to try and solve the population crisis created by the foolish and wicked social and economic policies followed under Mao Tse Tung.

The peculiar and varied ethics of certain death by execution, suicide, or euthanasia can only be understood in relation to the question "Who owns me?" If the answer is that the individual owns himself or herself and that the state or society ought to be primarily seen as the sum of our individual property rights in ourselves, then suicide and voluntary euthanasia are permissible but execution and demands that the individual face certain sacrifice in war or at any other time are not. At the center of the moral order is the autonomous individual with plans, hopes, expectations, and awareness who cannot be subjected to the suffering caused by the imposition of certain death but who has the right to choose certain death rather than to suffer an existence felt to be less than worthwhile. In this type of state, every man has the right to be unhappy in his own way. By contrast we have the view shared by reactionaries and revolutionaries, and by secular and religious dictators, that we are owned by the state or the social order and that those in power may legitimately force us to die *or* to stay alive.

NOTES

1. For details about relevant naval protocols and customs see Lord Russell of Liverpool, 1954, *The scourge of the swastika*, London, Cassell, pp. 63-79.

2. See Lothar-Gunther Buchheim, 1974, *U-boat*, London, Collins. (This is a fictional work but based on direct experience.) There were exceptions, e.g., a British attack on Rommel in North Africa and the deliberate shooting down of a plane containing a Japanese admiral by the Americans after they had cracked the Japanese code and knew where to find him.

3. See Jean Baecherl, 1979, *Suicides*, Oxford, Basil, Blackwell, pp. 175–176.

4. See Albert Camus, 1953 (1944), *L'Etranger*, Paris, Gallimard, pp. 158–159:

> C'est à l'aube quils veraient, je le savais. En somme j'ai occupé mes mes nuits à attendre cette aube. Je n'ai jamais aimé être surpris. Quand il m'arrive quelque chose, je préfere être la. C'est pourquoi j'ai fini par ne plus dormir qu' un peu dans mes journées et, tout de long de mes nuits, j'ai attendu patiemment que la lumiere naisse sur la vitre du ciel. Le plus difficile c'etait l'heure douteuse oui je savais qu'ils opéracient d'habitude. Passé minuit j'attendais et je guettais. Jamais mon oreille n'avait percu tant de bruits distingués de sons si ténus. . . . j'aurais pu entendre des pas et mon coeur aurait pu éclater. Même si le moindre glissement me jetait à la porte, même si l'oreille collée au bris j'attendais éperdument jusqu'à

ce que j'entende ma propre respiration, effrayé de la trouver rauque et si pareille au râle d'un chien, au bout du compté mon coeur n'éclatait pas et j'avais encore gagné vingt-quatre heures.

See also Stendhal (Henri-Marie Beyle), 1953 (1830), *Scarlet and Black* (*Le rouge et le noir*), Harmondsworth, Penguin pp. 489–493 and 497–509.

5. Charles Dickens, 1967, *A Tale of Two Cities*, London, Heron p. 406.

6. Fyodor Dostoyevsky, 1955 (1869), *The Idiot* [translated, David Magarshack], Harmondsworth, Penguin pp. 47–48. See also pp. 86–88.

7. King James Bible.

8. See Baechler pp. 19–20, 365–368.

9. Report of the Royal Commission on Capital Punishment 1949–1953.

10. Royal Commission, paragraph 769, pp. 266–267.

11. See Baechler p. 36.

12. Courtney Browne, 1969, *Tojo, the Last Banzai*, London, Transworld p. 225.

13. See Browne pp. 230–233.

14. See Browne pp. 252–255.

15. See F.T. Grossmith, 1984, *The Cross and the Swastika*, Worthing, Sussex, Walter pp. 23–24.

16. See Grossmith p. 84.

17. See Grossmith p. 66.

18. See Grossmith p. 83.

19. Douglas Botting, 1986, *In the Ruins of the Reich*, London, Grafton, p. 343.

20. Grossmith p. 84.

21. See Edwin P. Hoyt, 1985, *The Kamakazes*, London, Panth, p. 322.

22. Baechler pp. 331-332.

23. Hoyt pp. 15–16.

24. Baechler p. 409.

25. Hoyt p. 271.

26. See Hoyt pp. 45 and 207.

27. See Baechler p. 410, Hoyt p. 259.

28. See Baechler p. 411, Hoyt pp. 151, 187, 248.

29. See Baechler p. 409.

30. See Baechler p. 411, Hoyt pp. 165, 174–175, 235.

31. See Hoyt p. 35.

32. See Baechler p. 409.

33. See Baechler p. 409, Hoyt p. 137.

34. See Baechler pp. 359–360, 409.

35. Baechler pp. 408–409.

36. Edward David (ed), 1977, *Inside Asquith's Cabinet, from the Diaries of Charles Hobhouse*, London, John Murray, p. 187.

37. See Hoyt p. 67 and Lt. Hiroo Onoda, 1976, *No Surrender, My Thirty Year War*, London, Transworld, p. 105.

38. Onoda p. 34–35.

39. See Onoda pp. 67–68.

40. See Baechler p. 413.

41. See Baechler p. 284–287.

42. See Fred M. Frohock, 1983, *Abortion a case study in law and morals*. Westport, Connecticut, Greenwood, p. 16. For a curious example of just such a case, see Lord Patrick

Devlin, 1985, *Easing the passing, the trial of John Bodkin Adams*, London, Faber and Faber, pp. 195–210. Devlin is against euthanasia, and so is the law of England and Wales, but the view of the public is much more complex.

43. See Helga Kuhse and Peter Singer, 1985, *Should the Baby Live?* Oxford, O.U.P.

44. See Lord Russell of Liverpool pp. 183–184 and Gerald Reitlinger, 1967, *The Final Solution*, London, Valentine Mitchell p. 136.

45. See Norman Cohn, 1970, *Warrant for Genocide*, Harmondsworth, Penguin p. 234.

46. See Clarissa Henry and Marc Hillel, 1976, *Children of the S.S.*, London, Hutchinson p. 36. In 1933 there were a million abortions in Germany but in 1938 there were only 200,000 and they were hidden under the classification "miscarriages."

47. See *L'interruption voluntaire de grosseuse dans l'Europe des neuf, 1981*, Paris, Institut National d'études demographiques. Cahier No. 91, Presses Universitaires de France.

48. See *Royal Commission on Capital Punishment* pp. 340–341.

49. See William Moore, 1979, *The thin yellow line*, London, Leo Cooper.

50. See Cohn p. 234, Lord Russell of Liverpool p. 184.

51. Reitlinger 1967.

52. It is very difficult to make any accurate calculations in part because there are no figures for the deaths of the German insane and feeble-minded as a result of enemy action. The total number of them who eventually were killed through the euthanasia program was probably of the order of 200,000. The number of Germans killed in the war was 7 million, almost equally divided between the military and civilians. The ratio is about 1:35, which is of the same order of magnitude as the proportion of the feeble-minded and insane in the general population. In either case the death rate is well under 10%, in contrast to the loss of several million Jews who represented three quarters of the Jewish population in the countries occupied by Nazi Germany.

53. See Fred Taylor (ed), *the Goebbels Diaries 1939–1941*, London, Sphere.

54. See Cohn p. 234.

55. William Shakespeare, *The Merchant of Venice* Act 3, Scene 1. In the German-occupied British Channel Islands an attempt by the local people to put on this play during the war met with strong opposition from the Nazis because of the implications of such lines. The play was insufficiently anti-Semitic for the authorities: see Alan Wood and Mary Seaton Wood, 1976, *Islands in Danger*, London, New English Library, p. 203.

14

Do We Have a Right to Die?

John Beloff

What I shall be discussing in this chapter are essentially problems of ethics. I shall be asking what attitude we *ought* to adopt towards the claim that people have the right, not only to dispose of their lives at their own discretion, but, if necessary, to seek the help and advice of others to this end. I shall make no secret of the fact that I am an active supporter of the voluntary euthanasia cause but, at the same time, I shall refrain from indulging in polemics and I shall try to examine as impartially as I can the various objections that are repeatedly raised whenever this controversial topic comes up for discussion, whether in parliament or in the pulpit.

Let us start with the question of suicide as such. Clearly if one maintains that it is wrong to take one's own life whatever may be the circumstances, then, *a fortiori*, one will think it wrong to involve others in such wrong-doing. On the other hand, even if we grant that suicide may be justified in certain circumstances, we may still wish to draw the line at involving others. Objections to suicide as such have been based mainly on religious grounds although there has also been opposition on secular grounds of a sociopolitical nature. It is, however, the religious opposition that has been the most influential, the most implacable, and the most deeply rooted, so it is to this that we must turn first.

It is a fact that nearly all the well-known religions and religious sects condemn suicide (Larue 1985). There is, however, a marked contrast between the three great monotheistic faiths, Judaism, Christianity, and Islam and a polytheistic religion such as Hinduism which, like Classical Paganism, is more permissive.[1] Curiously, as David Hume was, perhaps, the first to point out, there is no scriptural authority for condemning suicide.[2] The commandment "thou shalt not kill" was almost certainly intended to proscribe murder. Killing, after all, has always been sanctioned in certain circumstances, notably in war and in the administration of justice. The Mosaic law lists a variety of capital offenses so there could be no suggestion that life as such was sacred. Indeed, the Old Testament mentions a number of cases of suicide, notably those of Saul and of Samson, without the protagonists being censured on that score. Nevertheless, post-biblical Judaism is explicit in rejecting suicide and, for the Catholic Church, first St. Augustine and later St. Thomas Aquinas imposed the final seal of disapproval Blázquez 1985; Sullivan 1975).[3] For Islam the condemnation was no less categorical and the suicide was excluded from the Moslem paradise. It is not hard to understand why this should be so. For all three faiths, God is conceived as the giver of life and man as no more than a trustee of that gift. Hence, in renouncing life, we at once betray that trust and insult our creator.

What is less easy to understand is the vehemence which suicide aroused down the centuries as can be gauged by the severity of the punishment meted out to a suicide or rather, since a successful suicide places himself beyond the reach of earthly retribution, on the unfortunate family and friends of the suicide. Not only was the corpse denied burial in consecrated ground but often various obscene indignities were heaped upon it. Thus, in the city of Toulouse, at the time of Voltaire, the body of the suicide would be tied to a cart and dragged naked through the streets. Even as late as the 19th century the property of the suicide could be confiscated by the state in many countries. Indeed, it was not until the Suicide Act of 1961 that suicide ceased to be a crime in England. Before that time, an unsuccessful suicide was liable to be punished for making the attempt! When I was in India in 1986 I discovered to my surprise that this situation still obtained, although this peculiar legacy of British rule was at last starting to be challenged by some of the state legislatures.

The only form of suicide, if one may call it that, which has the sanction of all the religions, is deliberate martyrdom.[4] Thus, the defenders of the Masada fortress who took their own lives rather than fall into the hands of the besieging Roman army were always heroes to the Jews and still are in modern Israel. Even the Church took a lenient view of those pious women who killed themselves rather than suffer violation. The recent spate of suicide bombers in Lebanon is a grim reminder that, for the pious Moslem, to sacrifice one's life in a holy war against the infidel ensured immediate entry into paradise. But, martyrdom aside, it still remains true that, for the three monotheistic world religions, suicide was regarded as an act of the grossest impiety. Indeed, for Aquinas, it was an even greater sin than murder inasmuch as it afforded no opportunity for repentance! All this is in startling contrast to the preceding Greco-Roman civilization where suicide was always held to be preferable to dishonor and where some of the most celebrated philosophers of antiquity, especially those of the Stoic and Epicurean schools, explicity commended it as the rational solution once life had become unbearable.

What we must now consider is whether the religious opposition to suicide is (a) theologically sound and (b) ethically defensible. I shall try to demonstrate that, on neither count, does it bear examination. It may, perhaps, strike some of you as impertinent for an agnostic like myself to pronounce on questions of theology. If so, I can but plead that, since a number of eminent Christian scholars have recently come out in support of voluntary euthanasia, the theological arguments are, to say the least, inconclusive. The crux of the theological argument, as I understand it, is that since God alone has the right to decide when our lives have come to an end, in committing suicide we, at one blow, usurp the divine prerogative and violate the sanctity of life. Now, this strikes me as bad theology for a number of reasons. First it implies that God is a capricious and callous despot who abuses his prerogative. If anything could be said to be common knowledge it is that there is neither rhyme nor reason in the whys and wherefores of dying. Geniuses like Mozart and Schubert die in the prime of life and at the peak of their creativity, while nonentities drag out their lives a burden to themselves and others. Epidemics cut swathes through the population regardless of age, sex, or merit.

I am not unaware that theologians have attempted to make sense of this state of affairs; it is part of the whole problem of evil with which the theologian has to contend. It would, indeed, be surprising if this were not so, considering that for centuries some of the nimblest intellects were employed to put a plausible gloss on what were basically absurd dogmas. What I contend is that no satisfactory answers have ever been forthcoming. Thus it was said that it did not matter in the long run if the innocent had to suffer, as they would reap their reward in the world to come. But this was to cast God in the role of some crazy millionaire who arrogates to himself the right to create havoc and mayhem among his fellow citizens always so long as, at the end of the day, he pays adequate financial compensation. The point is that suffering is no less real whatever may be the sequel. A favorite argument among Christian apologists is that suffering can have a positive value if we make it the occasion to acquire spiritual strength. Now, there is something to be said in favor of resignation. It is better to suffer in silence and in dignity rather than rage against the inevitable. But, having said this, the argument could at best apply to very exceptional cases and its weakness is that it is flatly contradicted by everything we actually do when confronted with the prospect of suffering. For what else, after all, is medicine if it is not the alleviation of suffering and the prevention of premature death? If we really believed that it is God who decrees when and how we are to die we would behave much more fatalistically. In practice of course, even the most fervent Christian apologist will do everything possible to postpone the advent of death and diminish the amount of suffering involved. But, once we admit that death is not divinely decreed, how can it be wrong to make it a matter of personal and rational choice how and when to die? We take for granted these days planned parenthood and we see nothing wrong in deciding when our offspring should be born; why should we not also decide when we are ready to retire from life?

I conclude that the theological objection is invalid. It involves imputing to the deity characteristics that are incompatible with his supposed benevolence. Thus a deity who, as in the story of Job, deliberately inflicted suffering on one of his creatures whether to test his character or for any other reason would be a fiend, not a God who deserved our worship. But, for the sake of the argument, let us suppose that I am here mistaken, that the theological argument *is*, after all, valid perhaps for some reason that I have overlooked or failed to mention. The question still remains whether this would constitute an ethical objection to suicide. To say, after all, that God forbids something is, at most, to state a fact; it cannot follow that God is right to forbid it or that the something is wrong. A value judgment cannot be derived from a statement of fact whether the fact in question is a theological truth or a truth of nature. Of course, if God is all powerful it would be prudent for us to obey him, but that does not make it ethical. God could only be right to forbid something if that something is in itself evil or a means to evil, and, in the case for suicide, it remains to be shown that this is necessarily the case. If it should transpire that suicide is always wrong, then the fact that God also forbids it would be irrelevant from an ethical point of view. If, on the contrary, it should transpire that suicide can sometimes be justified, then the fact that God forbids it would prove that God cannot be wholly good, which some would take as a contradiction in terms. Again, the theological objection turns out to be either irrelevant or invalid.

The secular objections to suicide in principle strike me as even weaker and more question-begging than are the theological objections. It is, however, an interesting sociological fact that suicide and voluntary euthanasia are almost as great an anathema in Marxist countries as they are in Catholic countries. A Polish philosopher I met who supports voluntary euthanasia told me that he had to contend with the twofold opposition of the Polish state and the Catholic Church. It is a reminder that the right to die, like so many other human rights we hold dear, is a product of the liberal ethos. The essence of liberalism, after all, is the belief that we have the right to do as we please, always so long as we harm no one else in the process and infringe no others' rights to do as *they* please. In totalitarian systems, on the contrary, rights are conferred on us by the state, community, or other supreme authority. Hence there can be no right to die since this would be tantamount to resigning one's membership of the collective. Aquinas pointed out that suicide violates not only God's right of ownership, since we are His creatures, but also the rights of our community which we are unilaterally depriving of one of its members. No such objections can arise under a liberal dispensation where the individual is the supreme arbiter of his own good. This is not to say that the individual cannot do wrong in committing suicide; for example, he may thereby leave his dependents destitute, but it is not society as such that is wronged but only other individuals.

The American philosopher Joel Feinberg (1980) has discussed at great length whether suicide could be considered a violation of the "inalienable right to life" as conceived by Jefferson and the founding fathers of the American constitution. He arrives eventually at the conclusion that, on any reasonable interpretation of that phrase, this is not the case. He points out that in waiving this right we are not gainsaying its inalienability, for we still have that right even though we choose not to exercise it in our own particular case. It is only if we chose to treat the right to life as a mandatory rather than a discretionary right that suicide would amount to such a violation. But there is no justification for such an interpretation. On the contrary, the right to life, he points out "is exactly like the most treasured specimens in the 'right to liberty' and 'right to property' categories. Just as we have the right to come and go as we please," he continues "to read or not to read, to speak or not to speak, to worship or not to worship, to buy or sell or sit tight, as we please, so we have the right within the boundaries of our own autonomy, to live or die as we choose" (p. 249). I do not know whether Jefferson himself would agree with this formulation, but I cannot imagine a clearer or more cogent statement of what I am calling the liberal position to which I, myself, subscribe.

Let us pass on now from the question of suicide to the more contentious question of assisted suicide, which forms the nub of the voluntary euthanasia issue. Suicide, after all, is no longer a crime in most civilized countries whereas assisted suicide still is. I gather that, under Swiss law and West German law, one cannot be prosecuted merely for supplying someone with the wherewithal to commit suicide or the advice on how to use it but, in Britain, the United States, and most European countries even that amount of involvement is a crime, no matter how compassionate or disinterested the motivation. Should assisted suicide be made legal? If we conceive of the right to die as being like most other rights, *e.g.*, the right to property, the right to an education, the right to travel, the right to go about our daily business in peace and so on, then we should, as in all these other cases, be able to call upon the resources of the community to help us in fulfilling that right. As things now stand, suicide is a do-it-yourself job which carries with it a grave risk of being bungled and is at best a lonely and terrifying business. What is needed to transform suicide into a genuine *eu*thanasia, or good death, is the expert cooperation of the medical profession. And the first step in that direction is to make assisted suicide legal. If necessary, medically qualified personnel would alone be authorized to assist.

There are, at the present time, a number of rational arguments against legalizing assisted suicide, but they can all be summed up under the rubric "dangers of abuse." Inevitably, there will always be the danger of abuse. One would be hard put to think of any reform which did not carry with it some danger of abuse if only because, however carefully the law is framed, it can always be abused by sinister and unscrupulous persons. The principal abuses that are cited in this connection by the opponents of voluntary euthanasia are the following:

1. By legalizing voluntary euthanasia you undermine the value we place on life. This opens a way to further insidious practices which could lead eventually, as it did with the Nazis, to the extermination of whole sections of the population deemed useless or undesirable.

2. It is the very old and the very sick who would be the obvious candidates for voluntary euthanasia, in other words, the weakest and most defenseless members of society. Once voluntary euthanasia became legal they would be unable to withstand the pressure to take that option which their grasping heirs, or others who may wish to be rid of them, would apply. In this way the dividing line between voluntary and involuntary euthanasia would soon become eroded.

3. Those who would most benefit from voluntary euthanasia would be those

who are least in a position to give their informed consent. Who, then, would decide? The doctor? The family or next of kin? Even in those fortunate cases where the patient had completed an advanced declaration specifying the precise conditions in which he or she would want euthanasia we still cannot be sure that he or she might not have changed his or her mind. It is one thing to contemplate a future contingency and quite another to be confronted with its actuality.

Two further objections from the standpoint of the medical profession may now be added:

1. It would fall to the doctor in charge to decide who was a suitable candidate for voluntary euthanasia. This would not only impose an unfair onus on the doctor but would poison the normal relationship between doctor and patient where the doctor's role has always been seen as that of a sustainer of life, not as a destroyer. In short, euthanasia would represent too grave a breach with the Hippocratic tradition in medical ethics to be acceptable.
2. With the development of new pain-killing drugs and with improvements in the care of the dying, as now being pioneered by the hospices, the need for voluntary euthanasia will disappear.

There may well be other objections, too, but these are, I think, the most common and taken together present a formidale array of problems for the advocates of voluntary euthanasia. Where, then, does this leave the right to die?

Perhaps the first point that needs to be made is that these hypothetical risks have to be weighed against the very tangible horrors that are the outcome of the existing situation. Most people, these days, die in hospitals, which means that they do not have the possibility of committing suicide of their own accord and so have no escape, however traumatic the process of dying. Bearing this in mind let us look again at our list of objections.

The view that life is sacred and that once we violate this taboo we are on the road to perdition may sound plausible, but what exactly is it that we hold sacred? If it is life in the full biographical sense, there is every reason to deplore its premature termination but it is hard to see what is sacred about the mere fact of biological existence. What value is there in being in an irreversible coma or in a vegetative state even if one is still breathing and one's heart is still beating? Talk about the sanctity of life too readily degenerates into a slogan that obscures the real issues (Rachels 1986). Of more weight is the argument that it is often difficult to distinguish between voluntary and involuntary; even at the best of times we may not know our own minds for sure.

But the argument, dear to politicians, that old people would succumb to pressures from unscrupulous relatives seems to me to overlook the sheer cussedness of old people who are not easily persuaded to do what they do not want. It further ignores the fact that the will to live is among the most powerful instincts we possess; it is only in very special cases that it is likely to be overridden.

As for the doctors' contention that voluntary euthanasia would constitute a grave departure from traditional medical practice, this ignores the considerable changes that have already come about. The tendency to resort to all the marvels of modern technology in order to prolong the life of a patient even when there is no chance of recovery is rapidly becoming a thing of the past. Already, in the United States, some thirty-six states now recognize the legal validity of a patient's advanced declaration, or "living will" declining the use of life-support systems if there is no prospect of recovery (Humphry and Wickett 1986). Indeed, even the Vatican, in its Declaration of 1980, no longer insists on the use of extraordinary measures to keep a patient alive at all costs.[6] Thus, so far as passive euthanasia is concerned, the battle is almost won. What is now at issue is the use of active euthanasia, that is to say the deliberate intervention by the doctor to expedite death, as opposed simply to letting nature take its course.

Some moral philosophers would say that there is no ethical distinction between active and passive euthanasia and would point out that, if we regard the patient's welfare as paramount, we should adopt active euthanasia as being the most humane option (Beloff 1986). That is now the opinion of the Royal Dutch Medical Association in their official report on euthanasia.[7] The trouble is that active euthanasia does impose a greater responsibility on the doctor in charge and that is, I suspect, the main reason why it is still opposed by the medical profession elsewhere.

Finally, the belief that advances in medication and in nursing care will eventually render the voluntary euthanasia issue obsolete, while understandable, is unrealistic. It is based on a number of misconceptions about the demand for voluntary euthanasia. Thus, pain is not, by any means, the only reason for wanting euthanasia. Even more important are the indignities of being kept alive artificially in a state of total helplessness.[8] That is why most of the societies for voluntary euthanasia like to call themseles societies *for the right to die with dignity.* I certainly do not want my wife and children to remember me as a grotesque travesty of a once rational human being. It is no comfort to me to be told, as I was recently told by a professor geriatric medicine, that some of his senile patients appear to be quite happy. It is simply an affront to my self-image to acquiesce in the prospect of ending my days as a contented vegetable! But, in the last resort it all boils down to a question of individual liberty. Even if everyone had the prospect of dying in a first-rate hospice, remote as such a possibility may be, some of us may still prefer to die in our own way and in our own time.

Every reform carries with it the possibility that it may produce consequences of an unforeseen and undesirable kind. My own attempts to assuage the misgivings voiced by the anti-euthanasia lobby are bound to be no less speculative than the hazards which they foresee. There is only one way of settling the dispute, and that is to put the matter to the test. I suggest that is why, at the present time, the Dutch experiment is being watched with so much attention and accorded so much publicity. As of this writing, the Dutch parliament has still not passed a law making voluntary euthanasia legal, but there already exists a perfect understanding between the public prosecutor and the medical profession that no action will be taken against a doctor practicing active euthanasia provided he observes all ten conditions which the profession itself has laid down as necessary safeguards. As a result, already some 5000 patients a year take this option.

So far as I can see, there is nothing very special about the Netherlands that makes it different from other advanced Western countries. Consequently, if the experiment works there and, to the best of my knowledge, it has so far produced no untoward consequences or public scandals, there is a reasonable prospect that it will catch on elsewhere. Already the Hemlock Society, which has its headquarters in Los Angeles, has prepared what it calls the "Humane and Dignified Death Act" which it proposes to put before the voters of California in 1989 as an amendment to the California Natural Death Act of 1976. The relevant clause reads: "the inalienable right of privacy includes the right of the terminally ill to voluntary, humane and dignified doctor assisted aid in dying" (Risley 1986; Risley and White 1986).

There remains one final objection to voluntary euthanasia which I have still to touch on. Even if we reject, as unduly alarmist, the idea that voluntary euthanasia may lead, by imperceptible degrees, to the involuntary euthanasia of those who are a burden on society, it can still be argued that once voluntary euthanasia has become legitimate, a presumption would be created in its favor that would make it very hard to resist. The more conscientious old people, realizing what a burden they had become on those whose responsibility they were, might opt for euthanasia even if, in their heart of hearts, they would prefer to go on living. At the risk of sounding callous, my own answer to this objection would be to say: so what? Is that such a bad thing? I have known enough women, in my time, whose lives were virtually ruined by the strain of having to look after some aged invalid parent. If we do freely decide, of our own volition, that the time has come for us to step aside and cease being a burden on others, that, surely, is something to be applauded rather than condemned. There are those, I know, who deplore suicide on the grounds that it makes the survivors feel guilty at not having done more to make the life of the suicide worth living. Of course, suicide may stem from a variety of motives. A large proportion of attempted suicides are thought to be a cry for help, a way of dramatizing an individual's despair. Likewise, many suicides amount to acts of aggression or revenge upon those whom the suicide felt were insufficiently caring. But there can be altruistic suicides. As someone who is approaching his three score years and ten I can no longer shirk the responsibility of thinking about my own demise. My hope is that, once I realize that I am no longer any use to myself and a nuisance to everyone else, I will not flinch from taking the necessary steps to end my life with the minimum of fuss.

So, for me the question is not just do we have a right to die, but do we sometimes have a *duty* to die?

NOTES

1. Buddhism, on the other hand, with its intense preoccupation with the sanctity of life and with the esoteric doctrine of karma and rebirth, strongly discourages suicide.

2. In his essay "On Suicide," first published in 1777, the year after his death. Like most men of the Enlightenment, Hume defends the right to die.

3. For two contemporary expositions of the Catholic position on suicide see Blázquez (1985) and Sullivan (1975).

4 According to a recent declaration by the Sacred Congregation for the Defence of the Faith, published in 1980: "One should draw a distinction between suicide and that sacrifice by which, for a higher cause — such as the glory of God, the salvation of souls or the service of the brethren — one's own life is offered in place of danger." See Blázquez (1985) p. 70.

5. For an excellent discussion of this point see Rachels (1986), Chap. 25 "The Sanctity of Life."

6. See Larue (1985) pp. 35–43 or Downing and Smoker (1986), Appendix 4, pp. 293–301.

7. For a spirited defense of active voluntary euthanasia, see Admiraal (1986). Dr. Pieter Admiraal, an anesthetist, was in the forefront of the reform that has taken place in the Netherlands.

8. The following statement admirably expresses my own sentiments: "Pain itself can be controlled, provided the doctor in charge is prepared to put the relief of pain before the prolongation of life; but analgesics will not help a patient to live with total incontinence, reduced to the status of a helpless baby after a life of independent adulthood. And for the person who manages to avoid these grave afflictions there remains the spectre of senile decay, a physical and mental travesty of the normal person" (Barrington 1986: 233). Miss Barrington, a lawyer, is a leading light of the Voluntary Euthanasia Society (London).

REFERENCES

Admiraal, P.V. 1986. Active Voluntary Euthanasia. In *Voluntary Euthanasia: Experts Debate the Right to Die.* eds. A.B. Downing and B. Smoker. pp. 230–249. London: Peter Owen.

Barrington, M.R. 1986. The Case for Rational Suicide. In *op. cit.* eds. A.B. Downing and B. Smoker. pp. 230–249.

Beloff, J. 1986. Killing or Let Die? Is There a Valid Moral Distinction? *The Euthanasia Review.* 1(4):208–212.

Blázquez, N. 1985. The Church's Traditional Moral Teaching in Suicide. In *Suicide and the Right to Die.* eds. J. Pohier and D. Mieth. Edinburgh: Stichting Concilium and T & T Clark.

Downing, A.B., and Smoker, B., eds. 1986. *Voluntary Euthanasia: Experts Debate the Right to Die, op, cit.*

Feinberg, J. 1980. *Rights, Justice and the Bounds of Liberty.* Princeton, NJ: Princeton University Press.

Humphry, D., and Wickett, A. 1986. *The Right to Die: Understanding Euthanasia*, pp. 103–109. London: Bodley Head.

Larue, G.A. 1985. *Euthanasia and Religion: A Survey of the Attitudes of World Religions to the Right to Die.* Los Angeles: The Hemlock Society.

Rachels, J. 1986. *The End of Life: Euthanasia and Morality.* Oxford: Oxford University Press.

Risley, R. 1986. What the Humane and Dignified Death Initiative Does. *Euthanasia Review* 1:221–225.

Risley, R., and White, M. 1986. Humane and Dignified Death Initiative for 1988. *Euthanasia Review* 1:226:239.

Sullivan, J.V. 1975. The Immorality of Euthanasia. In *Beneficent Euthanasia.* ed. M. Kohl. Buffalo, NY: Prometheus Books.

15

Voluntary Active Euthanasia:

An Individual's Right to Determine The Time and Manner of Death

Marvin E. Newman

Does a competent terminally ill adult have the right to choose the time and manner of death? This question underlies any discussion of voluntary active euthanasia. Participants in the debate, however, suggest answers bearing no such common thread. Legal, ethical, philosophical, religious, political, and social perspectives offer contrasting views on the validity of allowing an incurably ill patient the right to decide knowingly to be put to death. While some view any deliberate act leading to death as criminal and thus contrary to state interests, others argue that it is a valid state interest to recognize society's inherent respect for an individual's right to escape unavoidable suffering.

Voluntary euthanasia is performed with the informed consent or at the informed request of a legally competent patient. Competence is a prerequisite to allowing a patient to refuse treatment when life is at stake. Competence is the mental ability to make a rational decision, and includes the ability to perceive, appreciate, and make a rational decision based on all relevant facts. Applied to euthanasia, legal competence is an incurable patient's ability to understand that a request for active euthanasia is a choice of death over life. A terminally ill or uncontrollably suffering patient's rational decision to end life is an exercise of free will.

The nature of a second party's acts usually distinguishes active euthanasia from passive euthanasia. Passive euthanasia, caused by an omission of treatment, has been judicially approved both when voluntary and when involuntary (Sherlock 1982). Although unplugging a respirator and switching off a dialysis machine are arguably acts of commission, both have been accepted as permissible passive euthanasia in voluntary as well as involuntary settings. This judicial respect of a patient's "right to die," however, is limited to a patient's right to die naturally. This chapter will argue that it is legally inconsistent to honor a terminally ill patient's request for removal of life support equipment, but deny a similarly situated patient's request for an immediate and painless death merely because a second party's active assistance is needed. Furthermore, this chapter will argue that imposing legal sanctions on an involved second party effectively denies a patient the right to choose euthanasia.

To support a proposal for voluntary active euthanasia, this chapter will explore, among other issues, how euthanasia decisions are carried out in the Netherlands. Since 1973, courts in the Netherlands have responded to the loudly proclaimed rights of individuals to make decisions regarding their own lives by spelling out guidelines under which active and direct euthanasia may be justified. This chapter will discuss the legal, ethical, and social implications of personal and judicial euthanasia decisions in the Netherlands, and the effects on patients, physicians, and communities. In addition, philosophical, religious, and nonreligious questions are key to the debate and must also be explored. Finally, this chapter will recommend a series of guidelines to ensure that voluntary active euthanasia be carried out in a way that would fully protect the rights of the individual without offending societal interests.

Attitudes toward euthanasia are necessarily affected by our feelings about suicide. Indeed the morality of the latter is a threshold question in an assessment of the morality of the former. If it is concluded that any suicide is morally intolerable, it is impossible to make a case for voluntary euthanasia. If, on the other hand, it is morally acceptable for one to bring an end to one's life in some circumstances, there can be no moral fault in the refusal of life-saving aid so that one may die, and we can then inquire whether it should make any difference that one seeks one's end at the hand of another.

Though always a controversial subject among philosophers, the taking of one's own life was at one time viewed with understanding and tolerance (Lecky 1927). Indeed there have been societies and philosophical traditions in which it was regarded as an appropriate relief from some of the travails of the world (Pretzel 1977). In pre-Christian Western thought, philosophers viewed suicide as acceptable for the purpose of ending suffering wrought by disease. For some it was more than acceptable, or acceptable for more than this reason, though few were as enthusiastic as the stoic who was forbidden from lecturing on the subject when, as a result of his persuasive advocacy of suicide, some among his listeners killed themselves (Westermark 1908). However, his contemporaries did not have to share his enthusiasm to be reluctant to condemn the taking of one's own life outright.

To Christians, this was an intolerable attitude. Death for the Christian was not a law of nature and an end to suffering. It was punishment for sin and for much of mankind the beginning of even greater suffering. In earthly life there was preparation for eternity and the possibility of redemption and it was wrong to abbreviate the former or to preclude the latter. Although the earlier Christian authorities tolerated suicide in very limited circumstances, the doctrine of the sanctity of life eventually led to the unqualified condemnation of suicide (Lecky 1927:74).

The advent of Christianity with its severe view of suicide has been the single most influential factor in shaping our attitudes to it and the related subject of euthanasia. Yet sympathy for some who have killed themselves remained, and upon the revival of classical learning even some theologians viewed suicide as occasionally permissible (Williams 1957). As well, difficulties in distinguishing among killing, letting die, and seeking death at the hand of another have persisted and reveal a core definitional problem which makes any categorical judgment about attitudes precarious.

Though it has been religion with its mass appeal which has had the most profound impact on our attitudes to suicide, it has been philosophy which has carried the critical debate on the subject. Albert Camus was guilty at least of exaggeration in asserting that there is "but one truly serious philosophical problem and that is suicide" (Gillon 1971), but there is no doubt that it has been recognized by the more contemporaneous philosophers as it was by the ancients as one very serious problem (Pretzel 1977:389-). In this, philosophers lend elegant expression to the ambivalence about the subject which most of us feel. Though we may react to some instances of suicide which come to our attention with disapproval, we react to others with compassion and are reluctant to attribute moral blame to the perpetrator. Few of us hold that it is *always* wrong to kill oneself.

Reluctance to condemn suicide outright leads us to contemplate whether it is important that one who seeks to end one's life on this earth wishes to do so at the hand of another. One who commits suicide has demonstrated that in addition to a commitment to end one's life one had the means and the access to do so. Another who requests euthanasia acknowledges the inability, by one's own hand, to end one's life or to end it in a tolerable fashion. Historically, assisted suicide was not uncommon. In some primitive societies it was traditional for the family to assist in killing one of their number or to do it themselves (Gillon 1971:182, note 1). In ancient Greece a botanist advised his readers about potions of hemlock which were particularly suitable for use in suicide, and a medical historian recorded many instances of doctors giving a poison to their dying patients. We must acknowledge, however, that suicide and euthanasia are different in important respects. Some definitions and usages of the word "euthanasia" are not limited to requested death. Even under those definitions that are, ethical considerations peculiar to suicide are widened to include the morality of intervention of others in the dying process. Whether the desire to exercise a hypothetical moral right to take one's own life implies permission for a designated other to take it, or even a moral duty imposed upon that other to do so, is a serious question which raises distinct issues of ethics and public policy (Woods 1978).

Although many doctors may be willing to assist in carrying out a patient's informed and competent choice of euthanasia, laws criminalizing active participation in suicide deter doctors from providing such assistance. Consequently, the possibility of criminal prosecution inhibits a free and open exchange of information about euthanasia between doctors and their terminally ill patients. Inadequacy of information about the euthanasia option prevents the vast majority of terminally ill patients from exercising their rights of self-determination and infringes on their privacy rights.

The constitutional right to privacy, as established by the United States Supreme Court in a series of cases[1] culminating in the 1973 decision on abortion, *Roe v. Wade* (1973), protects the individual's fundamental right to self-determination. This protection is particularly important in areas of moral controversy such as abortion, contraception, and euthanasia, where the right to privacy acts to protect private decision making in personal matters.

Courts, concluding that the individual patient's interests outweigh those of the state, have extended the right to privacy to include the right of a terminally ill patient to refuse treatment. These cases balance an individual's interest in self-determination and relief from the "traumatic cost" of prolonged life against state interests which include protecting the sanctity of life (Supt. of Belchertown State School v. Saikewicz 1977). Upholding the right of a terminally ill leukemia patient to refuse chemotherapy treatments, the Massachusetts Supreme Court in *Superintendent of Belchertown State School v. Saikewicz* (1977) stated, "The constitutional right to privacy. . .is an expression of the sanctity of individual free choice and self-determintion as fundamental constituents of life. The value of life as so perceived is lessened. . .by the failure to allow a competent human being the right of choice" (at p. 742).

The New Jersey Supreme Court in a 1985 decision upholding a terminally ill patient's right to refuse life-sustaining medical treatment expanded on this balancing analysis. In *In re Conroy* (1985) the court stated that the most important state interest limiting this right is the preservation of life, which embraces the two separate but related concerns of an interest in the life of a particular patient and an interest in preserving all life. The state's indirect and abstract interest in preserving the lives of competent patients should generally give way to the patients' much stronger personal interest in directing the course of their own lives.

These decisions logically extend the *Roe* doctrine's protection of a competent individual's right to make decisions about personal and moral matters to that individual's decision to refuse treatment ("The Right to Privacy" 1980). They reflect judicial recognition of the value of human dignity.

Similarly, courts should apply the *Roe* doctrine to protect a competent terminally ill patient's request for voluntary active euthanasia. If the right to privacy protects the right to die naturally, it should also protect the competent, terminal patient's right to choose a quick and painless death. The difference beween a terminal patient's choosing to refuse treatment and choosing a faster means of dying does not offer a basis for a legal distinction. When a competent terminal patient chooses to die, the state interests balanced against that patient's right to privacy are virtually the same regardless of the means chosen. In fact, applying the *Roe* doctrine to decisions made for incompetent patients by others is far more difficult to justify and creates the risk of abuse. Self-determination by definition does not encompass decisions made for an individual by a third party. In contrast, competent terminal patients' right to choose the time and manner of their deaths fits squarely within the right to privacy doctrine and should be given effect unless there exists a compelling state interest in preserving the patients' lives ("The Right to Privacy" 1980).

In cases in which the terminal patient is unable to end life without another party's assistance, the other party's activities should also come within the constitutional penumbra of protection. Where the Constitution protects an individual's rights, it also protects from criminal sanction second parties whose assistance is necessary in exercising those rights. Constitutional protection extends to third parties whose action is necessary to effectuate the exercise of that right where the individuals themselves would not be subject to prosecution or where the third parties are charged as accesssories to an act which could not be a crime. A second party has standing to assert the constitutional rights of another when the second party's intervention is necessary to protect the other party's constitutional rights. Doctors assisting terminal patients in voluntary active euthanasia should be able to defend against prosecution by asserting the patients' constitutional rights to self-determination. In many instances, without such assistance, voluntary active euthanasia for terminal patients would be impossible.

Objections to sanctioning voluntary active euthanasia are based on both religious and nonreligious grounds. The religious arguments may be summarized briefly: God gives all life, only God has the right to take life, and suffering is a necessary part of living that is not to be avoided. This reasoning is similar to that expressed by those who oppose abortion. Religious objections to abortion, however, have been deemed irrelevant to the legality of abortion. Thus, religious objections to euthanasia should be irrelevant to the legality of voluntary active euthanasia. But religious objections cannot be overlooked, especially in societies where politics and religion are intertwined. Political parties with religious underpinnings favor legislation banning voluntary active euthanasia, just as they favor legislation outlawing abortions. Countries whose governments are controlled by the church will probably not even consider the subject. "Secular" political parties, especially those in the minority, may want to propose legislation permitting euthanasia but often find it politically cumbersome to do so. These political barriers to sanctioning voluntary active euthanasia leave to the judiciary the responsibility for setting guidelines.

Nonreligious objections to voluntary euthanasia often evolve from a risk–benefit analysis in which the risks of abuse outweigh the benefits that would accrue to a small number of patients (Kamisar 1979). One perceived risk is commonly known as the "domino" or "wedge" theory (Kamisar 1969:114). Its proponents contend that once society accepts diminished quality as a valid reason to terminate life, there is no rational way to limit euthanasia and prevent its abuse. According to this theory, voluntary euthansia is the narrow end of a wedge that, once in place, will be driven deeply into society. Legalized voluntary euthanasia would lead to legalized involuntary euthanasia because of the absence of a rational distinction between those who seek to die because their lives are a burden to themselves, and those whom society seeks to kill because their lives are a burden to others.

Opponents of the wedge theory do not find it persuasive. They contend that courts can establish functional guidelines to balance the free exercise of the right to self-determination against potential abuses. Although establishing such guidelines may be difficult, the courts could separate justifiable from unjustifiable euthanasia and thus protect both the innocent second parties and the competent terminally ill.

Nonreligious objectors to voluntary euthanasia perceive another risk in the potential for abuse or mistake in allowing euthanasia. Abuse can most easily occur in establishing voluntariness. The fear exists that unscrupulous doctors, nurses, or family members may improperly persuade a weakened patient into consenting to euthanasia even though the consent does not reflect the patient's true intent. During the latter stages of a patient's illness, family members may be incapable of making a rational decision with the patient's best interests in mind. Inevitably, uncertainty will surround the patient's true desires. But courts are often called upon to determine an individual's intent. In criminal cases, courts must often infer a defendant's state of mind. In contrast, a voluntary request for euthanasia is an express statement of intent. Imposing sanctions such as the death penalty on the basis of inferred intent is scarcely different from allowing voluntary active euthanasia on the basis of express desire.

Decisions about length of life do not necessarily demand more of a patient's capabilities than do other important decisions. In fact, patients do not always regard decisions to shorten life as difficult choices. A few additional hours of life may seem rather unimportant to a patient for whom treatment may temporarily alleviate suffering or briefly extend life, especially if the patient has taken leave of loved ones and is reconciled to the situation.

Related to the potential for abuse or involuntariness is the potential for mistake (Kamisar 1969:99). A doctor's diagnosis of terminal illness may be incorrect. Administering euthanasia on the basis of an incorrect prognosis would be a tragic error. Even if a diagnosis of terminal illness is correct, some relief or a full cure may become available before the patient's natural death. On the other hand, such medical discoveries are usually foreseeable, and doctors working with terminal illnesses are generally apprised of developing or experimental treatments. To be considered informed, a patient must have full notice of the risk of an incorrect diagnosis or the availability of a potential cure.

The practice of voluntary active euthanasia in the Netherlands is on the increase. The key to why this practice is accepted lies in the Dutch people's strong belief in self-determination—a belief so strong that it supersedes the influence of the church on a moral issue. Although the majority of the Dutch people profess faith in Protestantism or Catholicism, they are not a religious people. While the basic tenets of both the Protestant and Catholic churches clearly oppose any form of euthanasia, recent polls show that two thirds of Dutch society do not object to it. But this populist approval has not translated into legislative sanction. The majority Christian Democratic Party of the Netherlands, holding to its religious underpinnings, opposes active euthanasia because it violates Scripture. The majority Liberal Democratic Party favors active euthanasia, but the position has given way to political realities. In the last election, the Liberal Democrats had to trade away their pro-euthanasia stance in order to achieve other political goals. Because the mixture of religion and politics precludes the government of the Netherlands from taking any affirmative role in sanctioning euthanasia, the courts have been forced to set guidelines for justifying euthanasia.

In 1973, the Criminal Courts in the Netherlands, without suspending the criminal code, spelled out circumstances under which a physician could go unpunished for participating in voluntary active euthanasia. Although the Netherlands Courts will convict physicians who assist in ending the suffering of a terminally ill patient, the Courts impose a more or less symbolic penalty. Most cases, however, never reach the courts. Each year, approximately one thousand people in the Netherlands decide to be put to death with the aid of a physician. Dutch prosecutors, however, pursue only 20% of the cases that come before them. Those doctors who are prosecuted are often found guilty but not punished, on the theory that they took the only appropriate action under the circumstances. These cases are rarely appealed.

Emerging from the Netherlands courts' decisions on voluntary active euthanasia are conditions under which euthanasia will be justified. These guidelines apply to both the patient and the physician whose help is sought to terminate the patient's life. The first condition is that the patient's decision be voluntary. There must be clear and convincing evidence of enduring, free determination. A patient's decision in favor of euthanasia is only voluntary if made without coercion. The patient's motive for choosing euthanasia is irrelevant, but factors such as pain, debilitation, emotional and financial burdens on loved ones, and the quality of remaining life may influence the decision. If possible, the request should be in writing as evidence that the decision was a well-considered one.

The second condition is that the patient's decision be an informed one. A patient must have adequate information as the basis for a sound understanding of the situation. Candid exchanges between doctor and patient ensure the patient's decision is fully informed as well as volunatry. Doctors, often keeping a journal detailing all relevant facts, carefully document all evidence of informed consent.

The third condition is that the patient must face irreversible, protracted, unbearable suffering. This guideline does not limit active euthanasia to the terminally ill. The Netherlands has accepted active euthanasia for chronically ill patients even though the illness is not terminal. Such a patient may simply prefer not to live any longer. In one case, voluntary active euthanasia was approved for a patient who had attempted suicide thirteen times.

The final condition is that there must be, from the patient's point of view, an absence of reasonable alternatives to alleviate the suffering. Most patients choose among alternative courses on the basis of such factors as how many days or months the treatment might add to their lives and the nature of that extended life. For example, a patient might consider whether treatment will allow or interfere with pursuit of important goals, such as completing projects and taking leave of loved ones. Additionally relevant to the patient are the

degree of suffering involved and the costs, financial or otherwise, to the patient
and others. The relative weight to be afforded each factor is ultimately the
choice of the competent patient (Report of President's Euthanasia Commission
1969).

Dutch case law has also generated conditions governing the assistance of a
second party in performing euthanasia (Admiraal 1986a). First, the assistance
must come from a qualified physician. Second, the physician must act only
after consulting another physician or expert who also approves the assistance.
This approval must be independent and the result of the other party's own
judgment. Third, the physician must exercise due care in performing the
euthanasia. Finally, the euthanasia must be necessary or desirable from a
medical point of view.

To secure compliance with these standards the Netherlands Public Prosecutor's office and quality-control medical inspectors have entered into an agreement regarding the handling of euthanasia cases. Although physicians are
required to be frank in reporting the cause of death, euthanasia is nearly always
reported as death by natural causes to avoid prosecution as well as problems
for the patient's family. The prosecution policy evidences the belief that decisions to prosecute for participating in voluntary active euthanasia should not
run counter to the conditions for impunity developed in the administration of
justice by the Netherlands courts. From 1982 through 1984, 36 cases of
euthanasia were brought to the attention of the Public Prosecutor. Of these
cases, 78 % were dropped. This illustrates the deferential approach to euthanasia cases that eventually led the Netherlands Supreme Court to open the
door to the *responsible* practice of voluntary active euthanasia. The Supreme
Court decision, handed down in November, 1984, is a good tool for examining
the legal theories behind sanctioning voluntary active euthanasia. It also
presents a fact situation that presents pre-euthanasia moral and ethical questions
facing the doctor, the patient, and the patient's family.

Although only the physician who assists in euthanasia may face prosecution,
the patient is the central figure in euthanasia cases (Admiral 1986b). The
patient's life, illness, suffering, wish to die, and death create every euthanasia
issue. In the landmark case before the Netherlands Supreme Court, a 94-year-
old woman who always had been a vital, mentally strong person, setting great
store by her independence, had asked her doctor to help her die. At the time
of the request, the woman lived in a home for the elderly. Her body func-
tioned poorly and she could not walk or sit up. Speech was almost impossible,
and she was totally dependent on the nursing staff for the most elementary
activities. But in this case dependence did not preclude competence. The
patient was fully conscious and deeply aware of her progressive degradation.
Her understanding of her condition became increasingly acute as her failing
health took away her ability to communicate with her environment.

In the last week of this woman's life, her physical condition deteriorated
sharply, leaving her unable to drink or speak. She lost consciousness for some
time. After a slight remission, however, she urgently repeated to her doctor her

previous requests for euthanasia. After long and exhaustive discussions between them, the physician decided to administer a series of injections that would lead to the woman's death. The first put her to sleep. The second, administered ten minutes later, sent her into a coma. A few minutes later a final injection induced respiratory arrest, and the woman was dead. The doctor then informed the police and the medical examiner about the ethanasia. Because the doctor refused to report the death as resulting from natural causes criminal charges were brought. The judicial process that followed sheds light on the conflicts inherent in the practice of voluntary active euthanasia.

The lower court dismissed the charges against the physician because it could not find the doctor's conduct undesirable and because the doctor had satisfied the highest standards of conscientiousness. The Prosecutor's office appealed the lower court's decision. The Amsterdam Court of Appeal reversed, finding the doctor guilty. The appellate court reasoned that it could not accept public opinion as sanctioning euthanasia in direct opposition to the Netherlands Criminal Code. Section 293 of the Code makes it a crime to deliberately take the life of another. The court rejected the physician's defense that under the emergency conditions his loyalty to his patient superseded his loyalty to the law.

The Netherlands Supreme Court disagreed and quashed the appellate ruling. The Supreme Court held that the appellate court should have carefully weighed the conflicting duties and interests of the physician and then made an objective decision as to whether or not his conduct was justified. Therefore, holding that an emergency situation could have existed, the Court overturned the decision. Although the Netherlands Supreme Court was under no obligation to state the reasons for its holding, it chose to state expressly that euthanasia cases should primarily be judged, not by legal standards, but by medical standards. This choice indicates an intent to take the problem out of the courts and place it back in the discipline where it arose.

Because the Supreme Court of the Netherlands must refrain from inquiry into the facts and merits of cases it is strictly limited to judging whether lower courts remain within the law and follow proper procedures. If a case is remanded, another Court of Appeal addresses the points of inquiry.* Although the public prosecutor in the instant case stopped pursuing the case against the physician before it went to the second appellate court, the relevant points of inquiry provide the framework within which future cases will be decided. According to the Court, euthanasia must be medically justified and judged under medical ethics.

In determining justifiability, three questions must be considered. First, was the continued faltering health of the patient, disintegration of personality, and further deterioration of unbearable suffering to be expected? Because a personality factor is included, both physical and nonphysical suffering are relevant. There is no definite requirement that the patient be terminally ill. The

---

*The Court of Appeals in the Hague would have the final fact judgment in the case.

second question is, could it reasonably be foreseen that a dignified death would soon no longer be possible? This question indicates respect for the conscious, dying human being as well as the living. Finally, were there any alternative ways, acceptable to the patient, to alleviate the suffering?

Although the answers to these questions must be based primarily on objective medical views, this is only the first judgment. The final determination as to permissibility remains a legal one and must, therefore, rest with society. If any reasonable doubt exists, the Criminal Court may decide whether a physician's loyalty to the patient superseded loyalty to the law so as to justify the physician's decision to assist the patient in being put to death. The Netherlands Supreme Court's decision may be justified by medical, ethical, and legal standards without requiring amendment to the Netherlands Criminal Code. After the Supreme Court's decision, two district courts aquitted physicians who conformed with the Supreme Court's standards. In another case, however, a district court convicted a physician who performed euthanasia and sentenced him to one year in prison. The court found the doctor, although well-intentioned, had been careless and negligent. In such a controversial issue as euthanasia, strict adherence to the guidelines is essential.

While the Netherlands Supreme Court was still considering the 1984 decision discussed earlier, the Dutch Medical Society set forth its own standards, similar to those generated by lower court decisions, for practicing voluntary active euthanasia. The report states that only a physician may act to terminate a life but should never be compelled to do so. When a patient and doctor disagree about the propriety of euthanasia, the physician must allow the patient to contact another physician as soon as possible. The Medical Society report also requires a physician to exercise due care to ensure that the patient's decision is a voluntary, informed one that reflects a desire to end unbearable suffering. The report, however, does not fully explore the doctor's role in the patient's initial decision to choose death.

A patient can request euthanasia in one of three ways. First, a living will can explicity state the wish to euthanasia as a guarantee of a dignified death. This is voluntary passive euthanasia. Second, a patient can request euthanasia during the course of an illness. Finally, the patient can reply affirmatively if the physician suggests that euthanasia might be appropriate in view of the patient's condition. Although many patients accept such a suggestion as a valid alternative, most physicians hesitate to initiate the suggestion. Some find it contrary to their personal views; others see it as a violation of their medical ethics. Logically, a physician's primary duty is to preserve life and constantly fight death. Arguably, then, suggestions of euthanasia are directly contrary to the Hippocratic Oath. Some medical philosophers read Hippocrates' writings as prohibiting a physician from ever helping a patient to die. Other philosophers note that Hippocrates held the patient's interests to be of supreme importance. They view voluntary active euthanasia performed to end unbearable suffering as an act in the patient's best interests. Consequently, a physician who can do no more for a patient has an ethical responsibility to ease the patient's passing.

No amount of judicial acceptance of voluntary euthanasia will be sufficient to quell this debate.

The patient's family also plays an important role in the euthanasia decision (Admiraal 1986a:101). In fact, relatives of a patient who chooses death may play the most difficult role in the process. Some patients, especially older ones, hesitate to discuss euthanasia with their physicians but feel more at ease discussing the subject with relatives. If the request for euthanasia comes from the family, it can lead to the assumption that they, and not the patient, are actually behind the decision. In such instances, medical teams hesitate to carry out the euthanasia because reasonable doubt exists as to voluntariness.

But what if the family strongly opposes the euthanasia decision? The Netherlands Health Council, set up by the Dutch government to promulgate guidelines for active euthanasia, has issued a ruling which states that parents cannot stop euthanasia, even for a young child. A child 13 or 14 years old may therefore make the decision to terminate his or her life, and if the parents oppose it, only the decision of the patient will matter. Although the National Health Council did not develop any specific rule with regard to the age a child must be to make this decision, age will be a factor in determining the competence of the patient.

Opponents of voluntary active euthanasia cite those arguments mentioned earlier to support the premise that it is impossible to achieve true certainty of a patient's wishes. That is, a patient's weakened condition may create susceptibility to persuasion by others with improper motives. Because even genuinely concerned family members may not always be capable of making a rational decision under such emotionally charged circumstances, there remains doubt as to voluntariness. Those who sanction the process place great faith in the courts to determine state of mind. Courts look for evidence of voluntariness to determine the culpability of a physician who aids a patient in dying. But before acting, the physician must also determine whether the patient's decision is voluntary. Although the standard requires clear and convincing evidence of voluntariness, the question remains whether self-determination can ever be certain beyond a reasonable doubt.

While these euthanasia issues were being raised in the Netherlands Courts and the Dutch Medical community, the Dutch government was not remaining inactive. Because the early 1980s saw the judiciary paving the way for the practice of euthanasia the government appointed a commission to submit recommendations for application of existing law and formation of future government policy on euthanasia. In 1985, the Government Commission on Euthanasia issued its report (Admiraal 1986b:99, note 25). As is typical in other facets of the euthanasia debate, the report reflected contrasting opinions. Although a majority of the Commission agreed that euthanasia should be permissible, without criminal sanctions, under certain circumstances and certain conditions, members of the Commission disagreed over what those circumstances and conditions should be. Some members wanted a requirement that the patient's condition be terminal. Others, following the established judicial guidelines, would extend the practice to those who are in a "hopeless emergency situation." All those favoring active euthanasia agreed that it should only be administered by a physician using verifiable medical procedures. Recognizing that common law guidelines are not well defined until after the passage of time, the majority of the Commission also agreed that a legislative body should pass some judgment on euthanasia to eliminate uncertainty for physicians.

Although the coalition government of the Netherlands, consisting of Christian Democrats and conservatives, does not support legislation to reduce the tension between the present criminal code and the developing practice of euthanasia, one small, liberal political party has introduced a bill to amend the present law. Under the proposed law, voluntary active euthanasia would no longer be an offense if it was practiced with due care for the benefit of a patient who is suffering unbearably or is terminally ill. The proposed legislation incorporates most of the same guidelines set forth by the Netherlands judiciary, the Dutch Medical Society, and the Government Commission on Euthanasia. Although the bill garnered popular support, populism typically plays second fiddle to the political realities in the Netherlands, and no new legislation should be expected in the near future.

Many countries other than the Netherlands are seeing the practice of voluntary active euthanasia being carried on within their borders. Euthanasia is going on quietly in England, Sweden, Switzerland, and even the United States. Evidence of this continuing practice comes from the number of calls being received in the Netherlands from physicians asking how to do it. In Switzerland and England, it is not forbidden to give prescriptions for barbiturtes which are to be used by patients to terminate their lives. However, doctors can have no part in administering the drug as they can in the Netherlands. In Sweden and other Western European countries, there is a growing belief among the medical community that they have a duty to perform euthanasia on a patient who requests it and is suffering intolerably.

In the United States, the major barrier to doctors engaging openly in active euthanasia is the threat of being sued for malpractice. Although patients in the Netherlands never sue the doctor, the United States is a much more litigious society. This threat could supersede any justification for voluntary active euthanasia from the patient's point of view which evolves from the constitional right to privacy. Patients' rights to make a competent decision to end their lives and seek help from a second party in doing so is worthless if the second party views the professional risk as too great.

In addition to the threat of malpractice, the doctor also faces the threat of criminal sanctions for what might be viewed as assisting an individual in committing suicide. Thus, guidelines must be set and strictly adhered to so that patients' decisions to terminate their lives be distinguished as euthanasia rather than suicide. Those practicing voluntary active euthanasia must be required to demonstrate satisfactory compliance with these guidelines to avoid criminal liability and the threat of medical malpractice actions. The following are a series of five conditions which, if satisfied, should allow doctors and the judicial system to honor terminal patients' decision regarding the times and manner of their deaths.

1. *The patient must be terminally ill.* For a patient to be deemed terminal, two independent corroborative medical opinions must agree that the patient has less than six months to live. In termination of treatment cases, courts and hospitals successfully use the standard safeguard of verifying prognoses through two independent medical opinions.

2. *The decision must be voluntary.* A patient's decision in favor of euthanasia is voluntary only if made free of coercion. The patient's motive for making the decision is not important. Patients may choose to die in order to spare their families the trauma of watching them turn into suffering vegetables. Although the euthanasia decision may be made for the benefit of others, it is nevertheless the patient's own choice.

To ensure voluntariness, the patient should sign a request form in the presence of two disinterested witnesses. A witness should *not* be (1) one who signed the declaration at the behest of the patient; (2) related to the patient by blood or marriage; (3) entitled to any part of the patient's estate, whether by statute or by will; (4) directly financially responsible for the patient's medical care; or (5) the attending physician or an employee of the health care facility (President's Commission 1983). Although these parties may discuss the euthanasia alternative with the patient, a direct request on their part should raise a resumption of involuntariness.

3. *The patient must be legally competent.* Two independent psychiatric opinions must confirm the patient's competence. Euthanasia involving an incompetent patient is involuntary and in such cases the state interests in avoiding abuses weigh more heavily against the patient's right to privacy than they do in the case of a legally competent patient. Individuals fearful of being left incapacitated and without legal competence to terminate their lives may prepare living wills.

4. *The patient's decision must be informed.* Patients should be aware of the stages of degeneration accompanying their illnesses, the likelihood of temporary or permanent remission, the possibility of recovery, and any other medically relevant information. Full disclosure is essential to the unfettered exercise of the right to self-determination. Early disclosure provides terminal patients more time to consider their limited options carefully before their thought processes become inhibited by pain-relieving drugs. During this time period, the patient may want to participate in support-group discussions with other patients who, having suffered serious illness and contemplated euthanasia, have since recovered.

5. *The doctor must prescribe the least active means to effect death.* Because a fully informed request by a competent terminal patient for assistance in the act of self-euthanasia is presumptively acceptable the burden should normally rest on a prosecutor to demonstrate that the euthanasia choice was properly honored by a physician. People more capable of causing their own painless deaths need

less active second party participation. Thus, the use of a more active method when less active means are available suggests improper conduct by the doctor.

If a case falls within these guidelines, no sanctions should be imposed on individuals assisting terminal patients in ending their lives.

The constitutional right to privacy protects competent terminal patients' rights to determine for themselves the time and manner of their deaths. Recognition of the right of self-determination is the underlying concept of a community not based on force. Such a community can be termed an ethical community in that it is grounded on rationality and peaceful manipulation rather than force. An ethical community will not allow the use of force to impose certain views on individuals against their wishes. This view undergirds a peaceful accommodation to the fact that there is a pluralism of moral beliefs. Although it may be impossible to agree on what constitutes a good death, each person should be allowed to make a personal choice, so long as the choice does not involve direct violence against others. It should not be presumed that individuals have delegated authority to the state to prevent them from making intensely personal individual choices. The guarantees afforded such individuals by the Constitution compel no other result.

NOTE

1. For example, Eisenstadt v. Baird, vol. 405, United States Supreme Court Reports, p. 438 (1972); Loving v. Virginia, vol. 388, United States Supreme Court Reports, p. 1 (1967); Skinner v. Oklahoma, vol. 316, United States Supreme Court Reports, p. 535 (1942); Meyer v. Nebraska, vol. 262, United States Supreme Court Reports, p. 390 (1922).

REFERENCES

Admiraal, P. 1986a. Active Voluntary Euthanasia. In *Voluntary Euthanasia: Experts Debate the Right to Die*. Ed. A. B. Downing. Atlantic Highlands, NJ: Humanities Press Int'l., p. 1184.

Admiraal, P. 1986b. Euthanasia applied at a General Hospital. *The Euthanasia Review*. Summer 1986:97.

In re Conroy. 1985. *Atlantic Reporter*, Second Series. 486:1209.

Gillon, R. 1971. "Suicide and Euthanasia." In *Historical Perspective in Euthanasia and the Right to Die*. Ed. A. B. Downing. London: Owen, 1971. (Citing Albert Camus in *Le Mythe de Sisyphe*.)

Kamisar, Y. 1969. Euthanasia Legislation: Some Non-Religious Objections. In *Euthanasia and the Right to Die*. Ed. A. Downing. London: Owen.

Lecky, W. E. H. 1927. *History of European Morals*. New York: D. Appleton and Co.

President's Commission for the Study of Ethical Problems in Medicine and Biomedical and Behavioral Research. 1983. Deciding to Forego Life-Sustaining Treatment: A Report on the Ethical, Medical, and Legal Issues in Treatment Decisions, p. 3.

Pretzel, P. 1977. Philosophical and Ethical Considerations of Suicide Prevention. In *Ethical Issues in Death and Dying*. R. F. Weir, Ed. New York: Columbia University Press, p. 387, pp. 388-389.

Report of President's Euthanasia Commission. In *Euthanasia and the Right to Die*, op, cit., p. 99, note 21.

The Right to Privacy and the Terminally Ill Patient: Establishing the Right to Die. 1980. *Mercer Law Review* 31:603, note.

Roe V. Wade. 1973. *United States Supreme Court Reports* 410:113.

Sherlock. 1982. For Everything There Is a Season: The Right to Die in the United States. *Brigham Young University Law Review*, p. 545.

Supt. of Belchertown State School v. Saikewicz. 1977. *Massachusetts Reporter* 373:728,742; *Northeastern Reporter*, Second Series, 370: 417,426.

Westermrck, E. 1908. *The Origin and Development of Moral Ideas*, vol. 2. London: Macmillan and Co., pp. 247-252.

Williams, G. 1957. *The Sanctity of Life and the Criminal Law*. New York: Knopf, p. 311.

Woods, J. 178. *Engineered Death: Abortion, Suicide, Euthanasia and Senecide*. Ottowa: University of Ottawa Press, 1978.

16

Jungian Psychology and The Nature of Death

Alfred Ribi

An enormous amount of research work has already been done since the awakening of modern science's interest in the nature of death. People have always been eager to know what will happen after the physical end of life. Religions have given answers to the question from their point of view. But religions merely state as a matter of fact what one must believe. As the willingness to believe decreased in the age of Enlightenment, scientific investigation began into the nature of death. Many people's idea of the nature of death is still the same as former religious belief. You cannot avoid having a conception of the nature of death because this is one of the fundamental questions of mankind. Even if you do not consciously profess a definite belief you nevertheless have a preconceived unconscious opinion about death.

This makes it difficult to approach the question scientifically because there is always the danger of a priori unconscious concepts underneath rational arguments pro or con.

There is still another obstacle which concerns the nature of a scientific approach. Usually "scientific" nowadays is meant to be a pure rationalistic, conscious, logical approach having causality as a basis. Since C.G. Jung's (1971,1977) investigations into the four functions of consciousness and into the nature of synchronicity, such a notion of "science" has become too narrow. To consider facts scientifically, we need to broaden our view. We must also accept feeling and intuition along with sensation and thinking. This produces tremendous difficulties for old-fashioned scientists who cannot accept that the other functions are as objective as sensation and thinking. In particular, the feeling function, which does not argue and reason about its conclusions but *values* the facts, is said to be "only subjective." This judgment simply expresses the fact that until recently those who were experts in scientific matters were not of the feeling type, meaning that their feeling was inferior. Inferior feeling, as every inferior function, is closely connected with the unconscious whereby it gets an archaic touch. This cannot be generalized into meaning that feeling as a pure function is less objective than the other functions are. In this connection, sensation as the "fonction du réel," which states the "just-so" of a fact, has the tendency to exclude all the other functions. In fact it is quite perplexing, to ask more than just to describe accurately the phenomena as they happen to be. So sensation recommends itself as the function best fitted for scientific work. In fact much work has been done this way and merely describes the facts. Every interpretation of reality would then be open to subjectivism and error. Carrying this concept of "science" to its ultimate conclusion ends in meaninglessness. I think science has a "raison d'être" only if it helps one live one's life in some way.

This is the reason why we have to enlarge our notion of what "science" and "scientific" means and take into account all four functions, including intuition which is concerned with connections. Intuition is a function kept outside of science, but only as long you are not aware that most of the creative investigations in science are instigated by intuition. This is the reason why the results of scientific research have to be put in a rational form, which no longer shows or admits the original intuitive approach. When it comes to the "last questions" of mankind, intuition especially can no longer be omitted because the human soul feels a deep need for unlimited mysteries in life. In fact, "the last questions" are always beyond the reach of consciousness. If an interpretation does not take into account the fact of an intuitive opening towards the infinite, it is sentenced to incompleteness and is only of short duration. If you look at the history of scientific research, you realize how many ideas, very popular and clever in their time, look rather ridiculous to us nowadays because they did not issue from all the four functions.

So much for the role of functions in modern science. We now come to synchronicity as opposed to causality. Modern science until now has looked for causal interpretations of the facts. Researchers were satisfied if they could interpret a phenomenon as the effect of a cause. The experiment was the proof of a constant relationship between cause and effect. So if you could imitate in your laboratory the regular order of cause and effect you had reached the peak of "scientific" explanation. We often forget that not even in natural science can every matter be subject to experiment (*e.g.*, astrophysics) and not only experimental investigation is strictly scientific (*e.g.*, geography).

If science is not restricted to exact science but means careful observation of the phenomena we have still another category of facts which happen not regularly but sporadically. It is the category of meaningful coincidences. They are facts that are not caused by a psychological situation, but that are related to it by meaning. They of course may have causal origin, but that does not add anything to the most astonishing timing between the physical and the psychological event. You cannot "prove" a synchronistic event, but you experience it or rather it hits you as a meaningful coincidence. Meaning is experienced as an inner evidence connecting the psychic situation and the physical event. Meaning is an objective inner experience, not a subsequent construction of the mind. We often ignore synchronistic events because we are not used to watching for them. We should notice them much more carefully and realize how frequent they are in everyday life. Wherever archetypal situations are constellated and big emotions occur, synchronicities are frequent. You can produce synchronicities by experiment and it has been done since ancient times by oracles. If you throw the old Chinese *I Ching*, the answer to your question from the fall of the coins can only be the result of meaningful coincidence; causal origin is unthinkable. As the "last questions" are archetypal situations, we have to reckon with the possibility of synchronicities happening. I was told by a sceptic that synchronicity does not help to explain the phenomena. We are not yet used to this kind of connection. But it helps a lot if, in your state of desperation while dying, you experience a meaningful and comforting dream. The dream in extremis may not be caused by the chemical changes of the brain but is an important psychic manifestation coincident with dying. It may be a synchronistic manifestation of the unconscious which is related to death by its meaning.

Until now research into the nature of death has issued from an outdated understanding of "science" and "scientific." Its main concern was to register from outside what was happening or manifesting around the time of dying and death. Because the most unexpected things happened the trend was to "explain" them in a causal and rational way. And because the most unheard of things appeared it was the concern of the researchers to prove them by witnesses.

It was the forgotten knowledge of mankind which was rediscovered by Gurney, Myers, and Podmore (1886) in the early years of the Society for Psychical Research (SPR). The facts were so contradictory to their "Weltanschauung" that they had great trouble interpreting what they found. They decided that the living, at the moment of dying, could produce fantastic hallucinations in other living persons. Since then the question has come up whether it was the spirit of the dying or dead person that manifested itself or whether it was an activity in the psyche that visualized itself as the dying or dead person. The first is called the *spiritistic*, the second the *animistic* hypothesis. To be able to decide such a question as to the probability of one or the other hypothesis we would have to know what the psyche is able to produce or what the *nature of the psyche* is. To date the psyche has not been taken into consideration or has been implicitly identified with consciousness. Modern depth psychology has discovered that besides consciousness, or rather as the origin of it, is the unconscious. From the manifestations of the latter it becomes quite clear that it exhibits a totally different nature from consciousness. The uncanny thing about the unconscious is that we don't know it. What is known are contents of consciousness. We are therefore not surprised that the unconscious manifests where we would least expect it. It shows qualities of the trickster in that it always escapes our intentions to catch it.

The second big collection, which partially relies upon the former, Emil Mattiesen's three volumes (1937–1939), suffer from the same lack of psychological insight, although not in the sense that he did not discuss the psychological implications of the animistic or spiritistic hypothesis. However, he misses the unconscious situation of the witness or observer. This would be the view from within. It does not only answer the questions regarding what happened but additionally to whom and in what situation did it happen?

The more recent research of Kübler-Ross (1969) and Raymond Moody (1975)—just to mention two—have a more psychological standpoint as they are concerned with the reactions of consciousness to death or with the strange features of near-death experience (NDE). The latter especially can teach us something about the unconscious because they happen in deep coma. The most exciting results of NDE are phenomena that absolutely cannot be understood just from what we know of consciousness. The NDE can teach us how to approach the realm of unconscious phenomena. The uniformity of these reports points to a psychic stratum that is common to all people and is not very dependent on cultural background. It is what C.G. Jung calls the collective unconscious, which means a psychic structure common to mankind. The interpretation or meaning of what has been experienced in deep coma of course depends upon the person's religious and cultural background. It had escaped Moody's attention that C.G. Jung has long before published an NDE of his own in his *Memories, Dreams, Reflections.*

In the description of NDEs you will notice the shattering *emotional* impact connected with it, which belongs to the phenomenon. It is the danger of science to overlook the emotional reaction that is prominent not only in NDEs but in any experience around death. A fuller description has to take the emotion into account because it has an archetypal origin. Now, death is an archetypal situation in which deeper instinctive layers of the psyche enter into the function. When you are threatened by death your conscious reaction is not so important or even life-preserving as your instinctive response. People have on the one hand a tendency toward self-preservation, but on the other hand death is a fascination. One can become fascinated by death, either as suicidal tendency or as infection through suicide. I have treated several people who were in danger of jumping out of a high window although they did not want to do so. And, for example, an analysand of mine was so fascinated by an obstacle that she crashed her car into it.

Death in these examples is not a rational thing and the fascination by it may even be opposed to consciousness. Death is a mystery bigger than man can grasp. This leads to different attitudes in the researcher of which he or she should be aware: some accept it as a mystery that only the initiated can understand, but ordinary people cannot. Others are inflated in the way that they try to reduce death to some rational measure (chemical, psychological). Although the mystery is always bigger than we are, we are nevertheless drawn to investigate it. Every mystery of life has always challenged us to explain it. But it is not only for the sake of scientific insight but for practical reasons that we badly need an answer from death in order to be able to live. So, any investigation into the nature of death meets a deep need in man. If you favor a materialistic world view, then it is "the sad end of everything" on earth. But if you are looking for a modern approach to the problem, then you have to be aware of many unexpected difficulties, especially psychological. Recently modern physics has had to take psychology into its experimental considerations. How much more is it needed in a topic from which the deeper layers of the psyche cannot be excluded?

When I had made up my mind about future research in our field I came across a questionnaire about it which was sent to C.G. Jung in 1963 by the International Journal of Parapsychology, New York (Jung 1977:1213 ff). There he says: "The factor which favors the occurrence of parapsychological events is the presence of an active archetype, i.e., a situation in which the deeper instinctual layers of the psyche are called into action. The archetype is a borderline phenomenon, characterized by a relativation of space and time . . . ." He stresses that "the psychological significance of parapsychological events has hardly been explored yet." He continues that "the greatest and most important part of parapsychological research will be the careful exploration and qualitative description of spontaneous events."

It has not been realized thoroughly enough that in the collective unconscious there is no space or time. Whatever occurs in it somewhere occurs everywhere. And what occurs at a certain time may occur at the same time or before or after it. This is a difficult concept for our conscious minds which are used to identifying events at a certain place and at a definite time. Our physics relies on time and space. But the collective unconscious exhibits a, let us say, "non-Newtonian physics" insofar as the same event may happen at different places at the same time. Gurney and co-worker's (1886) collection has several examples of an apparition of a person who is dying appearing to a person nearby. For example, a five-year-old child appeared to his father, who was very fond of him, at a time when the father was in Paris, whereas the son was living in London. The father awoke one morning hearing his son's voice quite near. He saw a white translucent mass close in front of his eyes and in the center of it the face of the boy with shining eyes and smiling mouth. The apparition was only of short duration accompanied by the sound of the boy's voice. At the same time the child died in London (I:444).

I have chosen this example to show you that the apparition may communicate an event happening at the time in another place. But the unconscious is rarely just mirroring what really happens; it is communicating a message in a creative way. Thus the information exhibits a new and unpredictable form. It is not just a physical event happening at different places. It is as if death releases an impulse that is transformed by the receiver's unconscious in a form typical for the latter. But in my example you will notice too that typical collective symbols appear, such as the shining translucent mass. These symbols are more or less universal. Phantasms of the living as of the dead often exhibit light phenomena, which are typical symbols of the beyond. It seems that the beyond is represented by the unconscious as a land of pure light and the figures from it as beings of light, for example, in gnostic speculations (Apocryphon Johannis).

I have never encountered an apparition that could not just as well appear as a dream motif. There is no fundamental difference between any apparition and an innerpsychic manifestation because the unconscious is the medium through which we get the messages from the psychic and from the material world. A message from the material world must always be transformed into a psychic form in order to be communicated. This is the reason why, for example, a dying person may appear to his friend, not as he is on his deathbed but as he is in the friend's memory. The apparition is seldom an exact replica of a person. The "non-Newtonian physics" of the unconscious is only non-Newtonian concerning relativity of space and time, but it is not really physics at all.

The most impressive feature of the unconscious is its creativity. Even in dreams provoked by a sensory stimulus the latter is represented not as an optical image of the stimulus, but is interwoven into the happening of the dream in the most astonishing way. Therefore we have to stop thinking about parapsychological manifestations in terms of usual physics. They should instead be called paraphysical manifestations because their reigning laws are outside ordinary physics.

The time coincidence of an apparition and the death of a person is also not strict. Louisa E. Rhine gives the example of a lady combing her hair in front of a mirror in her bedroom in the morning. Suddenly the room became very light with a miraculous light. She felt a breath on her shoulder and heard a slight noise of wings. When she looked into the mirror she saw her mother standing behind her chair and looking beautiful, like an angel. She stood there for half a minute and smiled. The lady cried "mother" and hurried to her, but the mother had disappeared and the light was gone. A phone call soon after informed the lady of her mother's death at midnight. The time difference between the two places was about two hours. Therefore, death had occurred about eight hours earlier. C.G. Jung stresses the fact that the time coincidence must be strict to the extent that one event is psychologically experienced as belonging to the other. That means a *relative* coincidence in time. There are events in which the Newtonian time difference between the two is very short; they happen together or immediately one after the other. But for some it is sufficient even if there is a time interval of days. Because of the relativation of time we cannot count in the usual Newtonian fashion. All these "paranormal" manifestations around the time of death are nothing less than synchronistic events, or noncausal meaningful coincidences. We have to forget about our usual thinking in the category of causality. This type of thinking is no longer appropriate to the phenomena of the collective psyche. Causal reasons of course have to be excluded. As long as causality fits the facts it must be used. But, when it no longer fits and causal explanation is overstressed, then we have to think in terms of coincidences. However, this has hardly been acknowledged in our field.

The question, still debated, of whether the animistic or the spiritistic hypothesis holds true is the wrong question. In the realm of the collective unconscious there is, as stressed above, no space. This means that we no longer can attribute a place to an event. The consequence of this is evidently that it happens in the psyche as well as outside. There is no difference between inside or outside. These are categories of consciousness because it is a finite phenomenon. As the collective unconscious is infinite, there exists no border between inside and outside. C.G. Jung called this the *unus mundus*, the *one world*, before its division into psychic and physical worlds. This division makes categories necessary to consciousness. As soon as a content enters consciousness it can be differentiated as either physical or psychic. But outside the personal realm of the psyche the two are undifferentiated, that is identical. But as it is neither psychic nor physical, it is something beyond the differentiation, the splitting into the two: it is *psychoid*, meaning psyche-like.

The psychoid aspect of the archetype is a hypothesis evidenced from many facts. But it cannot be experienced. As soon as an archetypal content approaches consciousness, it divides into either physical or psychic. This is the reason why dead people in dreams sometimes manifest more in the animistic way, coming closer to a subjective experience, and sometimes in the spiritistic way, as if the activity stems from the libido of the dead person. Analysts with great experience in dream analysis are able to differentiate the two kinds of appearances in dreams. From this point of view the differentiation into animistic or spiritistic manifestations is valuable. In this respect spiritistic means behaving like a subtle body, that is, a semi-physical object.

If we are now looking for the message in dreams about death we have to do so more from the standpoint of synchronicity than from that of causality. If such dreams are stating something it is not because the beyond is "like that," but because it is meaningful for consciousness to understand the beyond in this way. When we ask about truth we have to reckon with the fact that there are several truths, not only one. We are used to looking for one truth. But at the border of our knowledge there may be several truths. As we know, the different religions of the world have different concepts of the nature of death and rebirth. In dreams of Westerners we sometimes find statements that point more to an Eastern religious belief than to Christian belief. Apparently for some people an Eastern concept would better fit their needs, or in other words, it is their truth. This is why Jungian analysts have to study comparative religion. As the collective unconscious is common to mankind, motives proper to other cultures may arise (Kennedy: 1988). As to the notion of truth, we can no longer state what is true and what is not. When it has come up through the unconscious and makes sense to the consciousness, then it is true. Truth in this field is always limited to the person in whom it arose. But it is nevertheless not only subjective truth, as the statement of the unconscious itself is an *objective* one. The statements of the collective unconscious are the uttermost objectivity we can ever reach. We have to be satisfied with this in order not to fall into general subjectivism. But as the statements of the unconscious in general are *compensatory* to the conscious standpoint, there is a certain concomitant *subjectivism*, too.

The other difficulty in understanding the statements of the unconscious is its *symbolic language*. The symbolism does not veil the message but is the best possible expression of truth. Therefore this is never simple, like a logical statement, but intuitive to express the unfathomable, which goes far beyond any reach of consciousness. Symbols always exhibit a multidimensional quality. The standpoint of thinking alone is never enough to understand symbols. Symbols appeal as much to intuition and feeling, and can only be understood when these functions are engaged too.

Dreams about the death or burial of the dreamer never point to physical death. They mean for consciousness to undergo transformation. The idea of rebirth is an archetypal idea. It primarily points to transformation of consciousness. Rebirth motives do not necessarily point to rebirth after death. So, when the motif appears in any manifestation of the unconscious, we have to consider the state of consciousness to be able to understand the way in which it must be conceived. To my understanding, this is especially true for "past life recall." We have no indication of what these experiences under hypnosis in the shape of past lives are pointing to. Since it helps, as a therapeutic tool, it must be meaningful for some people to take it as an experience of previous lives. I wonder, however, how the unconscious comments on such a therapy in dreams.

Previously I said that we can never attain absolute truth. Nevertheless, this must not be misunderstood: the collective unconscious conveys with it the feeling of absolute certainty. This is the reason why you cannot discuss this matter with a spiritistic medium. The medium takes all that s/he experiences in his unconscious as *the* reality, as we do during dreaming. As long as s/he takes it as his or her truth, it is all right. Or, as long as s/he takes the messages of dead people from the beyond as a therapeutic help for the survivor, there is no objection. But, if s/he takes it for granted as, or even as proof of, personal survival, it is not valid. I cannot decide how far the medium is picking up something from his or her or the survivors' unconscious according to the animistic hypothesis. Nevertheless, I know of a case where the medium's messages were regarded with a sceptical attitude. In this case the unconscious sent a dream ridiculing the dreamer's too sceptical attitude about survival after death. I would not take this as a proof that there is survival after death, but obviously the unconscious intended to correct the too-critical attitude. The unconscious apparently wants us to open up to this possibility. The reason for such an attitude might well be that we live better with it, as well as that it is so. But finally, this difference matters only from the standpoint of consciousness, which always wants to decide between the two possibilities. Why could it not be the one as well as the other? Rationally, one is excluding the other, but life is not only and not always rational.

There is another reason for difficulties with a medium. C.G. Jung in his work about synchronicity gave evidence about the absolute knowledge of the unconscious. By this he means that somewhere in the unconscious everything is known. This knowledge is not usually accessible to consciousness. Dreams bring up knowledge that has never been learned. This is especially evident in the intuitive search of mathematicians for the solutions to a problem. They sometimes find the solution and afterwards laboriously have to find the way to it. So, if a person speaks the old Egyptian language, it is not proof that he once lived in the time of the old Egyptians. His unconscious might have gotten access to this information. In the first half of this century a lot of work was done about personality splitting. Such partial personalities sometimes exhibit the most extraordinary faculties. From the psychology of primitives, we know that people may become possessed by ancestral spirits that endow them with extraordinary qualities.

We are used to understanding a person as a separate entity. We are not aware how much we are connected with each other when it comes to the unconscious. We identify the person with the unique qualities and acquirements of a lifetime. These, however, belong only to the realm of consciousness. The question arises whether the unconscious is part of the person too. There is no doubt for the personal part of the unconscious, the shadow. But as to the collective unconscious we are not so sure. It is the part of the personality common to mankind in the same way as we have anatomic organs, typically human as well as typically mammalian: shared with other human races and, allowing for some variation, with other species. In an individual these features also exhibit specific personal traits. We could define the person as a unique combination of specific qualities that are not entirely personal.

It is absolutely important to understand what makes the person a personality when we want to discuss the personal survival of death. From NDE we know that the person is undergoing a transformation at the threshold of death. The usual ego-personality is lost and another kind of personality is taking over. As personality does not consist only of the ego but of a totality of ego and the unconscious (called the Self by C.G. Jung) this is probably the personality we have to look for as surviving death. It is what the ancient alchemists called the philosopher's stone. To it they attributed the most marvelous qualities, especially incorruptibility. The philosopher's stone is something that has to be prepared during lifetime in order to resist the fire at death. Marie-Louise von Franz in her book *Dreams and Death* (1986) cites an impressive dream of this motif, which can be summarized as follows:

> I see that a devastating forest fire has ravaged the wood, everywhere there are only ashes. But in the midst of it there is a red fieldstone which exhibits no traces of the fire (1986:78).

In this dream the fieldstone is a genuine symbol of the incorruptible, whereas the wood symbolized the physical body being destroyed by the illness. Usually people do not know about alchemical imagery, but their dreams express themselves in this way. The dream is primarily a message for the terminally ill person, comforting by saying that there is something indestructible in him or her which will not be lost in the imminent death of the body. This could just be a personal message of the Self to this person were it not that this idea arises everywhere else, for example, in alchemy.

By comparing ideas and motifs, we become sure that this is not a singular experience but a collective one. We can only point out that ideas and motifs of the collective unconscious are ubiquitous. We do not know whether they point to a certain reality in the beyond. For practical reasons — and I can see no objection to this — we can believe that it corresponds to the state in the beyond. But any greater certainty is out of our reach.

I am struck by how meaningful these messages from dreams about the beyond are compared with mediumistic messages. Through the latter you usually get the same sort of messages as in a letter, a visit to a friend, or else very general instruction and advice that says nothing new. The only explanation I can devise for this fact is that it stems from a rather superficial layer of the unconscious. I refuse to accept that this mirrors any reality of the beyond. As long as the message does not transcend the usually known, it is not worthwhile.

Let's return to the kind of personality that from this point of view may survive death. If this sort of personality is a quintessence of the living person, as M.L. von Franz has shown, then it is unbelievable that it is committed to futilities in the beyond. Thus the messages must carry a deeper insight than we have. This is the experience of the aforementioned shamans or medicine men, possessed by ancestral spirits. As in the case of the Brazilian "Doctor Fritz," this spirit not only endows the medium with special faculties but constellates the archetype of the healer. This combination leads to the most incredible effects of healing. But there is nothing supernatural about it, because every single effect is known from other experiences, too. Parapsychological effects belong to the very nature of the collective unconscious; they are synchronistic events.

In conclusion, a quality of synchronistic events must be stressed: their uniqueness. Synchronicities are not regular phenomena, although they are frequent occurrences. They are singular events, exceptions, even miracles. We are not able to experiment and provoke certain synchronicities; they happen spontaneously. We draw our conclusions from one-time experiences, which gives us a certain feeling of insecurity although by comparing them to other similar experiences we feel more secure. Nevertheless, for the person who experiences a synchronicity it is self-evident and the truth. We have to be content with the singular evidence when it is *carefully observed*. We are not able to use statistics because these phenomena are the exceptions that are discarded by statistics. So, the despised is becoming the cornerstone of our research, in this case into the nature of death.

REFERENCES

Gurney, E., Myers, F.W.H., and Podmore, F. 1970. *Phantasms of the Living.* 2 Vols. Scholars' Facsimiles and Reprints. Gainesville, Florida (First published 1886).

Jung, C.G. 1980. *Synchronicity: An Acausal Connecting Principle.* Vol. 8 of *Collected Works.* London: Routledge and Kegan Paul, p. 416.

————. 1971. *Psychological Types*. Vol. 6 of *Collected Works*, *op.cit.*

————. 1977. *The Symbolic Life*. Vol. 18 of *Collected Works op.cit*, p. 510.

————. 1982. *Memories, Dreams, Reflections. Recorded and edited by Aniela Jaffe.* Glasgow: W. Collins, pp. 320,330.

Kennedy, E. 1988. "The Alchemical Transformation in Death: Dreams on the Psychic Origin of Death." Thesis, C.G. Jung-Institute.

Kübler-Ross. 1969. *On Death and Dying.* New York: Macmillan.

Mattiesen, E. 1962. Das persönliche Ueberleben des Todes. Eine Darstellung der Erfahrungsbeweise 3 Bde. Unveränderter Nachdruck der Ausgabe 1936–1939, ergänzt durch ein Vorwort von Dr. Gebhard Frei und E. Bauer. Berlin: W. de Gruyter.

Moody, R.A. 1975. *Life after Life: The Investigation of a Phenomenon - Survival of Bodily Death.* Atlanta, GA: Mockingbird Books.

Myers, F.W.H. 1903. *Human Personality and its Survival of Bodily Death.* New York and Bombay: Longmans, Green and Co., 2 Vols, vol. II, pp. 1–80.

Rhine, L.E. 1956,1957. Hallucinatory Psi Experiences. *The Journal of Parapsychology.* 20:233–256; 21:13–46.

von Franz, M. 1986. *On Dreams and Death.* Boston and London: Shambhala, p. 78.

17

Problems Raised by the Concept of the Survival of Personality After Death

Gertrude R. Schmeidler

For any important questions (and surely questions about death and dying are important) an emphasis on crossdisciplinary and crosscultural relations ought to be taken for granted. More and more of the studies of dying have been crossdisciplinary (though not crosscultural). The last few years show increasing recognition that neurologists and those in the medical professions share the study of dying with ethicists and jurists. There is even in some quarters recognition that psychological factors interact with the biological ones, although this recognition has grown more slowly. But death has seldom had crossdisciplinary investigations, although there is room for them.

A statement of our crosscultural interest is probably as much in need of emphasis now as it was fifty yeas ago, and this is embarrassing for those of us in psychology. Future historians of science will, I think, find it extraordinary that we have not yet learned the crosscultural lesson. The reason for what seems (but is seldom) a deliberate avoidance of the topic is probably a mix of laziness and of provincialism, or cultural blindness. It is all too easy to make our observations only on those around us, then theorize from what we have observed, and conveniently forget how our local constraints limited us to a special case when we thought we were examining a general one.

Two of the major psychological figures of the last century are all too vivid examples of this. Piaget (1954) watched Swiss children think and learn, generalized from them about the course of cognitive development, and had his generalizations largely supported by tests of other European or of American children. He was widely acclaimed for having found the Truth (with a capital T), but his generalizations had to be modified (Overton, 1983), most strikingly because of discrepant results from other children, for example, in Africa, who had not been affected by European ways.

Freud is another example. He was brought up in a middle-class Victorian household; his patients and associates were also raised in middle- or upper-class Victorian households; and he generalized as if the effect of that kind of child rearing was universal (Freud, 1900). Minor modifications of many specifics of his brilliant theory, and then some major modifications, had to be made when neo-Freudians such as Erikson (1950) studied those who were reared differently.

We should have learned by now, though it is a hard lesson, that crosscultural checks are a requisite part of any serious attempt to validate a theory that has to do with humans.

The major difficulty which prevents our putting together the necessary large assembly of research findings is, of course, that the reseach itself is done piecemeal. Any particular anthropologist or sociologist is likely to plan a project to study a particular question of interest, then report on it and on other incidental findings. The topic of dying is only of peripheral interest to most; thus, most of their writings give us sparse reports about it and no systematic crosscultural comparisons. And yet a scrap of information here or there indicates that cultural differences in dying have important implications for the healing arts.

Here are two examples. Mead (1937) shows us that those in one society often die after what seems only a minor illness and suggests that it is because a person who feels sick typically retires to a dark corner of a hut and stays there, passive and unattended. If there are causal relations between this response to sickness and an early death, they need to be traced. In other societies (Halifax-Grof, 1974) there is belief in hex death, and some evidence indicates that, with this belief, hex death occurs. This suggests one of two possibilities. One is that whoever casts the hex can directly cause death. The other is that the belief, the expectation of dying can cause radical body malfunction. Either of the two has important practical implications.

Is there also need for more crossdisciplinary research on dying? Yes; and here I suggest an unconventional possibility: research on dying as it relates to death. Death may or may not be the end of conscious experience. A considerable body of evidence that there is survival of consciousness after death has been gathered, chiefly by parapsychologists; the evidence is considered strong by some but by many is considered inconclusive. (There is more on this topic, later in the chapter.) I suggest that the evidence is strong enough that we should consider the possibility that consciousness continues after the body dies.

If it does, is it affected by the process of dying? Dying can be brief or prolonged; anticipated or not; accompanied by a variety of psychological reactions, from rage and resentment and fear to calm or even eagerness for the dying to end. Might changes in the dying process influence what occurs after death? Few parapsychologists have even speculated on this question, and, so far as I know, only Berger (1987) has attempted research on it. It also could be important.

Our scraps of information (or perhaps of misinformation) need to be assessed by specialists. The important variables need to be teased out and fitted together by crossdisciplinary teams or by the rare person who is well trained in more than one discipline. And the hypotheses that emerge then need further crossdisciplinary and especially crosscultural testing.

But no one can do everything at once. In the rest of this chapter I sketch out an overview of a single subtopic among those we are studying here: the topic of what death is thought to be. (The generalist, of course, can readily relate this question to the whole of our problems, both because what we hope or fear of death might well affect the biological process of dying and because of its crosscultural diversity.) After this overview of what death is thought to be, I will take a quick look at reasons for and against holding the particular view that is most common in our own society. This will at least be minimally crossdisciplinary; it partakes of both psychology and parapsychology.

WHAT IS DEATH THOUGHT TO BE?

When we think of death, the basic alternatives can be phrased like Hamlet's question: to be or not to be. Historians and anthropologists tell us that the majority opinion is overwhelmingly on the side of "to be," of a continuing existence after death. But this is consensus, not unanimity; I will make a brief mention of some exceptions.

Marxist ideology, for one example, denies that there is a future life. Presumably the convinced Communist accepts this part of the ideology along with the rest. For others who are nominally Marxists, however, we do not know what the beliefs are. No data from public opinion polls or large-scale in-depth interviews tell us how widely the party line is accepted.

There have been a number of similar exceptions: various sects, such as the Shakers, that take death to be the cessation of consciousness and of personality as well as of body activity. It is noteworthy, however, that the sects are usually small and shortlived.

A further set of exceptions will often occur within a cultural group: individuals who differ from the majority by considering that the "not to be" alternative is the more plausible. They are sometimes punished as heretics, sometimes reviled, sometimes heard respectfully (especially when they are considered spokesmen for science); yet even in our own society where science is often revered, they have not, according to poll results, changed the majority opinion.

Let us take it, then, that there is crosscultural consensus supporting survival after death; although obviously the mere fact of a majority vote in favor of a continuing postmortem existence is no evidence of validity. The vote can be explained away readily as mere wishful thinking.

Is there consensus, crossculturally, on the kind of future existence? No, there is remarkable diversity. In some societies, for example, it is expected that the spirit immediately departs from its body for a distant location; in other societies it is expected that the spirit will hover for some period in the neighborhood of its body. Within this second belief come further cultural differences. The period may be days or weeks or much longer. The hovering may be only near the corpse or it may also be elsewhere. The spirit's presence or departure is believed to be affected by such varied causes as type of death, especially death by murder, or mode of burial, or incantations, or the adequacy of propitiatory gifts.

There are many even more striking differences in expectations about the future life. Some give us descriptions of an afterlife that is an embodied continuation of present life. Two subclasses of this type are transmigration to a nonhuman but living being and reincarnation as another human. Other descriptions detach the spirit world from the world in which we live. These of course differ, as we see in the contrast between the sad, aimless netherworld of the ancient Greeks and the eternal agony and eternal bliss of the Christian hell and heaven. Still other descriptions straddle the difference between detachment and attachment, as when an ancestral spirit, different from what the person had been in life but still recognizable, is available for counsel or is a potential threat.

One common thread runs through all the discrepant ideas of future existence that I have been listing: the idea that the surviving spirit is recognizable. it might seem that this is inherent in the concept of survival and that it is given by the definition of surviving, but this is not so. Here too there is a different opinion, one that has been held for millenia. It is the thesis that the final, desirable form of survival after death, the ultimate goal of reincarnations, is absorption into the One, where individuality is lost.

It would be fascinating if we could trace the causes for these differing concepts, perhaps to some combination of temperament and child rearing and the external setting and historical events, but doing so is either hard or impossible. It may well be impossible for concepts that originated in the distant past because the historical record is not sufficiently complete. And it would surely be difficult even for comparatively recent concepts, such as those of Marx or the Shakers.

What if we turn to a narrower research goal? Instead of trying to determine the origin of a cultural or subcultural belief, we might try to trace the origin of the belief in an individual. We would then try to learn who, under what conditions, stayed with the expectation that was learned in childhood and also learn who, under what conditions, shifted to some other expectation. Even this would be a large, long, expensive task — and one likely not to have government funding. The question of why a group developed one concept rather than another, and the separable quetion of why an individual in the group accepts or rejects that concept, may be a challenge to some future reseach workers. At present they seem to be only matters for armchair speculation.

Now I present to you a different armchair analysis, one that is not crosscultural but instead examines one belief about death that is common in our own society. It is the expectation or even the subjective certainty that after death those who loved each other will be reunited. The belief typically extends the concept of survival to include a form of survival that keeps us recognizably the same in personality, memories, and even somehow in appearance.

Two assumptions underlie this common belief. One is explicit and has often been the subject of controversy. It is, of course, that each of us while alive has a spirit or soul, and that this part of us continues after death.

But the second underlying assumption has seldom been made explicit. In the expectation that after death we will recognize and be reunited with those we love lies the implicit presumption that each of us has been consistently recognizable while alive, at least to one's intimates; that each of us is a unique self, not to be confused with any other person. Without this assumption of a unique personality, there could be no expectation of recognizing a loved person after death.

The two assumptions need separate discussion. For each, two types of question will be raised. Is the concept defensible rationally? Is there evidence to support its validity?

ARE WE UNIQUELY IDENTIFIABLE?

The possibility that it would be difficult for us to recognize each other became a salient problem to me some years ago when Robert Ashby asked me to look at some puzzling questionnaire data that he had collected. His respondents were largely members of the Spiritual Frontiers Fellowship or else those who had come to hear him lecture on survival after death. His questionnaire asked about survival; and, as would be expected with these groups, the great majority of the respondents thought survival after death to be certain or at least possible. Their high level of cooperation was shown by their thoughtful responses to almost all of the long list of questions that Ashby posed — to all questions except one.

The exceptional question that most were unable or unwilling to answer seemed appropriate in its context. It came in the middle of the questionnaire and asked, in effect, "If you found yourself surviving death, and you wanted to communicate with someone alive, how would you identify yourself?" But to Ashby's astonishment, and to mine when he showed me the records, the majority of the respondents either left that item blank or gave an unresponsive answer, such as "I don't know." I suggest to you that it seems safe to infer that anyone who finds self-identification difficult would find it at least as difficult to identify another person.

A graduate student and I wondered if a different group of respondents would show the same pattern. He therefore administered a similar questionnaire to a large number of high school students in New York. Since high school students have learned that it is best to write something — anything — if they do not know an answer, this second questionnaire yielded fewer blanks than Ashby's, but it nevertheless showed essentially the same pattern. Instead of leaving the space empty, the students made answers such as "There's nothing special about me," or the familiar, "I don't know," or gave responses that seemed meaningless, like, "I would touch him." The sum of blanks and of nonresponsive answers added up to a percentage similar to the one Ashby had found (Schmeidler, 1977).

The problem of identifying oneself thus seems difficult or impossible to many laymen. How does it look to professionals? It is easily solved by biologists and those in medicine: they take a person's body to identify the person. It is only occasionally a problem for jurists who also use the body as basis for identification. The occasional exceptions come with a plea of insanity, a plea which essentially claims that at some time a man was "not himself."

It is a research question for psychologists, who have repeatedly investigated it. They may ask, for example, if individuals keep similar attitudes and show similar traits over long periods of the life span. When the responses are treated statistically, the question is likely to be answered in the affirmative for many traits and attitudes. For example, the answer might be yes, about two thirds of a sample are self-consistent for a particular trait like cooperativeness. But three issues immediately come to mind. One is that the exceptions are as interesting as the general pattern. Another is that environment and life experiences may have been relatively stable and thus be the primary cause for stability of the trait. And the third is that, in any event, so general a research question is almost irrelevant to the issue before us, the issue of individual uniqueness.

Other psychological research bears directly on that issue. Psychologists have often looked for evidence of a uniquely identifiable self but none, I think, claims to have found that evidence. A typical project might study some individuals intensively at a particular age, then make another intensive study of them at a later age, then try to match one set of records with the other. But again and again (unless the time interval is short) some matches are incorrect. Often, especially when there are drastic changes in a person's life, such as a disfiguring accident or a family breakup, there are marked differences between childhood and adolescence, or between adolescence and maturity. In short, the empirical evidence that has so far been collected does not support the thesis that each living self is uniquely recognizable.

Does absence of evidence disprove the thesis? No. Like any other theory, this one can be made so flexible that it is impossible to disprove. It needs, I think, only two additional postulates. One is that the self changes and grows; it is not static. The other is that the way the self shows itself is constrained by body and perhaps other processes, and of course by the environment. Given these, it is possible to explain away all the mismatches. Some are due to expecting identity at different ages, instead of expecting orderly growth. Others come when psychologists measure superficial changes, due to adventitious environmental or bodily influence, rather than the true, deeper characteristics of the self. The argument is that psychologists are misled by growth changes and external constraints.

Where does this defense leave the assumption that a unique self is continuous while alive? Can we rationally continue to hold that position? Only, I think, if we confront and try to account for the apparent anomalies. For example, can we specify which of the changes are orderly, rather than merely claiming that some will be? Can we specify which patterns are irrelevant to the true self so that shifts in them can legitimately be disregarded? We should be able to state when and under what conditions the later manifestations of one's self will differ from earlier ones. We should also consider a related question. Memories often change. Can predictions be made about which will vanish, and which will be modified, and which will remain intact?

None of these is an easy question, but they need to be answered to put the concept of a recognizable living self on firm ground. The assumption is defensible, now, only with an uncomfortably large number of appeals to ignorance.

Recent research on twins is adding new information and new complexities. It is possible to argue that part of each person's uniqueness stems from idiosyncrasies in preferences or outlook or ways of behaving. This was studied when identical twins who had been reared apart were reunited. Idiosyncrasies did indeed make one pair distinctively different from another, but astonishingly often, the two members of a pair showed the same unusual characteristics. Holden (1987) reports, for example, that two men in their 40s, identical twins who had been separated at birth, both liked to surprise people by sneezing in elevators, both had hasty tempers, and both came to the laboratory wearing wire-rimmed eyeglasses and blue shirts that were double breasted and had epaulettes. In a famous pair studied earlier, each had a wirehaired terrier named Trixie. Examples of oddities could be multiplied, like a preference for weaing many bracelets on the same arm along with an extraordinary abundance of other jewelry. Such similarities within a pair of twins obviously suggest that to find uniqueness, one's questions must be highly specific. They also leave us to wonder what questions would identify uniqueness for individuals with the same heredity.

In summary, the assumption so common in our society that survival after death implies reunion with those we love involves, when we examine it, a prickly, difficult set of questions. Can we identify some person we love as distinct from all other persons? If someone knew and loved a person at one stage of life, but someone else knew and loved that person at another stage, will the person be recognized by both? Let us leave this issue unresolved and turn to the question of survival.

IS THERE SURVIVAL OF CONSCIOUSNESS AFTER DEATH?

Now consider a related pair of assumptions: that a self or soul or spirit has informed our body during life and that this same self continues after death. The paired assumptions raise some general questions that should at least be mentioned before we turn to evidence relevant to them.

Was this inherent soul or spirit produced by some stage of body development? If so, how could something that transcends and is independent of the body originate from the body? If we reject that explanation of how the self began, we must assume it had an independent or prior source, but this gives rise to still further questions. How and when did it enter the body? How does it interact with the body? Is it separable from the body while the body is alive? Can it interact with other bodies rather than merely its own? And of course we can wonder if after death it develops further than it did in life, and whether then it has a different set of constraints. For these questions taken as a whole, the only self-consistent and complete set of answers, so far as I know, consists of attributing all that occurs to the will of God, and then stating that the will of God is unknowable and out of the reach of science.

This means that from the scientific point of view, the commonly held belief that a recognizable personality survives death has no coherent theory to support it. But this does not necessarily mean that the belief is false. Every science accepts many well-established facts that do not yet fit a theoretical structure. If there is factual, empirical support for the belief, we can expect that sooner or later, as more facts are learned, an adequate theory can be stated.

And there seem by now to be facts that bear on some of the questions in my list. One large set answers the question of whether the self can, without the intervention of its own body, interact directly with other bodies. This is a topic studied by parapsychologists, who often divide it into two subtopics: ESP, or information obtained without use of the senses, and PK, or physical changes produced without body intervention. There is by now clear evidence that such interaction can occur. I will cite a single example, chosen from many others that seem to me to be equally strong.

This example comes from one of the techniques that are used to study PK. Its method makes use of an instrument called a random number generator (RNG), which records events that physicists tell us are truly random and thus cannot be inferred. (It may, for instance, record the emission of radioactive particles or minuscule changes in electronic noise.) Further, physicists tell us that the events will not be influenced by any muscular or other body changes.

In RNG research, a subject is asked to push a button on the machine so that the next recording will show a particular change (e.g., a faster rate of particle emission on some trials; a slower rate on others). This is an impossible task for our bodies. Our senses cannot tell us what the next random event will be and our effectors cannot change it. Thus, when the machine records number of tries and number of successes, and there are only two choices, the expected outcome is an average near 50%, the chance level.

Radin, May and Thomson (1985) summarized the data of all published RNG research with binary targets from the time this method was introduced (Schmidt, 1969) to 1984. They found 75 reports, describing 332 experiments. When those experiments were evaluated as a whole, they showed success at odds astronomically higher than chance. But perhaps some experiments had been left unpublished because the results were null? Radin and colleagues used what is called a Monte Carlo simulation to estimate how many such experiments may have been performed. They found the number was 95, added those hypothetical 95 null experiments to the published ones, and evaluated the new batch of 427 by using an excellent statistical technique called meta-analysis. The meta-analysis showed that the results were clearly different from the expected 50% success, with odds of less than one in a trillion that they were due only to chance. I suggest to you that this demonstrates that some nonbodily part of ourselves can interact with an object in the external world.

This in itself tells us nothing about survival, but it and other evidence for ESP and PK seem to legitimize the concept that our self (whatever it is) includes something that has properties which our body does not have. This in turn seems to legitimize queries about the possibility of nonphysical existence after the body's death, and thus of the survival concept.

Other lines of research examine the survival problem more directly, but do not give such clearcut answers. They employ a surprisingly large number of methods. Each method has given results which some intelligent, well-trained scientists interpret as supporting or even proving the survival hypothesis but which other well-trained and intelligent scientists interpret as failing to support it. A short listing follows.

Two of the methods study living persons. One is the near-death experience (Sabom, 1982). Of those who revive after being considered clinically dead, perhaps half report having had vivid experiences while apparently dead. The experiences they report tend to have a good deal in common but are far from a complete overlap. Perhaps most impressive are the occasional cases where a person when revived describes accurately events that ocurred in a distant place during the time of apparent death.

The second method with living persons tests those who claim to have out-of-body experiences, that is, experiences of being at a location distant from one's body. Some have accurately described events at that distant place (Mitchell, 1981).

One method studies the dying (Osis and Haraldsson, 1977). Fairly often a dying person claims that a dead relative has come to help with the transition to an afterlife. Evidence, which some think supports the survival hypothesis, comes from a subgroup of these cases where the family at the bedside think the dying person's claim must be only fantasy because, so far as they know, that relative is still alive and well. We are told, however, that in all such cases that have been investigated, the family later learned that the relative had in fact died before the dying person described his or her coming to help.

Other methods study the dead (Gauld, 1982). Apparitions sometimes give information that is later found to be correct. Sometimes a group, perhaps using a ouija board, hopes to receive messages from spirits. At least one careful investigation has found that many messages gave correct and specific information known to no one who was present. And psychics or mediums, trying to obtain messages from a dead person, have often reported accurate information that was unknown to anyone present and (more rarely) that was known to no one alive until an attempt to check the message confirmed its correctness.

Each of these lines of evidence can be explained away by one or another counterhypothesis. The commonality among near-death experience is explained as a combination of physiological change and of wishful thinking. All the cases of accurate information are explained as extraordinary examples of effective ESP, sometimes embedded in a hallucination or in a fantasy of being out of one's body. The explanations are ad hoc and often seem forced; they often postulate more effective ESP than has otherwise been found. They are more parsimonious than the survival interpretation, but whether they are more intellectually satisfying than the thesis of a spirit, separable from the body and surviving death, is still controversial.

CONCLUSION

An evaluation of the expectation about death that is most commonly held in our culture must be only tentative. Its base in psychology is shaky, and few other scientific disciplines bear directly on it. Some evidence supports it, but the evidence can be interpreted in other ways. No adequate theory answers the questions it raises. It has not found a crosscultural consensus. This part of the problems we are examining demands further research before it can have a firm answer.

REFERENCES

Berger, A. S. 1987. *Aristocracy of the Dead: New Findings in Post-Mortem Survival.* Jefferson, N.C.: McFarland Press.

Erikson, E. H. 1950. *Childhood and Society.* New York: Norton.

Freud, S. 1953. *The Interpretation of Dreams.* London: Hogarth Press. (First published 1900.)

Gauld, A. 1982. *Mediumship and Survival: A Century of Investigations.* London: Heinemann.

Halifax-Grof, J. 1974. Hex Death. In *Parapsychology and Anthropology.* Ed. A. Angoff and D. Barth. New York Parapsychology Foundation.

Holden, C. 1987. The Genetics of Personality. *Science 237:* 598–601.

Mead, M. 1937. *Cooperation and Competition among Primitive Peoples.* New York: McGraw-Hill.

Mitchell, J. 1981. *Out-of-Body Experiences: A Handbook.* Jefferson, N.C.: McFarland Press.

Osis, K., and Haraldsson E. 1977. *At the Hour of Death.* New York: Avon Books.

Overton, W. F. (Ed.) 1983. *The Relationship between Social and Cognitive Development.* Hillsdale, N.J.: Erlbaum.

Piaget, J. 1954. *The Construction of Reality in the Child.* New York: Basic Books.

Radin, D.I., May, E.C. and Thomson, M.J. 1986. Psi Experiments with Random Number Generators: Meta-analysis part 1. In *Research in Parapsychology 1985.* Eds. D.H. Weiner and D.I. Radin. Metuchen, N.J.: Scarecrow Press, 14–17.

Sabom, M. B. 1982. *Recollections of Death: A Medical Investigation.* New York: Harper & Row.

Schmeidler, G. R. 1977. Looking Ahead: a Method for Research on Survival. *Theta 5:* 2–6.

Schmidt, H. 1969. Precognition of a Quantum Process. *Journal of Parapsychology 33:* 99–108.

18

Does Religion Need Immortality?

Paul Badham

From a historical perspective belief in a future life has been at the center of religious faith. According to J.G. Frazer (1913), belief in a life after death was simply taken for granted by the adherents of the primitive religions of the world, while in the major religions it forms an essential element in the historic structure of their beliefs. In Christianity, Islam, and developed Judaism, belief in a future life was part and parcel of belief in God, while in Buddhism and Hinduism the core doctrine of Karma requires belief in a sequence of lives as its necessary condition. Hence, writing in 1860 W.R. Alger could confidently assert that "the very nerves and sinews of religion is the hope of immortality" (p.57).

But this could not be said so confidently today. In contemporary Christianity and Judaism in the West and in Buddhism in the East, scholars acquainted with modern thought play down the notion of a future life and question the place of such a notion in their inherited traditions.

Most Christian intellectuals today, at least in Europe, presuppose that belief in God can be emancipated from the future hope, and the characteristic contemporary emphasis is that the Christian message is essentially concerned with the transformation of life on earth. Christianity is not concerned "merely" with life after death but with Faith in the City in the here and now (Badham, in press). Even the journal *Theology* classified life after death as a "fringe belief" in our society (Hammerton and Downing, 1979:433–436); and as for the immortality of the soul, the critical dissection of this concept is one of the earliest exercises given to a first-year philosophy student in a British university. Likewise, in many contemporary interpretations of Buddhism it is insisted that Buddha's "no-self" doctrine be interpreted as an absolute bar on any serious expectation of a future life, and hence the concepts of Karma and of rebirth must both be demythologized to fit with the vision of Buddha as a kind of precursor to Wittgenstein and contemporary philosophy of mind (Cook, in preparation; Parfit 1984).

But I believe that such movements of thought have not fully appreciated just how closely belief in a life after death is interwoven with the rest of these belief systems, so that when this element is removed the whole fabric of faith begins to unravel. Let me explore this by reference to the key beliefs of Western and Eastern religion respectively: belief in God, and belief in Karma.

Let us start with belief in God. The foundation of all religious faith in a personal and loving God is, I suggest, the conviction that women and men of faith have had of entering into a lively relationship of love and trust with such a God. Certainly this seems true of the biblical writers. As John Hick (1970:102,112) points out:

> They did not think of God as an inferred entity but as an experienced reali-ty....If we consider the sense of living in the divine presence as this was expressed by, for example, Jesus of Nazareth, or by St. Paul, St. Francis, St. Anselm or the great prophets of the Old Testament, we find that their "awareness of God" was so vivid that he was as indubitable a factor in their experience as was their physical environment. They could no more help believing in the reality of God than in the reality of the material world and of their human neighbours.

This sense of the supremacy of the personal religious experience is not confined only to the heroes of faith. Within all branches of the Christian Church it is acknowledged to be supreme as can be shown by reference to the hymns, prayers, choruses, or patterns of worship used in the differing traditions, as well as in the concepts of conversion, dedication, and vocation.

The supremacy of religious experience is important not only for belief in God, but also for belief in a future life. For as Edward Schillebeeckx (1980:797) says:

> The breeding ground of belief in life after death...was always seen in a com-munion of life between God and man....Living communion with God, attested as the meaning, the foundation and the inspiring content of human existence, is the only climate in which the believer's trust in a life after death comes, and evidently can come to historical fruition.

Within the biblical tradition it can be shown that the faith in a future life, which developed in Israel during the intertestamental period, was profoundly shaped by a growing belief that each individual mattered to God, and if this was so then the all-powerful God could be relied on to ensure that death did not ultimately triumph over that relationship, nor destroy forever the loved individual (Badham, 1977).

The stress on the importance of the individual person to God was further strengthened by the teaching of Jesus, and his constant use of the analogy of fatherhood to describe the human relationship to God. As a consequence of his teaching, and of the belief that God had raised him to new life, the Christian faith came into existence explicitly as a religion of salvation offering the first converts a sense of utter and joyful certainty about a life to come: "an eternal weight of glory beyond all comparison" (2 Corinthians 4.17) with our present earthly existence. All the first Christians thought of heaven as their true home and came to think of themselves as "no more than strangers and passing travellers on earth" (Hebrews 11.13). It was their absolute faith in a life beyond that enabled so many of the early Christians to embrace martyrdom with composure, and even with enthusiasm! Indeed, St. Ignatius of Antioch on his way to death in the Roman amphitheater could even write "I am yearning for death with all the passion of a lover" (trans. by Staniforth, 1968:106), so convinced was he that it was just the prelude to a glorious destiny. In the mission field too it was the claim to know of an eternal life that was perceived as Christianity's greatest attraction. Certainly, according to the Venerable Bede, it was this message that persuaded the Anglo-Saxons to embrace Christianity (trans. by Sherley-Price, 1955:125).

Throughout the centuries the hope of immortality has been so interwoven with the Christian understanding of God that it has been the central mode of interpretation of other doctrines, and integral to the Christian sacramental system. Thus, for St. Athanasius and the whole Orthodox tradition the motive behind the incarnation was to confer immortality upon humanity: God became what we are so that we might become immortal as he is (trans. by a Religious, 1963:93). In Catholic and Protestant Christianity the death and resurrection of Christ were seen as vitally connected with the opening up of everlasting salvation. In the Church's sacramental system a Christian was said to become an inheritor of the kingdom of heaven, and reference to God's everlasting Kingdom was made at the most solemn moments of confirmation, marriage, ordination, and absolution. In the Holy Communion service Christians are said to receive the "bread of immortality" in the Orthodox liturgy, or the bread of eternal or everlasting life in Catholic and Anglican formularies. Finally, in the last rites the Christian receives the Viaticum to nourish his soul for the journey through death.

However, to show that a belief was, in the past, absolutely central to Christianity is by no means a sufficient ground for supposing it to be relevant today. As T.S. Eliot put it, "Christianity is always adapting itself into something which can be believed (Hick, 1977:ix). And it is easy to point to a whole range of doctrines, from an infallible Bible to an historical fall, that were once perceived as central but that have since been discarded by all but the most wooden of fundamentalists. Should we then join the young Schleiermacher (1958:9) in categorizing the hope of immortality as part of the "rubbish of antiquity" from which Christianity must be cleansed if it is to speak to the modern world? That the "father of modern theology" subsequently changed his mind on the central importance of this doctrine (Schleiermacher, 1960) does not in itself remove the possibility that his first thoughts were correct. What has to be shown, therefore, is not merely that belief in a life after death was, historically speaking, an important belief in earlier formulations of Christian doctrine, but, far more importantly, that it remains vital to the intellectual coherence of the Christian vision.

My basic contention is that without belief in a future hope the Christian doctrine of God becomes irrelevant because it becomes vacuous. It is no accident that when William James (1902) surveyed *The Varieties of Religious*

Experience over eighty years ago he found that for almost all believers then, God primarily mattered as the provider of immortality. That God has ceased "to matter" to so many contemporary intellectuals may well reflect, at least in part, an intuitive awareness of the emptiness of claims about God in a context where there is little emphasis on a future hope.

This was brought home to many Christians by the challenge of the *Theology and Falsification* debate of the 1950s. In this Antony Flew (and A. MacIntyre, 1955) challenged Christian intellectuals to specify any actual difference their faith in God made to the way they looked at life. The only serious response to this challenge was that given by John Hick (1957;1967) and Ian Crombie (1955) who set out the notion of "eschatological verification," namely that there is a real difference in attitude between theists and nontheists in that the believer in God sees this life as a preparation for an eternal destiny whereas the nonbeliever does not, and this difference is real because, if the believers' hopes are realized, it will be verified after death. The importance of this can be made clear by posing the direct question "if belief in life after death is excluded, is there *any* significant difference between the substantive beliefs and expectations of well-educated and informed believers and nonbelievers in God?" I suggest there is not, and that without the otherworldly dimension Christian claims about the love and care of God die "the death of a thousand qualifications" when really probed by a searching inquirer. Hence I suggest that unless a Christian is willing to postulate a future life, any claim to believe in the fatherly care of an omnipotent God is without content.

Moreover, only in the context of belief in a life after death is it possible even to sketch a theodicy that could conceivably reconcile belief in an all-knowing, all-loving, and all-powerful God with the manifest evils of earthly existence. For, as John Hick (1966) has argued, if there is a life after death, it becomes at least conceivable that the changes and chances of this world with all its potential for joy and sorrow, for good and evil, may make sense as an inevitable part of an environment in which persons can develop as free and responsible agents. As a "vale of soul-making" the hardships and challenges of this life may serve a larger purpose; but if there is no soul to make, no larger purpose to serve, then the fact of suffering in general, and its random character in particular, simply makes nonsense of Christian claims about God's character and power. It should be stressed that Hick's theodicy does not in any way imply that suffering is in itself ennobling or redemptive, for the evidence would go flat against any so simplistic a view. But what this theodicy does say is that a real objective physical world governed by regular physical law provides an environment more suited to the development of responsible agents than would an environment in which divine intervention consistently saved humanity from the consequences of its folly, or from the heartache and challenge implicit in any finite and physical existence. John Hick's arguments do not "solve" the problem of evil, the extent and nature of which remains a persistent challenge to the integrity of Christian believing, but what Hick's work does make clear is that without a belief in a future life no approach to the problem of evil can even get off the ground. If death means extinction, then there is no question but that old age, suffering, disease, and death will gain the ultimate victory over each and every one of us, and thereby bring to nothing the belief that each one of us is eternally precious to an all-sovereign God.

But of course there are good reasons why many Christians feel unable any longer to maintain belief in a future life. The idea of a literal or quasi-literal resurrection of the dead seems almost impossible to reconcile with what we know of the nature of reality (Badham, 1987). And if resurrection is reinterpreted, as it is by almost all contemporary Christians (Badham, 1977), to mean that the person will receive a new and glorious body for the expression of itself in the unimaginably different life of heaven, vexatious problems of the identity of those resurrected persons inescapably arise. In fact, though this is not always fully appreciated by contemporary Christians, if material identity between present and future bodies is not affirmed, then some concept of the soul becomes essential to ensure continuity of the self between the two worlds. Yet the concept of the soul has been so criticized by contemporary philosophy that many Christians today feel they can no longer affirm such belief. And if life after death depends on the soul, then life after death must go. Consequently, for many contemporary Christians belief in a personal future life has become impossible, and the best that can be hoped for by an increasing number of Christian thinkers is that the eternal and omniscient God will forever remember us and we will thus live on in "the complete and infallible memory of God" (Hartshorne, 1961:252–253).

But this does not solve the dilemma. Not only because to be remembered is not at all the same thing as to live on, but also because, if dualism really is impossible, it is just as impossible for God as for the soul. And even if an immaterial God could be conceived, he could not actually relate to a soul-less person. The fundamental difficulty that many philosophers have with the concept of the soul is that they find it hard to give content to any claim that a "person" could exist as an immaterial or disembodied entity, for as Antony Flew (1964:4,12) puts it, "person words refer to people...people are what you meet...and what you meet are creatures of flesh and blood who can be pointed at, touched, heard, seen and talked to." But of course this applies to God, too, "a non-embodied mind active throughout the Universe," as Antony Kenny rightly points out; "most contemporary philosophers find immateriality problematic" (Kenny 1979:127), and this relates to God quite as much as the soul, for the two beliefs have a comparable logical structure.

The point I am making is this: If some Christians today give up belief in a life after death because they have become convinced that dualism is impossible, they cannot consistently stop simply at rejecting belief in a future life; God must go too. Furthermore, even if God is allowed to be an exception to the ban on "immaterial persons" this would not save religion, for religion is based on the view that persons can enter into a relationship with God, and this is not possible unless persons have souls.

The problem is that the religious grounds for belief in God are that men and women throughout the ages have believed themselves to have encountered God in prayer and worship and to have had their lives transformed by such an encounter. This experience of being encountered by God is the living heart of religion, but Christian spirituality has always insisted that this experimental awareness of God is "not mediated by the senses." According to Vladimir Lossky, "The divine light being given in mystical experience surpasses at the same time both sense and intellect. It is immaterial and is not apprehended by the senses" (Lossky, 1957:223). Lossky insists that all the greatest theologians of the Eastern Orthodox tradition stress the immediacy of the mystic's knowledge of God (Lossky, 1957:224). Eric Mascall, speaking for the Western tradition, emphasizes that "a very impressive body of religious thought has affirmed the possibility and indeed the occurrence of a cognitive experience which is not mediated by the senses" (Mascall, 1957:54). Paul Tillich has characterized this approach as the Augustinian–Franciscan solution to the philosophy of religion, which asserts that God is knowable in himself directly (Tillich, 1964).

This understanding of the divine–human encounter is not something that is confined to the great mystics. The whole of Christian spirituality is permeated by it. Historically the one indispensable element in a person wishing to offer himself for the Christian ministry in Catholic, Protestant, and Orthodox traditions has been whether or not he felt "inwardly moved" and "truly called" to this ministry (Ordination service in the Book of Common Prayer of the Church of England). Almost all books on prayer insist on the importance of quieting the senses and of opening oneself up to God. They urge the seeking out of a place of complete quiet, closing the eyes, and putting hands together. All such activities presuppose that the sense of the presence of God is only distracted if data from the senses continue to pour in upon the mind. Only when, as far as possible, has one closed off one's sensory input is one in a state where encounter with God is deemed to be likely.

This whole approach to prayer presupposes a dualist understanding of man as its necessary condition. For it asserts that God can make the reality of his presence felt other than through neural pathways. In other words, it implies that knowledge of God can be understood as communicated to us through some process akin to telepathy; direct to the mind and not via sensory stimuli. This is of immense importance for our consideration of the concept of the soul. In *Body and Mind*, his defense of materialism, Professor Keith Campbell argued that it was basic to belief in central-state materialism that "the brain is receptive only to information which arrives by neural pathways and so is confined to perception by way of the senses," hence "if some people are receptive to the contents of the minds of another by some more direct means such as telepathy then those minds are just not brains," (Campbell, 1971:191). My argument is that this applies just as much to claimed instances of non-sense–mediated awareness of God as it does to any alleged claims of telepathic rapport between other human minds, with the important difference that claims to communion with God are vastly more common, better attested, and more influential in human history than any claims to non-sense–mediated communication between human beings have been. For as I have sought to show, this religious experiencing is at the root of the deepest Christian commitment, and the Thomist way of moving from the world to God represents a second reflective stage in the person's religious development. Of course some religious experience takes the form of considering the beauty of the world, or of worship, or of a sense of duty, and abstracting from these experiences to the notion of a transcendent God. But I suggest that the movement of thought from the world to the transcendent depends upon a pre-existing mystical–intuitive immediate awareness of God, which can only be a reality if dualism is true.

However, in view of the difficulties facing the affirmation of dualism today, some Christians have suggested that Christianity should dispense with belief in a personal relationship with God, and focus entirely on the social and prophetic heritage of Christianity. This is indeed the line taken in the report by the Archbishop of Canterbury's Commission entitled *Faith in the City*. This commission points out that

> few philosophers now allow for a separate component or "soul," with which religion can be uniquely concerned, and modern philosophy encourages us to return to the idiom of the Bible, according to which, God addresses our whole person along with the social relationships amid which we live.... The suggestion that religion is an entirely personal matter of the relationship of an individual with God should now be... unacceptable (commission on Urban Priority Areas, 1985:50).

This is one of the few instances I know of any quasi-official organ of a Church tackling the difficulties of articulating Christian Faith in a strongly antidualist ethos, but I suggest its solution to the difficulty, namely the abandonment of the idea of a direct and personal encounter with God, has not considered with sufficient care the implications of doing this for the foundations of Christian belief, including the grounds on which the social Gospel itself also rests. For in a strict sense it is simply not true that God *addresses* the whole person. We do not see God with our eyes, or hear him with our ears; rather, as St. Paul said, "spiritual things are spiritually discerned" (1 Corinthians 2.14). We have no sense experience of God. Hence, if a thoroughly materialist understanding of the human person is adopted I do not see how the claim to "encounter" or enter into a relationship of love with a transcendent and immaterial God can be considered, quite apart from the fact that precisely the same philosophical majority rejects belief in God as rejects belief in the soul and for the same reasons.

I conclude therefore that the Christian religion needs belief in a future life and that this ought to be perceived as integral to any coherent version of Christian theism. I would also urge that for comparable reasons Islam and Judaism are in a similar situation. Both are just as committed as Christianity to belief in an immaterial, all-powerful, and all-compassionate God who has created the human race for his own purposes and has destined all of humanity to an eternal destiny. In the case of Islam the idea of a future life seems even more necessary than in contemporary Christianity. For Muslims continue to affirm a strong belief in the "Last Day," a day of Judgment in which all will receive their just deserts. And many Muslims also continue to affirm belief in the concept of *jihad* or holy war with its associated view that those who die in such a struggle are guaranteed immediate entrance to paradise. It is apparent from attempts made to restore the full rigor of Islamic law that the Quranic notion of the importance of absolute judicial principles is very much alive today. It is also apparent, from the readiness with which religious enthusiasts are ready to embrace martrydom in what they see to be the cause of Allah in Iran, Lebanon, and elsewhere, that the concept of Jihad is also a living contemporary conviction. I claim therefore that Islam, even more than Christianity, is committed to belief in a future life, and indeed few, if any, Muslims would question this.

Turning to Judaism, the situation changes. First, because it seems probable that a higher proportion of contemporary Jews do not actually believe in a future life than the adherents of any other religion. Secondly, because the Old Testament faith developed a profound and vivid sense of God, and a vibrant religious consciousness without any expectation of a future life (Badham, 1977: Chap. 1). There is a sense, therefore, that both Judaism today and the Old Testament faith of former times might seem to refute my thesis. But I don't think they do. The initial understanding of the Covenant was that it was between God and the whole people of Israel. Hence the survival of the individual was of no consequence provided the life of the nation remained. But once the religion of Israel came to be seen as entailing a relationship between God and the individual, the old theodicy came under increasing strain, and belief in a future life came to be regarded as an essential element in developed Judaism, such that the rabbis put the Afterlife at the center of their system. The abandonment of such beliefs under the pressure of contemporary thought raises major problems for Judaism. As Rabbi Dan Cohn-Sherbok (1987) puts it:

> The belief in a Hereafter has helped Jews make sense of the world as a creation of a good and powerful God and provided a source of great consolation for their travail on earth. Without the promise of Messianic redemption, resurrection and the eventual vindication of the righteous in Paradise, Jews will face great difficulties reconciling the belief in a providential God who watches over his chosen people with the terrible events of modern Jewish history. If there is no eschatological unfolding of a divine drama in which Jewish people will ultimately triumph, what hope can there be for the righteous of Israel?

Turning from the Abrahamic religions to the religions of the East, belief in reincarnation has always been central to the religions of Hinduism and Buddhism. In the case of Hinduism there is no need to discuss the importance of the doctrine, since no one doubts that the doctrine is fundamental; however, much discussion may focus on how it be interpreted. But in the case of Buddhism the situation is different. For Buddhism is frequently presented today as a religion that denies the existence of personal life after bodily death.

As we shall see, there are some grounds for this view in that it seems clear that the historical Buddha did repudiate the Hindu understanding of the soul (*atman*) and call into question too egoistic a stress on personal survival.

Nevertheless, I believe that interpretations of Buddhism which deny the eternal dimension do not do justice to the historic teaching of this faith. For, with the possible exception of some elements of the Zen tradition, Buddhism as a living religion has never equated death with extinction but has had a deep and abiding conviction of the reality of a future life. As Edward Conze puts it in his preface to the section of his edition of Buddhist Scriptures which deals with other worlds: "The horizon of Buddhism is not bounded by the limits of the sensory world, their true interests lie beyond it . . . many Buddhists believe they possess definite knowledge of life after death" (Conze, 1959:221). This is also true of popular Buddhism. The popularity of the tales of Buddha's former lives, the institution of Lamaism in Tibetan Buddhism, and the fascination of Buddhist monks and laity in reported claims to remember former lives only makes sense in a context of widespread belief in a fairly concrete understanding of rebirth. The Pure-land tradition, still the dominant form of Buddhism in Japan, is only intelligible if one assumes that its literature of heavenly states of being or its warnings of purgatorial hells has some content. Likewise, can one make sense of the *Tibetan Book of the Dead* (Evans-Wentz, 1960) unless one supposes that its detailed descriptions of the experiences the mind will undergo in the Bardo World are not merely descriptive of the processes of dying, but of a mind-dependent state into which it supposes the mind will enter after bodily death? And in the realm of culture the ethos of funerals in Thailand and Burma reveals an attitude of mind in which life after death is not simply "believed in," but is treated as an unquestioned "fact of life," a conviction far deeper than anything encountered today in the post-Christian countries of the West. Moreover, I believe that one contributory factor to the American defeats in Vietnam and Cambodia was the failure of their strategists to take account of the fearlessness of death that a still living tradition of belief in reincarnation had given to their opponents.

The question remains, however, is belief in rebirth integral to Buddhism as such? It is clearly integral to Lamaism, since the whole notion that the present head of a monastic order can in some sense "be" the reincarnation of a former head requires a doctrine of rebirth as its necessary condition. Likewise, the notion that Amida Buddha or some other Bodhisattva functions as a savior figure bringing eternal life to those who trust in him also demands belief in the existence of the "pure-lands" to which the soul will ultimately move. But of course neither the Tibetan nor the Pure-land form of Buddhism can realistically claim to represent what the historical Buddha taught. However, it is clear that the Buddha himself accepted and taught a belief in karma. This is the view that we are all involved in a cycle of life. What we are now is the product of what we have done in the past, and what we will be in the future depends on what we do now. This belief is to be found in the earliest Pali traditions and is indisputably part of what the historical Buddha believed. He also believed that it was important to rid oneself of egoism[80] so that one would escape from this cycle and enter the deathless state of parinirvana. The foundation of Buddha's ethical system and the foundation of his total world-view is utterly bound up with these notions of karma, rebirth, and parinirvana. Hence, to reject rebirth or to deny the reality of parinirvana would be to reject elements in Buddhism that are central not only to the main Buddhist traditions of today, but also to what the Buddha himself saw as vital to his whole understanding of the meaning of life.

However, scholars who interpret Buddhism as denying immortality do have a prima facie case. For Buddha explicitly denied the immortality of the soul and taught a "no-self" doctrine, which many see as parallel to the view of many contemporary Western philosophers of mind who see talk of the self as simply a convenient term for talking about our dispositional behavior patterns, which are inescapably dependent on our ever-changing physical embodiment (Cook, in preparation; Parfit, 1984).

But this ignores crucial elements in the Buddha's teaching. For though Buddha did indeed deny the immortality of the soul, he went on in the very next verse (Visuddhi-Magga XVIII) to deny the extinction of the soul at death (Warren, 1973:132–135). In this as in other doctrines he taught a "middle-path." We may wonder how a middle path is possible in such a context, yet on reflection it does make considerable sense. In one sense death clearly marks the end of life, but if one assumes the reality of rebirth as the Buddha did,* then in another sense death is not the end.

Every denial has to be understood against its opposing affirmation. Buddha's denial of the self was a denial of one very specific understanding of the self, the concept of *atman*. Buddha denied that there is a permanent unchanging spirit that can be considered self or soul or ego as opposed to matter. He believed that the idea of an abiding, immortal substance called atman was a mental projection. In particular he objected to an identification of this atman with a supposed world-soul. As he taught, "The speculative view that the universe is atman, and that I shall be atman after death—permanent, abiding, everlasting, unchanging, and that I shall exist as such for eternity, is not that wholly and completely fooish" (Rahula, 1967:59).

It seems to me that the Buddha was wholly right in what he denied. The concept of atman is just not a valid understanding of what it means to be a human self. To be human is to be developing, changing, moving on. Only a dynamic understanding of human selfhood does justice to experience or empirical reality. But to affirm this, as the Buddha did, in no sense excludes the notion of a future life and indeed Buddha (in Samyutta-Nikaya XXII 85) repudiated the idea that it did as a "wicked heresy" (Sarvepalli and Moore, 1957). Buddha believed the doctrine of complete annihilation at death or at the

---

*Buddha refers to the doctrine of rebirth in his First Sermon, in his Fire Sermon, and in the Dhammapada. As such it is present in the most ancient documents of earliest Buddhism.

entry to parinirvana as undermining the whole structue of his belief system. I believe he was right to take this line because, if rebirth were ruled out, then neither the principle of karma as a means of interpreting life nor the spiritual goal of achieving parinirvana, the deathless state, by escaping from the cycle of life could be intelligible.

I conclude therefore that however difficult it may be to affirm any kind of belief in today's world, it is religiously essential to do so. For Christianity, Judaism, and Islam, life after death seems inextricably interwoven with what those faiths wish to affirm about God. For Hinduism and Buddhism, rebirth or reincarnation seems wholly interwoven with what those faiths wish to affirm concerning the meaning of life. These observations do not exclude the possibility that these faiths may not at some point in the future abandon such beliefs as outmoded, and we have in fact noted that many contemporary apologists wish them to do just that. All I do wish to affirm is that the cost has not been weighed, and it is not adequately appreciated what a profound transformation would be involved at the thoroughgoing removal of so central a feature of their respective understandings of reality.

REFERENCES

Alger, W.R. 1968. *The Destiny of the Soul.* New York: Greenwood Press, p. 57. (First published 1860.)

Badham, L. 1987. A Naturalistic Case for Extinction. In *Death and Immortality in the Religions of the World.* Eds. P. Badham and L. Badham. New York: Paragon House.

Badham, P. (in press) Some Secular Trends in the Church of England Today. In *Religion, State and Society in Modern Britian.* Ed. P. Badham. New York: Mellen.

———. 1977. *Christian Beliefs about Life after Death.* New York: Barnes and Noble, pp. 13–17, Chapters 1 and 5.

Bede (translated by L. Sherley-Price). 1955. *A History of the English Church.* Harmondsworth: Penguin Classics, Book 2, p. 125.

Campbell, K. 1970 *Body and Mind.* London: Macmillan, p. 191.

Cohn-Sherbok, D. 1987. Death and Immortality in the Jewish Tradition. In *Death and Immortality in the Religions of the World.* Eds. P. Badham and L. Badham. New York: Paragon House.

Conze, E. 1959. *Buddhist Scriptures.* Harmondsworth: Penguin Classics, p. 221.

Cook, H. The Buddhist Thinks about Death. In *Death and the Afterlife* (in preparation). Ed. S. Davis. London: Macmillan.

Crombie, I. 1955. Arising from the University Discussion. In *New Essays in Philosophical Theology.* Eds. A. Flew and A. MacIntyre. London: SCM Press, p. 129.

Evans-Wentz, W.Y. 1960. *The Tibetan Book of the Dead.* London: Oxford University Press. (first published 1927.)

Flew, A. 1964. *Body, Mind and Death.* London: Macmillan, p. 4, p. 12.

Flew, A., and MacIntyre, A. 1955. *New Essays in Philosophical Theology.* London: SCM Press, Chapter 6.

Frazer, J.G. 1913. *The Belief in Immortality and the World of the Dead,* Vol. 1. London: Macmillan, pp. 138–139.

Hammerton, M., and Downing, A.C. 1979. Fringe Beliefs among Undergraduates. *Theology* 82 (690):433–436.

Hartshorne, C. 1961. *The Logic of Perfection*. LaSalle, IL: Opencourt, pp. 253–253.

Hick, J. 1977. *The Myth of God Incarnate*. London: SCM Press, p. 1x.

———. 1970. *Arguments for the Existence of God*. London: Macmillan, p. 102, p.112.

———. 1966 *Evil and the God of Love*. London: Macmillan, Part 4.

———. 1957/1967. *Faith and Reason*. Ithaca, NY: Cornell; 2nd ed, London: Macmillan, p. 175.

James, W. 1963. *The Varieties of Religious Experience*. London: Fontana, p. 498. (first published 1902.)

Kenny, A. 1979. *The God of the Philosophers*. Oxford: Clarendon, p. 127.

Lossky, V. 1957. *The Mystical Theology of the Eastern Church*. London: James Clarke, pp. 223,224.

Mascall, E.L. 1957. *Words and Images*. London: Longmans, p. 54.

Parfit, D. 1984. I Find Buddha's Claims to be True. In *Reasons and Persons*. Oxford: Oxford University Press.

Rahula, W. 1967. *What the Buddha Taught*. London: Gordon Fraser, p. 59.

Report of the Archbishop of Canterbury's Commission on Urban Priority Areas. 1985. *Faith in the City*. London: Church House, p. 50.

St. Athanasius. (Translated by a Religious of C.S.V.M.) 1963. *On the Incarnation*, Chapter 54. London: Mowbrays, p. 93.

St. Ignatius of Antioch, (Translated by M. Staniforth.) 1968. Epistle to the Romans, Chapter 7. *Early Christian Writings*. Harmondworth: Penguin Classics, p. 125.

Sarvepalli, R., and Moore, C.A. 195. *A Sourcebook in Indian Philosophy*. Princeton, NJ: Princeton University Press, p. 286.

Schillebeeckx, E. 1980. *Christ, the Christian Experience in the Modern World*. London: SCM Press, p. 797.

Schleiermacher, F. 1960. *The Christian Faith*. Edinburgh: T. and T. Clarke, pp. 696–720. (First published 1830.)

———. 1958. *On Religion*. New York: Harper, p. 9. (First published 1799.)

Tillich, P. 1964. *Theology of Culture*. Oxford: Oxford Univesity Press, p. 12.

Warren, H.C. 1973. *Buddhism in Translations:* New York: Athenaeum, pp. 132–135.

19

The *Ars Moriendi* and Breaking
The Conspiracy of Silence

Michael Perry

Both birth and death are mysteries. When we touch either of them, we touch the roots of the numinous awareness, and, in the words of T. S. Eliot (1935/1937:20), we experience

A fear like birth and death, when we see birth and death alone
In a void apart.

That fear is a numinous fear, because "the awesome change from person to corpse is a unique event and stirs deep and complex feelings" (Woodward 1987); so deep and so complex that we cannot properly analyze them within the parameters of a single discipline. We need multidisciplinary and multicultural cross-fertilization.

The journal I edit is called *The Christian Parapsychologist*,[1] so I suppose multi-disciplinary cross-fertilization is meat and drink to me. When I was a young student of theology in Cambridge University in the early 1950s, I met a fellow undergraduate who explained that he had decided to study theology because it gave him the opportunity of getting to know something about a very wide selection of subjects: ancient languages, history, literary criticism, poetry, music, philosophy, psychology. The range of necessary competences in a good theologian is almost as wide as that required of a parapsychologist. Parapsychologists have to add statistical mathematics, the laws of evidence, anthropology — you name it, and it is not hard to see how the parapsychologist needs it if he is to be a master of his subject. It seems to me that the study of death can join theology and parapsychology as an inextricably interdisciplinary enterprise. What I intend to do in this chapter is to show how this must be, and how many areas of study impinge upon our search for an understanding of death.

Death is an embarrassment to the majority of people. There is a conspiracy of silence about it. We cannot say the word "death" out loud without the kind of *frisson* that indicates we are breaking a powerful taboo. You only have to think of the number of euphemisms we have invented to prevent us from having to speak the word "death," to be assured of that. Like the ancient Hebrews who found it intolerable to use the name of their God in conversation, we go to great lengths to prevent the frightening syllable from passing our lips.

And yet we know that, for all our attempts, death is the worst-kept secret in the world. Like sex used to be in Victorian society, everybody does it but nobody is supposed to talk about it. What is more, once the taboo has been overcome, the floodgates are open. I can testify from having talked about death to scores of groups and hundreds of individuals, that once the initial reticence has been surmounted, once the embarrassment is over and people's tongues are loosed, there is no end to the questions that people are longing to ask.

How did this taboo originate? How, for that matter, does *any* taboo originate? The taboo — for instance — against revealing one's personal name. We all know that a person who knows our name has a certain power over us. From my earliest schooldays I realized that when the teacher looked up from her desk and said, "Michael Perry, come out to the front of the class!", I had been detected in some misdemeanor and could expect the punishment due. Even on those rare occasions when there *was* no misdemeanor, the sound of my own name on the teacher's lips sent a spasm of panic through my whole body. If it wasn't something I had done, it was — even worse — something I didn't know, and my inability to answer the question would show me up in front of my classmates. From such experiences does the taboo against revealing a personal name originate.

Other taboos arise because there are certain things about which we feel very deeply, and we do not want them opened up to profane gaze. We are not emotionally prepared to have them questioned — or, even worse, ridiculed — so we clam up, until we are assured that our questions will be taken sympathetically and we will not be shown up as fools for asking them. Death is one of those subjects. Try as we may, we cannot approach death in general, let alone the particularity of our own death, with the calm detachment that we feel should be appropriate to a pure biological datum. It touches us emotionally and stirs dormant religious feelings within us.

If this is true, we immediately realize that this attitude is culturally and historically conditioned. Although it is probably true that no society is without its taboos, the exact nature of a constellation of taboos is a function of the particular culture under consideration. The strength of the taboo about personal names, for example, will be felt very differently by a Trobriand islander, a diffident English gentleman, and an extrovert citizen of the United States of America.

So it is with the taboo on naming or talking about death. Maybe it is an artifact of a late twentieth-century, post-religious, Western culture. Certainly it was not strongly felt by our great-grandparents. There are certain contemporary cultures (or subcultures) where it has remarkably little power. So we need to ask some questions about it. In what kinds of society, at what periods of history, has it been strong? Has it anything to do with the strength of

religious tradition? Or with the uncertainty of life? Is it weaker in times of war
or widespread pestilence? Is it a function of medical competence or confidence?
With what personality characteristics is it correlated? Is it a Western rather than
an Eastern or third-world phenomenon? How and why does the taboo
originate? What are the psychological mechanisms behind it?

We are already thick into our need of interdisciplinary insights. We need
anthropological, historical, and religious perspectives to help us understand the
conspiracy of silence with which death is surrounded in our contemporary
polite middle-class Western society, and we need the insights of psychology
to enable us to unravel the reasons behind it.

Two factors may in part explain this feeling of being ill-at-ease about death.
Death confronts us with our own impotence, and with our own ignorance.
Neither impotence nor ignorance is easy to face up to or to live with. Let me
deal with them in order.

In his book *Health is for People* (1975), Michael Wilson writes about the way
in which people's beliefs about man in society influence the kind of hospitals
they build. He lists six basic common assumptions about humankind, health,
and hospitals:

1. The cure of disease is more important than the care of patients.
2. Staff members need to have power over patients.
3. Individuals are separate from one another.
4. The provision of health is a task for experts.
5. Every problem has a solution.
6. Death is the worst thing that can happen to anyone.

Wilson subjects each of these assumptions to critical scrutiny, and gives each
of them some rough handling. We are, in our hospitals, reluctant to speak
about death or to tell patients about a fatal prognosis. Wilson writes (p. 29):

> We are a death-fearing society, and the practice of medicine and nursing is
> influenced by such social fears and expectations. . . .The status and power of the
> doctor in hospital derives from his skill, real and imaginary, to prevent
> death. . . .But the hospital is a place of truth where the facts of mortality must
> be faced.

If death is seen as the supreme failure of the physician's art, then it is not
surprising that in a place built to assert and affirm the physician's skills, death
is treated as an unspeakable obscenity.

But do we *need* to think of death in terms of human impotence? It all depends
how we define the term "health." Michael Wilson complains that "our
understanding of health is based on our knowledge of illness" and that the
National Health Service in Britain is founded upon the idea "that health is
obtained by getting rid of disease" (1975:1). This is to get off on the wrong foot
altogether. *Must* we define health by a double negative—the absence of

dysfunction? Or can we find a positive definition of health that will lead us to a positive valuation of death?

I would like to propose, as a definition of "health," "a state of harmony that has to be operative in four directions or dimensions if it is to be complete." You would expect me, as a minister of religion, to begin with the upwards dimension, and to stress that until a person is in harmony with God he cannot be fully healthy. In Christian terms this involves the analysis of humanity as being fundamentally at odds with God (the doctrines of the Fall and of original sin) and needing a reconciliation that cannot be effected by humanity alone but that needs the atoning death of Christ upon the cross to make it possible. Other religions will have their own analysis of the ills of humanity, but all (with the possible exception of pure Buddhism, or the philosophy of Confucius) see the solution of them in terms of a reconciliation with the divine or with whatever is understood as the invisible power behind the phenomenal world.

Nor can there be health without harmony between man and his fellows — what we might term the horizontal direction or dimension. Healthy societies need healthy interpersonal relationships, not only at the macro-level of international politics and the meso-level of local communities, but also at the micro-level of the family and of day-to-day living. The stresses of living at odds with our fellow humans are as great a cause of ill-health as any.

The third direction or dimension in which harmony is required for there to be health is the "downwards" dimension; our relationship with the material universe of which we form a part. This is to be seen not only in the sphere of ecology and conservation, where our selfish greed as imagined Lords of Creation has been all too balefully evident in the past,[2] and the need for penitent reconciliation with our material environment has been powerfully drawn to our attention in the last decade or two; it is also evident in the realization that we are physical beings with physical bodies. When we neglect or misuse those bodies, through overindulgence, through allowing noxious materials into our metabolism, through workaholism and the lack of adequate exercise, through unwise diet or unbalanced intake, we force ill health upon ourselves.. And, besides what our own folly brings upon us, there are the ravages of disease and the manifold conditions to which our physicians and surgeons devote their skills. All these show us that until we are in harmony with the physical universe — of which our material bodies are a part — we will not enjoy full health.

Finally, there is the "inward" dimension. No person can be at health unless he has come to terms with himself and is able to accept himself as a person worthy of respect. Religious persons, in particular, are prone to the sin of so loving others as themselves that they forget to love themselves as well as they love others. Many people are so dissatisfied with themselves, or even disgusted with themselves, that their whole lives go sour. A healthy person appreciates himself and enjoys being the kind of person he was created to be.

If our aim is to achieve health in this total and positive sense, then we will need to employ an enormous diversity of approaches to our human condition.

Harmony with the divine is the business of religion. Harmony with humankind involves politics, sociology, interpersonal skills, and a knowledge of the psychology of relationships. Harmony with the material world is the business of ecology. Our physical bodies, to be at harmony, need the skills of every conceivable branch of medicine. If we are to be at harmony with ourselves, besides the knowledge of psychology, psychiatry, and psychotherapy, we need to realize that the human being is a Gestalt who must be treated as a whole person and not a collection of ill-assorted and separable aspects. If health is to be set forward, nothing less than a multidisciplinary cross-fertilization will suffice.

As a corollary to this understanding of a positive definition of health, however — and here we come back to the main thrust of this chapter — we see death in a very different light, and it no longer taunts us with a sense of our human impotence.

When health is seen as the achievement of harmony in every relationship of life, then "suffering" is not the same as "pain," and "healing" is not the same as "cure." Pain can be eliminated by adequate analgesia; suffering only disappears when the scars left by bad relationships have been healed; and healing, in the sense of a restoration of harmony, can be found whether or not there has been a cure for the specific ailment that has been affecting the patient's body. Healing may even come about through death, in which case it no longer sounds so bizarre to be told about the patient who said to his doctor, "There's no need to worry; I'm not dying of anything serious." Death can become the opportunity for a superb and self-fulfilling act of total reconciliation to, and harmony with, God, humanity, the physical world (and our failing physical body), and our own inner self. If that happens to us, we die a healthy death.

That does not come without being learned. The medievals knew as much, and coined a phrase to describe the spiritual and ascetic work that had to be accomplished before a person could make what was known as a "good death." The phrase is *ars moriendi*: the art of dying. It is, by and large, a lost art, but we need to recover it. The first stage in its recovery is to overcome our taboo on talk about death. Only if we may freely speak of death may we prepare ourselves for it.

Before we come to that, however, we have other territory to explore. I said that we find the thought of death unacceptable because it exposes our impotence and our ignorance. Having said something about the harm that comes from repressing all thought of death because it reminds us of our impotence, let us now address the equal dangers of being afraid of death because of our ignorance.

There are two areas of ignorance: the process of dying and the status of death. Enormous inroads have been made into both in the last few decades, but equally enormous questions remain.

We certainly know more now about dying than we did in previous generations, even though we seem to be less able to cope with it than we did in the "ages of faith." For all the reticence in bringing up the subject in conversation, writing about it seems to be one of the great growth industries of our time. There is a lovely throwaway line at the head of the bibliography to Michael Simpson's book *The Facts of Death* (1979), where he writes that "having read and reviewed over 800 books in the area of death, dying, and bereavement, I can recommend the following as the most valuable for the general reader." And that was eight years ago!

The two great pioneers, one in the area of understanding the psychodynamics of the approach to death, and the other in the practical aspects of enabling patients to die with fully human dignity, are Elisabeth Kübler-Ross and Cicely Saunders. The dying process has been increasingly well-charted since Kübler-Ross first published *On Death and Dying* in 1969, and the hospice movement grows in its understanding of the needs of dying patients, their relatives, and those who give them support and professional care (duBoulay, 1984). When people know they are dying, they can pass through five stages: denial (and remember that "truth is a vital drug, but the big problem is getting the dosage right"), anger, bargaining, weeping (mourning), and acceptance. The stages do not always come in the "right" order, and dying people, like the rest of us, often regress to a logically earlier and less mature stage in the process; but if we are to come to the stage of acceptance, there is a great deal of work for dying patients to do, and many different professional skills are needed in order to help them. This is where the hospice can do so much. It is still hard to get health care professionals to put enough of their scarce resources into so labor-intensive a unit. Perhaps this is because it is a service that so often does not conform to their own defective models of what "health" is all about. They tend to think that once an illness becomes terminal, there is "nothing more that the doctors can do," and resources are allocated instead to the scenes of more frenetic medical and surgical activity. How wrong can they be?

To move towards death as what Kübler-Ross has called "the final stage of growth," we need careful nursing, careful pain control, and a very great deal of counselling. It is counselling, in particular, of which we are most short. The Cruse organization trains grief counsellors for bereavement therapy after the death of a loved one, but there are still few people around who have been trained to help people who want to mourn their own passing. It cannot be done within a five-minute consultant's ward-round visit. Hospital chaplains can do it, except that in many hospitals they are expected to shoulder an impossibly large caseload, so that their work with the individual tends to suffer. Macmillan nurses on domiciliary visits can do it, and if the staffing ratio is right (which it is in a hospice, but often is not on a general or acute ward), the ward nurse can do it. But the opportunity to minister must be taken as soon as it is presented. Delay usually means the boat has been missed. Best of all, relatives can do it, if they know what to expect, and how to guide the dying person through the stages. If we could only recover the *ars moriendi* and make it widely known, how much more human and humane our last journey could be! With pain control, with proper nursing, through the acceptance of mortality as natural and to be expected, we could allow death to be properly managed within a therapeutic environment, and we could help the dying to die a healthy death, reconciled to God, the world, nature, their fellows, and themselves.

I must move from the process of dying to the status of death, which is the other area of ignorance mentioned earlier. We cannot really frame an adequate *ars moriendi* until we know whether death is a terminus or a transition. And that question is as far from solution as ever.

That may sound a pessimistic conclusion. After all, have we not come an enormous way in thanatological studies, in the last ten or twenty years in particular? There have been studies of deathbed visions, the near-death experience, the use of the technique of hypnotic regression, as well as the hardy annuals of parapsychological research such as the data of mediumship, apparitions, and haunts. What is obvious is that every advance in the sophistication of our gathering of data seems to be countered by an equivalent (or greater) advance in the sophistication of the questions asked about those data.

Thus: deathbed visions have been known from time immemorial. Their interpretation depended upon whether the person thinking about them regarded them as odd coincidences or clues to the nature of reality. The first stage was to collect so many examples that the hypothesis of coincidence began to look overstretched. This was done by W. F. Barrett in 1926 in a book that has only recently been reprinted as a classic of the early history of scientific parapsychology. Then the questions begin to be asked: what causes deathbed visions? The activity of the departed who are welcoming a new member to their community? Or the activity of the dying person who is hallucinating in a way that is determined by an amalgam of his medication and his own cultural and religious background? That led to the researches of Karlis Osis and Erlendur Haraldsson (1977). They examined the deathbed vision by phenomenological analysis and tried to see whether there were any statistically sustainable correlations between the presence of hallucinogenic chemicals in the bloodstream, or cerebral anoxia, or between the visions reported and the cultural and religious beliefs of the experients.

Meanwhile, others were examining, not the secondhand reportage of observers at the deathbeds of others, but the firsthand reports of those who had a close brush with death and returned with their own experiences. Again, the stories had been circulating from time immemorial (there is a good example in Bede's *History of the English Church and People*, written in the seventh century AD (1955/1958),[3] so the first stage in scientific validation was to collect so many examples that it could not be argued that such stories were no more than near-unique and puzzling "sports." Raymond Moody did this in the mid-1970s (1975,1977). Stage two was the attempt to subject the accounts to statistical analysis, to see whether the experience was an objective glimpse into another dimension of existence, or a side-effect of the psychological state of the near-death experient. We are still in the phase of arguing whether the near-death experience is an ego-defensive reaction to intolerable somatic stress, whether the out-of-body experience is a slip-over to an alternative explanation of conflicting sense data, whether the dark tunnel is an archetype or a culturally determined pre-expectation, whether the light at the end of the tunnel is a reliving of the birth trauma (and if so whether it is experienced by those who were born by Caesarean section), whether temporal lobe seizures are not characterized by ecstatic feelings so frequently that it is likely the visions of those suffering such severe trauma are similarly caused, whether the reported visions are or are not affected by religious teachings about the afterlife, and so on.

We could tell an almost identical story about the developments in the technique of hypnotic regression, or about mediumship, or about the experiences of those who have reported apparitions or hauntings. It is clear that if we want to answer the question of the status of death (whether it is a terminus or a transition) we have a plethora of disciplines to consult: parapsychologists, psychologists, physicians; cultural anthropologists, folklorists, historians of comparative religion — no one discipline can give us the answer we are looking for. But, above all, we need the help of the philosopher.[4] It is, nonetheless, inescapably true that experience is sacred, interpretation free, and we shall not come to the end of our quest until we have satisfied ourselves as to the interpretation we put on the mass of data which we are considering.

The International Institute for the Study of Death was originally set up under the provisional title of the "International Institute for the Study of Death and Immortality." The words "and Immortality" have quietly disappeared. Why, I wonder? Because they were too limiting of the postmortem possibilities, which could include immortality, temporary continued existence, reincarnation, or a host of other possibilities?[5] Or because death itself is enough to be studying for the present, let alone the questions of what (if anything) follows it? The quesions are intriguing. What is certain is that we will not get very far in considering the enigma of death until we have faced the questions of the interpretation of the phenomena I have been briefly reviewing. And the trouble is that it looks as if we shall never reach certainty, because the data we are surveying cannot logically have one single and unequivocal explanation. We shall always be dealing with the balance of probabilities between different sets of possible inferences.

As soon as we start thinking philosophically, we are beset by radical doubt. I argued some years ago in *The Resurrection of Man* (1975)[6] that parapsychology cannot provide us with an argument whereby a set of necessary inferences leads us from empirical data to that interpretation of them which speaks of human survival of death, let alone to anything like a Christian belief in immortality or resurrection. There do not seem to be any absolutely necessary inferences from sense perception. For example, I am aware of my self *as* my self, as an experiencing, feeling, thinking unit. And I am aware of interactions between my self and other selves. But how far are the inferences I draw from my experience of other selves, necessary inferences, and how far are they the result of (conscious or unconscious) choices between several possible sets of inferences—some, admittedly, more likely than others, but none either necessary or impossible? One possible position is solipsism: the belief that I am the only thinking substance in the universe and that the apparently external universe is merely a thought-projection arising from the electrical impulses within my own skull. Not very likely, but logically impossible to refute. One step less radical than that is epiphenomenalism, according to which the mind is something that arises out of a certain degree of physical complexity associated with the human brain, but that when that complex instrument decays, the mind that has been its epiphenomenon ceases to exist. Epiphenomenological explanations of the out-of-body experience have been much canvassed of late. They argue that there is no "soul" to travel "out" of the body, but that the phenomenon is explicable in terms of abnormal interpretations of conflicting sense perceptions in situations of particular trauma (Blackmore, 1984).

Perhaps the answer to solipsism and epiphenomenalism is that they are not impossible, but unlikely, and that in this world we find truth by taking the more likely and rejecting the less likely alternatives. We live, not by certainty but by a balance of probabilities. That is not far from saying that we live by faith rather than by sight. I argued in an earlier paper entitled "Faith, Reason, and Evidence in Religion, Science and Psychical Research" (Perry, 1984) that scientific hypotheses and theories are inferences that follow from observation and experiment, and I tried to show how a coherent system of beliefs is built up on foundtions that are always (at base) inferential rather than necessary. Part of the fascination of parapsychology is the way in which it continually reminds us that we work by inference rather than by necessary deduction. In the end, a scientist has faith in his paradigm about the nature of reality; so does the religious person. All paradigms are provisional, and experience is continually challenging us to refine our paradigms so as to incorporate more and more of our experience and experiment. The study of death and the question of whether death is a terminus or a staging-post raises this whole set of questions about inference and paradigm in its most acute form.

We take heart from the knowledge that there are some logically impeccable positions (solipsism, for example) that, in practice, no philosopher ever holds. They are possible, but they are not likely. It should be our aim in the study of death to reach a position which becomes more and more likely. We shall never get to a position where it is logically impossible for anyone rationally to disagree with us. But—and I am sure you take my point—we need sophisticated philosophy to help us get anywhere near that point.

I also claimed in that book *The Resurrection of Man* (1975) that our ultimate certainty in the face of the problems set by death would have to be a religious certainty. Those who accept the God-paradigm as their explanatory model for the universe, and those who put their trust in the God whose nature is such as to make it likely to believe that he intends a resurrection life for the humans he has created, and that he has raised Jesus from the dead as a first-fruits, have a certainty that is practical and sufficient. I still hold by that, as my own personal statement, while realizing that it is not a stance which can be reached by necessary logical argument. But then, neither is any metaphysical stance that anybody holds—and everybody holds *some* stance or other.

Meanwhile, there is life to be lived, and death to be died. In our present provisional position, bereft of certainties, but teased by signposts and indications and hints and possibilities about death, what do we do about it?

I have already spoken of the *ars moriendi*, and the way in which we should try to help people die a good death. This is not enough. A great mystic of the fourteenth century, the Blessed Henry Suso (1328,1910) taught that if we put off learning to die till the last moment, we should find it too late. If we are to die properly, it is a lifetime's learning. The old Church of England Litany (going back to 1548) prayed that we might be delivered from "sudden death." I take a modest pride in having successfully proposed an alteration of that phrase in our church's Alternative Service Book of 1980.

No one wants a lingering death, but no one ought to die without preparation. The A.S.B. Litany prays that we may be delivered "from violence, murder, and dying unprepared" (p. 99). That involves bringing one's whole life into healthy harmony with God, with one's fellows, with physical nature, and with one's own self in such a way that one is not caught unawares by death but can be ready for the ultimate adventure when it comes. That will not be to demystify death, nor to empty it of its significance. Death is, in the profoundest sense, a mystery, and a significant mystery, to which we can direct our life, and in which we can sum up its meaning. By practicing the art of dying during our life, we may consummate it in a proper manner when the time comes to do so. It is worth working on!

To think of death in this way will not take the grief from parting. We will still need to understand loss and bereavement, and will welcome the insights of Cruse counsellors, hospital chaplains, pastors, and the bereaved and dying themselves. Since it will for most people involve a complete reversal of their instinctive attitudes towards death, there is an enormous educational task ahead of us, so that yet another professional discipline is involved if the work of an International Institute for the Study of Death is to be properly set forward.

Truly, nothing less than a multidisciplinary and multicultural cross-fertilization will suffice for the work that lies ahead of us. But it is worthwhile. Through it, we may come to a greater understanding of death and its significance (whether that significance is seen as a moment of final harmony or as a rite of passage to whatever lies beyond it). We work towards ending that conspiracy of silence and recovering a contemporary *ars moriendi*. Our lives make sense in our deaths, and death completes the perfect round of which our lives are but a broken arc.

NOTES

1. Published quarterly by the Churches' Fellowship for Psychical and Spiritual Studies, 44 High Street, New Romney, Kent TN28 8BZ.

2. A mistaken exegesis of Genesis 1.28 ("Be fruitful, and multiply, and replenish the earth, and subdue it") and Psalm 8.6 ("Thou makest [man] to have dominion of the works of thy hands: and thou hast put all things in subjection under his feet") has got a lot to answer for. A recovery of the Biblical understanding of lordship as implying a balance of rights over, and responsibilities towards, creation, has been too long coming in the twentieth-century West.

3. See the mention of this account in *The Christian Parapsychologist*, June 1987 (7:42–3).

4. At Lampeter, Wales, where this paper was originally given, Paul Badham and others have set up an M.A. course on "Death and Immortality in Western Thought." See the accounts in, for example, *The Christian Parapsychologist*, March 1983 (5:31) and December 1985 (6:155–157).

5. Eight possible scenarios are discussed in "Theories about Survival" by R.H. Thouless (1979).

6. The inaugural volume in *Mowbray's Library of Theology*.

REFERENCES

Alternative Service Book. 1980. (The Church of England) p. 99.

Barrett, W.F. 1986. *Death-Bed Visions.* In the *Colin Wilson Library of the Paranormal.* Wellingborough, Northants., UK: Aquarian Press. (First published 1926.)

Bede. (Trans. by L. Sherley-Price.) 1955. (Rev. ed. 1968.) *History of the English Church.* London: Penguin Books, pp. 289–294.

Blackmore, S. 1984. "A Psychological Study of the Out-of-Body Experience." *Journal of Parapsychology* 48:201-218.

du Boulay, S. 1984. *Cicely Saunders.* London: Hodder & Stoughton.

Eliot, T.S. 1935/1937. *Murder in the Cathedral.* London: Faber and Faber, p. 20.

Moody, R. 1975. *Life after Life.* Atlanta, GA: Mockingbird Books.

———. 1977. *Reflections on Life after Life.* Atlanta, GA: Mockingbird Books.

Osis, K., and Haraldsson, E. 1977. *At the Hour of Death.* New York: Avon Books.

Perry, M. 1975. *The Resurrection of Man.* London & Oxford: A.R. Mowbray & Co., Ltd.

———. 1984. "Faith, Reason and Evidence in Religion, Science and Psychical Research." In *Psychic Studies - a Christian's View.* Wellingborough, Northants., UK: Aquarian Press, pp. 52–65.

Simpson, M. 1979. *The Facts of Death.* Englewood Cliffs, NJ: Prentice Hall.

Suso, H. (the Blessed) (Trans. by C.H. Mckenna.) 1910. *Das Büchlein der ewigen Weisheit.* London: O.P. (First published 1328.)

Thouless, R.H. 1979. "Theories about Survival." *Journal of the Society for Psychical Research* 50:1–8.

Wilson, M. 1975. *Health is for People.* 1975. London: Darton, Longman and Todd.

Woodward, J. 1987. "Pastoral Work with the Dying." *Theology* 90:119.

20

A Postmodern Mythology of Death

Michael Grosso

A man should be able to say he has done his best to form a conception of life after death, and to create some image of it — even if he must confess his failure. Not to have done so is a vital loss. —*C. G. Jung*

The somewhat plastic term "postmodern" is increasingly in vogue these days. In this essay I use it to refer to a new worldview currently taking shape. This emerging worldview or paradigm draws on many sources. One of the most important is modern physics, especially quantum mechanics. From a religious standpoint, it draws on the tradition of the so-called perennial philosophy, the mystical and experiential core of the great religions. Postmodernism, as I see it, is a quest for reconciliation between the new physical science and the new catholicity of the world spiritual traditions.

It is a worldview growing out of a concern for the fate of the biosphere; it sees humanity at an evolutionary crossroads and seeks to cooperate with, as it learns to discover, the upward tendencies of the evolutionary process; it wants to restore mind and meaning to the heart of the cosmic process; it respects the indigenous dimension of world culture; it tends toward a holistic or specific politics: that is, a politics that looks beyond the stereotyped opposites of "left" and "right," "progressive" and "conservative," that presupposes not merely a free and educated electorate but one with vision and higher consciousness.

This nascent worldview is eager to right the injuries that come from male domination, hierarchism, mechanism, authoritarianism, tribalism, dualism, moralism, nationalism, egoism, false collectivism, pessimism, and nihilism. Postmodernism, in short, represents a collective dream of world transformation. It expresses a family of disaffections and aspirations, geared toward realizing what is often boldly referred to as a "New Age."

Our postmodern world demands a new vision of the meaning of human death. Myth, as I use the word here, is the realm of stories that image transcendent meanings. "Myth" and "mythology" denote extremities on a spectrum of possibilities. Myth is usually thought of as a spontaneous production of the unconscious mind; mythology is the reflective study of these spontaneous products. In reality, no myth can be pure; that is, the moment an unconscious product acquires a form, in language or any medium of communication, it becomes subject to the influences of conscious mind. Myth, in short, is inseparable from mythology. Myth (less reflective) is characteristic of the early phases of a culture; mythology (more reflective) thrives during the more mature phases. Given that we are in the ripe stages of a highly reflective, scientific civilization, our stress, as a culture, is on the reflective approach to myth. That is why I speak of a postmodern *mythology* of death. Such a mythology would have to be multidisciplinary and multicultural.

OBSERVATIONS ON NEANDERTHAL CAVE BURIALS

Mythology begins with the cave burials of Neanderthal Man. The remains of a youth of about sixteen years of age were found in a grotto of Le Moustier, France, in 1908; arranged in a sleeping posture, they were surrounded by a hand ax and the charred bones of sacrificed animals. In this primeval confrontation with death, we find evidence of the first metaphor invented by *Homo sapiens*. Death, it would appear, was pictured as a kind of sleep. I assume that the Neanderthals knew the difference between a dead and a sleeping man. To represent a dead man as sleeping was, I conjecture, therefore to create a metaphor. The metaphor was a myth in germ; it told a story, and a story unfolds in time. The story this myth told was that the dead, who are really only sleeping, will one day awaken. In this bold metaphoric stroke, the first humans discovered a way to free themselves from the tyranny of appearances. For the metaphor–myth–story implied tacit awareness of a breach between appearance and reality, between the presentations of sense and a hidden world of extrasensory goings-on. The first Neanderthal myth was a death-transcending myth.

The dawning recognition of death awakened the spiritual imagination of *Homo sapiens*. The evidence from these first traces of human consciousness— dating back about 70,000 years—supports the claim of Giambattista Vico, who wrote in his great seminal work, *The New Science* of 1744 (Bergin and Fisch, 1961): "We observe that all nations, barbarous as well as civilized, though separately founded because remote from each other in time and space, keep the following human customs: all have some religion, all contract solemn marriages, all bury their dead" (para. 333). For Vico these "customs" are coeval with the founding or evolution of humanity itself, and are grounded in a common substratum of human consciousness. "For, by the axiom that 'uniform ideas, born among peoples unknown to each other, must have a common ground of truth,' it must have been dictated to all nations that from these three institutions humanity began among them all, so that the world should not become again a bestial wilderness." Vico's axiom about uniform ideas being born among people unknown to each other anticipates Frazer's (1922:386) idea of the "similar constitution of the human mind in different countries," as well as the more familiar Jungian archetypes of the collective unconscious.

In the words of Joseph Campbell (1983:57), a great postmodern mythologist, ". . . it does look very much as though Vico's three elementary institutions of religion, marriage, and burial may have come simultaneously to manifestation in that period when, in the course of the evolution of life, the first degree had been attained of the 'sapien' mind." Laying aside Vico's claim about religion and marriage, I want here to stress that evidence from anthropology and comparative religion shows a universal belief in some form of postmortem survival. As reflected in burial customs, it appears to be a constant built into the groundlayers of the human psyche.

Yet even at the earliest stages of history we see signs of faltering belief in this "uniform idea." For instance, the oldest epic in work history tells of Gilgamesh's (Sanders, 1977) discovery of death and his tortured quest for immortality. The end result is soul-wrenching disillusion. The oldest epics of the Western tradition, the *Iliad* and *Odyssey*, at best offer an unappetizing view of postmortem survival. In the *Odyssey* (Fitzgerald, 1963), for instance, Achilles admits to Odysseus his horror of the listless shadowlike existence in Hades.

On the other hand, the Greek and Babylonian epics contained answers to the archetypal quest for immortality: the epics themselves, which glorify and enshrine the deeds of great heroes. The heroic world, evoked in verse by the epic poets, offers to anyone sufficiently equipped a chance at surrogate immortality in the collective memory.

Needless to say, the early heroic attempts at self-perpetuation through *pheme*, the disembodied voice of "fame," were not the last word in the history of the immortality project. They were stopgaps preceding renewal. The Homeric form of heroic immortality through "fame" gave way to the Platonic quest for immortality, rooted in shamanic ecstasy, the practice, that is, as Socrates said in the *Phaedo* (Plato, 1961), of the soul separating itself from the body.

In part, the originality of Platonic philosophy is the claim it makes for the immortality of the soul, for already during the heyday of Periclean Athens, scepticism over survival was common among the educated. But this scepticism was not terminal. It was followed by the Platonic renewal of the survival myth. It is worth remembering here that it was Plato who inspired Saint Augustine and made him receptive to the teachings of the early Christians.

THE IDEA OF DEATH AS SPIRITUAL STIMULUS

My object here is not to review the checkered history of the survival myth but to state the hypothesis that it possesses what Vico called a "common ground of truth," which, in spite of changing climates of thought and opinion rises periodically, like the phoenix, from the ashes of unbelief. Arguably, the historical records might bear out the truth of what Spengler (1932:89) wrote: "Here, too, the higher thought originates as meditation upon death. Every religion, every scientific investigation, every philosophy proceeds from it. . . . And thus every new Culture comes into existence with a new view of the world, that is, a sudden glimpse of death as the secret of the perceivable world." The example of Plato's philosophy comes to mind; surely we have here a "new view of the world," and one that glimpses "death as the secret of the perceivable world." Consider, for example, Plato's account of philosophy as the practice of death. No less a compelling example of Spengler's thesis is Christianity, whose secret spell over the world is its promise of a general Resurrection.

But history moves on. In the course of our struggle for self-mastery we discover the technical magic of scientific rationalism. We use it as a weapon for subduing nature. By the time we come to the 17th century Scientific Revolution, we have created a worldview that goes entirely against the grain of the elementary needs of the collective psyche. Modern physicalist theories of reality end by leaving no room at all for mythologies of mind, spirit, soul, the divine, and so forth. Yet, once again, on the Vichian–Jungian assumption of a deep psychic groundplan, we cannot suppose this to be the end to the Immortality Project. A broad look at history suggests that the Scientific Revolution may be the latest replay of Homeric or Babylonian scepticism, destined to be eclipsed by a renewal of spontaneous forces from the deep structure of the collective psyche.

I want to look more closely at this historic meeting of Western science with the immortality instinct that appears to be so deeply ingrained in human behavior. Modern science, so much at odds with traditional myths of death and the soul, places us back in the position of the first Neanderthals: that is, back in the presence of death, stripped of tradition, without inner resources. Modern science has forced us to rediscover death, as if for the first time. Stripped of traditional mythologies, we fall back into a state of primordial helplessness before nature. But unlike the first paleolithic hunters facing the terrors of the receding Ice Age, we face altogether new terrors such as collective extinction from nuclear war.

A POSTMODERN MYTHOLOGY OF DEATH?

Given that the myth of survival possesses what Vico calls a "common ground of truth," — is built, that is, into the needs of the collective human psyche; and given Spengler's hypothesis that the creative moments of culture are responses to the consciousness of death, I cannot help wondering if we are witnessing the emergence of a new postmodern mythology of death.

Modern science has challenged the great spiritual traditions on the most sensitive points; in the light of physicalist science, death pretty much implies personal extinction. Technology complicates matters by threatening us in new and deadly ways. It confronts us with the idea of total extinction in a historically unprecedented way. The combination of inner resources severely taxed and outer threats magnified as never before is what tempts me to talk of a second discovery of death. (The first discovery of death was coeval with the dawn of human consciousness.) The hypothesis I want to place before the reader is this: this *second discovery of death*, due to the rise of modern science, is stirring up the psychic and cultural forces pushing us toward a postmodern world. Here I concentrate on one possible piece of evidence for this: the emerging postmodern mythology of death.

REFLECTIVE DATA FOR THE NEW MYTHOLOGY

Thanatology

New movements of thought bear on this new mythology. The rise of "thanatology" may be seen as part of a response to the second discovery of death. The merit of thanatology is that it tries to confront, rather than deny, the idea of death. My general impression, however, is that academic thanatology remains tied to the dogmas of scientific materialism. Moreover, academic thanatology tends to focus on themes that are peripheral to the central question of the nature of death itself. As far as the question of a postmodern mythology of death is concerned, more promising material lies elsewhere.

Quest for the New Paradigm

There is a broad movement of thought, hard to categorize with a label, which rotates around the quest for a "new paradigm." The main hope is to harmonize science and religion, a hope almost endemic to the Western tradition. Ever since Western rationality turned into a force at odds with traditional mythologies of death and the soul, there have been efforts to realign reason with the transcendent goals of humanity.

The quest for a new paradigm is at least as old as Xenophanes, the pre-Socratic philosopher, who criticized anthropomorphic Homeric theology and sought to purify it with monotheism. Medieval philosophy carried on the search for an integrated paradigm; the search has continued from Descartes through Kant and Hegel to contemporary times. Two typical moves in the contemporary quest are, first, the attempt to purify religion of its historical and sectarian limitations. One tries to exhibit what Leibniz called *philosophia perennia*, focusing on the mystical core of the world religions. The second move is to try to show that this purified experiential core is congruent with contemporary physics.

I am not concerned with the validity of these moves but with their mythic outcome. The picture emerging from the new paradigm quest indirectly favors a postmodern mythology of death. What we see is an attempt to reinstate consciousness at the center of the cosmic process. No longer an irrelevant epiphenomenon or complex of "secondary qualities," human subjectivity, according to certain interpretations of quantum mechanics, is portrayed as constituting, participating in, or somehow creating, by observing, the external world. This portrayal provides an intellectual milieu that hints at a more hopeful status of human consciousness vis-a-vis the objective fact of death.

Psychical Research

Data *directly* bearing on a postmodern mythology of death come from psychical research (or parapsychology). Psychical research began in late nineteenth century England, originally as an attempt to use scientific method to investigate, and possibly to revalidate, the traditional view of the soul. In this scholarly enterprise, we note the collective will to create a survival myth reasserting itself; science, which appears at first to negate that will, is here enlisted to reaffirm it. In psychical research we observe a dramatic, but intellectually purified, return of the repressed need for a survival myth.

The outcome of this rather extensive, but not widely known, research remains inconclusive for reasons that need not detain us here. Let me at least say that anyone who studies the evidence with an open mind will be forced to hesitate before dismissing the idea of postmortem survival. The consensus of careful students is that, although the case for survival remains unproven, there is a case for some probability of survival, though few would wish to be too precise in assigning specific values to this probability.

Probabilism and Survival

However, the probabilistic nature of survival evidence is suited to the needs of a survival myth. In other words, a myth of the beyond, as Plato said of his own great myths, gives only a probably picture of outcomes. The Platonic myth did not intend to give cognitive certainty but emotional assurance, sometimes moral guidance (see Stewart, 1904;1960; Reinhardt, 1927). The reason we need myths in the first place is that there are domains of human experience where we are condemned to ignorance but where at the same time we are driven to form some image, to make some claim.

Even the person convinced that death is personal extinction is working with a mythical image, more or less probably true. Since we are bound to entertain *some* image, *some* myth of death, psychical reseach at least offers a fertile strand of data for questioning the nihilistic myth, and for beginning to sketch a postmodern mythology.

Jungian Depth Psychology

Another area of research with direct implications for a new mythology of death is Jungian depth psychology (von Franz, 1986). The depth psychologists have charted an area of the human psyche — called archetypes of the collective unconscious — that seems to operate free from the restrictions of time and space. This area is now called "transpersonal." Transpersonal psychology investigates experiences in which we apparently make contact with regions of being beyond ordinary time and space. Such experiences offer data for exploring a postmodern mythology of death (see, for instance, Grof, 1985).

Psychology, Philosophy, and Theology

Contemporary writings in psychology, philosophy, and theology offer much that may be of use to a new mythology of death. A number of writers have traced the impact on the modern world of what I have called the second discovery of death: Ernest Becker (1973) and Miguel de Unamuno (1954), for instance, detail the distortions in politics; N. O. Brown (1959), in our relation to the body and in our capacity for love. Martin Heidegger (1962) relates the consciousness of death to human authenticity. John Hick (1976), who attempts a global theology of death, insists on the importance of openness to all the relevant data and stresses the theoretical importance of parapsychology.

SPONTANEOUS MATERIAL RELEVANT TO THE NEW MYTH

Nineteenth Century Spiritualism

In addition to reflective efforts, there is a wide array of spontaneous data relating to the new mythology of death. Modern spiritualism provides much data. Nineteenth century spiritualism may be thought of as "postmodern" in that the survival myth it nurtured derived neither from nineteenth century materialism nor from Christianity. It was a myth based on alleged empirical data, derived, for instance, from mediumship. The spiritualist afterlife myth differs from the Christian myth; gone, for instance, are ideas that stress hell, judgment, and damnation.

The myth of spiritualism contains three beliefs relevant to the new myth: first, that survival is a demonstrable fact; second, that intercourse between incarnate and discarnate spirits is a genuine possibility; third, that opportunities for postmortem spiritual evolution await all who are rightly prepared.

Sociologist Andrew Greeley and his colleagues at the University of Chicago's National Opinions Research Council (NORC) report that either more people are having psychic experiences or more are talking about them; for instance, 11 years ago 27% of American adults believed they had been in touch with someone who died, usually a dead spouse or sibling. In a recent national poll, conducted by Greeley and his associates, the figure jumped to 42%. This is a dramatic increase. Apart from the question of evidence for these beliefs, the fact is that the belief—the myth—of contact with the dead is growing.

The twentieth century has witnessed the rise of several types of phenomena that bear on the formation of a new mythology of death and transcendence. One could indeed argue that in face of the second discovery of death, the collective mind is predictably in the throes of creating new myths and images of death.

The Near-Death Experience

The near-death experience (NDE) is a widely reported phenomenon. According to a Gallup poll (1982), it appears that millions of Americans have

had the archetypal NDE. NDEs, while not good evidence for postmortem survival, are undoubtedly changing the image of death. The archetypal NDE,
perhaps more than any other recent phenomenon, provides a rich harvest of
materials for a new mythology of death. As Kenneth Ring (1984) has pointed
out, the effect of these phenomena is to change the image of death as the Grim
Reaper to the image of death as the Being of Light (Raymond Moody's phrase).
Ring and Moody (1975) have been exploring resources for radically transform-
ing the collective imagination. The images or archetypes they have been focusing upon have enormous psychodynamic potential which, in a true Vichian
spirit, offers potent material for our evolving consciousness of death.

Movies, novels, short stories, television programs, and magazine articles are
cropping up everywhere featuring this new image of death. The NDE is extraordinary in its power to transform the image of death. Scientific materialism
images death as extinction, nothingness. The classic NDE seems almost determined to reverse that image; in place of nothingness, it images light, God,
higher guides, unconditional love — in short, contact with a higher and fuller
reality. The material garnered by the Victorian psychical researchers is far more
compelling as evidence for postmortem survival than near-death studies; but
that material has not had the same impact on the collective imagination. One
reason may be that near-death survivors, attesting to their encounters with
another world, are still among us.

Near-death mythology is postmodern in that it breaks with traditional Christianity in certain ways. Some conservatives and fundamentalists identify the
Being of Light with Lucifer, on grounds of its deceptive affability. Like nineteenth century spiritualism, current near-death visionaries play down traditional judgmental motifs and project images of optimism, growth, universalism
and spiritual evolution. NDE, because of its gnostic overtones, might well
irritate church authoritarianism; experiencers claim to possess direct
knowledge of postmortem survival and even of God. The church might appear
superfluous under such conditions of epistemological intimacy.

Channeling

Another phenomenon related to our new mythology is so-called "channeling." Increasing numbers of people claim to be "channels" of information
thought to emanate from a higher order of being. Contemporary channeling
is similar to late nineteenth century spiritualism in some ways; for instance,
both claim the operation of guides, entities, or inner teachers as conduits to
the unseen source. There are notable differences, however. Spiritualism was
concerned with evidence (good, bad, or fraudulent) for postmortem survival;
channeling focuses on this-worldly advice and shows little concern for
evidence.

Another difference is that present-day channelers accent the belief in reincarnation. Again, the sense of evidence, as well as the awareness of the
philosophical problems that beset the notion of reincarnation, is weak.
However, the mythic import seems fairly clear to me; the belief in reincarna-

tion provides a vague feeling of continuity with the past and an equally vague feeling of meaningfulness for the present. The intellectual content of the "revelations" of current channelers, like the intellectual content of most popular mediums, is painfully banal; and we notice a similar penchant for exploiting the gullible. I think, however, that modern channelers outdo the old spiritualists in banality and commercial ruthlessness.

The success of modern channeling, in my view, supports the idea that a myth is emerging from the collective unconscious. It is as though large masses of people are in a semi-trance; they hear the same cliches, the same threadbare proclamations of hope, love, and higher reality. They respond without any sign of conscious censorship, cheerfully embracing, absorbing, and regenerating a living myth from the debris of a handful of cliches. They do not want proof, logic, evidence; they want consolation, meaning, inspiration. Above all else, they grasp at any sanction of their own sense of self, apparently so fragile and so menaced. They want to establish contact with the vital instincts of the unconscious that, as Freud once said, does not believe in death; that is why they are easily persuaded, and why they are not put off by moral or rational scruples.

UFOs and the New Death Mythology

The mythology of channeling tends to blend with the mythology of UFOs; higher guides are often cast in the personae of extraterrestrials or, more vaguely characterized, "interdimensionals." The UFO phenomenon also contains material for a postmodern mythology of death. The question of UFOs is quite complex. Whatever one may think of this baffling phenomenon, there is little doubt of the psychic component (Jung, 1964; Wallee, 1969; Hynek and Vallee, 1975; Keel, 1971). There are at least three types of UFO reports: distant sightings, contactee cases, and the more ominous, recently stressed, type of abductee case. They contribute to the growing mythology of death in various ways. They raise questions about certain absolutes in contemporary cosmology (the speed of light, the nature of space); they project images of higher types of being and higher technologies. In a general way, they suggest the incompleteness of our present worldview and so imply that the orthodox scientific myth of death as extinction may not be true.

It is also true that much of the "contactee" literature, which documents telepathic communications with "space brothers" and other mysterious beings, reinforces the general spiritual thrust of the new myth: for instance, that *Homo sapiens* is at the threshold of an evolutionary quantum leap, and that human consciousness has the collective capacity to change the structure of physical and social reality. The important thing about these widespread phenomena is that they suggest to the collective imagination a vastly expanded picture of what is possible in nature.

Although reports of unidentified flying objects date back through history, it was in 1947 that the first modern global wave of UFO reports began. These reports occurred soon after the first explosion of the atomic bomb, and some of the most striking sightings revolve around nuclear testing sites and other military installations (Lazzari, 1980). This fact is consistent with the idea that the new mythology is a reaction to a new consciousness of death, a consciousness aggravated by the threat of nuclear annihilation.

Apparitions of the Virgin Mary

Another type of psychic phenomenon with global dimensions began to accelerate during the same year of 1947 (McClure, 1983). Visions of what is taken to be the Virgin Mary have, since the nineteenth century and especially since 1947, been increasingly reported all over the world. More than one researcher (see Vallee) has noticed similarities between Marian visions and UFO phenomena; elsewhere (1985) I have looked at some of these similarities. Some of the more obvious are the luminous and numinous character of the entities that manifest; the nature of the message, which involves warnings of global cataclysm and pleas for spiritual transformation; and the aftereffects, which so often end in missionary, if not messianic, fervor. As far as the sketch of postmodernism I began with is concerned, the Marian visions fit nicely, once they are detached from their peculiar religious ideology, as symbolic epiphanies of the feminine dimension of the collective psyche.

TOWARD A HEALING VISION

In my view, emerging patterns of psychic phenomena give us raw materials for a new mythology of death. My examples are meant to be suggestions. Besides these spontaneous phenomena, there is a growing mass of research on problems of death and dying. It is my contention — discussed in my book, *The Final Choice* (1985) — that our attitude toward death has evolved in a unique way. Scientific materialism has, in effect, rendered obsolete our traditional mythologies of an afterlife. The same scientific materialism has spawned a technology that threatens (1) to poison the biosphere to death and (2) to destroy it through nuclear war. Is there then a linkage between scientific materialism's nihilistic myth of death and the threat to the biosphere? Whatever the answer to this question, my point is that these historically unprecedented threats to life on earth are mobilizing forces of the collective imagination. The global crisis has evoked new and profound reflections on the meaning of death and new and profound patterns of psychic phenomena meant to compensate for the nihilistic image of death.

I believe the collective unconscious "rejects" this nihilistic image. A process is underway directed toward forging a new image. This new image, I believe, is part of a spontaneous self-healing. Observations of the near-death experience offer a model of how this self-healing may be taking place. In short, the mechanism of individual near-death may contain clues to what is happening on a collective scale. We may, in short, be in the throes of a *planetary* near-death experience (Grosso, 1986).

If so, the ensemble of responses we have outlined in this paper, spontaneous and reflective, individual and collective, are part of a systemic evolution toward a postmodern mythology of death. That mythology is part of the total postmodern paradigm shift taking place. Touching, as it does, on the most fundamental question of human being and nonbeing, it is central to all talk of paradigm shifts.

CONCLUSION

Let me conclude by stating what I believe to be some desirable features of the new mythology. First, it should be consistent with science, but with the whole of science: with depth psychology and parapsychology; with the new physics; and with the new evolutionary paradigm that is beginning to surface (see, for instance, Denton [1985]). We would hope that the vision of death would not be a product of mere wish-fulfillment; but neither should we expect ironclad certainties from it. Myth can only give probabilities. Psychical research could provide the probable truth content of a new mythology of death.

The new mythology of death should be consonant with the needs of life. It should not be otherworldly at the expense of this world; in short, its ruling imagery would celebrate the values of the here and now as well as open a path toward futuristic or otherworldly evolution. It should stir the hope and creative forces of our deepest vital being, without clashing with the pacific and adaptive needs of technological man.

I would hope for something practical from a new myth of death. Every myth, as Mircea Eliade (1963) has shown, has a ritual component. The purpose of the rite is to bring us back to the healing source, the patterns and forces that can orient us to live and die well. Our new life-enhancing mythology of death should be, like the native American Indian quest, individual and pluralistic. We already have, I believe, hints from the near-death experience of a deep reservoir of archetypal healing energies within us. A postmodern mythology of death would, let us hope, explore practical ways of awakening those energies, and of weaving them into the fabric of everyday life.

REFERENCES

Becker, E. 1973. *The Denial of Death.* New York: The Free Press.
Bergin, T. H., and Fisch, M. H. 1961. *The New Science of Giambattista Vico.* New York: Doubleday.
Brown, N. O. 1959. *Life Against Death.* New York: Vintage Books.
Campbell, J. 1983. *The Way of the Animal Powers.* New York: Harper & Row.
Denton, M. 1985. *Evolution: A Theory in Crisis.* Bethesda, MD: Adler & Adler.
Eliade, M. 1964. *Myth and Reality.* New York: Harper & Row.
Fitzgerald, R. 1963. *Homer's Odyssey.* New York: Anchor Books.
von Franz, M. L. 1987. *On Dreams and Death.* Boston & London: Shambhala.
Frazer, J. G. 1922. *The Golden Bough.* New York: Macmillan.

Gallup, G. Jr. 1982. *Adventures in Immortality*. New York: McGraw Hill.

Grof, S. 1985. *Beyond the Brain*. New York: Suny.

Grosso, M. 1985. *The Final Choice*. Walpole, NH: Stillpoint.

Grosso, M. 1986. The Planetary Near-Death Experience. Paper presented at conference, Mind, Matter, and Meaning, sponsored by the Psychology Department of West Georgia College, Carrollton, Georgia, April 11–12, 1987.

Heidegger, M. 1962. *Being and Time*. New York: Harper & Row.

Hick, J. 1976. *Death and Eternal Life*. New York: Harper & Row.

Hynek, J. A. and Vallee, J. 1975. *The Edge of Reality*. Chicago: Henry Regnery Company.

Jung, C. G. 1964. *Civilization in Transition*. New York: Bollingen Foundation.

Keel, J. A. 1971. *UFO's: Operation Trojan Horse*. London: Abacus.

21

People and the Paranormal

David Cockburn

NEAR-DEATH EXPERIENCES

It is sometimes suggested[1] that certain parapsychological phenomena have a crucial bearing on our understanding of what a person is and that these phenomena do, or could, provide support for the idea that people live on after what we call "death." I believe that these suggestions, at any rate in their most familiar form, involve serious confusions. In the first half of this chapter I will look in some detail at the use sometimes made of the phenomenon known as the "near-death experience" (NDE) and, in particular, of the "out-of-body experience" (OBE) often associated with this. In the second half, I will try to bring out what I believe are a number of more general misunderstandings that repeatedly arise in this area.

To have a near-death experience is to have thoughts, feelings, visual sensations, or some other experience while in a state in which one shows (more or less) no external behavioral or physiological signs of life. The grounds for thinking that these occur are the reports of individuals who have recovered after being in such a condition. While it is sometimes suggested that NDEs do in themselves indicate that a person is something quite distinct from the extended, tangible human being that we encounter in normal life, the reports of these patients often have a further striking feature. Those concerned insist that they did, for a period, observe the room, or indeed some other place, from a position external to their body. Furthermore, they are sometimes able to give accurate reports of events that were taking place while they were apparently unconscious and that, in some cases, could not have been observed from the point where their body was at the time. It is concluded that the individual "left the body" for a period, and so that a person must be something other than the familiar bodily being. This opens up the possibility that I should survive the destruction of this bodily being. Indeed, it might be thought to suggest that it is likely that I will in fact survive what we call "death." The grounds for this claim would be that it is clear that in these cases the individual lives on, in a fully conscious state, through a period in which the body is in a state which is very similar to that of death.

Now I do, as I said, believe that all of this involves serious confusions. I do not, in fact, believe that any empirical discoveries could throw doubt on the idea that a person "the self" is the extended, tangible human being, any more than they could throw doubt on the idea that a table is an extended, tangible entity. These questions are the business of philosophy, not science, and developments within philosophy during the last fifty years do, I believe, show such dualist views of persons to be quite untenable. It is not scientific discoveries that have created the important difficulties for dualist views and no empirical evidence could do anything to rescue such views. I will not, however, attempt to defend these claims directly. I will argue only for the more modest claim that, at the very least, a considerable amount of work needs to be done at a number of points if it is to be shown that phenomena of the kind I have mentioned bear on our picture of ourselves in anything like the ways suggested. I should stress that I will not be calling into question any of the data which is appealed to. My suggestion will, rather, be that enormous care is needed in taking even a first step beyond that data.

The claim that NDEs occur does, in one sense, appear to go beyond the best evidence for them that we could conceivably have. We can, by definition, have no contemporary evidence; we are, of necessity, dependent on the memory reports of the subject, since the supposed significance of NDEs lies in the fact that the individual shows no external signs of life at the time. Should this concern us? Well, consider an imaginary example. Suppose that when rhododendron wine was first produced and drunk it was found to have rather unusual effects. Instead of making people drunk in the normal sense it led them, after one sip, to make a lot of remarkable claims about what they had been experiencing for the last half hour. While they have in fact been sitting in Lampeter talking with us they claim to have had a totally different set of experiences, perhaps of things that have been happening thousands of miles away. Furthermore, it turns out that their reports correspond in a striking fashion to things that were, during that period, happening somewhere else. This would, of course, be an extraordinary phenomenon. Would we, however, be justified in concluding that these people *had* been having the experiences of which they have memory impressions? At the very least we must say that we would not be compelled to draw this conclusion. We could think of the wine as inducing false memory impressions that are, in a way which we do not yet understand, influenced by things that have been happening in another part of the world during the last half hour. Further, despite the embarrassing incompleteness of such an account there would, on the face of it, be serious difficulties with the suggested alternative. For we would have overwhelming evidence, in the form of his behavior over the last half hour, that the subject was experiencing nothing resembling what it now seems to him that he was.

One obvious difference between my imaginary example and NDEs lies in the fact that in the latter case the subjects do not, during the relevant period, show unambiguous signs that they are experiencing something *else*. Rather, they show what we would normally take to be fairly unambiguous signs that they are experiencing nothing at all. It is not, however, immediately obvious why this difference should be thought to be of decisive importance. In any case, some work needs to be done here to show that we are right to take the extraordinary memory impressions of these patients as evidence for the occurrence of NDEs.

In the remainder of this chapter I will assume that we have strong grounds for the claim that NDEs do occur. What bearing would such experiences have on our picture of ourselves? One thing they might show (depending on the details of the physiological data) is that what we experience at a particular time is not totally dependent on the state of our brain at that time. While that will, no doubt, come as a surprise to many we need to sharply distinguish *this* question, the question of what my consciousness is *dependent on,* from the question of what it *is* that is conscious. Consider an analogy. We normally assume that how well a car goes is crucially dependent on the state of the engine. Suppose, however, that we were presented with startling evidence strongly suggesting that the performance of a car could be affected by influences of a kind which are totally alien to contemporary science. Would such a discovery do anything at all to suggest that my car is not that familiar thing with four wheels, a roof, and so on? Would it support the idea that it is possible for my car to live on after the disintegration of the extended, tangible thing parked outside? This, I take it, is obvious nonsense.

Now on the face of it, it is the same with people. It is one thing to ask what a person's states are dependent on. That is a question for science. It is quite another to ask what those states are states of; to ask, that is, what it *is* that thinks, sees, is happy or sad and so on. Whether the answer to the first question is "the brain" or something quite different is totally irrelevant to the second question. Neither way will it affect the suggestion that it is the human being that thinks, sees and so on. NDEs cannot in this way give any support to the idea that the person, the "real me," is something distinct from this extended, tangible being and so might survive the destruction of that being.

Perhaps, however, these remarks do not give sufficient weight to the way in which patients are able to give accurate reports of what was happening at the time in places not observable from the bed where the human being was lying. Does not this at least suggest that the individual "left the body" for a period; and so that the "real person" is something quite distinct from this bodily being? Well, this would be moving a bit too rapidly. The facts so far described are quite consistent with the suggestion that the patient was able to give these reports as a result of signals picked up while she was located where she appeared to be, namely, in bed.

It might be argued that this talk of "signals" does not really do justice to the way in which the individual's perspective on the world was for a period from a point external to the body. It is not merely that she knows what was happening, say, next door. For a period she saw things from a point in the next-door room; or, at least, it now seems to her that she did. Does not this suggest that part of the patient was "outside her body" for that period? Well, even if we agree that it does suggest this (and I will have more to say about this later) there would be no pressure at all on us to identify what left the body with the "real person." If my eyes were on the ends of long stalks I could observe what was going on next door. I would, no doubt, when particularly absorbed in what I was seeing, half think of myself as being in that room; or perhaps even, momentarily, come to believe that that was where I was. None of this would put any pressure on us to say that I really was next door.

I am not offering an alternative account of OBEs. I am simply suggesting that we do need to be given some reason for thinking that their occurrence should move us in the direction of a dualist view of people. Now it might be said in reply that the relevance of OBEs to this issue lies in the fact that they simply cannot be fitted into the current materialistic scientific world view; that the terms employed by modern physics are quite incapable of providing any explanation of the observed facts. Assuming that this is correct, what conclusions should we draw? We certainly cannot move immediately from here to the conclusion that a person is something distinct from the solid, extended entity which others can see. I can hold that a person is a material being in that sense and yet deny that modern physics has the resources to explain everything that we might want explained. (Few, I take it, would be tempted to conclude from spoon-bending of the kind attributed by some to Uri Geller that the things affected, namely spoons, are not in fact material entities. It may be worth noting here that it is no use responding to such analogies with the observation that "people are not spoons or cars." Certainly the difference could hardly be more fundamental. The question is: Which difference is relevant to the particular argument which the analogy is used to illustrate?)

Nevertheless, it might be said, a dualist view of persons *can* provide an explanation of the observed phenomena in a way in which no alternative view can. Thus, at least until we have an adequate explanation consistent with the view that the bodily being is the real person, these phenomena should be regarded as grounds for accepting the dualist view. In response to this I should concede first that I have no idea whatsoever how these phenomena might be explained. I spoke of "signals" that the patient, in his/her bed, might be picking up. Let us suppose, however, that we have good reason for ruling out any such explanation; *nothing*, at least of the kind now recognized by physics, is passing from the relevant point in space to the patient in bed.[2] I am left thinking in terms of action at a distance; what happens at one place (the event on which he is able to report) is affecting the patient even though there is *no mechanism whatsoever* that connects the events with the patient.

Let us turn now to how the dualist theory would explain such veridical OBE reports. We are perhaps inclined to see it like this: "On the dualist theory I am something quite distinct from this body. This opens the possibility of explaining veridical OBE reports in terms of the fact that the individual left his body and observed the world from a position external to it." Traditional philosophical dualism, of the kind associated with Descartes, does not, I think, leave room for such an explanation since it does not leave room for the idea that the "real me" has any spatial location;[3] I cannot leave my body since I was never in it. I will not pursue the question of whether some other form of "dualism" could leave room for the idea that the "real me" has spatial location since I believe there are further problems.

Perhaps the most notorious objection to dualism concerns the question of the interaction between mind and body. To the extent that one holds that the "real me" is something quite different in kind from this extended, solid entity, one appears to rule out the possibility of there being any intelligible mechanism that links what happens in the one substance with what happens in the other. Descartes, in my view rightly, was apparently quite unimpressed by this supposed objection to dualism. My point at the moment, however, is that the dualist "explanation" of veridical OBE reports (indeed, of everything that people do) is going to contain a gap of exactly the same kind as that which is present in my nondualist account of the situation. Given that this is so, the dualist can apparently have no legitimate complaint against my "explanation," which involves an undisguised appeal to action at a distance. So we have no reason at all to move towards a two-component picture of persons.

One further point can be made here. The suggestion is that veridical OBE reports support some kind of dualism because dualism would allow us to explain the reports in terms of the fact that the individual was for a period located at the relevant place. Now, in normal circumstances we do, of course, take the fact that I was at a certain place at a certain time as explaining the knowledge that I have of what happened there. In a particular case, however, this would be no explanation at all if it was discovered that I had lost my eyes, ears and so on before going there. Would it, then, be an explanation if I had, temporarily, "lost my body?"

From my point of view it is a striking fact that we are all, myself included, tempted to interpret the reported phenomena in terms of the individual "leaving their body." Many will no doubt feel that it *must* be quite easy to meet the points I have made since, it will be said, this interpretation of the phenomena is so obviously the most natural one. I suspect that this feeling reflects a curious ease with which we slide between two quite different pictures of what a person is. At the same time as trying to bring this out I can, I hope, further undermine our wayward temptations here.

Assume that we have strong evidence for the claim that for a period the individual's visual perspective on the world was from a point outside the physical body. Assume too that for a period the person felt himself to be located at that point. My question is: Should this lead us to say that for that period the person was (or it is likely that he was) situated at a point outside this body? To draw this conclusion we would need to have independent grounds for the following claim: people are (generally) situated at that point from which their visual perspective on the world is.[4] Without this claim, the inference is quite unjustified. Do we have any grounds for it? On the face of it we do. We might say that we have overwhelming grounds for the claim that, with the exception of cases involving mirrors and the like (which we will assume can be dealt with somehow), people are always situated at that point from which their visual perspective on the world is. Now I think that is right. Leaving aside for the moment the phenomena we are dealing with, namely OBEs, this seems to be a very well-supported universal truth. But then my thinking so is dependent on my view that people are *human beings*. For we seem to have strong evidence for the claim that human beings — these visible, tangile entities — are always situated at that point from which their visual perspective on the world is. Now this is no use at all for the person who wants to use OBEs to establish some form of dualism. He cannot use *that* generalization to reach his desired conclusion because the phenomena to which he appeals are simply a counterexample to it. To put the same point in another way, someone whose aim is to prove that the real person is something distinct from the visible, tangible human being can hardly use an argument that is only valid on the assumption that people *are* human beings. (I say "can hardly." My suspicion is that this is precisely what most of us are inclined to do.)

So the question is: If one thinks that the person is something distinct from the human being — as one must if one is going to claim that in these cases "people do leave their bodies" — what grounds can one have for the claim that people are (generally) situated at that point from which their visual perspective on the world is? What one needs is the following: People are generally situated inside human beings. Assuming that we are dealing with a form of dualism within which this *makes sense*, it is not at all clear what could count as evidence for it. At any rate, until we are shown how this claim might be supported we appear to have no grounds at all for moving from the suggestion that the individual's perspective on the world was, for a period, from a point of view external to this body to the idea that the individual was, for that period, situated at that point. The idea that the "real person" is the crying, talking, sleeping, walking human being is quite untouched by these phenomena.

I must make one further point here. To say that there is a confusion in the way in which NDEs are sometimes appealed to as "evidence of the spiritual" is *not* to say that there need be a confusion in the thought of those whose lives are turned around by their own experience when they come close to death. For the effect which this has on their view of life need not run through any theory about what a person is. Indeed, quite independently of the kind of experience which I have been discussing, I would be rather surprised if an individual's life was not significantly affected by his recognition that he had been close to death. We might even think that a failure to be moved in this way would be evidence of a certain shallowness in the person. But of course the change in him would not normally have anything to do with a new piece of "evidence" that he has acquired.

HUMAN BEINGS AND SCIENCE

My claim is not that we do not *have* to draw from the reported phenomena the conclusions that commonly are drawn. It is, rather, that further work needs to be done at a number of points if it is to be shown that the phenomena give us *any reason at all* to draw these conclusions. I do not in fact believe that this work can be successfully done since, as I remarked at the beginning, I do not believe that the really important questions in this area are ones to which empirical evidence, of this or any other kind, is of any relevance. While I cannot attempt to argue this point in any detail here, I hope that some very general remarks will at least serve to raise some doubts about the way in which these issues are commonly viewed. More specifically, I want to try to bring out in a more general way the confusion involved in the idea that the discoveries of some science might, by showing us something about what a person is, open up the possibility that we live on after death. At the same time I hope to suggest — though no more than that — that this conclusion is not a purely negative one. For to say that parapsychology cannot help us here is not to say that we must accept the "materialistic" view of ourselves commonly associated with the more conventional sciences. We need to take seriously the possibility that this picture of the options involves fundamental misunderstandings of the relations between science and philosophy, and between each of these and questions concerning the value and significance of human life. (I should stress that the generality of what I say may contain dangers. I will speak of "science" and of "value," or "the spiritual," as if these terms picked out clearly defined, unified notions that have certain, generally agreed features. Since things are clearly not quite that simple, what I say can be no more than suggestive.)

Opposition to traditional dualism within contemporary philosophy has come from two radically different directions. One form of criticism is motivated largely by an enormous respect for the achievements of modern science. In its pure form this approach suggests that the problem with dualism of Descartes' variety was its assumption that human behavior cannot be explained in "physical" terms. Since it is now clear, so the argument goes, that all human behavior *can* be explained in such terms, in particular in terms of the workings of the brain, we no longer need to postulate the existence of any mysterious "non-physical" entity such as the Cartesian soul. The "mind," the essential person, has now been shown to be the brain. Now, to the extent that parapsychological phenomena suggest that important features of our lives *cannot* be explained in terms of the workings of the brain, this line of argument will be undermined.

From the point of view of another strand in contemporary philosophy, however, what the two sides in that dispute agree on is very much more important than what they differ over. What they share is the assumption that something other than the living human being, the being that we encounter in daily life, should be thought of as "the essential person." To be more specific, it is assumed that the being to which pains, thoughts, emotions, and so on are to be attributed is that thing, whatever it turns out to be, which explains the observable movements of the human being. Once it is assumed in this way that "the essential person" ("the self," "the mind," or whatever you like to call it) is something that lies behind and animates the human being that others can see and touch, one will be left with a genuine question concerning what kind of entity this is; a question to which empirical evidence of the kind produced by the neurophysiologist, and, perhaps, the parapsychologist, will be relevant. If, however, there is no reason to make that assumption none of this empirical data, however interesting it may be in other ways, will have any bearing on the question of whether a peson is a being of the kind that can be seen and touched. For one will insist that the person is not that which *explains* the movements of what we observe but the very thing that we observe: namely, the human being. Now I have not directly defended this position. I hope, however, that some of my points help to highlight the fact that there is an assumption which might be questioned behind the idea that we must choose, in the light of the evidence, between the claim that I am a lump of matter inside this skull and the claim that I am an "immaterial" entity somehow connected with that lump of matter.

It might be thought that I have exaggerated the difference between the two lines of development in contemporary philosophy. For what they share, the claim that a person is an extended, tangible being — in the one case the brain, in the other the human being — is the most significant feature of each of them. This common strand represents a dramatic contrast with traditional dualism in that in placing the person in the familiar world of stones and trees the possibility of thinking of ourselves as in any fundamental way marked off from the rest of nature is removed. For example, the identification of the person with the human being rather than with the brain does not alter the fact that any talk of "life after death" is automatically excluded; for while it may once have been possible to hold that the human being might rise again after death, our greater scientific knowledge today simply excludes this possibility.

This line of reasoning encourges us to abandon far too rapidly the attempt to find sense in the idea that we are in some fundamental way marked off from the rest of nature. It is assumed, for example, that to reject one familiar way in which talk of "life after death" might be understood is automatically to exclude the possibility that such talk could have *any* sense. Since, however, I have no idea how to make my doubts about that particular move plausible, my remarks will focus on the more general form of the worry.

Much of the interest in parapsychological phenomena is, I think, motivated by something like the following thought: "As soon as one grants that a person is an extended, tangible, observable being — a being that exists in the world of stones, trees, and mountains — one is committing oneself to the view that the world as described by modern physics is *the* world. This has dramatic implications for our conception of ourselves. For example, it rules out the possibility of our thinking of ourselves as in any way responsible for what we do; what we do must be accepted as being the product of the impersonal mechanisms described by the physicist. More generally, the idea that we are fundamentally 'spiritual' beings, beings that have the kind of value which is traditionally associated with talk of 'the soul,' must be abandoned."

The idea that value can seep into the world through the cracks in physics has a long history. A question that can and needs to be asked quite independently of any investigation into whether there are such cracks is this: Why should it be thought that whatever seeps in through such cracks is of any value? Consider the question of responsibility. Suppose that we could accept that a person is essentially an "immaterial" being. How would this help the idea that we are in some sense responsible for what we do? If the claim that something is "immaterial" simply means that you cannot see it, touch it, weigh it, and so on, then it needs to be shown why an immaterial being should not be every bit as determined by "impersonal mechanisms" as a material being can be. The rigid laws to which it is subject won't, perhaps, be those of the physicist, but there appears to be no reason to think that immaterial beings could not be subject to rigid laws.[5] Roughly parallel remarks apply to the idea that we are fundamentally "spiritual" beings. On the face of it, there is no reason to suppose that a being that cannot be seen or touched is likely to be more morally or religiously elevated, more worthy of respect, than one that can. The linking of the immaterial in that sense with the idea of "spiritual" value stands in need of defense. *If* there is a difficulty in the idea that value is to be found in the normal world of stones, trees, and human beings, it needs to be shown that exactly the same difficulty does not arise for the world which it is suggested is revealed to us by the paranormal.

But *is* there a difficulty in the idea that value is to be found in the world of extended, tangible, observable beings? We can approach this question by way of the following suggestion: "The world as described by the natural scientist, and in particular by the physicist, is a world without value. We must, then, find gaps in the physicist's description if we are to leave any room for what is of value." There may be nothing wrong with that thought in itself. To conclude, however, that we *must* turn to the paranormal if we are to find room for what is of value is to overlook the fact that "finding a gap in another's description of a situation" can take a variety of forms. Consider a careful description of Leonardo da Vinci's *Madonna of the Rocks* entirely in terms of the color of paint at each point on the canvas; without, that is, any mention of what is *in* the painting. Most, I take it, will agree that this description leaves out the most important thing. Yet in its own terms it may contain no significant gap; there is no splash of red we can point to and say "You didn't mention that." We have, then, two quite different kinds of gap here. The kind of work needed to bring someone to see the gap in his description will be quite different in the two cases. For example, a magnifying glass may be a help if someone has failed to mention a tiny patch of green in one corner, but is unlikely to be of much help to someone who simply cannot see the faces in the picture. (No doubt the latter deficiency is difficult to imagine in this case. We could think instead of a more abstract painting where for many there is a real difficulty in discerning the patterns.)

The parapsychologist I am speaking of insists that what is wrong with the claim that modern science gives us "the fundamental truth about how things are" is the fact that the modern scientist systematically overlooks a certain kind of evidence. He does not question the claim (which no scientist need make) that what we might call "the scientific method" is *the* method of determining the "basic truth" about the world; that the world is that which is revealed to us by the most careful application of that method. Thus, he thinks that what we need is a bit of "super-science," an investigation into "super-nature." If we are to tell the whole story about the world, and, in particular, about people. Now the point of my analogy with a painting was this. There is at least room for the view that any change in my picture of the world that could be brought about in *that* way, that is by a simple confrontation with some new empirical data, could not be a change that goes "deep" in an ethical sense. The man who speaks of "the soul," it might be said, is separated by an enormous gulf from the one who speaks of us as, for example, "complex stimulus–response systems." The work needed to "correct" the latter view must, therefore, be of quite a diferent order.[6] We could compare here the gaps which separate the views of three people on capital punishment. One defends capital punishment on the grounds that "It is an effective deterrent." Another rejects it on the grounds that "It is not an effective deterrent." A third rejects it on the grounds that "The taking of human life is an act of such horror that it can never be justified in terms of its effectiveness in promoting some social purpose." For the third, the empirical evidence appealed to by the others is wholly irrelevant. Precisely because of that we might say that he is separated from the other two by a much deeper gulf than that which separates them.

I asked: Is there a difficulty in the idea that value is to be found in the world of extended, tangible, observable beings? One thing that stands in the way of clear thinking on this issue is the use we make of various contrasts: in particular, the "material" "immaterial" and "body" "mind" contrasts. Thus, the notion of the "material" becomes connected in our thought with that of the "materialistic" in the moral sense, with the idea of the world as described by the physicist, with the idea of what has mass, size, and shape, with the idea of the observable, and perhaps others. The notion of the "immaterial" is defined in our thought in terms of a contrast with that group of ideas. Powerful imagery helps to preserve such groupings of ideas in our minds. That which has no mass is free from the force of gravity and so is morally elevated.[7] Once one becomes aware of the role of this imagery, however, it should become clear that there is no reason to suppose that "reality" carves up neatly along these lines. For example, the warm smile on her lips is, I take it, a feature of the world of extended, tangible, observable things. Does *it* figure in the physicist's description of the world? And what of the child's exclamation of joy on opening a birthday present, or the terror in the face of the man facing execution.

Some will have doubts about these samples. Do we really see the warmth of the smile, the terror in the eyes and so on? In giving such descriptions are we not already employing a language which takes us beyond the world with which we are actually confronted in experience? Must we not agree that what I "really see" is not a warm smile but flesh arranged in such and such a way? Well, that needs to be argued. On the face of it there is no reason why we should defer to the natural scientist's description in this way. I do, after all, respond to it immediately *as a smile*.

Finally we can turn to the "human being" of which I have repeatedly spoken. It might be thought that this term is just a fudge. Have I not got to admit that my view is that people are simply their bodies; they are simply complex lumps of matter? The term "human being" disguises the unpalatable side of this in so far as in certain contexts it carries connotations of a more elevated kind. "He is a real human being." Well, suppose it is said that Bach's music is "just a lot of noise." What is the correct response to *that* suggestion? Compare this with "People are simply bodies." If that means "You can see them, touch them, and weigh them" that is one thing. If it means, for example, "There is no difference between being interested in her and being interested in her body," where the latter phrase is tied up with lust or doctors, it is quite another. The term "body" does, in certain contexts, allow one to slide too easily from one to the other. I use the term "human being" in order to discourage moves of just this kind. Of course, if one thinks such moves are quite legitimate one will have worries about my use of the term "human being"; but grounds for this worry do need to be established.

Developments in various sciences over the last hundred years have had an enormous impact on popular conceptions of the kind of beings that we are. It can, no doubt, be said that it is largely as a result of such developments that a great many people now have a picture of the person within which there is no room for the kind of value associated with talk of "the soul." My central point has been that to hold that this is a loss, that there is a serious deficiency in such pictures, is not yet to commit oneself to a particular view of the kind of work which is needed to correct the deficiency. Those who pursue an interest in the paranormal with the idea that this *must* be the key to the "spiritual" would do well to remember that their activities might be viewed in the light of the following analogy. Confronted with a description of *The Madonna of the Rocks* in terms of colour patches, and the insistence that "that is all there is to it," a man protests that several patches with subtle shades have been left out of the description. He knows that something very important is missing from the description but he is looking for what is missing in quite the wrong dimension. Of course, this analogy might be totally unfair. It does, however, need to be shown that it is. It does, that is, need to be shown that we should be looking to the empirical sciences for our model of the enquiry which may provide us with another way of understanding ourselves and our relationship to the natural world.

NOTES

1. An earlier verson of this chapter was written in response to an earlier version of the chapter by David Lorimer, which is included in this collection. I have rewritten my chapter in a way that makes it independent of Lorimer's, but many of my targets should still be recognizable in his paper. I am grateful to David Lorimer for the

stimulation that his paper provided and also, in a variety of different ways, to discussions with Paul Badham, Robert Edwards, Maureen Meehan, and Bryn Browne.

2. This, of course, leaves us with the possibility that something of a kind not now recognized by physics is travelling to the patient (just as the dualist "explanation" involves things of a kind not now recognized by physics travelling in the other direction). So I may be conceding too much in my next sentence.

3. "I thence concluded that I was a substance whose whole essence or nature consists only in thinking, and which, that it may exist, has need of no place..." (Descartes, *A Discourse on Method*, Part IV). It is true that Descartes does not always speak in ways that are consistent with this. The important point, however, is that his defense of dualism seems to commit him to that position. Contemporary dualists had, then, better think carefully before abandoning that feature of Descartes' thought.

4. It might be said that this is not simply an empirical generalization but a necessary truth of some kind. That claim, however, will only help if it can be defended without implicity rejecting dualism. I cannot argue here that this cannot be done, so I must leave this as a challenge to those whose work I am criticizing.

5. It might be said that at least this would open up the *possibility* that what we do is not the product of deterministic laws. In reply, however, it must be said that deterministic laws are, apparently, a thing of the past in modern physics. Whether or not that helps to leave room for the idea of human responsibility, it still needs to be shown what problem is overcome by the supposition that we are "immaterial" beings.

6. It might be replied that the relevant paranormal data is *not*, as I am suggesting, easily come by. All right, *as it happens*, it is not; but it might have been. It is possible that, in this curious way, the difficulties in producing really compelling data play an important role in sustaining the idea that it has an importance of the kind in question.

7. One might also think here of the imagery associated with the idea of "the body": for example, the body ties us to Earthly things, the pleasures of the flesh. I should stress that I do not wish to deny that such imagery can have its place. My point is just that it can seriously mislead us if we do not handle it with care.

REFERENCES

Badham, Paul and Linda. 1982. *Immortality or Extinction?* London: MacMillan.

Cook, John. 1969. Human Beings. *Studies in the Philosophy of Wittgenstein*, Ed. Peter Winch. London: Routledge and Kegan Paul.

Descartes, Rene. 1962. *A Discourse on Method*. (Trans. by John Vietch.) London: Dent.

Lorimer, David. 1984. *Survival? Body, Mind and Death in the Light of Psychic Experience*. London: Routledge and Kegan Paul.

Ryle, Gilbert. 1966. The World of Science and the Everyday World. In *Dilemmas*. Cambridge University Press.

Squires, Roger. 1974. Zombies v. Materialists. *Proceedings of the Aristotelian Society*. Supplementary Volume XLVLIII.

Winch, Peter. 1980/81. Eine Einstellung Zur Seele. *Proceedings of the Aristotelian Society*. Vol. LXXXI.

Wittgenstein, Ludwig. 1953. *Philosophical Investigations*. Oxford: Basil Blackwell.

22

The Near-Death Experience:

Crosscultural and Multidisciplinary Dimensions

David Lorimer

As a separate discipline, near-death studies goes back to the publication of *Life after Life* by Dr. Raymond Moody in 1975. The book achieved an unexpectedly large sale all over the world and prompted other researchers to enter the field. The principal scientific studies of the phenomenon have been carried out by Professor Kenneth Ring, whose *Life at Death* appeared in 1980 and by Dr. Michael Sabom with *Recollections of Death* in 1982. The International Association for Near-Death Studies (IANDS) was set up by Professor Ring in the United States in 1980 and has since produced an academic journal, *Anabiosis*, now called *The Journal of Near-Death Studies*, and a newsletter, *Revitalized Signs* (formerly *Vital Signs*). In 1984 a referenced textbook, *The Near-Death Experience* (Greyson and Flynn 1984) containing many of the articles from *Anabiosis* was published in the United States. In the United Kingom pioneering research was carried out by psychologist Margot Grey, herself a near-death experiencer. Her findings were published in 1985 as *Return from Death*. In 1986 IANDS (UK) was incorporated. It now has a membership of about 150, with public interest growing all the time.

The near-death experience (NDE) can be defined as the sequence of conscious experience that continues in spite of the fact that the subject is showing no external signs of life in terms of skin resistance, breathing, heartbeat and, occasionally, flat EEG. Opinions are still divided as to the exact interpretation of the experience: whether it should be taken at face value, or as a psychological compensation, or as a sign of a malfunctioning brain resulting from cerebral anoxia or hypercarbia. Few people, however, actually doubt that *something* is going on. Moreover, as far as we can tell at present, the components of the experience continue to show regular patterns, in any event in the United States, the United Kingdom, and France. Such observations have led to the adoption of certain scales and classifications for the purposes of statistical analysis.

Ring (1980) proposed two schemes, one in terms of stages, and the other a "weighted core experience index" (WCEI). The rationale of Ring's stages is that his respondents reported the "later" stages less frequently than the earlier one, and, broadly speaking, those experiencing these stages were "unconscious" for a longer period of time. The first stage, experienced by 60% of the respondents, is characterized by a sense of peace. Stage 2 (37%) features a sense of psychological and physical separation from the physical body. Stage 3 (23%) is entering the darkness, a tunnel enveloping the subject who sometimes has the impression of travelling at great speed. In Stage 4 there is an encounter with a being of light who may initiate a life review; there is frequently a feeling of oneness with the light — 16% report this stage. Stage 5 (10%) is entering the light or, rather, the world contained in the light; here the subject may meet deceased relatives with whom (s)he communicates telepathically. At some point subjects are told that it is not yet time for them to die, or else they encounter a barrier (stream, door, etc.) beyond which they know they cannot proceed and subsequently return to earth. Equally, they may decide to return in order to live more authentically (being more true to themselves) or because they realize that they still have obligations to undertake. The actual return is often painful and only reluctantly undergone. There is a bleak contrast between the world of light and freedom and the semiconsciousness of pain and limitation. On the other hand, the few subjects who report negative experiences are relieved to return. Margot Grey (1985) has given a corresponding classification for these: 1, fear and feeling of panic; 2, out-of-body experience (OBE); 3, entering a black void; 4, sensing an evil force; 5, entering a hell-like environment. It is not yet clear how frequent such negative experiences are. Rawlings (1978) speculates that they may be more frequent than reports suggest as the subjects may repress or be ashamed of these negative elements.

The components and weights of Ring's WCEI are:

Subjective sense of being dead:	1
Feeling of peace, painlessness, pleasantness:	2*
Sense of bodily separation:	2*
Sense of entering a dark region:	2*
Encountering a presence/hearing a voice:	3
Taking stock of one's life:	3
Seeing, or being enveloped in light:	2
Seeing beautiful colors:	1
Entering into the light:	4
Encountering visible "Spirits":	3

The asterisked numbers would score 2 or 4, depending respectively on (1) the strength of the feeling, (2) whether or not a clear out-of-body experience (OBE) is described, and (3) whether or not the void was accompanied by a noise. This scale enabled Ring to isolate degrees of the NDE, ranging from "non-experiencers" below 6, "moderate experiencers" between 6 and 9, and "deep experiencers" above 9. In his sample, 27 (26%) were deep experiencers,

22 (22%) moderate experiencers, and the remainder (53 [52%]) non-experiencers. This last category does not actually mean that the subjects experienced nothing but simply that, at best, their experience was not high enough in terms of the scale. Greyson (1984) compiled an NDE scale in which he classified components under the four headings of cognitive, affective, paranormal and transcendent. The cognitive includes speed of time and thoughts as well as the impression of understanding life; the affective refers to the feelings of peace and joy and the sensation of being surrounded by light; the paranormal phenomena were extrasensory perception (ESP) and the OBE, with the occasional precognition and the impression that one's senses were more vivid than normal; and the transcendent phase comprises encounters with deceased relatives or spiritual beings after entry into another world, and coming to a point of no return. For the sake of cross-cultural comparison, however, I propose to use Ring's scale.

CROSS-CULTURAL DIMENSIONS

Little work has been carried out to date in this field so that any conclusions drawn from the analysis which follows will require corroboration and elaboration through further research. So far, IANDS exists in the United States (US) and the United Kingdom (UK) only, as indicated above, and the bulk of the research has been done in the US. Nevertheless, death being a universal occurrence and condition of biological life, we might expect to find some common psychological characteristics as well as culturally determined differences. In a survey published in 1978, Sheils found that 51 of 54 cultures surveyed believed in the possibility of an OBE (one of the components of the NDE); he did add, however, that belief did not guarantee occurrence. We also know that the mystical experience, corresponding to Stage 4 of Ring's classification, is a cross-cultural phenomenon although details and interpretations may vary. Brown (1986) found that the stages leading to enlightenment exhibit cross-cultural and cross-traditional patterns although there was a perceptual conditioning in the ultimate experience. We shall now examine some material from India, Tibet, Chinese and Japanese Pure Land Buddhism, and Melanesia.

India

The most recent report was published by Stevenson and Pasricha in 1986. The conclusions of Osis and Haraldsson in an earlier work (1977) indicated a greater fear of dying and more frequent incidence of religious imagery than does Ring's work together with interpretations of religious figures consistent with Hindu tradition. There is no indication of the first factor in Stevenson and Pasricha; the second factor's presence would have to be judged inconclusive; while the third is very much in evidence. Their analysis is based on a small sample of eleven men and five women encountered in the course of their research into cases of the reincarnation type; four of these cases are cited in some detail. At present we have no surveys on the frequency of NDEs in India, nor can we know how representative the sample is.

The relevant cultural background information consists of the Hindu figures prominent in the afterworld: the king of the dead, Yamraj; his messengers called Yamdoots; and "the man with the book," Chitragupta. His book is thought to contain a complete record of all the person's deeds in the incarnation which has just ended. The special features of the Indian cases are partly related to this cultural backdrop. Messengers are described as coming to take the subject away and bringing him back; there is an element of force absent from all but a few negative Western cases. Experiencers find themselves in the presence of a man or a woman with a book which is then consulted. In ten of the cases there seemed to have been a bureaucratic error — the wrong person had been brought; and in six of these cases, another person (with the right name this time) is supposed to have died as the subject revived to tell the tale. One of the cases almost suggests a sort of hexing: as the gardener was informed that he should have died instead, he then did. The substitution idea also recalls Jung's NDE in 1944 when he became convinced that his doctor was in some sense obliged to die in his stead. At the time of Jung's recovery, the doctor seemed in perfect health, but he did in fact die within six weeks. The idea of a mistake having been made is indirectly related to a feature of Western cases, namely, that experiencers are often told that it is not yet time for them to die; in other words, the NDE indicates that death at that point would be premature. The return to earth life in Western cases can be voluntary or else as advised by the being of light.

One further fascinating peculiarity of Indian cases is the presence in four of them of some kind of mark on the physical body, which seems to have been the indirect outcome of the NDE. In one case, it is a boil, and in another a mark on the leg. Parallels to be drawn here would be the effect of hypnotic suggestions and the finding in Stevenson's own work that subjects who claim to be the reincarnation of particular individuals in the past either carry scars relating to some traumatic event in the purported previous incarnation or even, in some cases, identical birthmarks to those of previous personalities. Each of these instances suggests, if taken at face value, some kind of causal connection between mind and body.

If we look at the ten items on Ring's WCEI, we find that only the tenth feature, meeting visible spirits, is definitely present. Even the subjective sense of being dead is doubtful as the subjects comment on the likeness of the experience to a dream, something usually vehemently denied by Western experiencers. (This may, however, be due to the innuendo that a dream is more unreal in Western eyes.) There is no sense of bodily separation; this sense is by no means universal in Western cases, either, where many subjects go straight into a "transcendental" environment. The predominant feelings in Indian subjects are by no means peace and contentment; although feelings are not specifically mentioned, the dominant tone is one of confusion and harassment by the messengers. There is no life review; this event is actually relatively infrequent in the West as well. And, finally, there is certainly no encounter with the light, still less a melting into it. This might strike the researcher as curious, given the mystical and yogic tradition in India, but none of the subjects seemed particularly religious, nor, for that matter, are the Western experiencers. The structure of the Indian NDE rarely seems to extend beyond the discovery of a mistake and the sending back of the subject in order to rectify it. Although Pasricha and Stevenson conclude that differences in the NDE experiences correspond to different prevailing ideas in the US and India, they are rightly cautious about making any hard and fast statement at this stage.

Tibet

For years the best known source on the Tibetan tradition of death and dying has been Evan-Wentz's edition (1957) of *The Tibetan Book of the Dead*. In 1986 this was complemented by a book by Mullin, *Death and Dying in the Tibetan Tradition*, which has given us a much fuller picture and sets the earlier book in a broader context. Mullin shows how the tradition of meditations on death, arising from the fundamental Buddhist insight into impermanence, plays a central role and how these meditations lead to a pure practice of dharma, a concentration of spiritual resolve. Close parallels are drawn between travel in meditation and the final journey of death. The consciousness-principle returns to the physical body in the first instance but vacates it for good in the second.

The first reaction of the consciousness-principle on leaving the body is one of confusion. It cannot make out whether or not it is dead because it sees and hears relatives as before. The position is clarified when it realizes that the relatives do not reply to questions and are clearly distressed by the death; it then concludes that it is dead and feels "great misery." A comparison is in order at this point. The feeling of misery is certainly inconsistent with beatific Western experiences. The features of the OBE, however, are strikingly similar. The senses of sight and hearing are the most frequently reported. Sight may be so accurate that subjects report events that had occurred on the spot (and occasionally elsewhere) while they were ostensibly unconscious. The space experienced appears to duplicate physical space although the lighting may seem different: some subjects speak of a yellow or gold light. As for hearing, many of the impressions seem to be telephathic; the thoughts are seen as opposed to the words heard.

In the interlife cycle the consciousness-principle first comes face to face with the Fundamental Clear Light. If it is able to recognize and achieve unity with this Light, enlightenment and release from the cycle of births is attained. Subsequently there are opportunities to identify with various manifestations of the Buddha, but these too may be passed by as the consciousness-principle has not attained a high enough degree of spiritual development. A similar "measurement" of the soul (Western term) can be found in Swedenborg, who explains that the dying person is attended by celestial, then spiritual, angels in a descending hierarchy. (S)he may or may not be able to endure the purity of being; if not, the intensity diminishes until a comfortable level is reached.

Some Western experiencers have ardently wished to melt into the Being of Light but have known that they could not return to earth if this supervened; in this instance the Western light is more personal and less abstract than this Buddhist light. We shall, however, see more personal constructions in the Pure Land tradition.

After the peaceful deities come the wrathful deities. The consciousness-principle is terrified by the spectre of terror and awe, the product of evil propensities. Those reading the book are encouraged to realize that these haunting visions are simply products of the mind; they have no independent reality. The externalization of good and evil is present in Swedenborg, also, who maintains that the inner becomes the outer in the spiritual world and in the Koran, where the soul meets a beautiful or ugly maiden who is the embodiment of its deeds. Grey (1985), in her chapter on negative NDEs, comments that such terrifying experiences may be explained psychodynamically as a confrontation with the contents of the unconscious; in a parallel fashion, it would be possible to interpret beatific NDEs as journeys into the superconscious realms.

In the third part of the Book of the Dead comes the judgment. The Lord of Death consults the mirror of karma "wherein every good and evil act is vividly reflected. Lying is of no avail" (p. 166). In a footnote Evans-Wentz adds that the judge is effectively conscience and the mirror memory. This phase is closely paralleled in the NDE life review where the subject sees his/her life unroll in a series of vivid images. (S)he is both observer and experiencer; the higher impartial self assesses the intentions as well as the actions, and the subject experiences not only the images, but sometimes also the effects of thoughts, feelings and actions on others in his/her sphere. Joy and sorrow, kindness and cruelty are reflected and echoed back to the source: ecstasy and torture at the extremes.

Becker (1985) points out that the Tibetan sequence of a descent from light and perfection towards the darker side would be consistent with the Western finding that the majority of NDEs are beatific. This would not necessarily indicate the spiritual status of the subject but might simply represent the first stage of a general progression. Such a conclusion is supported by the findings of Whitton and Fisher (1986), who observed that hypnotically regressed subjects related an ecstatic state of mind at death, with a form of assessment following on, and the circumstances of the present life reflecting the karma of the individual with uncanny accuracy — if one concedes the psychological reality and consistency of the case histories.

Examination of the Western NDE in the light of the Tibetan tradition is instructive in revealing a number of cross-cultural patterns in terms of the Light, OBEs, judgment, and encounter with spirits. The phenomenology is all the more remarkable if one considers that the NDE may or may not be postulated to describe events in the first stages of the afterlife. There is at least a participation in a common archetype and perhaps even a genuine link in the common structure of consciousness and experience.

Pure Land Buddhism

Becker (1981, 1984) has written a couple of papers on near-death experiences in Chinese and Sino-Japanese Buddhism. A good deal of his analysis is concerned with the devotional tradition revolving round the figure of the savior Amida Buddha with whom disciples hoped to identify at death. Some of the deathbed descriptions of famous disciples make interesting reading in the light of modern NDE research. One (Becker, 1984:16) speaks of a "dream" in which the disciple proceeds through the void to meet the Buddha Amitabha who places him on the palm of his hand and "[in this position] he went through the whole [universe] in all directions (or: its light spread everywhere in all directions)." Then he suddenly wakes up and recounts the episode. We seem to have a description of a mystical expansion of consciousness, symbolized by the light, which resembles accounts of the extension of knowledge and awareness to a unitive state in which one knows everything because one is in a sense everything. This may be stretching the point somewhat, but the metaphor of expansion certainly holds.

An eleventh-century Chinese text refers to visions of hell and the Pure Land being common and adds that the Pure Land involves the synesthesia of "mysterious fragrance, light, clouds, music, or colours" (Becker, 1984). Light and colors we have already come across, but the elements of fragrance and music (the music of the spheres) are also referred to from time to time, the latter being a good deal more common than the former. As in his paper on Tibet, Becker concludes with some reflections on the mind-dependent nature of postmortem reality and stresses that the idea of the common-sense world as more "real" than the visionary is an unprovable assumption. Reality depends on the present focus of consciousness. And encounter with the visionary reality of the Pure Land tradition as well as with the world of modern Western NDE research has a profoundly transformative effect on the subject. We shall examine the issue of mind-dependence again in the context of philosophical implications.

Melanesia

Counts (1983), a Canadian anthropologist, examined a tiny sample of three NDEs and compared the content with one account of a dream and one of a vision. She begins by explaining that the Kaliai regard death as more of a process than a distinct event, a process that is complete with the cessation of heartbeat and breathing. The three cases cover different ground and exhibit some of the features of the WCEI. Frank describes an encounter with a being of light who turned him round and sent him back. Like Andrew, he does have a subjective sense of being dead. Andrew is told in typical Western fashion that it is not yet time for him to come while, by contrast, a woman whom he had seen walking on the road was actually expected. He returns along a beam of light and has the further thought that he will not return if his family has already started mourning. It turns out that his father had not realized what had happened during the six hours of his "absence." He did not see his physical body and, like many Westerners, was reluctant to return. Luke has rambling experiences in the course of which he meets a deceased relative and sees a sorcerer being judged; as in many primitive societies, sorcerers are held responsible for any death which is not regarded as a wholly natural occurrence.

In her conclusions Counts points out that there is no feeling of peace and pleasantness, that none of her respondents speaks about a tunnel, and that only the most westernized subject meets a being of light. These findings are on the whole consistent with Pasricha and Stevenson in India. The subjects do not see their physical bodies, the peaceful emotion is absent, there is no tunnel, and the subjects travel on foot; on the other hand there are no escorts, no hints of cumbersome bureaucratic incompetence and no traces of post-NDE injury on the physical body. So while there are some similarities among the West, India, and Melanesia (*e.g.*, meeting deceased spirits), and some features that India and Melanesia share which are absent in the West, residual factors appear to be peculiar to particular cultures. This suggests a complex interweaving and layering of human experience. As I indicated at the outset, it is early days in cross-cultural NDE research. A start has been made, but much more data will be required if detailed pictures are going to emerge. Analysis will be further complicated by the ubiquity of modern Western secular culture as an overlay on traditional ethnic and religious views. Who knows whether the conscious, unconscious, and superconscious minds will tell the same story?

MULTIDISCIPLINARY IMPLICATIONS

According to Grosso (1983) the NDE is an interdisciplinary field of study that touches on neurology, psychiatry, religion, philosophy, anthropology, mythology, psychology, and parapsychology. It is clearly impossible to treat all these areas in depth here. We shall therefore limit our analysis to certain key issues in philosophy, psychology, theology, and ethics in the hope that our observations will stimulate further discussion and research.

Philosophy

One key area of philosophical debate concerns the mind/body or mind/brain issue; related to this are questions of the nature of the self and individual identity that border on psychology. One way of putting the question is to ask whether consciousness is produced by the brain or whether the brain acts as a transducer or filter of consciousness, which it shapes and conditions in certain specific ways. The former position is widely held in modern philosophy and medicine. It forms the basis of most philosophical and medical training. Consciousness is a by-product of brain processes and therefore perishes with brainstem death. It follows that the only lines of interpretation of the NDE are either psychological or materialist. The psychological explanation, which supposes that the ego is attempting to deny its imminent dissolution, invokes such mechanisms as depersonalization or ego defense. The physicalist theories are based on the premise that the reported effects of the NDE arise from the malfunctioning of the brain owing to such conditions as cerebral anoxia or hypercarbia. It is important to note that the materialist premises actually preclude any explanations that take the NDE more or less at face value.

Materialist theories of the NDE come under pressure when cases are reported where a flat EEG has been measured during the relevant period. While it is clearly true that no irreversible brain damage has taken place, waking consciousness is associated with recognizable EEG patterns; one would hardly expect a person showing no clinical signs of life to report vivid quasi-sensory experience. Sabom (1984) has six cases where the OBE report can be shown to correspond closely with the medical account. Other cases indicate recognition of faces seen only in the OBE state and accurate information about events invisible from the patient's bed. This really should not happen if consciousness is totally dependent on the brain. So much for the objective angle. On the subjective side, subjects report vivid sensory and mental processes, often a good deal sharper than their state of mind prior to and after the NDE. They also insist that the "real me" that still thinks, senses, and feels is the part outside the body. This conclusion is quite a revelation for some patients who previously identified themselves with their physical bodies. By contrast the physical body is seen as the instrument of the self, the vehicle of expression used in the physical world. Such considerations indicate two general conclusions: that the dualist theory of a self-conscious mind using the physical instrument (which it discards at death) is a more adequate hypothesis to explain the veridical OBE accounts and the sense of self in the NDE; and that self-conscious mind is not merely the by-product of brain processes but is capable of existing even more intensely when freed from the space–time confines of the physical body. Elsewhere (1984) I have pursued this question in greater depth.

Copleston (1980, 1982) discusses the question of mysticism and sources of knowledge. He argues that if perception implies a distinction between perceiver and perceived, subject and object, "and if ultimate reality transcends the subject–object distinction, perception must obviously belong to the sphere of appearance, to the level on which the One appears as the Many" (1980:25). In analyzing Shankara's metaphysics and theory of knowledge, Copleston observes that a theory of degrees of reality implies a theory of degrees of knowledge and truth. And if the absolute can be known (i.e., experienced) then such knowledge and apprehension must transcend our cherished subject–object distinction. This transcendence is just the sort of state reported in stage 4 of the NDE (encountering the light). Subjects speak of being immersed or engulfed in it to the extent that they become the light and the light becomes them. They are all-knowing because they become part of everything and everything becomes part of them — from the inside, a glimpse into the oneness of cosmic consciousness. In this state they recall understanding the context and purpose of life and death, good and evil, joy and suffering, all of which make up an indivisible and comprehensible whole. In some cases the content of the knowledge is more specific. Subjects claim to have an extended time-sense that enables them to penetrate the past and sometimes the future; in the latter case they are given to understand that the future is not predetermined but consists of a number of lines of probability depending on present behavior and reactions. Free will expresses itself creatively but always within the limits of the possible. A future epistemology of mysticism will set sensory perception in a wider perspective; debates on free-will will be extended to include the relationship between consciousness and reality, that is, the nature of the mind-dependence discussed by Becker in his papers, will be a burgeoning field of study as we in the West realize our intellectual arrogance in assuming that we have all the answers.

Psychology

The nature of identity and consciousness is a border area between psychology and philosophy. The NDE suggests that the behaviorist theory is a gross misrepresentation of the human condition. Far from being sophisticated stimulus–response chickens with no responsibility for our actions, human beings are in essence spiritual, operating at present in a material dimension. The question of ethical responsibility will be pursued further below.

The models developed by humanistic and transpersonal psychology are much more consistent with the findings of NDE research than are behaviorist models. Maslow's peak experience is exemplified in the NDE, and Wilber's spectrum approach is mirrored in the different levels of consciousness experienced. The core NDE is also associated with a powerful transformative effect on the personality akin to religious conversion insofar as the subject finds a new center and purpose in life. Grosso (1983) refers to this transformative effect as the archetype of death and enlightenment (ADE), which he detects in other contexts where there is a dissolution and reconstruction, a disintegration preparing the way for a breakthrough. Subjects tend to lose any fear of death (also reported by those who attain mystical consciousness without being near death) and are convinced of life after death. This realization gives their lives a new slant, allied as it is with a transformation of values away from materialistic having towads spiritual being: living fully in the present, appreciating nature and beauty, having a sense of the inner presence of God, and extending unconditional love to all who come within reach.

Theology and Ethics

We have already seen how some subjects consider that they have met an extremely evolved spiritual being, which on occasion may even be interpreted as God himself. Traditionally such a meeting would be impossible, for "no man hath seen God and lived," but the manifestation of the divine qualities of love, wisdom, beauty, peace, and power is both vivid and transformative. The qualities encountered are those that the subjects attempt to bring back and incorporate in their lives. The experience is direct; it is not a mediated intellectual doctrine. Hence the tendency of subjects to place less emphasis on the formal side of religion and more on the inner connection with God. On occasion, however, subjects can find their original lukewarm faith kindled and deepened. In any event, the stress lies on the spirit rather than in the letter.

The NDE naturally touches on matters of Christian eschatology, the "last things" of death, judgment, heaven, and hell. For centuries theology has struggled with the muddle arising out of the attempt to combine the Platonic teaching of the immortality of the soul with the Hebrew idea of the resurrection of the flesh: Origen versus Tertullian. St. Paul speaks of a spiritual body germinating from the natural one, the higher emerging from the lower; commentaries on the passage in 1 Corinthians 15 have only served to stir up further confusion. One of the basic issues is the nature of the "person." Does a person by definition have to have a material body? Or is the person essentially an immortal and "immaterial" soul, in which case can (s)he have another bodily vehicle of different constitution and adapted to a different environment? This latter theory is favored by the NDE although the matter of a bodily vehicle, a form necessary for the differentiation of individuality, remains an open question, especially in a mind-dependent world where thought seems to have instant creative power. In the mystical union the "body" becomes the universe, as it were, as being and awareness are part of everything and everything a part of them: the universe as the body of God.

Ethically speaking, two experiences found in the NDE are central: the immersion in love, being-in-love, so that love permeates the very fabric of individual existence; there is no sense of separation, alienation, and division; they melt into and cohere with the unitive principle of life, paralleled in the gravity (*attraction* in French) that holds the universe together. The second crucial experience is the life review where the individual finds that nothing has been forgotten. Detachment from the brain brings a flood of impressions to mind. If the mystical immersion in love suggests an underlying oneness of being, the life review makes the connections between individuals quite explicit. It is clear how one's thoughts, feelings, and actions have affected others, especially if the feelings are now experienced sujectively by one. The judgment is by the "higher self" of the "lower self" or empirical personality. There are no excuses. Everything is distinctly perceived as it is; secret motivations are exposed under the testing searchlight of love. "Is there love in your heart?" "Have you always acted lovingly towards other life-forms, putting yourself in their place?" You now are in their place. The profound significance of this review is that it shows how the love and justice of God are reconciled. It is love that gently administers the justice of truth, that shows how the individual is responsible even for his/her thoughts and feelings. And it is love that points to the potential power of prayer as a concentrated form of healing and creative thought.

Although the NDE shows glimpses of paradise and hell as states of consciousness, I regard it as premature to draw any conclusions about the ethical and spiritual progress of the individual from studies which can, ipso facto, reach only the margins of postmortem existence. Studies such as those of Whitton and Fisher (1986) indicate that God is not mocked, karmic seeds are harvested once sown, but that we are offered repeated opportunities to learn, perfect, and balance where we have disturbed the cosmic harmony.

CONCLUSION

As indicated at the outset, the implications of the NDE raise questions so significant and complex that they cannot be fully treated within the scope of the present exploration. As near-death research has proceeded, work has focussed more on the meaning and implication of the NDE. Scholars in particular disciplines are now in a position to enrich their own fields with some of the insights gained in the NDE, while researchers concentrating on the NDE can begin to unfold the interdisciplinary aspects latent in this form of human experience.

REFERENCES

Becker, C.B. 1981. The Centrality of Near-Death Experiences in Chinese Pure Land Buddhism. *Anabiosis* 1:154–171.

———. 1984. The Pure Land Revisited: Sino-Japanese Meditations and Near-Death Experiences of the Next World. *Anabiosis* 4:51–68.

———. 1985. Views from Tibet: NDEs and the Book of the Dead. *Anabiosis* 5:1–20.

Brown, D.P. 1986. Stages of Meditation in Cross-Cultural Perspectives. In *Transformations of Consciousness*. Eds. Wilber, K., Engler, J., and Brown, D.P. New York: Shambala.

Copleston, F. 1980. *Philosophies and Cultures*. Oxford: Oxford University Press.

———. 1982. *Religion and the One*. London: Search Press.

Counts, D.A. 1983. Near-Death and Out-of-Body Experiences in a Melanesian Society. *Anabiosis* 3:115–135.

Evans-Wentz, W.Y. 1960. *The Tibetan Book of the Dead*. London: Oxford University Press.

Grey, M. 1985. *Return from Death*. London: Arkana.

Greyson, B., and Flynn, C. 1984. *The Near-Death Experience*. Springfield, IL: Charles C. Thomas.

Grosso, M. 1983. Jung, Parapsychology and the Near-Death Experience: Toward a Personal Paradigm. *Anabiosis* 3:3–38.

Lorimer, D. 1984. *Survival?* London: Routledge and Kegan Paul.

Moody, R. A. 1975. *Life after Life*. Atlanta, GA: Mockingbird Books.

Mullin, G. 1986. *Death and Dying, the Tibetan Tradition*. London: Arkana.

Osis, K., and Haraldsson, E. 1977. *At the Hour of Death*. New York: Avon Books.

Ring, K. 1980. *Life at Death: A Scientific Investigation of the Near-Death Experience*. New York: Coward, McCann and Geoghagan.

Ring, K. 1984. *Heading toward Omega: In Search of the Meaning of the Near-Death Experience*. New York: William Morrow.

Sabom, M. 1982. *Recollections of Death*. London: Corgi Books.

Sheils, D. A Cross-Cultural Study of Beliefs in Out-of-Body Experiences, Waking and Sleeping. *Journal of the Society for Psychical Research* 49:697–775.

Stevenson, I., and Pasricha, S. 1986. Near-Death Experiences in India, a Preliminary Report. *Journal of Nervous and Mental Diseases* 174(3):165–170.

Whitton, J., and Fisher, J. 1986. *Life between Life*. London: Collins.

INDEX

African perspectives, 14-23
    immortality, 27-28
Afterlife
    African concept, 17-18, 34-37
    Buddhism, 108-124
    Chinese, 128-129
    Hinduism, 87-88
    Islamic concept, 48-49, 55-64
    religious attitudes and concepts,
        209-219
    survival of consciousness, 203-208
    survival of personality, 199-208
Angel of death, 59-60
Ars Moriendi (the art of dying),
    9, 221-230
Attitudes toward death
    African, 21-23, 24-37
    Mayan,131-145

"Books of the dead," 8-9, 91, 260
Buddhism, 108-124,216-219
    Japanese, 121-122
    Karma, 111-112
    nirvana, 119-120
    no-soul theory, 110-112
    Pure Land, 262
Burial, 262
    Neanderthal caves, 233-234
    Necropoli, 142

Channeling, 239-240
Chinese perspectives, 126-130
    Confucius, 127
    Taoism, 127
    I Ching, 127-128, 190
Cultural aspects
    African, 14-23, 24-37
    American Indian 3
    Aztecs, 4
    British Hindu, 66
    Buddhism, 108-124
    Chinese, 127-128
    cross-cultural views, 101-107
    Greek, 5
    Hindu, 84-88

Islamic, 38-54, 54-64
Mayan, 131-145
MesoAmerican, 131-145
Micronesia, 5-6

Denial of death, 5, 66-67
    Becker, Ernest, 9-10
    elaborate cemeteries, 7-8
Divine judgment, 10-11

Eschatology, 28
    Upanishadic, 89-99
ESP, 206-207
Ethics
    of certain death, 149-162
    of suicide, 164-166
    right to die, 163-171
Euthanasia, 156-160, 173-186
    ethics, 167-171
    execution, 149-160
    in the Netherlands, 178-186
    Islamic view, 40
    legal aspects, 173-186
    Mayan concept, 43
    Nazi practices, 157-159
    passive, 173
    voluntary, active, 173-187
Execution
    ethics, 149-160

Fear of death, 221-230
Forest Lawn Memorial Park, 7-8
Funeral rites, 7-8
    African, 20-21, 32-33
    Islamic, 47-48, 60-63
    Hindu, 73-75

Good death, 69-71

Hinduism, 66-883, 84-88, 89-100
    karma, 76-77, 85-86, 93
    mourning, 75-76
    nirvana, 119-124
    reincarnation, 84-86
    samsara, 82,89

Immortality and religion, 209-219
Islamic perspectives, 38-54, 55-64
    resurrection, 50-52

Judaism, 216
Judgment day, 28
Jungian psychology of death, 12,
    188-197, 237-238
    synchronicity, 189-197

Koran (see also Quron), 55-58

Mayan cosmos, 131-145
    Mayan pyramid temples, 141-142
    Popul Vuh, 132-133
Mercy killing, 156-160
Meso-American culture, 131-145
Myths about death, 3-13
    channeling, 239-240
    death-denying, 7-9
    postmodern mythology, 235-242
    preparation for death, 5
    religious, 10-12

Near-death experience, 191, 207,
    238-239, 240-241, 244-254, 256-267
    cross-cultural views, 258-263
    ethics, 265-267
Nirvana, 119-124

Out-of-body experience, 245-248

Parapsychology, 206, 228-230, 237,
    244-254

Phoenix fire mystery, 84, 103

Quran (see also Koran), 42-51, 216

Ramananda, teachings of, 94-96
Rebirth
    Buddhism, 108-124
Reincarnation, 115-117
    in Hinduism, 84-86
    Phoenix fire mystery, 84, 103
Religion and immortality, 209-219
Religious traditions, 10-12
Resurrection
    Christian doctrine, 27-28
    Islamic view, 50-52
Right to die, 163-171
    voluntary, active euthanasia, 173-187

Suicide, 149-160, 164-167
    assisted suicide, 167-171
    kamikazes, 155
    philosophical attitudes toward, 174,
        178
    religious attitudes toward, 163-166
Survival of personality of the death,
    199-208

Thanatology, 236

Underworld, Mayan, 140-141, 144
Upanishad, 85-86, 89-100, 105, 113